Studies in the Social and Cultural History of Modern Warfare

In recent years the field of modern history has been enriched by the exploration of two parallel histories. These are the social and cultural history of armed conflict, and the impact of military events on social and cultural history.

Studies in the Social and Cultural History of Modern Warfare presents the fruits of this growing area of research, reflecting both the colonization of military history by cultural historians and the reciprocal interest of military historians in social and cultural history, to the benefit of both. The series offers the latest scholarship in European and non-European events from the 1850s to the present day.

A full list of titles in the series can be found at:
www.cambridge.org/modernwarfare

The Soviet Myth of World War II

How did a socialist society, ostensibly committed to Marxist id
internationalism and global class struggle, reconcile itself to not
patriotism, homeland, Russian ethnocentrism, and the glori
of war? In this provocative new history, Jonathan Brunstedt
this question through the lens of the myth and remembrance o
in World War II – arguably the central defining event of th
epoch. The book shows that while the experience and lega
conflict did much to reinforce a sense of Russian primacy an
dominated ethnic hierarchy, the story of the war enabled an a
supra-ethnic source of belonging, which subsumed Russia
Russian loyalties alike to the Soviet whole. The tension and
between Russocentric and 'internationalist' conceptions
which burst into the open during the late 1980s, reflec
struggle over the nature of patriotic identity in a multie
that continues to reverberate in the post-Soviet space. Th
new light on long-standing questions linked to the polit
brance and provides a crucial historical context for the p
of the war's memory in Russia today.

Jonathan Brunstedt is Assistant Professor of History
University.

The Soviet Myth of World War II

Patriotic Memory and the Russian Question in the USSR

Jonathan Brunstedt
Texas A & M University

CAMBRIDGE
UNIVERSITY PRESS

CAMBRIDGE
UNIVERSITY PRESS

University Printing House, Cambridge CB2 8BS, United Kingdom

One Liberty Plaza, 20th Floor, New York, NY 10006, USA

477 Williamstown Road, Port Melbourne, VIC 3207, Australia

314–321, 3rd Floor, Plot 3, Splendor Forum, Jasola District Centre, New Delhi – 110025, India

103 Penang Road, #05–06/07, Visioncrest Commercial, Singapore 238467

Cambridge University Press is part of the University of Cambridge.

It furthers the University's mission by disseminating knowledge in the pursuit of education, learning, and research at the highest international levels of excellence.

www.cambridge.org
Information on this title: www.cambridge.org/9781108498753
DOI: 10.1017/9781108595773

First published 2021

Printed in the United Kingdom by TJ Books Limited, Padstow Cornwall

A catalogue record for this publication is available from the British Library.

ISBN 978-1-108-49875-3 Hardback

. . . for both the number of those who fell and the monuments which were erected over them are proofs that the victory was won by the combined action of all the Greeks. Besides, if the men of these three cities alone had fought, while the rest sat by and did nothing, the altar would not have been inscribed as it was:

Here did the Greeks, whom with Ares' aid they had triumphed in battle,

Driven the Mede from their frontiers and delivered their country from bondage,

Set up an altar *together* for Zeus, Liberator of Greece.

– Plutarch, The Life of Aristides

Contents

Figures

Acknowledgments

This book would not have been possible without the tremendous support of a number of individuals and institutions. The History Department at Texas A&M University has been a welcoming new home and provided late-stage funding as I finalized the manuscript. My TAMU colleagues have been universally supportive, but I would like to single out Terry Anderson, Carlos Blanton, Olga Dror, Brian Linn, Trent MacNamara, Roger Reese, Stephen Riegg, and Adam Seipp for their encouragement and friendship. I am indebted as well to the History Department at Utah State University, where I previously served as assistant professor of modern European history. In particular, I would like to thank Lawrence Culver, Victoria Grieve, Jamie Sanders, and, especially, Tammy Proctor. At USU, Tammy was an unrivaled mentor and faculty advocate. Her hypercompetence and prodigious knowledge of Belgian beers came in especially handy during our co-taught program abroad. I am grateful for Tammy's continued friendship.

The project benefited immensely from the insights and assistance of a number of outstanding colleagues in the field. I met David Brandenberger as I was still formulating many of my ideas. From the outset, he provided reassurance, thoughtful criticism, and counsel as I navigated both the process of completing the book and establishing an academic career. He did so, moreover, always with the knowledge that my project's thesis diverged in key respects from that of his own first monograph. Without David's sage advice and generosity of spirit, this book would have been inconceivable. I also owe an outstanding debt of gratitude to Gregory Carleton, Steve Norris, and Karen Petrone – all of whom I met very early on in this project's development – for their perceptive critique and friendship over the years. Karen was particularly gracious with her time and helped me avoid several potentially embarrassing mistakes. For their commentary on draft sections of the manuscript, I am indebted to Seth Bernstein, Steven Jug, Anatoly Pinsky, Stephen Riegg, Brandon Schechter, and Nina Tumarkin. Rewarding conversations and exchanges with Şener Aktürk, Franziska Exeler, Juliane Fürst,

Adrienne Harris, Justus Hartzok, Erin Hochman, Kristy Ironside, Jesse Kauffman, Lisa Kirschenbaum, Kelly Kolar, Sharon Kowalsky, Steve Maddox, Yan Mann, Dan Orlovsky, and Laurie Stoff have also shaped my thinking on this project and history more broadly.

The origins of this book date to my time as a graduate student at Oxford. For their guidance during these years, I thank Jane Caplan, Richard Crampton, Robert Gildea, Catriona Kelly, Margaret MacMillan, Eugene Rogan, Robert Service, Andreas Umland and, most of all, David Priestland. David was a model advisor, encouraging me to think broadly and comparatively about the project. I am also grateful to my fellow Antonians, and especially Karin Heissler, Justinian Jampol, Sasha Polakow-Suransky, Catherine Porter, and Ray Sontag. Dan Healey offered me my first lectureship as his sabbatical replacement at Swansea University in Wales. I thank Dan for entrusting his home and office to me and for his advice on teaching.

I humbly acknowledge the funding bodies that sponsored my research, including the Higher Education Funding Council for England (HEFCE), the International Research and Exchanges Board (IREX), the Kennan Institute, the Scatcherd European Fund, the Andrew Smith Memorial Foundation, the Ilchester and Colin Matthews funds, St. Antony's College, and the Faculty of History and the School of Global and Area Studies at Oxford. Funds were provided by the United States Department of State through the Title VIII Program. None of these organizations is responsible for the views expressed herein. The Association for Slavic, East European, and Eurasian Studies and the School of Russian and Asian Studies provided additional grants. Parts of the book were completed during a fellowship at the Aleksanteri Institute at the University of Helsinki. I am grateful to Markku Kangaspuro, Anna Korhonen, and Eeva Korteniemi for their support while in Finland.

For seeing the book's potential and shepherding its production, I would like to thank Michael Watson, Emily Sharp, and Ruth Boyes at Cambridge University Press. I am grateful as well to Jay Winter and the Studies in the Social and Cultural History of Modern Warfare series editors, many of whose works directly inspired this book. I am indebted to Valery Shchekoldin for allowing me to use his incredible photographs; to Liza Zubyuk for tracking down materials at the last minute in Russia; and to the Wende Museum, a hidden gem of a repository in Southern California, which allowed me to republish some of its rare late-socialist artwork. Sections of this book first appeared in unrevised form as "Elder Brother, Loyal Friend, and the Stalinist Myth of War," *Ab Imperio*, no. 3 (2019): 88–116; "The Soviet Myth of the

Great Fatherland War and the Limits of Inclusionary Politics under Brezhnev," *Nationalities Papers*, 41, no. 1 (2013): 146–165; and in the volume *Excavating Memory: Material Culture Approaches to Sites of Remembering and Forgetting* (2016), edited by John Roby and Maria Theresia Starzmann, reprinted with permission of the University Press of Florida.

Most importantly, I thank my family. My parents, Diane Moore and William Brunstedt, provided constant love and support, as they have my whole life. Their spouses, Dick Moore and Kok Lan Tan, graciously opened their homes to me and my family over the years in California, Singapore, and Costa Rica. My two wonderful sisters, Ashley and Alexis, provided endless laughter and perspective. My in-laws in Italy, Mauro Serra and Marta Lattanzio, continue to embrace me as the albino "German tourist" son they never had.

My greatest debt will always be to my wife, Danila Serra. She made incalculable sacrifices over the course of this project, all while excelling in her own academic career. During the more difficult stages of research and writing, separated geographically and institutionally, and struggling to balance professional aspirations with family life, we often mused about life "after the book." Sometimes we would add fantastical flourishes to this invented reality, such as living in the same city or, less plausibly, working at the same institution. And when our imaginations ran wild, we would conjure two beautiful boys, with their mother's blue eyes and classical names, like Alexander and Nicholas. It is wholly thanks to Danila that this little myth we made has become the history we now live, together.

Abbreviations

APRK	Archive of the President of the Republic of Kazakhstan
ARAN	Archive of the Russian Academy of Sciences
ARAN IRI	Archive of the Institute of Russian History of the Russian Academy of Sciences
ASSR	Autonomous Soviet Socialist Republic
CC / TsK	Central Committee of the Communist Party
Cominform	Communist Information Bureau
Comintern	Communist International / Third International
CPSU / KPSS	Communist Party of the Soviet Union
Dashnaktsutyun	Armenian Revolutionary Federation
DOSAAF	Volunteer Society for Cooperation with the Army, Aviation, and Navy
GARF	State Archive of the Russian Federation
GDR	German Democratic Republic
KGB	Committee of State Security
Obkom	Regional Party Committee
OKhDOPIM	Department for the Preservation of Documents of the Socio-Political History of Moscow
RGALI	Russian State Archive of Literature and Art
RGANI	Russian State Archive of Contemporary History
RGASPI	Russian State Archive of Social and Political History
RSFSR	Russian Soviet Federative Socialist Republic
Samizdat	Literally "self-publishing": a form of underground publishing and distribution that attempted to circumvent state censorship
SSR	(Titular) Soviet Socialist Republic
TsGAIPD RT	Central State Archive of Historical-Political Documentation of the Republic of Tatarstan
TsGAGA	Central State Archive of the City of Almaty

TsGARK	Central State Archive of the Republic of Kazakhstan
TsMAMLS	Central Moscow Archive-Museum of Personal Collections
USSR / SSSR	Union of Soviet Socialist Republics
VLKSM	All-Union Leninist Young Communist League (Komsomol)
VOOPIiK	All-Russian Society for the Preservation of Historical and Cultural Monuments

Map 1 Map of the USSR, ca. 1989

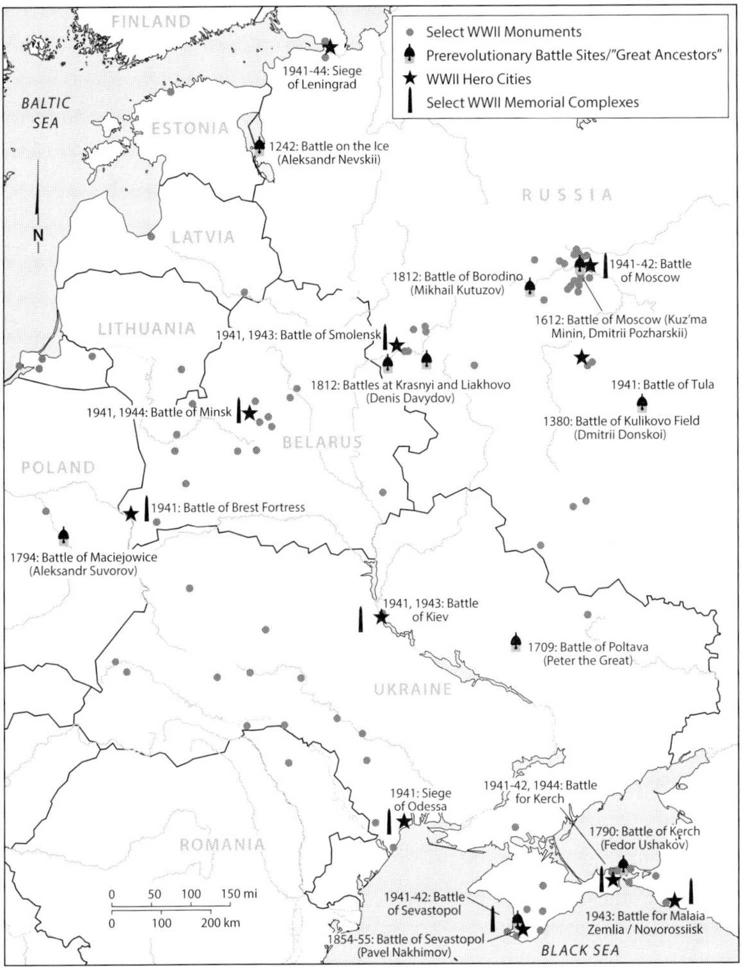

Map 2 The geography of Russian war memory in the western USSR

Introduction
War and the Tensions of Patriotism

> There was below the surface something of a conflict at that time between "Holy Russia" and the "Soviet Union." Sometimes compromises were reached between the two.
>
> – Alexander Werth, *Russia at War*[1]

> Our masters the Bolsheviks set up the Third International, and our masters the Bolsheviks developed the theory of so-called Socialism in One Country. That theory's a contradiction in terms – like fried ice.
>
> – Vasily Grossman, *Life and Fate*[2]

In late November 1941, as the Battle for Moscow raged, Soviet newspapers heralded a remarkable act of bravery at a place west of the capital called Dubosekovo. According to reports, twenty-eight members of the 316th Rifle Division (later redesignated the 8th Guards "Panfilov" Division) stood their ground against a column of fifty-four German tanks, destroying as many as eighteen in the process. Although all twenty-eight men perished in the fighting, their gallantry had forced the withdrawal of the much larger and better equipped German force. This story, repeated in various iterations throughout the war, proved extremely popular. As the Germans advanced on the city of Stalingrad in the late summer of 1942, for example, one political officer noted in his diary that he was suddenly compelled "to call out to the soldiers of the south: 'Fight like the twenty-eight! Crush tanks as they were crushed by the Panfilov-Guardsmen outside Moscow. Stand to the death, and the enemy will flee as it fled from Moscow.'"[3] Only later did it emerge that a few of the twenty-eight Panfilovtsy had not died in the fighting at Dubosekovo. While the story was easily modified to accommodate the new details, the matter was further complicated when one of the survivors later admitted to military prosecutors that the Dubosekovo encounter was largely a

[1] Werth, *Russia at War*, 741. [2] Grossman, *Life and Fate*, 299.
[3] P. Logvinenko, "Traditsii 28 geroev (Iz dnevnika politrabotnika)," *Krasnaia zvezda*, Aug. 27, 1942, 3.

fabrication, the invention of frontline newspaper reporters and editors. The Prosecutor's Office passed this information to the Politburo, which continued to promote the invented and sensationalized account as a highly effective source of agitation. The legend of the twenty-eight Panfilovtsy survived the war's end and Stalin's death; it would thrive for decades as an important component of the Soviet myth of World War II.[4]

The appeal of the story of the twenty-eight heroes derived in large part from the unit's multiethnic composition. Assembled in Soviet Central Asia, the Panfilov division had recruited heavily from the local population, with Russians constituting a small percentage of the overall formation.[5] Although the first newspaper articles devoted to the engagement at Dubosekovo made no mention of the participants' ethnicities, by 1942 the central press was specifying that among the twenty-eight "were Russians, Ukrainians, and Kazakhs," as well as troops of other nationalities. "Their martial comradeship, sealed in blood, became the epitome of the great fighting friendship of the peoples of our country," wrote Aleksandr Krivitskii, the literary secretary of the Red Army newspaper *Krasnaia zvezda* and the man most responsible for the myth's creation and perpetuation.[6] Such an emphasis on multiethnic friendship dovetailed with a broader mobilizational campaign highlighting the heroic pedigree of "non-Russian" men-at-arms.[7] In fact, it was the head of the Red Army's Political Directorate and Soviet Information Bureau, Aleksandr Shcherbakov, rather than Krivitskii, who first publicly emphasized the unit's diverse ethnic makeup.[8]

At the same time, the myth of the twenty-eight reinforced the more Russocentric themes of Soviet wartime culture. Most significant in this regard was the Russian political commissar supposedly in charge of the unit, Vasilii Klochkov. According to an expanded version of the story published in 1942, a few days before leading his men into battle,

4 GARF R-8131/37/4041/306–320. The location of Dubosekovo was not mentioned in the first article. See V. Koroteev, "Gvardeitsy Panfilova v boiakh za Moskvu," *Krasnaia zvezda*, Nov. 27, 1941, 3; A. Krivitskii, "Zaveshchanie 28 pavshikh geroev," *Krasnaia zvezda*, Nov. 28, 1941, 1. See also Luzhkov, *Moskva prifrontovaia*, 533–540; Petrov and Edel'man, "Novoe o sovetskikh geroiakh," 140–151. For an analysis of the actual engagement and the myth's origins, see Statiev, "La Garde meurt mais ne se rend pas," 769–798.

5 See Table 13.2 in Glantz, *Colossus Reborn*, 594.

6 Krivitskii, *28 geroev-panfilovtsev*, 5, 11–13. The outline of the story's initial publication is recounted in the memoirs of *Krasnaia zvezda*'s managing editor, David Ortenberg. See Ortenberg, *God 1942*, 47–48.

7 As Brandon Schechter points out, "non-Russian" was a catchall term to denote non-Slavic (Caucasian, Central Asian, etc.) peoples. Schechter, *The Stuff of Soldiers*, 1–2.

8 "Pod znamenem lenina. Doklad tov. A. S. Shcherbakova 21 ianvaria 1942 goda na torzhestvenno-traurnom zasedanii, posviashchennom XVIII godovshchine so dnia smerti V. I. Lenina," *Krasnaia zvezda*, Jan. 22, 1942, 2–3.

Klochkov took part in the famed November military parade on Red Square, during which Stalin delivered one of his most famous wartime addresses. "Let the heroic image of our great ancestors inspire you in this war," Stalin urged, "Aleksandr Nevskii, Dmitrii Donskoi, Kuz'ma Minin, Dmitrii Pozharskii, Aleksandr Suvorov, Mikhail Kutuzov."[9] The author then recounts how, standing in formation, Klochkov felt as though he was following in the footsteps of Russian warriors through the ages, such as the forces of Dmitrii Donskoi before defeating the Mongol–Tatar horde at the Battle of Kulikovo Field, or the militiamen of Kuz'ma Minin and Dmitrii Pozharskii, who ousted Polish–Lithuanian forces in 1612. Alongside these young Red Army volunteers "are the mustachioed fellow-fighters of Suvorov," and with them "Mikhail Kutuzov will soon pursue Napoleon's vaunted grenadiers." The story's narrator then ponders whether it was this moment, admiring the ancient Kremlin walls, that inspired Klochkov's legendary battle cry nine days later as German tanks bore down on the twenty-eight: "*Russia* is vast, but there is nowhere to retreat – Moscow is at our backs!"[10]

The figure of Klochkov is instructive. While the 1942 account described the political commissar deriving inspiration from prerevolutionary Russian sources, by 1952 authoritative treatments were attributing the man's bravery and sacrifice to a decidedly Soviet pedigree: "At the head of the platoon stood political instructor [Vasilii Klochkov]. The son of a poor Russian peasant, Klochkov passed through the difficult school of life. The Soviet Motherland opened before him a path to a happy future. But war broke out, and Klochkov left for the front to defend the Motherland." It was in the name of a homeland that symbolized emancipation from the prerevolutionary epoch, as much as continuity with it, that Klochkov and his men sacrificed their lives. "I will fight to the last breath," Klochkov's 1952 iteration declared shortly before the fateful engagement, "for the Motherland, for Stalin."[11]

As the war experience receded further into the past, the multiethnic, even universal, aspects of the Panfilovtsy story often took precedence over its Russocentric and historical features.[12] By the 1960s, delegations of young communists from around the world were identifying with this

[9] "Rech' Predsedatelia Gosudarstvennogo Komiteta Oborony i Narodnogo Komissara Oborony tov. I. V. Stalina na Krasnoi ploshchadi v den' XXIV godovshchiny Velikoi Oktiabr'skoi Sotsialisticheskoi Revoliutsii," *Krasnaia zvezda*, Nov. 9, 1941, 1. Also, Merridale, *Red Fortress*, 329.

[10] Krivitskii, *28 geroev-panfilovtsev*, 7–10 (emphasis added).

[11] Pankratova, *Velikii russkii narod*, 2nd ed., 180.

[12] On the transition from living, "communicative" memory to "cultural" and "political" remembrances, see Assmann, "Re-Framing Memory," 35–50.

Figure 0.1 Communist youth commemorate the last stand of the Panfilovtsy at Dubosekovo, early 1980s (courtesy of Valery Shchekoldin)

"socialist Thermopylae" (Figure 0.1).[13] Cuban youths visiting Moscow in 1965, for instance, took an oath at the site of the battle, declaring: "As the twenty-eight Panfilov-Guardsmen defended Moscow, so too shall we protect Cuba from American imperialism."[14] All the while the legend of the twenty-eight resonated among the USSR's multiethnic population. It should come as no surprise that one of the most revered Soviet war memorials still standing outside the borders of present-day Russia, one that has avoided the waves of post-Soviet iconoclasm that saw the toppling of other such monuments, is Kazakhstan's Memorial of Glory, dedicated to the feat of the twenty-eight. Unveiled in 1975, at the peak of the late-socialist commemorative cult of the war, the monument consists of a massive sculptural depiction of representatives of each of the country's fifteen republics wrought into the shape of the USSR (Figure 0.2). A popular venue for afternoon strolls and wedding processions, the memorial is situated in a leafy park in the center of Almaty that also bears the name of the Panfilovtsy.

[13] I take the Thermopylae metaphor from Kozlov, *The Readers of Novyi Mir*, 265.
[14] RGASPI M-1/32/1193/39.

Figure 0.2 Monument of Glory, Almaty, Kazakhstan (author's photo)

Like the legend of the twenty-eight Panfilov-Guardsmen in particular, the larger Soviet myth of victory embodied the fundamental tensions of wartime mobilization, which incorporated seemingly contradictory "Russian" and "Soviet," ethnocentric and "internationalist," transhistorical and postrevolutionary tendencies. The tensions and contradictions between these countervailing patriotic currents did not dissipate after 1945. Rather, they underpinned later Soviet debates about the meaning of victory; about the nature of patriotism and patriotic identity in a socialist society; about the place of the Russian people, their history and culture, within a supranational entity that presented itself as a renunciation of the old imperial order. How the war's "official" memory refracted these tensions of patriotism between the 1940s and 1980s is the subject of this book.

* * *

This is a history of the Soviet myth of victory in World War II from its Stalinist origins to its emergence as arguably the supreme symbol of state authority during the late-socialist period. The book argues that the war's memory encapsulated a range of competing ideological tendencies that gradually coalesced to form a "pan-Soviet" counterpoint to broader notions of Russian leadership and Russian-led ethnic hierarchy. While

Russocentric historical narratives of the prerevolutionary and early Soviet eras continued to stress Russian benevolence and assistance on the path to modernity, the story of the war evolved as a parallel but countervailing ideological current, which flattened hierarchical configurations among Russians and non-Russians alike. At the same time, many contested the notion of a horizontally integrated "Soviet" political community. The book shows how a "Russophile" faction of party elites, nationalist-oriented intellectuals, and even some non-Russian party organizations in the republics, perpetuated a Russocentric understanding of the war "from below." The competition between Russocentric and pan-Soviet conceptions of victory, which burst into the open during the late 1980s, reflected a wider struggle over the nature of patriotic identity in a multiethnic society that continues to reverberate in the post-Soviet space.

The book challenges a commonly held view that official war memory embodied and reinforced the fundamentally Russocentric basis of Soviet multiethnic governance.[15] Particularly in the years after Stalin's death, the Soviet leadership looked to the war's memory to bolster lateral "friendship" bonds and a supra-ethnic sense of belonging, one that did not succumb to, but remained in constant tension with, state-sponsored Russocentrism and a centuries-long narrative of Russian exceptionalism. In highlighting the fluid and ambiguous nature of the state's informal ethnic hierarchy, the present study sheds new light on long-standing questions linked to the politics of remembrance and provides a crucial historical context for the patriotic revival of the war's memory in twenty-first-century Russia.[16]

[15] This view is discussed in the following sections. Here, I distinguish between linguistic Russification, which was an assimilationist and homogenizing policy, and "Russocentrism" as the more general promotion of the Russian people as a distinct, leading entity vis-à-vis other Soviet peoples. On this distinction, see Aspaturian, "The Non-Russian Nationalities," 143–198.

[16] In 2014, the war served as a framing device for the annexation of Crimea and the Russian-backed separatist movement in eastern Ukraine. In both cases, Russian state media cast the Russian-speaking near abroad as the heirs to the Soviet generation of victors while branding the Ukrainian government and its supporters "fascists" and "banderovtsy" (a reference to followers of the Ukrainian nationalist leader and Nazi collaborator Stepan Bandera). Ukrainian media took part in its own war-related framing of events. See, for example, McGlynn, "Historical Framing," 1058–1080. In Russia, the rekindling of the war's public memory has not been an exclusively top-down process, but has ridden a preexisting wave of popular enthusiasm for victory and grassroots efforts to remember the dead of war, conferring an air of authenticity on this official endeavor. On government cooption of popular commemorations, see Bernstein, "Remembering War," 422–436. The tradition of the Immortal Regiment, to take one example, began as a journalist-led, grassroots movement in the city of Tomsk in 2012. The political leadership has since appropriated and politicized the tradition to the dismay of its originators. See Gabowitsch, "Are Copycats Subversive," 297–314; Fedor, "Memory, Kinship,"

The Myth of the War Victory

As in other countries that experienced the devastation of war and occupation, the Soviet leadership fashioned a self-serving "myth of the war experience," which recast the conflict as an event with profound meaning and sanctity.[17] Although national myths are always selective and grounded in forgetting as much as remembering, this book is less interested in ferreting out "myth" from "reality" than in looking at how myths structure reality.[18] As the cultural historian Michael Kammen proposes, even where there is a willful distortion of the past, "description and explanation serve us in more satisfactory ways than cynicism about bad faith or evil intent on the part of dominant elites." War myths reflect "a normative desire for . . . national unity, stability, and state-building." They are, moreover, hardly confined to authoritarian regimes.[19] This is to say that the Soviet myth of the war victory, like all officially sanctioned mythologies of war, reflected the universal drive for social cohesion in the wake of national upheaval.[20]

And yet, in the Soviet Union, the collective remembrance of World War II attained a significance arguably without parallel.[21] This was due in

307–344; Edele, "Fighting Russia's History Wars," 90–124. For an excellent overview of these processes under Putin, see Walker, *The Long Hangover*.

[17] Mosse, *Fallen Soldiers*, 3–11.

[18] Barthes, *Mythologies*, 142–145; Bouchard, *National Myths*, passim; Dany and Freistein, "Global Governance," 229–248.

[19] Kammen, *In the Past Lane*, 200, 204. In the United States, politicians, journalists, novelists, and many historians engaged in a mythmaking of their own after the war, which perpetuated a sense of American exceptionalism rooted in the wartime experience. Of course, liberal-democratic societies have produced other, more problematic war-related myths. See, for example, the "Lost Cause" erasure of slavery from Civil War memory in the southern United States or the blotting out of collaboration and communist participation from the Gaullist myth of resistance in postwar France. On these issues, see Blight, *Race and Reunion*; Golsan, "The Legacy of World War II in France," 73–101; Lagrou, *The Legacy of Nazi Occupation*; Rousso, *The Vichy Syndrome*; Bodnar, *The "Good War" in American Memory*.

[20] On the Soviet drive for a "homogeneous and harmonious" postwar society, see Weiner, *Making Sense of War*, 133–138; Weiner, "Nature, Nurture, and Memory," 1114–1155. Following Gérard Bouchard, I take myth to mean "enduring, deeply rooted, inclusive representations that suffuse a nation's past, present, and future with a set of values, ideals, and beliefs expressed in an identity and a memory": Bouchard, *National Myths*, 277.

[21] Although there are various labels used to describe the phenomenon of group memory, each expressing a slightly different nuance, this book generally uses the terms collective, social, or cultural memory or remembrance interchangeably to mean "the body of beliefs and ideas about the past that help a public or society understand both its past, present, and by implication, its future." Following John Bodnar, the book takes this "body of beliefs" to be the outcome of a dynamic interaction between "official" and "vernacular" cultures; the former advanced by authorities in positions of power, the latter reflecting "an array of specialized interests that are grounded in parts of the whole." See Bodnar, *Remaking America*, 13–15.

Figure 0.3 Artist at work on an official portrait of Leonid Brezhnev (courtesy of Valery Shchekoldin)

no small part to the sheer scale of Soviet losses. By most estimates, close to twenty-seven million Soviet citizens lost their lives as a direct result of the conflict. The Germans and their allies destroyed as many as seventy thousand Soviet villages and nearly two thousand towns and cities, leaving some twenty-five million people homeless by war's end.[22] Beginning in the 1960s, the public celebration of victory acquired the characteristics of a state-sanctioned cult, which included ubiquitous monuments, commemorative rituals, and mass media productions devised, in part, to legitimate the aging political elite (Figure 0.3).[23] Official portraits of Leonid Brezhnev increasingly tied his personal authority to supposed wartime service and heroics, a connection reflected in the almost comical number of military and other decorations adorning the general secretary's uniform.[24] By 1984,

[22] See Krivosheev, *Rossiia i SSSR v voinakh XX veka*, esp. 115–121. Critics of Krivosheev have given considerably higher figures for military losses. See, for example, Mikhalev, *Liudskie poteri v Velikoi Otechestvennoi voine*. For a useful discussion of Western biases concerning the Soviet war effort, see Davies, *No Simple Victory*, 9–72.

[23] On the war's veneration as constituting a state cult, see Tumarkin, *The Living & the Dead*.

[24] On Brezhnev's connection to the late-socialist war cult, see Davis, *Myth Making*.

according to official figures, the CPSU had helped to establish as many as one-hundred thousand monuments and memorial sites dedicated to the war, with more than forty thousand of these falling within the territory of a single republic – the Ukrainian SSR.[25] Even amid the USSR's collapse, the war remained, in the words of one Western chronicler at the time, the only "unquestionable victory of the regime."[26]

The "Great Patriotic War," as Soviet media dubbed the conflict, emerged as the central defining event of the Soviet epoch.[27] It was the lens through which Soviet citizens made sense of everything that had come before. From the vantage point of 1945, the brutality of collectivization, headlong industrialization, the Gulag, show trials, and purges became necessary measures to prepare the country for the long-anticipated showdown with the forces of imperialism, among which Nazi Germany embodied a particularly monstrous strain. Although the war's mythology fluctuated with the evolving political landscape, several key ingredients to victory remained constant: the Soviet political and economic system, the unity and unwavering patriotism of the Soviet people, socialist ideology, cooperation among Soviet nations, and the leadership of the Communist Party.[28]

Long dismissed for its blatantly propagandistic function and its association with both Stalin's cult and late-socialist gerontocracy, the war's public memory has become the object of sustained scholarly investigation over the past two decades.[29] Grounded largely in the theoretical and methodological approaches of the "memory boom" of the 1980s and 90s,[30] studies focusing on the Soviet Union have shed light on the often-dynamic role the war's commemoration played in shaping individual and

[25] Anderson, "Voprosy okhrany," 4. [26] Remnick, *Lenin's Tomb*, 400.

[27] On the war's longer-term impact on Soviet society and political culture, see, for example, Weiner, *Making Sense of War*, esp. 7–39; Lovell, *The Shadow of War*; Zubkova, *Russia after the War*; Druzhba, *Velikaia Otechestvennaia voina*; Fitzpatrick, "Postwar Soviet Society," 129–156.

[28] To this list, many scholars would certainly add the fraternal guidance and unique historical provenance of the Russian people. In a recent overview of victory culture in the USSR, for example, Mark Edele cites the Soviet system and Russian leadership theme as more or less equal factors: Edele, "The Soviet Culture of Victory," 787.

[29] Indeed, for many years, Tumarkin's *The Living & the Dead* was the only monograph to deal exclusively with the war's public memory. Other early works to identify the significance of the war's memory in Soviet society include Lane, *The Rites of Rulers*, esp. chap. 9; Vail' and Genis, *60-e mir sovetskogo cheloveka*, esp. 88–100; Gallagher, *The Soviet History of World War II*; Arnold, *Stalingrad im sowjetischen Gedächtnis*; and individual chapters in Stites, *Culture and Entertainment in Wartime Russia*; Garrard and Garrard, *World War 2 and the Soviet People*; Barber and Harrison, *The Soviet Home Front*; Linz, *The Impact of World War II*.

[30] Professional historians were responding to a confluence of circumstances that included the *Historikerstreit* in West Germany and renewed interest in Holocaust memory, the fiftieth anniversary of V-E Day, and the collapse of Communism in Central and Eastern

group recollections and identities.[31] In recent years, pathbreaking monographs have explored both the production and reception of Soviet war memory from a variety of perspectives.[32]

Europe. For an overview of the memory boom, see Ashplant, Dawson, and Roper, "The Politics of War Memory," 4–7. Key works in the English-language literature include Calder, *The Myth of the Blitz*; Mosse, *Fallen Soldiers*; Sherman, *The Construction of Memory in Interwar France*; Thomson, *Anzac Memories*; Winter, *Sites of Memory, Sites of Mourning*. See also important discussions in Adorno, "What Does Coming to Terms with the Past Mean?," 114–129; Gillis, "Introduction," 3–26; Herf, *Divided Memory*; Huyssen, *Twilight Memories*; Koonz, "Between Memory and Oblivion," 258–280; Koshar, *From Monuments to Traces*; Passerini, *Fascism in Popular Memory*. This wave of scholarship was attuned to modernist developments in the study of nationalism, which conceptualized the nation as a fundamentally modern construct: Anderson, *Imagined Communities*; Gellner, *Nations and Nationalism*; Hobsbawm, *Nations and Nationalism*; Hobsbawm, "Introduction: Inventing Traditions"; Hroch, "From National Movement to the Fully-Formed Nation." More recently, theorists of nationalism have highlighted the quotidian aspects of nation and ethnicity: Brubaker, *Ethnicity without Groups*; Billig, *Banal Nationalism*. Likewise, they incorporated insights from the bourgeoning field of memory studies, namely the idea that memories are given distinct shape and meaning in relation to the group or groups within which one is embedded: Nora, "General Introduction: Between Memory and History," 1–20; Assmann and Czaplicka, "Collective Memory and Cultural Identity," 125–133. These ideas were rooted in the work of Maurice Halbwachs, who argued in the 1920s that memories are "socially framed": Halbwachs, *On Collective Memory*.

31 In her excellent study of war memory in Leningrad, for example, Lisa Kirschenbaum reveals how official remembrance practices produced a framework within which individuals structured their conceptions of the past, "endowing loss with meaning as the necessary and terrible price of victory." See Kirschenbaum, *The Legacy of the Siege*, 11–17, 186–228, qt. 320; Peri, *The War Within*, passim; Merridale, *Ivan's War*, 189, 264, 373–395.

32 Perhaps no single monograph has done more to invigorate scholarly interest in the war's political and cultural legacy than Amir Weiner's work on the west-central Ukrainian region of Vinnytsia. Weiner demonstrates the conflict's profound impact on the nature of political authority and legitimacy, state violence, and collective identities. Weiner also revealed the war's place as a key milestone in Soviet eschatology: Weiner, *Making Sense of War*, 16–17; Weiner, "When Memory Counts," 167–188; cf. Lane, "Legitimacy and Power," 213. On the eschatological features of Marxism in Russia, see also Halfin, *From Darkness to Light*. The relatively recent literature on Soviet war memory includes important examinations of the local dimensions of memory in Leningrad and other urban and regional milieux (e.g., Mijnssen, *Russia's Hero Cities*; Donovan, *Chronicles in Stone*; Peri, *The War Within*; Davis, *Myth Making*; Maddox, *Saving Stalin's Imperial City*; Hellbeck, *Stalingrad*; Amar, *The Paradox of Ukrainian Lviv*; Risch, *The Ukrainian West*; Qualls, *From Ruins to Reconstruction*; Kirschenbaum, *The Legacy of the Siege*; Weiner, *Making Sense of War*); the war's treatment in Soviet cinema, literature, and historiography (e.g., Dobrenko, *Late Stalinism*, esp. 35–86; Kozlov, *The Readers of Novyi Mir*, esp. 263–283; Jones, *Myth, Memory, Trauma*, esp. 173–211; Ellis, *The Damned and the Dead*; Youngblood, *Russian War Films*; Markwick, *Rewriting History*); the evolution of Victory Day (e.g., Gabowitsch, "Victory Day before Brezhnev" as well as his forthcoming edited volume, *Pamiatnik i prazdnik: etnografiia Dnia Pobedy*; and on post-Soviet Victory Day: Norris, "Memory for Sale," 201–229); the plight of veterans and their part in propagating war memory (e.g., Edele, *Soviet Veterans of World War II*; Fieseler, *Arme Sieger*; Merridale *Ivan's War*, chap. 11); the impact on women, gender, and youth (e.g., Fraser, *Military Masculinity*; Krylova, *Soviet Women in Combat*; deGraffenried, *Sacrificing Childhood*;

But whereas the scholarly literature has tended away from high politics and the Party's central mythmaking apparatus to shed light on regional and societal variation and lived experience, the present study focuses on the production of what Amir Weiner called the "dominant myth" and its relationship to the most numerous Soviet nationality – the Russian people. That is to say, *The Soviet Myth* is primarily concerned with the mechanisms of rule, the outlook and intentions of political elites, and the methods whereby those elites sought to forge a sense of common identity through remembrance of war.[33] As Krishan Kumar observes, far from ignoring popular attitudes and perceptions, a focus on "rulers" and "ruling peoples" can elucidate the process of negotiation between state and citizenry, "to see it not simply in oppositional terms but as a matter of a shared enterprise that could unite rulers and ruled as much as it divided them."[34] Even one-party political systems depend on their capacity to connect with their subjects, to – as Frederick Corney puts it – implicate "the listeners in the telling of the story."[35] The myth of victory in the Great Patriotic War, and its relationship to the Soviet Union's "first among equals," played a central role in this official endeavor. But before examining the book's argument in greater detail, it is necessary to first

Fürst, *Stalin's Last Generation*; Markwick and Cardona, *Soviet Women on the Frontline*; also Bernstein, *Raised under Stalin*, chap. 8; Harris, "No Nastas'ias on the Volga," 99–130; Harris, "Memorializations of a Martyr," 73–90; Conze and Fieseler, "Soviet Women as Comrades-in-Arms," 211–234); the role of wartime mobilization in bringing non-Russian – and especially non-Slavic – communities into the Soviet fold (e.g., Carmack, *Kazakhstan in World War II*; Berkhoff, *Motherland in Danger*, 202–222; also Florin, "Becoming Soviet"; Shaw, "Soldiers' Letters to Inobatxon and O'g'ulxon"; Shin, "Red Army Propaganda"; Rudling, "For a Heroic Belarus!"; Yekelchyk, *Stalin's Empire of Memory*; Yilmaz, "History Writing"; Schechter, "The People's Instructions"; Stronski, *Tashkent*, chap. 4); the war's place within a specifically Russian martial longue durée (e.g., Carleton, *Russia: The Story of War*; Petrone, *The Great War in Russian Memory*; Hosking, *Rulers and Victims*, esp.189–223; Brandenberger, *National Bolshevism*, 183–239; Vujačić, *Nationalism, Myth, and the State*, 185–193); the changing nature of citizenship viewed from the "stuff" soldiers carried (Schechter, *The Stuff of Soldiers*); among other works cited throughout this book.

33 For important critiques of the state-centered approach to social memory, see Confino, "Collective Memory," 1386–1403; Winter, *Remembering War*, 135–153; Winter and Sivan, "Setting the Framework," 6–39. However, in authoritarian societies where a small political elite controls the mechanisms of social memory, analyses of the "official" production of memory are especially relevant; they elucidate the framework within which memory is made. As Winter concedes, "political groups and institutions inject collective memory . . . into the process." Winter, "The Performance of the Past," 17.

34 Kumar, *Visions of Empire*, 6. A similar point is made in Blitstein, "Nation and Empire," 204–205.

35 Corney, *Telling October*, 10–11. Among scholars who have revolutionized our understanding of the relationship between the Soviet state and its citizenry by demonstrating ways official messaging helped structure popular perceptions, behaviors, and actions, see, for example, Hellbeck, *Revolution on My Mind*; Halfin, *Terror in My Soul*; Kotkin, *Magnetic Mountain*.

consider the party-state's evolving posture toward its most prominent (one might even say "awkward") national community, ethnic Russians, in the years leading up to and during the war.[36]

The Russian Question

Having emerged victorious from the bloody civil war that came in the wake of the Bolshevik seizure of power in 1917, Russia's Communist government faced the daunting challenge of transforming a vast former empire into a structure that claimed not to be one. The Bolsheviks unveiled their novel approach to this problem in 1923, following the establishment of the Union of Soviet Socialist Republics the previous year.[37] Based on the Marxist assumption that national identity was a transitory, bourgeois phenomenon that needed to be traversed and transcended before advancing to the purely class-based consciousness of socialism the regime granted forms of nationhood to the inherited ethnic minorities of the former Russian Empire in hopes of defusing their politically charged aspirations and antagonisms. This "anti-imperial state" was conceived not only to assist in the revolutionary drive toward socialism, but also to facilitate trust between the state's various ethnic groups and the former oppressor nation of Great Russians. To this end, the regime introduced measures that positively discriminated against the state's ethnic Russian core. In the cultural sphere, this meant the denigration of tsarist military heroes and Russian literary icons. At an institutional level, the Bolsheviks denied the Russian people their own communist party, academy of sciences, state security service, and ethnically delineated territory. They were granted a federative (SFSR) rather than national (SSR) republic. And while this encouraged Russians to more closely identify with central, all-union institutions – and thus territorially with the USSR as a whole – the objective was to hamstring Russian cultural and political nationalism, which both Lenin and Stalin initially identified as the greater threat than the "local" nationalisms of non-Russian peoples.[38]

During the 1930s, Stalin reversed the official line on Russians in what has been cited as an important facet of a more general conservative "retreat" from the internationalist and class-based precepts of the prior

[36] This is in reference to Terry Martin's apt description of the RSFSR as the "awkward republic." Martin, *Affirmative Action Empire*, 394–402.

[37] This outline of early Soviet nationalities policy is indebted to pioneering studies emphasizing the Bolsheviks as nation-builders rather than destroyers. For several, now-classic examples, see Edgar, *Tribal Nation*; Hirsch, *Empire of Nations*; Martin, *Affirmative Action Empire*; Smith, *The Bolsheviks and the National Question*; Slezkine, "The USSR as a Communal Apartment"; Suny, *The Revenge of the Past*; Simon, *Nationalism.*

[38] Martin, *Affirmative Action Empire*, 19; Vihavainen, "Nationalism and Internationalism," 79.

decade.[39] The very creation of the Soviet Union in 1922 and Stalin's subsequent thesis of "socialism in one country" reflected the gnawing sense that revolution in the industrially advanced West was unlikely anytime soon; hence, the fledgling Union would need to fend for itself.[40] The War Scare of 1927 and especially Hitler's rise to power in 1933 appear to have convinced Stalin that Marxism-Leninism alone lacked the mobilizational potential necessary to successfully defend the Soviet state.[41] Just as troubling were indications that indigenization policies, far from accelerating the obsolescence of ethnonational identities, were fueling anti-Soviet "bourgeois" nationalism within the USSR's borders. Thus, throughout the decade, the regime took a hard line against perceived instances of non-Russian nationalist activity, resulting in the "unmasking" of several dozen real or imagined nationalist conspiracies across the country.[42]

At the same time, Soviet cultural production shifted attention away from abstract social forces as the drivers of history toward individual agency and everyday heroism. Following Stalin's decimation of the Old Bolshevik ranks in the latter part of the decade, the focus shifted more thoroughly toward Russian cultural and historical themes. The press celebrated Russians as "first among equals" while touting Russian cultural, scientific, and, especially, military achievements of the prerevolutionary era. Films, histories, and monuments depicting Russian and proto-Russian heroes such as Aleksandr Nevskii, Dmitrii Donskoi, and Mikhail Kutuzov complemented official appeals to patriotism and patriotic devotion to motherland.[43] Russian language instruction became mandatory in schools in 1938 while the introduction of the internal passport (1932) had fixed one's sub-state national identity, which was based on the nationality of one's biological parents. Such "cultural technologies of rule" helped imbue both Soviet officialdom and the broader citizenry with an increasingly ethnonational outlook and self-perception. By the end of the decade, the concept of nationality had displaced the former preoccupation with class identity, a phenomenon Terry Martin

[39] The classic work arguing that there was a retreat from Soviet socialism toward a more traditional Russian nationalism is Timasheff, *The Great Retreat*, esp. chap. 7 and 378–382.

[40] The term is based on Stalin's 1924 thesis, which argued for developing socialism within a Soviet framework rather than prioritizing revolution abroad.

[41] Brandenberger, *National Bolshevism*, 21–24; Brooks, *Thank You, Comrade Stalin*, 76; Dobrenko, "The Disaster of Middlebrow Taste," 153–164.

[42] Service, *Stalin*, 326–328; Suny, "Stalin and His Stalinism," 37–38.

[43] This outline is drawn primarily from Brandenberger, *National Bolshevism*, 29–42, 77–94. See also Service, *Stalin*, 205–206.

goes so far as to describe as a turn toward ethnic primordialism.[44] During the war, as we will see, these processes helped render whole ethnic groups vulnerable to accusations of collective treason.

But the turn to Russocentrism and prerevolutionary patriotic imagery signified neither an abandonment of socialism nor an embrace of Russian nationalism.[45] The Stalinist leadership, like all revolutionary elites, continued to legitimate itself through a revolutionary metanarrative that emphasized the cleavage between the old and the new orders and that often explained away negative social phenomena as "remnants of the old regime."[46] Not unlike the nineteenth-century American magazine editor John O'Sullivan, who pointed to his country's revolutionary break as justification for its unfettered westward expansion, Stalinist authorities regularly signaled their antipathy toward "monarchies and aristocracies of antiquity" and nostalgic "reminiscences of battle fields [*sic*]."[47] As Marxists, however, the Bolsheviks did not reject the past wholesale. Instead, they viewed their movement as the culmination of a process centuries in the making. History even offered a blueprint that, if properly deciphered, could illuminate the inexorable march toward communism.[48] Although Russian history was rife with "reactionary" elements, Stalin believed it was entirely appropriate to celebrate its "popular" features, including pre-Soviet proletarian struggles and wars fought in defense of the homeland.[49] Far from irrelevant to the revolutionary project, the Communists saw "progressive" historical subject matter as vital to comprehending the prehistory of the Great October Socialist Revolution, even if there was not always a consensus over whether tsarist commanders and proto-Russian warriors constituted acceptable models of revolutionary patriotism.[50]

Stalinist Russocentrism might best be appreciated as a pragmatic and populist shift in the method of ideological indoctrination. As David Brandenberger has argued, at a time of rapid industrialization and mobilization for war, the new line "cloaked a Marxist-Leninist worldview within russocentric, etatist rhetoric" in order to more

44 Hirsch, *Empire of Nations*, 99–227; Martin, *Affirmative Action Empire*, 442–451.

45 For the view that Stalin embraced a variation of Russian nationalism, see, for example, Lewin, *The Soviet Century*, chap.12; Tucker, *Stalin in Power*, 41–43.

46 Hunt, *Politics, Culture, and Class in the French Revolution*, 19–51.

47 O'Sullivan, "The Great Nation of Futurity," 426–430; Hopkins, *American Empire*, 191–193. I thank Lawrence Culver for first pointing me to O'Sullivan's text.

48 For an illuminating discussion of this issue, see Bergman, *The French Revolutionary Tradition*, esp. i–xiv, and passim.

49 Walicki, *Marxism*, esp. 398–454.

50 This issue became particularly acute in the post-Stalin era. David Hoffmann makes a similar point about the challenges Stalin's Russocentrism presented in the longer term: Hoffmann, *Stalinist Values*, 165.

effectively "propagandize state-building and promote popular loyalty to the regime."[51] Such an interpretation is especially apt given the official declaration, following collectivization and the First Five-Year Plan, that socialism had been "built in its foundations."[52] In light of the purported elimination of capitalist exploitation within the Soviet Union, the shift in policy of the mid 1930s – observed in the promotion of traditional familial roles, in the move from avant-gardism to neoclassical monumental forms, and in the seemingly un-Marxist notion of a Soviet homeland – could now be justified as legitimating and consolidating the revolutionary order.[53] The Russian national revival was selective and largely adhered to Stalin's doctrine of national cultures, which mandated that they be "national in form" but "socialist in content."[54] Pushkin's rehabilitation, to take one example, recast the poet-aristocrat as a true "people's poet," largely alienated from the ruling class to which he belonged.[55] Similarly, authorities rehabilitated certain tsars – Ivan IV and Peter the Great, but not Catherine – for having enabled a strong central state in which to build socialism.[56] Put simply, the turn to Russian prerevolutionary cultural and patriotic motifs was, from its inception, highly pragmatic and instrumental; it was a provisional means of ideological indoctrination and mobilization at a time when the country was about to face an existential threat.

War and Ethnic Hierarchy

It was during the war that the Soviet state most effusively co-opted tsarist symbolism and Russian historical motifs.[57] The Soviet leadership cast the war as a struggle for national liberation, as a "Great Patriotic War"

[51] Brandenberger, *National Bolshevism*, qt. 6, 62; Brandenberger, "Stalin's Populism," 723–739.

[52] On the profound significance of this claim, see Hoffmann, *Stalinist Values*, 4, 152–153, passim.

[53] Hoffmann, "Was There a 'Great Retreat' from Soviet Socialism," 651–674; Kotkin, *Magnetic Mountain*, 357.

[54] Brandenberger, *National Bolshevism*, chaps. 2–3.

[55] Petrone, *Life Has Become More Joyous, Comrades*, 131–134.

[56] As Erik van Ree notes: "Stalinist attention to Russian struggles against foreign invaders in late medieval times ... can be similarly interpreted as highlighting not the primordial character of the Russian nation but precisely the fact that this nation was a historical creation." Ree, "Stalin as Marxist," qt. 176; Brandenberger, *National Bolshevism*, 51–52; Perrie, *The Cult of Ivan the Terrible*, 29–33, 98.

[57] For example, Berkhoff, *Motherland in Danger*, 202–222; Maddox, "These Monuments Must Be Protected!"; Norris, *A War of Images*, 179–185; Brandenberger, *National Bolshevism*, chaps. 7–10; Brooks, *Thank You, Comrade Stalin*, 159–194; Kirschenbaum, "Our City, Our Hearths, Our Families," 825; Barber, "The Image of Stalin," 38; Edele, "Paper Soldiers," 89–108. See also the various entries in Platt and Brandenberger, *Epic Revisionism*; Stites, *Culture and Entertainment in Wartime Russia*. On wartime loyalties, particularly among Russians, see, for example, Enstad, *Soviet Russians*; Budnitskii, "The

evocative of the 1812 Patriotic War against Napoleon. State media touted traditional Russian soldierly virtues as a model for new recruits. These included "physical stamina," "sense of duty," "self-sacrifice," "hatred of oppression," and, most of all, "steadfastness [*stoikost'*]" and "love for the motherland [*rodina*]."[58] Iconography depicting prerevolutionary Russian commanders urging on Red Army troops became a mainstay of wartime propaganda. In early 1944, the state adopted a new patriotic national anthem to replace the old "Internationale," one that made explicit reference to the role of Russia, which "united forever" [*splotila naveki*] the country's various peoples.[59] Meanwhile, chauvinistic and anti-Semitic attitudes among party functionaries, such as the head of the Department of Propaganda and Agitation (Agitprop), Georgii Aleksandrov, only added momentum to the Russocentric surge unleashed by the war.[60]

But the Russocentric propaganda of the war years did not target Russians exclusively. As late as 1945, the Soviet leadership remained committed to mobilizing non-Russians through the deployment of local national-patriotic imagery, albeit within a Russocentric historical framework.[61] This campaign stemmed primarily from complications presented by the recruitment and arrival at the front of soldiers from Central Asia and the Caucasus who often lacked knowledge of the Russian language and among whom political indoctrination before the war had met with limited success. The program sought to localize and contextualize the war for non-Russian recruits in several ways. The military created

Great Patriotic War and Soviet Society"; Edele, *Stalin's Defectors*; Reese, *Why Stalin's Soldiers Fought*.

58 GARF 6903/12/87/637. On "steadfastness [*stoikost'*]" as a particularly important Russian historical virtue, see Carleton, *Russia: The Story of War*, esp. chap. 4. On "love for the motherland," see Merridale, *Ivan's War*, 91, 99, 201, 380–381, and passim.

59 Service, *Stalin*, 442–448.

60 The Russians as "elder brothers" and "first among equals" built on prewar declarations and thus appeared very early in the war. See, for example, "Velikaia druzhba narodov SSSR," *Pravda*, July 29, 1941, 1; V. Kruzkhkov, "Velikaia sila leninsko-stalinskoi druzhby narodov," *Pravda*, Feb. 21, 1942, 3. On Aleksandrov's chauvinism, see Berkhoff, *Motherland in Danger*, 163. Additional Russocentric measures included the limited revival of the Russian Orthodox Church and the disbanding of Comintern. The more general Russocentric thrust of wartime propaganda and policies proved extremely popular among frontline soldiers, where, alongside Tolstoy's *War and Peace*, one of the most popular stories was that of a Russian peasant soldier, the titular *Vasilii Terkin*, by Aleksandr Tvardovskii. See Tvardovskii, *Vasilii Terkin*, 35–36, 122–127, 203, and passim; Carleton, *Russia: The Story of War*, 86–88; Hosking, "The Second World War," 162–187. Other popular writers, such as Aleksei Tolstoi, Ilya Ehrenburg, and Konstantin Simonov, conflated Soviet and Russian loyalties. Examples include Simonov, *Russkie liudi*; and the various entries in Erenburg, *Voina: Aprel' 1942 – Mart 1943*. On the popularity among soldiers of Russocentric propaganda, see Merridale, *Ivan's War*, 381.

61 Recent explorations of this campaign include Carmack, *Kazakhstan in World War II*, passim; Florin, "Becoming Soviet"; Shaw, "Soldiers' Letters to Inobatxon and O'g'ulxon"; Shin, "Red Army Propaganda."

a number of national formations within its ranks while central authorities deployed bilingual political instructors to articulate Soviet objectives in recruits' native languages. In addition, training in the Russian language intensified during the war to improve communication between the predominantly Russian and Slavic officer corps and the new arrivals.[62]

Along with these measures, mobilization involved the selective resurrection of non-Russian national pasts. Georgian writers produced histories on state-building monarchs like eleventh-century King Davit Agmashenebeli. Uzbeks were reminded of the hero Tarabi, who "struggled for freedom against the Mongol invaders."[63] Ukrainian newspapers traced the fighting traditions of the Ukrainian people to the seventeenth-century Cossack leaders Petro Konashevich-Sahaidachnyi and Bogdan Khmel'nitskii, who, in 1654, pledged Cossack allegiance to the Muscovite tsar. In 1943, the state went so far as to establish the Order of Bogdan Khmel'nitskii for outstanding combat service leading to the liberation of Soviet territory. Patterned on military orders named for Nevskii, Suvorov, and Kutuzov established in 1942, this order remained the only military decoration recalling a historical figure of non-Russian lineage.[64] The advancement of non-Russian national pasts supplemented the central media's emphasis on the present-day heroism of non-Russian Soviet citizens in defense of the motherland – the myth of the twenty-eight Panfilovtsy being the most famous example.[65] However, authorities intended such measures to reinforce rather than replace a sense of ethnic hierarchy. Indeed, Stalin approved the introduction of the Order of Bogdan Khmel'nitskii mainly because of the latter's role in promoting the "sacred union" between Ukrainians and Russians.[66]

Such efforts to mobilize non-Russian groups through targeted propaganda accelerated the essentialization of ethnic categories that began

[62] For excellent treatments of this subject, see Schechter, "The People's Instructions," 109–133; Dreeze, "Stalin's Empire." On national formations in the Red Army, see Glantz, *Colossus Reborn*, 548–51, 600–604. On the way these wartime processes fostered a Russified sense of Soviet national belonging, see especially Shaw, "Making Ivan-Uzbek."

[63] Stronski, *Tashkent*, qt. 84; Shin, "Red Army Propaganda," 55.

[64] On the introduction of historically themed military decorations and the incorporation of elements of tsarist uniforms, see Schechter, *The Stuff of Soldiers*, 58–72. In terms of the timeline of their appearance, naval decorations were an exception. As late as 1944, the state approved decorations bearing the names of the Russian admirals Fedor Ushakov and Pavel Nakhimov. See also Vdovin, *Russkie v XX veke*, 150.

[65] Among numerous other publicized examples of multiethnic cooperation in the defeat of Nazi Germany, see the defense of the so-called Pavlov House during the Battle of Stalingrad, which purportedly involved nearly a dozen Soviet nationalities. Rodimtsev, *Gvardeitsy stoiali nasmert'*, 84–105.

[66] Yekelchyk, "Stalinist Patriotism," 51–80.

before the war.[67] If the leadership considered certain nationalities useful in the fight against Germany, it looked upon others with suspicion and came to regard whole ethnic groups as irredeemable "enemy nations."[68] For example, in 1944, authorities deported nearly half a million Chechen and Ingush peoples to Central Asia. Given their "enemy" status, wartime and postwar commemorations downplayed the contributions of these groups. Soviet media gave strikingly little recognition to the numerous fighters of Chechen origin who participated in the defense of Brest Fortress in June 1941.[69] Amir Weiner describes such a ranking or outright "excision" of peoples based on their perceived wartime contribution as "hierarchical heroism," one of two major cornerstones of the emerging war myth.[70]

The other cornerstone Weiner identifies is the principle of "universal suffering," which applied most directly to the uniqueness of the Jewish wartime experience. Jews were well represented throughout the Red Army and industry and Soviet media acknowledged the Jewish contribution to the fight until very late in the war.[71] Readers of Soviet newspapers, moreover, could find in the journalism of Ehrenberg and other published reports direct references to the Nazi extermination program.[72] While not a full-throated appeal to the Soviet Union's Jews, the sporadic release of such information probably contributed to a general sense of outrage, a reaction that occasionally provoked calls for the creation of Jewish military formations within the Red Army.[73] Nevertheless, public representations typically cast the Nazis' campaign against Soviet Jewry as being waged against "citizens of the USSR."[74] This was in part an effort to counter German characterizations of the Soviet Union as a bastion of

67 Martin, "Modernization or Neo-Traditionalism? Ascribed Nationality and Soviet Primordialism."

68 Smith, *Red Nations*, 147–162; Naimark, "Ethnic Cleansing"; Weiner, *Making Sense of War*, chaps. 3–4; Nekrich, *The Punished Peoples*.

69 An exception among Chechen soldiers was the celebrated machine-gunner Khanpasha Nuradilov. Merlin, "Remembering and Forgetting," 37; Tishkov, *Chechnya*, 200.

70 Weiner, *Making Sense of War*, chap. 4.

71 Weiner, 216–235. Likewise, the Jewish Anti-Fascist Committee in Moscow, under the leadership of Solomon Mikhoels and Shakne Epshtein, operated a relatively successful propaganda campaign geared toward audiences abroad.

72 Berkhoff, "Total Annihilation"; Berkhoff, *Motherland in Danger*, 136–166.

73 As one Soviet soldier mentioned in a letter to Ehrenburg, "I am convinced that the Jews will fight the Fascists with a hatred ten times greater, both as patriots of the motherland and as the avengers of the blood of their brothers, sisters, fathers and mothers, wives and children." Quoted in Arad, *In the Shadow of the Red Banner*, 9. There is also evidence that many Soviet citizens welcomed news of the systematic killing of Jews. See Berkhoff, *Motherland in Danger*, 162–166.

74 Arad, *In the Shadow of the Red Banner*, 7–11; Arad, "Stalin and the Soviet Leadership: Responses to the Holocaust."

"Judeo-Bolshevism."[75] It also stemmed from anti-Semitic attitudes among the party rank and file, further complicating representations of Jewish heroism. It was quite common, for instance, to encounter rumors that Jews were evading military service. As a sign of things to come, public accounts increasingly glossed over the Jewish identity of soldiers as the war drew to a close.[76]

Hence, Weiner and others contend, the war not only furthered the essentialization of ethnic identities, it also reified their hierarchical configuration. Russians, through their wartime service, remained the paramount Soviet collective, while groups suspected of disloyalty were consigned to political oblivion.[77] Between these two poles stood everyone else, grouped into Soviet nations arranged vertically in the order of their supposed contribution in wartime.[78]

Interpreting Victory

The relationship between the hierarchical mode of heroism detailed in the preceding section and the fledgling myth of victory has divided historians. A number of scholars have argued that the war victory fostered a transcendent, pan-Soviet identity, one that superseded hierarchical ethnic particularism.[79] As Barbara Epstein asserts in her study of the Minsk Ghetto, "The Great Patriotic War became the basis of a new or at least refashioned and revived Soviet identity, transcending the various

[75] Manley, *To the Tashkent Station*, 83.

[76] Manley, 229–235; Weiner, *Making Sense of War*, 216–235.

[77] This is certainly not to equate Soviet ethnic hierarchy with the racial ideology and biological determinism of the Nazis. As Weiner is careful to point out, in the Soviet case, "individuals maintained the right to appeal and often did so successfully," while "the fear of allowing biological-familial heredity to dictate the prospects of redemption continued to haunt the regime." Weiner, *Making Sense of War*, 201–202.

[78] Among "loyal" national communities, the war reinforced a Sovietized sense of ethnic identity. This process involved its own hierarchical complications and reconfigurations. Tarik Cyril Amar has demonstrated that the official history of the Ivan Franko People's Guard, an underground organization based in the western Ukrainian city of L'vov (Lviv), came to promote a distinctly Soviet-Ukrainian national myth. This was achieved in part by diminishing the very prominent role played by Polish Communists, Jews, and other groups within the organization. See Amar, *The Paradox of Ukrainian Lviv*, 282–297. More generally, see Weiner, "Nature, Nurture, and Memory," 1149–1154.

[79] See, for example, Epstein, *The Minsk Ghetto*, passim; Whittington, "Making a Home for the Soviet People," 147–161; Lovell, *The Shadow of War*, 231; Kotkin, *Armageddon Averted*, 44–45; Szporluk, *Russia, Ukraine*, xxxv–xxxvi; Szporluk, "The Fall of the Tsarist Empire," 82; Dunmore, *Soviet Politics*, 130; Lane, *The Rites of Rulers*, 145–146. Similarly, Lisa Kirschenbaum argues that the war's memory helped perpetuate "such (unrealized) visions of Soviet citizenship and the Soviet person." Kirschenbaum, *The Legacy of the Siege*, 13.

ethnic groups, or nationalities, composing the Soviet Union."[80] Amir Weiner, too, contends that the emerging myth of the war nurtured a "supraclass, cross-ethnic" sense of belonging that provided "the polity with a previously absent integrating theme." Yet precisely how this wider sense of Sovietness impacted the war myth's hierarchy of heroism – and in particular the notion of Russian wartime primacy – is less clear. Weiner notes, for example, that toward the end of the war the inclusive all-Soviet mode of heroism was reinstated in Ukraine so as to "curtail the mistaken assumption ... that Ukraine was liberated from the Nazis 'under the banner of [Taras] Shevchenko and [Panteleimon] Kulish.'" Here, Weiner frames mobilization as a "balancing act" between ethnonational-oriented appeals and what he calls the "Soviet component." Should it grow too strong, the national factor threatened to destabilize the Soviet component; at the same time, the Soviet component offered a means of tempering ethnonational assertiveness linked to wartime mobilization.[81] But how this intriguing framework, taken from Ukraine, applied to Russians and to Soviet multiethnicity more generally remains unexplored.

An investigation into the relationship between the "Soviet component" and the concept of Russian hierarchical primacy seems especially appropriate given that scholarship on postwar ideology, mass culture, and nationalities policy has largely interpreted the war's official memory to be an extension of the Russocentric hierarchy of the war years.[82] It is in its attention to the war myth's bearing on the so-called Russian Question – defined here as "the role and status of the Russian people, language, and culture within the Soviet Union" – that the present study builds on the important groundwork laid by Weiner and others.[83]

The most important scholarly examination of this issue to date is David Brandenberger's *National Bolshevism*, which explains the trajectory of the Stalinist turn toward Russocentric etatism from 1931 to 1956. Brandenberger affirms the link between the war's memory and the

[80] Epstein, *The Minsk Ghetto*, 228. [81] Weiner, *Making Sense of War*, 354–356, 385.

[82] As Yuri Slezkine remarks of the first postwar decade, "Every day and every hour, in every classroom and at every meeting, the Soviet people ... were told that the war had been won by the Russians and their friends; that the Russians had won the war because they were a great nation; that they had been a great nation for as long as Russian had been spoken." Slezkine, *Arctic Mirrors*, 309. For other examples, see Kozhevnikov, *Russkii patriotizm*, esp. 399–403; Plokhy, *Lost Kingdom*, 274–275; Carleton, *Russia: The Story of War*, esp. 85–89; Shin, "Red Army Propaganda," 39–40; Yekelchyk, *Stalin's Empire of Memory*; Manley, *To the Tashkent Station*, 235–237; Dobrenko, *Stalinist Cinema*, 136–137; Brandenberger, "Stalin, the Leningrad Affair," esp. 247–248; Brandenberger, *National Bolshevism*, 183–225; Hosking, "The Second World War," 162–187.

[83] This is following Terry Martin: Martin, *Affirmative Action Empire*, 24.

Russian people's enduring status as the paramount Soviet nation.[84] As he observes, ideologists' main preoccupation in the immediate postwar period involved reconciling "the previous decade's emphasis on prerevolutionary Russian history with the war's undeniably modern, 'Soviet' character." For Brandenberger, this ideological reconciliation hinged on the emerging war myth, which presented the 1941–5 conflict "as a fundamentally Russian experience." In this view, nuanced distinctions between the Soviet war effort and Russia's much longer history of patriotic struggles against foreign aggressors mattered little, as a broader Russocentric ideological framework quickly subsumed the victory narrative.[85] The war victory thus enabled the Stalinist leadership to craft an ideological amalgam of sorts, which paired Russian-led victory in 1945 and a millennium of Russian exceptionalism in a patriotic double axis, offering ideologists an "evocative vocabulary of myths, imagery, and iconography with which to rally the population."[86]

A similar emphasis on the Russocentric basis of Soviet patriotic identity has dominated the historiography of the late-socialist period.[87] Groundbreaking studies by Yitzhak Brudny, Nikolai Mitrokhin, and others, have exposed the sometimes-intimate relationship between Russian nationalist-oriented intellectuals and the late-socialist party leadership, as well as the state's continued reliance on Russian national-patriotic motifs for popular mobilization. As Brudny argues, faced with a decline in revolutionary fervency, the Brezhnev-led Politburo of the 1960s and 1970s made an ideological compromise, co-opting elements of the Russian nationalist intelligentsia in order to bolster the state's mobilizational capacity. The official support for a limited, pro-Soviet Russian nationalism was, Brudny contends, most apparent in the increased print runs of nationalist "thick" journals and in the protection and elevation of so-called village prose writers. Likewise, Mitrokhin has charted the permeation of Russian nationalist attitudes among the middle echelons of the Party and state. The development of an informal network of Russophiles in positions of authority, and the likeminded artists, writers,

[84] Brandenberger, *National Bolshevism*. The most recent iteration of Brandenberger's argument is Brandenberger, *Stalinskii russotsentrizm* (2017).

[85] Brandenberger writes that postwar attempts to discern between the prerevolutionary and Soviet eras while nevertheless capturing a sense of Russian historical exceptionalism "was remarkably awkward, if not totally finessed. Ultimately, this prescription proved to be impossible to enforce and was quickly forgotten." Brandenberger, *National Bolshevism*, 193.

[86] Brandenberger, esp. 183–196.

[87] One, introductory textbook summarizes the era thusly: "Soviet civilization was firmly under the sway of a Russian cultural pantheon and a Russian-dominated cult of World War II." Lovell, *The Soviet Union*, 111.

historians, and veterans they cultivated, constituted nothing less than an informal "Russian Party" embedded within party-state structures. Although Mitrokhin notes in passing that Russian nationalist cultural figures were instrumental in shaping the war's memory, the connection between state-supported Russian nationalism and the late-socialist victory myth has remained almost wholly unexplored. This omission is particularly glaring given that the war's memory was the subject of perhaps the largest propaganda campaign of the late-socialist era – the cult of World War II. The few authors who do touch on the war's remembrance in this context tend to view it as an outgrowth of broader Russian national-patriotic tendencies.[88]

This book makes three significant contributions to this literature, which will be explicated in detail in the following sections. Together, these interventions – which I categorize as "wartime threads," "discursive tension," and "the doctrine of the Soviet people" – form the core of the book's argument.

Wartime Threads

The book's first major contention is that Stalinist Russocentrism was merely one of several competing patriotic strands unleashed during wartime mobilization that vied to define the war's memory in the postwar era. By the war's end, as Agitprop terminated certain wartime appeals, such as those pertaining to non-Russian heroic pasts and Orthodox Church-inspired proclamations, the various remaining mobilizational threads coalesced to form two prevailing ideological paradigms. The first, which this book terms the "Russocentric paradigm," was a direct extension of the wartime Russocentric line. Epitomized in Stalin's "great ancestors" speech of 1941, its essence involved positioning the Great Patriotic War along a thousand-year continuum of Russian martial struggles. This tendency was multiethnic in the sense that it highlighted the state's ethnic diversity and Russians' leading place within a highly variegated population. It was "Soviet" in that it cited the Soviet system, party leadership, and socialism as important wartime factors. But the Russocentric

[88] Brudny, *Reinventing Russia*, 3–4, 57–80, and passim; Mitrokhin, *Russkaia partiia*, 114–116, 276–283, 291–293, and passim; Kozhevnikov, *Russkii patriotizm*, 404–499. Brudny does not address the Russian nationalist link with the war's official veneration at all, while Donovan implies a subtle connection, rooted in late-socialist reflections on the Nazi destruction of Russian cultural artifacts. Hosking sees the war cult as partly emerging from the broader "Russianist outlook." See Donovan, *Chronicles in Stone*, 31–105; Hosking, *Rulers and Victims*, 324–337, 361–371, qt. 362. For classic treatments of the growth of Russian nationalism during this period, see Dunlop, *Faces*; Yanov, *The Russian Challenge*; Yanov, *The Russian New Right*; Zaslavsky, *The Neo-Stalinist State*, chap. 5.

paradigm presented Russian leadership and historical pedigree as fundamental, even overriding, ingredients to victory.[89]

The other dominant postwar tendency this book identifies, one that is often glossed over in the scholarly literature by the more evocative nationalistic imagery, was an ideological line firmly rooted in the Soviet era, its unique achievements, and the motif of a "socialist motherland" inhabited by a supra-ethnic community of "Soviet people."[90] This "pan-Soviet /internationalist paradigm" was highly statist and patriotic in the sense that it advocated the "patriotism of socialism in one country."[91] It was Russified in its emphasis on Russian as the language of interethnic communication and in its veneration of the Russian cultural canon. Its internationalism was domestic – that is, reflecting "friendship" bonds among Soviet peoples.[92] But unlike the Russocentric paradigm, the pan-Soviet /internationalist tendency maintained an uneasy if not antagonistic relationship to both Russian-led hierarchy and pre-Soviet patriotic motifs. The concept nearly always served to underscore the depth of the revolutionary divide, the novelty (as opposed to antiquity) of the Soviet people, and the primacy of a supranational and postrevolutionary sense of political identity.[93]

The pan-Soviet line portrayed the state's various ethnonational constituencies as bound not by Russian leadership but by lateral loyalties: "Russians, Ukrainians, Belarusians, Turkmen, Uzbeks, Tajiks and other peoples of the multinational Soviet Union" defending their motherland

[89] In addition to Brandenberger's "russocentric rubric," this paradigm is similar to both Gregory Carleton's notion of a "Russian myth of exceptionalism" and Mischa Gabowitsch's concept of "panhistorical militarism." See, respectively, Carleton, *Russia: The Story of War*; Gabowitsch, "Russia's Arlington," 89–143.

[90] For an important discussion of the wartime evolution of the term "motherland," see Merridale, *Ivan's War*, 131–136, 373, 380–381. Regarding the concept of the "socialist motherland," Roger Reese observes perceptively how it signified that "not only was the USSR in danger; as the only socialist country, socialism itself and its potential for saving humankind were threatened." See Reese, *Why Stalin's Soldiers Fought*, qt. 188, 197.

[91] Malia, *The Soviet Tragedy*, 235–236.

[92] On the concept of "domestic internationalism," see Scott, *Familiar Strangers*, 29–36.

[93] See "Geroicheskii sovetskii narod," *Pravda*, Nov. 11, 1944, 1. This paradigm was evident from the outset of the war: "Nash otvet: smert' vragam! Nash lozung: pobeda!" *Pravda*, Jun. 23, 1941, 2; "Sviashchennaia nenavist' k vragu," *Pravda*, Jun. 23, 1941, 2; "Vse sily na zashchitu rodiny," *Krasnaia zvezda*, Jul. 3, 1941, 2; V. Iakutenok, "Moia mechta – bit' fashistskikh gadov," *Krasnaia zvezda*, Jul. 4, 1941, 2; V. Stavskii, "Armiia, dostoinaia svoego naroda," *Pravda*, Jan. 21, 1942, 3; P. Iudin, "Lenin – Osnovatel' sovetskogo gosudarstva," *Pravda*, Jan. 21, 1942, 3; "Za Rodinu, za stalinskuiu konstitutsiiu!" *Krasnaia zvezda*, Dec. 5, 1942, 1; "Nerushimaia sem'ia narodov SSSR," *Pravda*, Dec. 30, 1942, 1. On the importance of inclusive "Soviet" themes, see also Brooks, "Pravda Goes to War," 20–21; Florin, "Becoming Soviet," 495–516; Shaw, "Soldiers' Letters to Inobatxon and O'g'ulxon," 517–552; Hellbeck, *Stalingrad*, 18–68; Berkhoff, *Motherland in Danger*, 206–207.

"arm in arm, shoulder to shoulder," as one wartime article in *Pravda* phrased it.[94] Such appeals minimized ethnonational particularities as the multiethnic "friendship" and "family" of nations became a monolithic "fortress" and "ferocious wall."[95] The pan-Soviet paradigm was distinct from the closely related doctrine of the "friendship of the peoples." As initially conceived, the friendship of the peoples formula functioned to perpetuate notions of ethnic hierarchy and primordialism.[96] It was the Russians, according to the friendship narrative, who first cast off the yoke of old regime oppression and whose guidance and cultural achievements led non-Russians along the path to modernity. As *Pravda* explained in February 1942, "The Great Russian people – elder brother and first among equals in a single Soviet family – lent tremendous assistance to other peoples. With its help, formerly oppressed peoples achieved their liberation, [and] economic and cultural golden age."[97] The opening stanza of the new national anthem, adopted in January 1944, reflected this aspect of the friendship of the peoples doctrine: "An unbreakable union of free republics, / Great Rus' has united forever to stand."[98]

However, by mid-1944, press accounts were commonly attributing the impending victory to a homogeneous "Soviet people" [*sovetskii narod*] rather than to metaphors underscoring ethnonational diversity and variegated hierarchy. Allusions to the war as the "trial" [*ispytanie*] or "crucible" [*surovoe ispytanie*] of the Soviet people appeared frequently, while rote formulations such as "Great Patriotic War of the Soviet people" and "great feat of the Soviet people" routinized the link between victory and the overarching Soviet community.[99] One *Pravda* editorial reacted to a speech in which Stalin honored the "great Soviet people"[100]

94 "Ot sovetskogo informbiuro (vechernee soobshchenie 15 iiulia)," *Pravda*, Jul. 16, 1941, 1.

95 "Boevoe bratstvo narodov Sovetskogo Soiuza," *Pravda*, Oct. 31, 1942, 1.

96 Martin, *Affirmative Action Empire*, 432–461.

97 V. Kruzhkov, "Velikaia sila leninsko-stalinskoi druzhby narodov," *Pravda*, Feb. 21, 1942, 3.

98 Dubrovskii, "Glavnaia pesnia," 181. Tellingly, Shcherbakov and Voroshilov's original call for proposals for a new anthem specified that while the hymn should have a "national" rather than party character, it should reflect Soviet-era motifs, which included the friendship of the peoples. See ibid, 170.

99 See, for example, "Torzhestvennoe zasedanie moskovskogo soveta deputatov trudiashchikhsia, posviashchennoe prazdnovaniiu XXVII godovshchiny Velikoi Oktiabr'skoi Sotsialisticheskoi Revoliutsii," *Krasnaia zvezda*, Nov. 7, 1944, 3; Iudin, "Lenin – Osnovatel' sovetskogo gosudarstva," 3; "Velikii pod''em," *Krasnaia zvezda*, Nov. 25, 1943, 1; "Besprimernyi podvig naroda v zashchite Rodiny," *Krasnaia zvezda*, Jan. 7, 1944, 1.; "Za Rodinu, za stalinskuiu konstitutsiiu!" 1.

100 "Doklad Predsedatelia Gosudarstvennogo Komiteta Oborony tovarishcha I. V. Stalina," *Krasnaia zvezda*, Nov. 7, 1944, 2. First applied to the Russian people in 1937, the epithet "great" was typically reserved for Slavic ethnonational communities. On the use of this designation for Ukrainians, see Yekelchyk, "Stalinist Patriotism," 62–63.

by exclaiming that "[t]hese simple words ... speak of a fervent *Soviet* patriotism," characterized by "boundless love of the Soviet person for the Soviet Motherland and Soviet state," a "superior worldview," and a "deeply civic identity." In contrast to the virulent ethnonationalism of the Nazis, "[o]ur patriotism," the author specified, "is Soviet, socialist patriotism." The article concluded by looking to the Soviet people's venerable past:

Twenty-seven years ago, the workers and peasants of our country, heeding the appeal of the Party of Lenin and Stalin, began to build a new, Soviet society ... They defeated their domestic enemies – the imperialists. They defended their state from fierce attacks by foreign invaders. They overcame all deprivations and tribulations, and gave the world the most striking demonstration of their ability to govern, organize domestic life, [and] advance the cause of their country and world civilization. Today the Soviet people have shown they are able to defend the Soviet cause and the cause of all humanity on the battlefield against fascism.[101]

While Russian military exploits in 1242, 1380, 1612, and 1812 continued to provide ideologists with convenient images of heroism in wartime, with the pan-Soviet paradigm such distant connections were no longer requisite.[102] It was not inspiration from prerevolutionary models that facilitated victory in the present but rather the radical transformations that had begun a mere "twenty-seven years ago" (Figure 0.4).

By the time the historian M. V. Nechkina proposed what she saw as the emergence of a "fundamentally new" community of Soviet people in the summer of 1944, she drew on what had become a commonplace pan-Soviet/internationalist model of patriotic identity, one that, though difficult to define, was certainly "higher" than any one nation, Russians included:

The formation of the "Soviet people" has passed through significant stages during the [Great] Patriotic War. The Soviet people is not a nation [*natsiia*], but something higher ..., fundamentally new and novel in the history of mankind, a stable community of people. It combines a unity of territory, a fundamentally new, shared economic system, the Soviet system, [and] a type of single new culture despite a multiplicity of languages. However, this is not a nation, but something new and higher. This is quite a new phenomenon in human history.[103]

[101] "Geroicheskii sovetskii narod," 1 (emphasis added).

[102] As Alexis Peri observes, Leningraders sometimes interpreted analogies with 1812 subversively, which might partly explain some of the privileging of the pan-Soviet line. Peri, *The War Within*, 217–222.

[103] "Stenogramma soveshchaniia," no. 2, 80–81. Although careful to specify that the narod was "not a nation," her definition certainly conforms to Western modernist and older Bolshevik formulations. Şener Aktürk argues that the term is better translated into English as "Soviet nation." See Aktürk, *Regimes of Ethnicity*, 198.

Figure 0.4 "Glory to the valiant Soviet fighters who are smashing the fascist beast in his lair!": 1945 poster pairing the impending victory with Soviet-era precedents (Vyacheslav Prokofyev/TASS via Getty Images)

Nikita Khrushchev's 1961 declaration that the Soviet people constituted a wholly "new historical community," sharing a "common socialist motherland," "a common economic base," and a "common worldview" was not, as is often suggested, an invention of the post-Stalin era.[104] Rather, it embodied one of two contrasting mobilizational strategies that would go on to shape official conceptions of victory for decades.

[104] For example: Evans, *Soviet Marxism-Leninism*, 88. Indeed, a variant of such a project began at least as early as the 1930s. See Brandenberger, *Propaganda State*, esp. 98–119; Sanborn, *Drafting*, 96–131.

Discursive Tension

How authorities attempted to reconcile the Russocentric and pan-Soviet/internationalist tendencies after 1945 is the book's second major theme. While many scholars have pointed to the wartime and postwar emergence of a Russified ideological amalgam, this book argues that the two mobilizational paradigms did not so much fuse as constitute a set of divergent patriotic discourses.[105] Starting late in the war, the ideological establishment worked to harmonize the competing Russocentric and pan-Soviet threads through what might be called discursive tension. A set of norms rather than an explicit policy prescription, discursive tension involved positioning what were two distinct patriotic paradigms at the opposite poles of an ideological spectrum.[106] In the postwar era, the war narrative itself embodied this tension. Late Stalinism tolerated the coexistence of rival Russocentric and "internationalist" victory narratives, enabling a surprisingly fluid mobilizational repertoire that the leadership could use to promote either Russian leadership and ethnic diversity or the idea of a homogeneous "Soviet" people as the changing domestic and international landscape required. Despite the victory myth's continued multivalence under Stalin, the Cold War saw many Soviet ideologists confine Russocentric dynamics to prerevolutionary and early Soviet historical narratives, while advancing the emerging victory myth as an overwhelmingly pan-Soviet/internationalist ideal. It would take over a decade after the war for the pan-Soviet victory myth to prevail over its Russocentric counterpart. Nevertheless, this more compartmentalized form of discursive tension, in which the war became the exclusive domain of the pan-Soviet end of the ideological spectrum, was already observable in some of the mobilizational strategies of the latter half of the war. To illustrate the concept, it is useful to examine its initial, wartime manifestation.

[105] On the emergence of an amalgam, see Suny, "The Contradictions of Identity," 27; Gill, *Symbols and Legitimacy*, 145–153; Hosking, "The Second World War," 178. Roger Reese contends that propaganda organs treated the motif and sanctity of the revolutionary divide as a secondary motivation for soldiers, and in some cases entirely jettisoned the theme. See Reese, *Why Stalin's Soldiers Fought*, 188, 197. David Brandenberger's sophisticated argument that the use of the Russian national past was first and foremost a "populist flirtation," supports the view that there was a longer-term amalgamation in which Russocentric concerns fused with Marxist-Leninist and proletarian internationalist ambitions: Brandenberger, *National Bolshevism*, 6–7; Brandenberger, "Stalin's Populism," 730. As indicated, my own reading of Soviet wartime propaganda suggests that, after 1941, Agitprop only sporadically reconciled "Russian" and "Soviet" aspects of patriotic culture in anything like a stable fusion, although these twin tendencies both broadly pointed in the direction of social cohesion.

[106] Following Jesse Kauffman, I take "norms" to mean "usually unspoken and unwritten but generally shared habits, values, and assumptions." Kauffman, *Elusive Alliance*, 221.

For instance, both the new state hymn and the "friendship of the peoples" narrative limited the scope of Russian exceptionalism to the period leading up to and during the establishment of Soviet power. In the case of the national anthem, following the single mention of the Russians' part in uniting the peoples of the USSR, the chorus and subsequent verses stressed ostensibly supra-ethnic, Soviet ideals: the revolution, Stalin's cult, and war against a foreign enemy.[107] Likewise, the course of the war reconfigured the friendship metaphor in subtle but not insignificant ways. Representations of the friendship of the peoples increasingly concentrated the theme of Russian leadership around the events of the revolution and the spheres of cultural and technological advancement. As an article in *Pravda* asserted in November 1944,

> The Russian people rallied the other peoples of Russia on to the Great October Socialist Revolution, liberating working people from bondage to industrialists and imperialists ... [Revolution] put into practice the humane ideas of Lenin and Stalin on the self-determination of peoples, on the equality, brotherhood, and friendship of the peoples.[108]

The war, according to the same article, embodied not Russian leadership but "the common cause of all working people regardless of national distinction." The author continues,

> The [Great] Patriotic War has expanded and strengthened ties between our peoples, between the republics belonging to the Soviet Union ... Today the RSFSR, the Kazakh SSR, and the Georgian SSR help to rebuild Ukraine. People in Tashkent and Ashgabat think about the revival of Kiev. The residents of Baku, Yerevan, Kazan, Novosibirsk, [and] Vladivostok are avidly interested in the fates of Minsk, Riga, Vilnius, Tallinn, Kishinev and Petrozavodsk.

The article pointed to the legendary twenty-eight Panfilovtsy as the exemplification of this newfound wartime unity between peoples. In a telling omission, the author cited the battle cry of the commander of the twenty-eight, Vasilii Klochkov ("There is nowhere to retreat – Moscow is at our backs!"), shorn of its original reference to "Russia."[109]

By 1945, many ideologists were asserting that victory represented the fulfillment of 1917 and the rejection of the tsarist inheritance, even those aspects that were celebrated as emblematic of a heroic pedigree.[110] This

[107] Stalin personally helped cultivate the draft of what would become the new official state hymn, submitted by S. V. Mikhalkov and G. El'-Registan. See Dubrovskii, "Glavnaia pesnia." Reports from 1946 indicate the Soviet public had not yet fully embraced the new patriotic anthem. See "Bol'shinstvo liudei ne znaiut slov Gimna," 95.

[108] "Nerushima stalinskaia druzhba narodov nashei strany," *Pravda*, Nov. 5, 1944, 1.

[109] "Nerushima stalinskaia druzhba narodov nashei strany," 1.

[110] For an excellent example, see the February 1945 meeting of *Pravda* ideologists presided over by the paper's chief editor, Petr Pospelov: RGASPI 629/1/83/1–71, 105–127,

variation of the war myth stressed the political, socioeconomic, and ideological sources of victory over notions of Russian leadership, ethnic hierarchy, or the association with prerevolutionary Russian military exploits. Indeed, as victory became more certain, elite conceptions of the war's significance often portrayed it as a uniquely Soviet feat, as the basis for an imagined political community disengaged from any prerevolutionary inheritance.

None of this is to suggest the elimination of the Russocentric paradigm either during or after the war. Historical narratives continued to underscore prerevolutionary Russian benevolence and Russian-led industrial and agricultural modernization in the Soviet era. Moreover, Stalin reiterated the Russocentric understanding of victory on multiple occasions between 1945 and 1946. These statements, together with memories of wartime propaganda highlighting Russian historical precedents, assured that the victory myth would itself contain Russocentric and pan-Soviet vectors.

However, within the deeply Russocentric ideological ecosystem of the late 1940s, Soviet patriotism's discursive tension facilitated a variant of the war's memory that diminished the primacy of Russians in favor of an aspirational and undifferentiated Soviet people.[111] The Soviet state remained committed to fostering multinationalism within its borders. Yet victory in the war offered the party leadership an alternative wellspring of heroic imagery with which to bridle ethnonational identities and emphasize their transitory rather than primordial nature. In this way, late-Stalinist war memory would work to collapse the heroism hierarchy in certain contexts while reinforcing it in others.[112]

The Doctrine of the Soviet People

The book's third major assertion is that a doctrine of the Soviet people reconceptualized how discursive tension operated throughout the post-

where discussants even rejected analogies with 1812. For other examples, see "Ob ideologicheskoi rabote partorganizatsii," 4–8; "Lenin i Stalin o sovetskom patriotizme," 15–17; Solodovnikov, "Za vysokuiu ideinost' sovetskogo iskusstva," 54. See also Burdei, *Istorik i voina*, 157–159; Orlov, "Natsional'nyi i internatsional'nyi komponenty," 406–415.

[111] This was part of a wider European quest for social homogenization in the wake of war and occupation. As Weiner acknowledges, crafting an image of the nation as an "undifferentiated entity" was a goal of most European states after the war. Weiner, "Nature, Nurture, and Memory," 1126. For Western European efforts toward homogenization, see Lagrou, *The Legacy of Nazi Occupation*.

[112] The promotion of ethnic particularism and hierarchy persisted, of course. The point here, and where this study diverges from Weiner, is that it persisted mainly outside the realm of the war myth.

Stalin era. During the late 1950s and early 60s, destalinization conflated much of the wartime Russocentric imagery and messaging with the excesses of Stalin's personality cult, discrediting the Russocentric victory narrative in the process. Thus, rather than tolerate contrasting Russocentric and pan-Soviet/internationalist variations on the war's memory as Stalin had done, Khrushchev and his successors put forth the pan-Soviet myth as the sole official expression of victory. They did so by way of the Soviet people doctrine.

First enunciated by Khrushchev in 1961, the doctrine of the Soviet people reified the practice, described previously, whereby the Russocentric and pan-Soviet/internationalist paradigms were tethered to specific narrative spheres along an ideological spectrum. The doctrine therefore contained both homogenizing and variegating discourses. The reformulated victory myth became the exclusive purview of the doctrine's pan-Soviet/internationalist pole, advancing a picture of the Soviet people as a unified, nation-like entity. At the same time, narratives of the Soviet Union's formation and consolidation, which rested at the opposite pole, emphasized Russian-led ethnocultural diversity and hierarchy.

Such a framework helps explain the prominence of the war's commemoration beginning in the late 1960s. While state policies deliberately stoked pro-Soviet Russian nationalistic expression during this period, the theme of the war and its cultic commemorative edifice provided a countervailing pressure that authorities could draw upon as needed to curtail both Russian and non-Russian national assertiveness. As the book argues, neo-Stalinists in the Party, Russophile intellectuals, and cultural preservationist movements were hesitant to openly engage the subject of the war from a Russocentric, much less nationalistic, perspective. Instead, authorities encouraged these groups to silo their nationalism within the designated spheres of prerevolutionary patriotic culture and early Soviet development.

At the same time, the expansion of the war cult was partly geared toward bringing Russian nationalist sympathizers into the fold, not to cater to nationalist concerns but rather to steer Russian cultural nationalism in a pan-Soviet direction. The war's commemoration emphasized key areas of overlap with nationalist priorities, such as devotion to motherland, patriotism, and, most importantly, the dissemination of these values among Soviet youth. Over time, this attention to overlapping areas of interest with nationalistic-oriented intellectuals created ambiguities that eroded the foundations of the Soviet people doctrine. It was precisely those areas of ambiguity that some nationalist writers focused on to cultivate a vaguely Russocentric, even national-patriotic, version of the war narrative. Although this remained a marginal tendency, it nevertheless perpetuated a Russocentric memory of the war that was increasingly irreconcilable with the dominant myth of state, a fact made all too apparent when Mikhail Gorbachev lifted many censorship restrictions in the mid to late 1980s, hastening the USSR's demise.

* * *

In short, the book argues that the state employed two distinct mythologies of integration in the decades after 1945, which represented contrasting expressions of collective belonging and loyalty. The first, which the book describes as a Russocentric tendency, promoted Russian leadership of an ethnically diverse and hierarchically configured collection of nations; the second – a pan-Soviet/internationalist tendency – limited displays of the singular role of the Russian people and heterogeneous hierarchy more generally in favor of a laterally united and Russian-speaking "Soviet people." In the initial years after 1945, the war narrative itself reflected these divergent paradigms. Soviet leaders and ideologists could craft accounts of victory that hewed to either end of the ideological spectrum. Following Stalin's death and denunciation, authorities reformulated the discursive tension contained within the war narrative. The new doctrine channeled Russocentrism toward the themes of prerevolutionary and early Soviet ethnic relations while the pan-Soviet paradigm centered on the myth of the war victory.[113]

Although these twin mythologies each served the ends of social integration, they represent contradictory approaches to Soviet multiethnic governance.[114] This is not to suggest that ethnic and Soviet identities were incompatible. Studies of empire have shown that citizens often effectively negotiated local, national, and supranational identities.[115] Recent scholarship on the USSR has likewise demonstrated that non-Russian communities routinely balanced local and all-union loyalties in a way that stabilized relations between the center and the ethnically defined periphery.[116] Rather, the present study locates this contradiction in the practices and outlook of the regime itself, as it

[113] This closely follows Peter Blitstein's notion of simultaneous "imperial" and "nationalizing" practices: Blitstein, "Nation and Empire," 197–219.
[114] On the contradictory nature of the state's practice of "*both* empire maintenance *and* nation-building," see Blitstein, qt. 217; Suny, "The Contradictions of Identity," 29; Hoffmann, *Stalinist Values*, 165.
[115] See, for example, Judson, *The Habsburg Empire*; Monger, *Patriotism and Propaganda in First World War Britain*.
[116] For important case studies focusing on the South Caucasus, see, for example, Johnson, "Speaking Soviet"; Scott, *Familiar Strangers*; Lehmann, "Apricot Socialism."

simultaneously elevated and subjugated the status and identity of its Russian national core.

The argument unfolds chronologically and thematically. Chapters 1 and 2 explore ideological production and commemoration in the late Stalinist era through the lens of the fledgling victory myth. Specifically, Chapter 1 pursues the afterlife of Stalin's oft-cited toast to the Russian people in both Russian and non-Russian contexts to tease out its rather inconsistent and ambiguous connection to the official war narrative. Chapter 2 analyzes late-Stalinist commemorations and the victory myth's coexistence with the wider celebration of Russian prerevolutionary themes. It argues that in spite of the highly Russocentric atmosphere, the late-Stalinist leadership tolerated a certain dynamism and multivalence in the war's memory, which preserved the pan-Soviet line as an "internationalist" counterpoise to the otherwise Russian-dominated mobilizational agenda. Chapter 3 focuses on efforts to de-Stalinize the war's memory and recalibrate Soviet identity in the wake of Khrushchev's denunciation of Stalin's personality cult. As destalinization linked the Russocentrism of the war to the figure of Stalin, the leadership elevated the pan-Soviet/internationalist version of the war's memory via the doctrine of the Soviet people. Defenders of Stalin's war record meanwhile contested this process, recasting Stalin as a protector of Russian national-patriotic values. Chapter 4 centers on the production of the commemorative war cult of the mid-1960s to the 1980s. Together, Chapters 3–4 show that the political establishment saw the large-scale veneration of 1945 as a means of diffusing neo-Stalinist and nationalist-oriented resistance to the ideological formula elaborated in the Soviet people doctrine. Finally, Chapter 5 examines Russian nationalist engagement with the state war cult and the limited way nationalist intellectuals sought to Russify the content of the war's memory, while nonetheless adhering to its officially endorsed, pan-Soviet configuration.

This book does not claim to be a comprehensive study of the war's representation in the Soviet Union. It centers squarely on the interrelationship between the Russian Question and the politics of the war's memorialization. *The Soviet Myth* is necessarily selective, therefore, in its sources and lines of inquiry. While the analysis does not ignore films, television, novels, theater, memoir literature, and paintings – all mediums that helped shape the Soviet victory myth – it gives far greater attention to debates among ideologists, historians, anniversary committees, and party leaders. It was these deliberations that most directly engaged the Russian Question and that generated the official framework within which Soviet cultural production operated. Likewise, the book's emphasis on the tension between national and supranational identities precluded an in-depth treatment of many other important aspects of the war's memory, including the gendered nature of the war's representation, the memories of deported peoples, local and family commemorations, veterans' gatherings, among other themes. The chapters that follow pursue those voices that, I believe, best shed light on the Russian people's evolving place within official war memory.

The book's analysis aligns broadly with an interpretation of the Soviet Union as a unique type of modern polity, one that exhibited characteristics of both empire and a multiethnic national state.[117] In many ways, patriotic mobilization in its pan-Soviet guise resembled the "imperial patriotism" practiced by certain dynastic empires. Just as the Habsburg and Romanov monarchies sometimes promoted a form of patriotic identity that obscured the dominance of their respective Germanic and Slavic cores, the Communist Party leadership often utilized the war's memory for a similarly dissociative function, to project a supra-ethnic, socialist version of what Clifford Geertz called "the inherent sacredness of sovereign power."[118] But the subordination of a dominant people for the sake of the political community as a whole is also a feature of multiethnic nationalizing states, where, as Anthony Smith observes, myths that advance lateral bonds serve to "weld an ethnically disparate nation together" and "draw in other *ethnies* who have no connection with the communal past of the dominant *ethnie*."[119] Such rhetorical similarities with nationalizing states have convinced a few scholars that the term "Soviet people" is perhaps better rendered in English as "Soviet nation."[120]

[117] It might be, as one important contribution to this matter argues, that the USSR was a "mobilizational state that seeks to sculpt its citizenry in an ideal image." See Khalid, "Backwardness and the Quest for Civilization," 232.

A recent overview of this debate summarized the dominant position that the USSR constituted "an anti-imperialist state that nonetheless exhibited imperial qualities." Goff and Siegelbaum, "Introduction," 3. See also Siegelbaum and Moch, "Transnationalism in One Country," 971–976; Edgar, "Bolshevism, Patriarchy, and the Nation," 252–272; Beissinger, "Demise of an Empire-State," 93–115.

[118] Geertz, *Local Knowledge*, 123. On the monarchical image as transcendent of ethnic categories in the Habsburg and Romanov contexts, see Wortman, *Scenarios of Power*, 1–72, 411–414 and passim; Unowsky, *The Pomp and Politics of Patriotism*. In the Romanov case, this circumstance changed during the late 19th century, when the tsarist administration experimented with a more Russian national image: Hosking, *Russia*, 120–150. On the Russians' nebulous place in the Soviet imperial context, see Scott, *Familiar Strangers*, esp. 29–36; Oushakine, *The Patriotism of Despair*, 10; Hosking, *Rulers and Victims*, passim.

[119] Smith, "The 'Golden Age' and National Renewal," 38–54. On the role of war in forging an imperial sense of nationhood, see Colley, *Britons*.

[120] See especially Aktürk, *Regimes of Ethnicity*, 198.

Whether patriotic mobilization in the Soviet Union constituted an imperial or nationalizing outlook, its persistent tensions lent a remarkable fluidity to the state's "repertoire of rule," which alternated between the "production of difference" and the promotion of social homogeneity.[121] On the one hand, these tensions proved irreconcilable in the long term and fueled competing rather than symbiotic notions of what it meant to be at once Soviet *and* Russian. On the other hand, this dynamic enabled Communist authority to assert, reconfigure, or ignore outright ethnic particularism and hierarchy as circumstance dictated.[122] This book argues that the adaptability of Soviet identity hinged on the Russian Question. The pan-Soviet model of patriotism encouraged Russians to subsume their unique sense of identity in the name of a higher "Soviet" sense of belonging. While not the only approach to mobilization and state-building that the regime employed – Russian-led hierarchy and ethnic diversity remained constant themes – the present study contends that such a logic was most fully on display in the myth and remembrance of the Soviet victory in World War II.

[121] Kivelson and Suny, *Russia's Empires*, 4.
[122] Burbank and Cooper, *Empires in World History*, 3–8; Scott, *Familiar Strangers*, 12–19, 29–36.

1 Stalin's Toast

Victory and the Vagaries of Postwar Russocentrism

> I am surprised that C[omrade] Stalin, who always stressed the significance of internationalism in our country, has now specifically singled out the Russian people.
>
> – Pasmannik, Moscow factory inspector, 1945[1]

> We are no longer the Russians we were before 1917; our Russia [*Rus'*] is no longer the same, our character is no longer the same.
>
> – Andrei Zhdanov, 1946[2]

Few of Joseph Stalin's public statements have been as scrutinized as an address he delivered at a banquet in the Grand Kremlin Palace in late May 1945. Organized to honor the commanders of the Red Army and Navy for their role in the recent victory over Germany, roughly a thousand military officers and leading representatives of the Party and state attended the event. The mood was festive, even raucous. Performances by cultural luminaries like the ballerina Galina Ulanova and the opera singer Mark Reizen punctuated the evening, as did frequent toasts. It was well after midnight when Stalin rose from the Presidium table to give one final address.[3] "I would like to raise a toast," he declared, according to the account given in the official press, "to the health of our Soviet people [*sovetskogo naroda*] and, most of all, the Russian people [*russkogo naroda*]." The Russian people, through their "clear mind, staunch [*stoikii*] character, and patience" had "earned in this war general recognition as the guiding force of the Soviet Union." The "trust of the Russian people in the Soviet

[1] TsKhDOPIM 3/61/46/135–136, publ. in Gorinov, *Moskva poslevoennaia*, 52–53.

[2] "Doklad t. Zhdanova o zhurnalakh 'Zvezda' i 'Leningrad'," *Literaturnaia gazeta*, Sep. 21, 1946, 2–3.

[3] This description is based on Iakovlev, *Tsel' zhizni*, 395–400; Shtemenko, *General'nyi shtab*, 268–270; Nevezhin, *Stalin o voine*, 226–283; Gusliarov, *Stalin v zhizni*, 521–523.

government" was "the decisive force that ensured the historic victory over the enemy of mankind – over fascism."[4]

Printed on the front page of *Pravda*'s May 25 edition, reactions to Stalin's words varied. Many welcomed the formal acknowledgment that the Soviet victory rested on a Russian foundation. "Often such powerful feelings take possession of the soul," one soldier wrote in his diary on May 27. "[H]ow much I contemplated, experienced, reading Comrade's Stalin's address ... He spoke about us Russians with such warmth."[5] Others were more ambivalent. A reported conversation between Moscow factory employees conveyed confusion: "It is unclear why C[omrade] Stalin only spoke about the Russian people; in fact, Ukrainians, Belarusians and other peoples endured greater difficulties and fought heroically against the enemy." Another worker expressed concern that Stalin's statement might lead to "excessive pride [*zaznaistvu*] and the contraposition of one [Soviet] nation against another." One agronomist argued that "[h]ad such a speech about the merits of the Russian people been made not by C[omrade] Stalin but by someone else, he would be accused of great-power chauvinism."[6] The writer Ilya Ehrenburg purportedly found the toast so offensive that he was brought to tears.[7] In the West, where "Russian" had long served as shorthand for "Soviet," media reports simply ignored the toast's symbolic implications. The *New York Times*, for example, emphasized Stalin's admission of the Soviet government's mistakes and the fact that the leader appeared to be "in one of his jolliest moods in years."[8]

Scholarly interpretations have noted the toast's foundational role in defining the emerging war myth as "unambiguously russocentric."[9] In the

[4] "Vystuplenie tovarishcha I. V. Stalina," *Pravda*, May 25, 1945, 1. The heavily edited shorthand record upon which the published speech was based is located under RGASPI 558/11/1098/17–18, publ. in Nevezhin, *Stalin o voine*, 264–268.

[5] Bushin, *Ia posetil sei mir*, 118–119. [6] TsKhDOPIM 3/61/46/135–136.

[7] Chukovskii, cited in Gusliarov, *Stalin v zhizni*, 522.

[8] "Stalin Salutes Russians for Faith in Regime Despite Errors During Darkest Days in War," *New York Times*, May 26, 1945, 5.

[9] Brandenberger, *National Bolshevism*, 183, 227. See also Kostyrchenko, *V plenu*, 23. Both Zubkova and Roberts downplay the toast's importance and suggest it was overshadowed the following month by Stalin's toast to "the screws in the great machine of state." Compare Roberts, *Stalin's Wars*, 266–267, and Zubkova, *Russia After the War*, 29, with Yekelchyk, *Stalin's Empire of Memory*, 88–89; Brandenberger, *National Bolshevism*, 130–131, 200–201, 233–234; Burdei, *Istorik i voina*, 45–48; Kostrychenko, *V plenu*, 23; Barghoorn, *Soviet Russian Nationalism*, 42. Erik Scott argues that Stalin's Georgian identity allowed him to confidently toast the Russian people's role in the war since, to do so as a Great Russian, would have amounted to chauvinism. However, this does not explain why other Russians within the party leadership continued to single out the Russians as "first among equals" in other contexts. See Scott, *Familiar Strangers*, 87–88. The toast's implications are not discussed in several leading works on the war's memory,

words of one leading historian, Stalin's Russocentric verdict on the war "flowed together" with the veneration of a thousand years of Russian history.[10] This apparently went hand-in-hand with a campaign unfolding in non-Russian republics, where an overriding trope of Russian wartime liberation and guidance undergirded official war memory among non-Russian Soviet peoples.[11] This ideological campaign, the so-called Zhdanovshchina, also brought unique republican historical narratives in line with a centuries-long "Russian grand narrative."[12] Among non-Russian national communities, authorities curbed explorations of distinct martial traditions while promoting an exclusively Sovietized sense of ethnic identity.[13] Historians have suggested that, by disproportionately restricting heroic narratives aimed at non-Russians, Soviet patriotic culture after the war was marked by what remained: the glorification of Russia, its people, and its centuries-old history.[14] The late-Stalinist war myth, in this reading, functioned primarily to remind the multinational Soviet people that Russians have "always been the greatest, wisest, bravest, and most virtuous of all nations."[15]

However, a closer inspection of early authoritative treatments of the war complicates this picture. Amid the widespread public glorification of Russian history and culture that accompanied late Stalinism, postwar accounts of victory offered varied and at times contradictory depictions of wartime patriotism, which often departed from the theme

including Kirschenbaum, *The Legacy of the Siege*; Weiner, *Making Sense of War*; Tumarkin, *The Living & the Dead.*

10 Brandenberger, *National Bolshevism*, 187–196, qt. 196; Brandenberger, "Stalin, the Leningrad Affair," 247–248.

11 See, for example, Hnatiuk, "How the Soviet Union Suppressed the Holocaust"; Manley, *To the Tashkent Station*, 235–237; Yekelchyk, *Stalin's Empire of Memory*, 53–71; Slezkine, *Arctic Mirrors*, 309. Recent studies have questioned the extent to which postwar Sovietization constituted deliberate Russification. As Tarik Cyril Amar writes in his study of the western Ukrainian city of Lviv, "Sovietization cannot be reduced to Russian imperialism in a new guise." He continues, "In postwar Lviv, more important than any Russification tendencies was the ongoing struggle between Ukrainians over who was 'liberator' and who was 'backward.'" Amar concedes, however, that the postwar Ukrainization of the enlarged Ukrainian SSR was rooted in subordination to the Russian elder brother. See Amar, *The Paradox of Ukrainian Lviv*, chap. 4, qt. 7, 145.

12 Associated with party secretary Andrei Zhdanov, the Zhdanovshchina has been traditionally understood as a cultural and ideological crusade against Western influences in the arts and sciences. For a now-classic treatment, see Hahn, *Postwar Soviet Politics*. On the implementation of a "Russian grand narrative" among Ukrainians, see Yekelchyk, *Stalin's Empire of Memory*, 10–11, 22, 27.

13 See Shin, "Red Army Propaganda"; Yekelchyk, *Stalin's Empire of Memory*, 53–71; Carmack, "History and Hero-Making"; cf. Brandenberger, *National Bolshevism*, 196.

14 Brandenberger, *National Bolshevism*, 187–196; Schechter, "The People's Instructions," 119. For a contrasting example, see Vujačić, "Stalinism and Russian Nationalism."

15 Yekelchyk, *Stalin's Empire of Memory*, 59, 88.

of Russian guidance and liberation.[16] Indeed, Stalin's toast was hardly the final word on the war's significance; the following year, the leadership issued two equally foundational statements. First, Stalin delivered a widely publicized address to a meeting of Moscow voters during elections for the Supreme Soviet. In his comments, Stalin explained what he considered to be the ultimate "summation" of victory in the war. Nearly a year removed from Germany's capitulation, Stalin's overall analysis highlighted the superiority of the socialist system, the multinational state, and the fighting prowess of the Red Army, all the while remaining silent on the singular role of the Russian people.[17]

It was left to Zhdanov to clarify the place of the Russian nation in the postwar account of victory, which he did in a major publication for *Literaturnaia gazeta* in August. "We are no longer the Russians we were before 1917," the party secretary asserted. "Our Russia [*Rus'*] is no longer the same. ... We have changed and have grown along with the great transformations that have radically altered the face of our country." The article then characterized the war along purely ideological lines as a "brilliant victory for socialism" and a "brilliant victory for Marxism."[18] Delivered from a blatantly Russocentric point of view, Zhdanov's article nevertheless invited multiple interpretations. On the one hand, it confirmed the close link between the Russian people and the Soviet state ("*We* are no longer the Russians we were," "*Our* Russia," and so on). At the same time, the article could be read as an attempt to restrict Russians' sense of self. To be Russian in the postwar era, Zhdanov affirmed, had little to do with primordial ties to the distant past. Rather, the article proposed that Russianness should be understood and celebrated in its purely Soviet condition. While not a rejection of the Russocentrism of the victory toast, Zhdanov's article together with Stalin's summation speech reflected a certain flexibility in the leadership's commitment to the Russocentric paradigm. Indeed, following multiple Russocentric assessments of the war in 1945 and 46, Stalin rejected outright a reference to the Russians' leading role from the draft of the newly proposed party program in July 1947.[19]

16 On the highly Russocentric atmosphere and the persistence of prerevolutionary heroes in postwar patriotic culture, see Brandenberger, "Stalin, the Leningrad Affair," 241–255, esp. 247–248; Kenez, *A History of the Soviet Union*, 182; Slezkine, *Arctic Mirrors*, 304. Cf. Kirschenbaum, *The Legacy of the Siege*, 143; Lovell, *The Shadow of War*, 231.

17 Stalin, *Rech'*, 9–13.

18 "Doklad t. Zhdanova o zhurnalakh 'Zvezda' i 'Leningrad,'" *Literaturnaia gazeta*, Sep. 21, 1946, 3. Stalin emphatically embraced Zhdanov's formulation. See Ree, *The Political Thought of Joseph Stalin*, 181. For further analysis, see Clark, *The Soviet Novel*, 198–199.

19 RGASPI 558/11/123/23, cited in Popov, *Bol'shaia nich'ia*, 69. Although the motivation behind this rejection is unclear, it was a departure from the sentiments contained in Stalin's toast and a sign of inconsistent thinking on the Russian Question. In 1946, Stalin had given a speech declaring, "In the Patriotic War, the friendship of the peoples grew

It was not merely that postwar public culture had to accede to Stalin's toast; in many respects, the Russocentrism of the toast had to accommodate later official pronouncements that reiterated the broader "Soviet" sources of victory and that stressed a curtailed role for Russians within the hierarchy of heroism. It was the task of central and republican ideologues, in the first instance, to square the various patriotic currents unleashed by the war and its victorious conclusion. This endeavor met with only partial success but preserved a robust, pan-Soviet/internationalist conception of victory that ran alongside – but in marked contrast to – state-promoted Russocentrism and Russian-dominated accounts of the prerevolutionary past.

Thus, despite Stalin's unambiguous assertion of Russian wartime leadership in his toast of May 1945, there was nevertheless significant variability in late-Stalinist representations, both among central ideologues and between center and periphery. While many central authorities portrayed the war as advancing lateral "friendship" ties of the pan-Soviet mode, others promoted the wartime Russocentric paradigm. Ideologues and cultural intelligentsia in the republics were similarly inconsistent. Using Kazakhstan as a case study, we see that certain local agitators and party officials adhered to the pan-Soviet narrative, homing in on the themes of multiethnic friendship and shared Soviet heroism without a mention of Russian wartime leadership. Others, meanwhile, articulated a decidedly Russocentric understanding of victory and cast the war as evidence of Russian primacy and "elder brotherhood," likely to assuage the center's concerns over potential manifestations of "local" nationalism. As a result, some of the most noteworthy efforts to steer the war narrative in a more Russocentric direction came, paradoxically, from non-Russian party organizations.

Far from a consistent Russocentric ideological rubric, this chapter shows that the Stalinist leadership refused to commit to an exclusively Russocentric understanding of the war. Rather, it allowed the pan-Soviet /internationalist paradigm to coexist with its Russocentric counterpart in discursive tension throughout the era. As Stalin's toast was eliciting mixed reactions, party ideologues shaped a divergent set of postwar narratives geared toward mobilizing local populations along contrasting ideological planes. So long as the core ingredients of victory – Stalin's leadership, party guidance, the Soviet system, the unwavering heroism of the Red Army and citizenry – remained in place, the myth's articulators were free to promote a range of competing narratives, from accounts

stronger, as they rallied around their elder brother, the Russian people." Quoted in Brandenberger, "Sovetskii patriotizm," 23.

emphasizing a united Soviet people bound laterally in "friendship" to those stressing Russian "elder brotherhood" and ethnic diversity. Ultimately, these contending metaphors for Soviet collective identity would do much to shape later contests over the meaning and nature of victory.[20]

The Varieties of Postwar Patriotism

Stalin's victory toast to the Russian people reverberated in official culture. It was famously the subject of an award-winning painting by the Ukrainian artist Mykhailo Khmelko.[21] References to the Russian people as the USSR's guiding force peppered the public statements of high-ranking officials.[22] Leading theoreticians struggled to include Stalin's toast in their works. The *Pravda* editor-in-chief Petr Pospelov, for example, made last minute alterations to his inclusive treatise on multi-ethnic patriotism in order to accommodate quoted material from the toast, even while Stalin's words fit incongruously with the remainder of the piece.[23] In late 1945, the first postwar edition of A. V. Shestakov's standard primary school textbook capped its coverage of the recent war by noting that "[t]he heroic feats of the Soviet people, and first of all the Russian people, who are the most outstanding nation of all the nations belonging to the Soviet Union, achieved victory for our country."[24] Perceived as a clear signal from above, ideologues continued to reproduce the toast in various iterations throughout the early postwar era.[25]

Most notably, Stalin's declaration provided a point of departure for a January 1947 public lecture by the Ministry of Higher Education entitled "The Great Russian People." The speaker was the historian Anna Pankratova. An orthodox Marxist with an "internationalist" bent, Pankratova had come under attack during the war for the critical interpretation of tsarist colonial policy offered in her coauthored volume *History of the Kazakh SSR*. In the Ministry's lecture hall, she now proclaimed the Russian nation the eternal "friend and liberator of oppressed

[20] On "friendship" and "brotherhood" as contending metaphors, see Suny, "The Contradictions of Identity," 26.
[21] Yekelchyk, *Stalin's Empire of Memory*, 88–89.
[22] Burdei, *Istorik i voina*, 45–48; Barghoorn, *Soviet Russian Nationalism*, 42.
[23] See RGASPI 629/1/68/11–124; RGASPI 629/1/67/50–57; Pospelov, *Sila*, 38. Compare also Mitin, "Lenin i Stalin o sovetskom patriotizme," *Krasnaia zvezda*, Jan. 21, 1945, 3, with Mitin, *Voprosy patriotizma*.
[24] Shestakov, *Istoriia SSSR* (1945), 274. Shestakov died in 1941; the publishing house prepared the postwar volume.
[25] Brandenberger, *National Bolshevism*, 196. For one extreme example, see "Russkii narod – rukovodiashchaia sila sredi narodov nashei strany," *Bol'shevik* 10 (1945): 3–12.

and weak peoples." Pankratova recounted in some detail the thousand-year process by which the Russian people's national character was forged. Russians displayed their unique brand of courage, honed through countless struggles "against conquerors of all eras," during the Great Patriotic War. Parroting Stalin's toast, Pankratova reminded her audience that it had been the Russian people who most "believed in the correctness of the Soviet government's policy" and possessed a "steadfast faith" in Soviet power. The Pravda publishing house released Pankratova's lecture as a brochure with an initial print run of 85,000 copies. By 1952, for its second edition, she had expanded the work into a full-length book with a print run of 100,000.[26]

The same year, the historian Isaak Mints, whose dissolved Commission on the History of the Great Patriotic War was prohibited from publishing a major documentary account, issued a concise volume on the war featuring an extended passage linking previous military exploits with Russian leadership in the defeat of Germany.[27] As in Pankratova's lecture, Mints's discussion of Stalin's toast transitioned into a paean of Russian military prowess through the ages:

> The Russian people have defended their existence in the long hard struggle against foreign enemies. It endured the full weight of the Mongol invaders, and thus saved Europe from their yoke. It put an end to the eastward spread of aggression from the German Teutonic Knights. It defeated the troops of the conqueror Napoleon – contender for world domination.[28]

Given Pankratova's prior sins and Mints's identity as a Jew in an increasingly anti-Semitic postwar milieu, both now obediently played the part of Russian national patriots.

However, a broad reading of postwar histories suggests that the larger sweep of postwar Russocentrism never fully consumed the war narrative.[29] Indeed, the sentiments expressed in Stalin's May 1945 toast and echoed in key writings by figures like Pankratova and Mints represented merely one pole in a spectrum of competing victory narratives. Alongside odes to the "great Russian people" were patriotic texts that departed from the framework of Russian primordial heroism and wartime

[26] Pankratova, *Velikii russkii narod*, 4–5, 28–30. See also Pankratova, *Velikii russkii narod*, 2nd ed.

[27] Foundational material on the Commission can be found under RAN IRI 2/1/22/11-55ob. For a recent work based on documents collected by the Commission, with details on the Commission's work and fate, see Hellbeck, *Stalingrad*, esp. 70–84, 436–440.

[28] Mints, *Velikaia Otechestvennaia*, 63–69.

[29] Brandenberger argues that Stalin's toast defined the early war myth "as a fundamentally Russian experience." See Brandenberger, *National Bolshevism*, 183, 196, 227.

primacy. Crucially, these could claim an equally authoritative lineage. Whether the 1946 clarifying remarks by Stalin or Zhdanov noted previously, or the late-wartime strand of pan-Soviet appeals discussed in the book's Introduction, postwar victory narratives grew out of seemingly contradictory discourses. By drawing on certain canonical statements while excluding others, ideologues exerted no small amount of agency in developing the victory myth's discursive tension. Not only did late-Stalinist treatments of the war regularly contextualize wartime Russocentrism in a way that rendered it more palatable to the multinational population, but various other cases demonstrate that the pan-Soviet/internationalist understanding of victory persisted intact within an otherwise highly Russified official culture.[30]

Even at the Russocentric extreme, embodied by the Pankratova and – to a lesser extent – Mints texts, ideologues had to work through the contradictions of wartime and postwar official messaging. At the very least, this involved a shift in emphasis away from the primordial Russian heroism of the early war years toward a principally Soviet martial identity and pedigree. Postwar histories nearly always refracted landmark Russocentric pronouncements, such as Stalin's great ancestors speech, through a Marxist–Leninist lens, subjecting them to endless hairsplitting over the uniquely revolutionary character of Soviet patriotism. Mints, despite fawning over Russian military victories of the past, devoted far more attention in his history to outlining the late-wartime consensus that the "Soviet social system gave its peoples the great, all-conquering power of our country." In his words:

> The Soviet government . . . quickly eliminated the reasons for the weakness of old Russia – its political, economic, cultural and military backwardness. All the power and might of the Soviet social system clearly manifested during the Great Patriotic War.
>
> . . . The war showed all the superiority of the Soviet social system over any other social system.
>
> . . . The Soviet state system gave us victory over the enemy. History is replete with attempts to formulate multinational states. Most of these were created by force and disintegrated under the blows of the sword.
>
> . . .Headed by the Russian people, and next to them, Ukrainians and Belarusians, Georgians and Armenians, Uzbeks and Tajiks – all the peoples of our vast Union fought heroically. Many of them have never before participated in wars [and] had no combat experience because the tsarist government was afraid to put weapons in their hands. And now the children of these people showed

[30] See, for example, Mitin, *Voprosy patriotizma*; Kolesnikova, *O sovetskom patriotizme*; Shepilov, *Velikii sovetskii narod*; Matiushkin, *Druzhba narodov SSSR*; Sobolev, *O sovetskom patriotizme*; Vyshinksii, "Sovetskii patriotism"; Shatagin and Osipov, *Velikaia pobeda sovetskogo naroda*.

miracles of bravery on the battlefields. Among their ranks arose Heroes of the Soviet Union, combat commanders and generals.

Following a reference to Stalin's toast and a brief survey of the heroic past of the Russian people, Mints pivoted to warning against unqualified praise of the Russian military legacy:

[Russian soldiers] have written many glorious pages in the history of their people. ... But at that time, it was rare that the objectives of war were near and dear to the soldiers. The old army was an instrument of the rule of the landowners and the bourgeoisie, a tool for the colonial enslavement of many peoples of tsarist Russia. She served the predatory policy of tsarism ... The Great Socialist Revolution created a new army, [and] turned its weapons from the oppression of workers and peasants into an instrument of liberation ... The strength of the Red Army lies in the fact that wonderful military equipment is in the hands of politically conscious fighters, fully aware of what they are fighting for. The strength of the Red Army lies in its consciousness, in its devotion to the ideas of Lenin and Stalin.

While the Soviet system, its progressive ideological underpinnings, and the "wise leadership" of Stalin provided the crux of victory, Mints devoted nearly as much attention to lauding the Soviet Union's wartime allies – Great Britain and the United States – as he did to celebrating the pre-socialist legacy and centrality of the Russian people.[31]

The treatment of the war in Pankratova's *The Great Russian People* similarly adhered to Zhdanov's formulation of a Sovietized Russian identity. Indeed, Pankratova was careful to adjoin the text of Stalin's toast with Zhdanov's remarks.[32] In the book's second edition, which greatly expanded her analysis of the 1941–5 period, Pankratova mined Stalin's toast for its underlying Soviet message. Regarding the innate "clear mind, staunch character, and patience" of the Russian people, for instance, Pankratova insisted that these were "only effective" under conditions of Soviet power. Likewise, while Pankratova acknowledged that Russians have always displayed devotion to their Motherland, "in the past, this love ... was poisoned," she wrote, "by the knowledge that the country was dominated by landowners and capitalists, the tsar and [his] officials." It was only after 1917 that "our Motherland ... acquired a completely different meaning. Now the Soviet people have something to defend."[33] It was in the pages of *The Great Russian People*'s second edition that Pankratova transformed political instructor Klochkov, the Russophile leader of the twenty-eight Panfilovtsy, into a decidedly Soviet hero with

[31] Mints, *Velikaia Otechestvennaia*, 63–71.
[32] Pankratova, *Velikii russkii narod*, 3–5; Pankratova, *Velikii russkii narod*, 2nd ed., 4.
[33] Pankratova, *Velikii russkii narod*, 2nd ed., 176–177, 198.

a strictly postrevolutionary pedigree.[34] Thus, in Pankratova's volume, perhaps the most thorough official acclamation of Russian history ever published, we see an effort to reconcile, rather than supplant, the pan-Soviet/internationalist paradigm with the Russocentrism of Stalin's toast.

But where Pankratova and Mints emphasized a qualified Russocentrism, other authors presented a discernably pan-Soviet victory myth. Emblematic of these is Aleksandr Sobolev's 1948 lecture-turned-pamphlet *On Soviet Patriotism.* With an initial print run larger than that of Pankratova's *The Great Russian People*, Sobolev's text eschewed any direct discussion of Stalin's toast, focusing instead on the war's role in forging a supra-ethnic Soviet people. Thanks to the victory of socialism and success in the war, Sobolev observed, "there has arisen a new historical community of people, the 'Soviet People,' having a common socioeconomic structure of life, a common worldview, common goals and challenges in the construction of a communist society." Aping the pan-Soviet rhetoric of the later war years, Sobolev emphasized that the new patriotism was "qualitatively different" from its prerevolutionary forebear. "It is," wrote Sobolev, "a new, higher form of patriotism" and "a deeply conscious patriotism ... based on an understanding of the superiority of the Soviet social and political system over any other, non-Soviet systems." "Our superiority," he concluded, "is not national, not biological, but historical and social."[35]

For writers of this ilk, it was not chiefly the Russian people or their "great ancestors" that animated patriotism during the war, but rather socialism, the Soviet social system, and the new imagined community – the "great Soviet people."[36] The Soviet people had fought to defend "Soviet soil," the "socialist motherland," and the "great achievements of the socialist revolution."[37] It was not Russia's thousand-year-old history that made possible the defeat of the Wehrmacht but rather emancipation from this history. As another text put it, "The victory of the Soviet people ... is due most of all to the fact that our state ... strode forward out of the times of tsarist Russia and turned into a progressive and mighty socialist power."[38] None of this is to deny the special place these authors accorded Russians within the friendship of the peoples, particularly with regard to prerevolutionary cultural and technological achievements.[39] However, their ability to reiterate a generally pan-Soviet

[34] Pankratova, 180. [35] Sobolev, *O sovetskom patriotizme*, 15–20.
[36] Shepilov, *Velikii sovetskii narod*. [37] Shatagin and Osipov, *Velikaia pobeda*, 9, 12, 16.
[38] Shatagin and Osipov, 33.
[39] Sobolev, for his part, devoted part of a sentence to Russian leadership, stating that "the Soviet peoples of our country, led by the Russian people, together defeated the insidious

/internationalist conception of the war victory amid the broader Russocentric political and cultural atmosphere indicates a surprising ambiguity, even heterodoxy, to late-Stalinist war memory.

Although ideological production generally hewed somewhere between the Russocentric and pan-Soviet poles, attempts to harmonize the two dominant ideological paradigms tended to muddle the clear Russocentric line of Stalin's toast. Texts frequently used the Russian leadership theme selectively, stripping it of its prerevolutionary historical conceits. It was only "under Soviet conditions" that this new supra-ethnic community could "pass through the fire of ... the Great Patriotic War," wrote S. G. Kolesnikova. Russians, like the various other ethnonational constituencies that made up the Soviet people, "are no longer their former selves" [*uzhe ne prezhnie liudi*].[40] Such works remained, for the most part, broadly inclusive and deferential to the shared Soviet sources of victory, even those that explicitly granted the Russians a leading role. Along these lines, Pankratova's standard high school textbook is worth quoting at length:

> Under the leadership of the great Russian people, Ukrainians and Belarusians, Georgians and Armenians, Uzbeks and Turkmen, all the peoples of our vast Soviet country fought heroically on the fronts of the [Great] Patriotic War. Within the glorious family of Heroes of the Soviet Union, there are many names of Soviet patriots of various nationalities. The Russian pilot and three-time Hero of the Soviet Union Aleksandr Pokryshkin, the Ukrainian partisan Sidor Kovpak, the Belarusian partisan Sosnovskii, the Kazakh Tulegen Tokhtarov, the Georgian Mikhail Pakhokidze, the Latvian Ianis Vil'khel'ms, the Estonian Meri, the Jew Gorelik and many others are now the pride of the peoples of the Soviet Union. The courageous representatives of all peoples of the USSR fearlessly went into battle with the cry "For the motherland! For Stalin!"[41]

The Pankratova school text and others like it thus balanced notions of Russian leadership and ethnic difference (for instance, the order in which ethnic heroes were listed) with distinctly Soviet elements: the leadership of Stalin, the Party, supra-ethnic friendship, the Soviet system, socialism.[42] The relative importance bestowed upon these factors, and the degree to which they edged in either a Russocentric or pan-Soviet direction, varied depending on the individual authors and editors involved in producing such narratives.

and hated enemy, defended their social achievements, freedom, honor, and national independence." His primary focus, however, was very clearly the postrevolutionary and all-Soviet sources of victory. Sobolev, *O sovetskom patriotizme*, 18.

[40] Kolesnikova, *O sovetskom patriotizme*, 29–30.

[41] This quote was retained in each of Pankratova's history textbooks between 1946–52. See her *Istoriia SSSR* (1951), 403.

[42] Pankratova's *Istoriia SSSR* (1951). See also Shestakov, *Istoriia SSSR* (1945), 264–274.

Even Stalin's toast could be channeled in a pan-Soviet direction. P. E. Vyshinskii, for instance, prefaced his coverage of Stalin's toast with nearly twenty pages of exposition clarifying the vast differences between Soviet patriotism and that of the prerevolutionary Russian variety. "Soviet patriotism," Vyshinskii reminded, "is *qualitatively* different from the patriotism of the old society ... Most of all, Soviet patriotism is the love for the *Soviet*, socialist motherland, where working people, freed from exploitation are the absolute masters of their country."[43] After reiterating Stalin's recognition of the Russian people's decisive "patience, perseverance, courage, clear mind, [and] trust in [the Soviet] government" during the war, Vyshinskii immediately placed these sentiments into a larger context. The toast had signified that "Soviet patriotism is not anational." While the Russian people's national character was on display during the war, so too, Vyshinskii pointed out, was the Georgian people's innate "spirit of freedom," and the Ukrainian "tradition of courageous struggle for freedom" against external enemies. Stalin chose on the occasion of the Kremlin reception to single out the Russian national contribution to victory. But the more salient point was the way certain national traditions "unite and bring all the peoples of the USSR closer together into a single multinational Soviet people." Soviet patriotism, Vyshinskii continued,

> presupposes the love of Russians for their great national culture, for their language, for their national traditions; the love of Ukrainians for their nation and their culture; the love of Georgians for Georgia, for the national culture of the Georgian people, etc. However, the most important feature of Soviet patriotism is the love of Russians, Ukrainians, Belarusians, Georgians, Armenians and all other peoples of the USSR for their common socialist homeland, for the Soviet state, and for a single socialist culture. Soviet socialist patriotism is the feeling of international brotherhood among Soviet peoples, it is the shared concern for the welfare of the USSR, the readiness of each Soviet nation to defend the interests of the other Soviet peoples as their own.[44]

By positioning the two dominant ideological paradigms – a Sovietized Russocentrism on the one hand and pan-Sovietism on the other – in tension with one another, Vyshinskii and other such activists offered readers a rather malleable framework for making sense of victory and patriotic identity. Whatever the effects of Stalin's toast, the pan-Soviet /internationalist understanding of the war remained a viable, if not dominant, ideological paradigm within the late-Stalinist ideological milieu.

[43] Vyshinskii, *Sovetskii patriotizm*, 436 (emphasis in the original).
[44] Vyshinskii, 443–447. See also Weiner, *Making Sense of War*, 336.

Thus, while authors often structured their texts around Stalin's toast and implied a close link between victory in the war and centuries of Russian exceptionalism, this approach was neither requisite nor congenital to the postwar victory myth. Ideologists such as Sobolev and Kolesnikova chose not to reference the toast, whereas others did so in passing, extracting only the most vital mention of the Russian people's faith in the Soviet government.[45] This pattern is not entirely surprising. Stalinist priorities had never been to foster Russian nationalism but rather to couch Marxist-Leninist themes in patriotic forms accessible to the widest swaths of the multinational population.[46] What is striking is the way theoreticians of the late 1940s translated this objective as it related to the war. Where prerevolutionary and early Soviet narratives continued to center on the idea of Russian historical preeminence and leadership of an ethnically diverse population, victory in the war enabled a more diverse set of patriotic narratives, including some that had little explicitly to do with Russian greatness in the past or hierarchical primacy in the present. Indeed, taken together, early postwar histories suggest a great deal of ambiguity at the heart of official war memory throughout the late 1940s. To be sure, such narrative ambiguity bred many highly Russocentric and historically informed accounts of the 1941–5 conflict. But it also afforded ideologists the leeway to recast Soviet society along pan-Soviet/internationalist lines, as a fundamentally civic, supranational body, born in revolution and forged in war.

The latitude granted many of the war myth's articulators to deviate from the Russocentric framework of Stalin's toast served an important mobilizational function. As the threat of an ideological Cold War intensified, there was evidently a growing concern among the leadership that prerevolutionary imagery and Russocentric phrasemaking were hampering the consolidation of a supra-ethnic patriotic identity beyond the confines of the RSFSR.[47] While the selective celebration of Russian history and culture continued unabated across the USSR, the victory myth's multivalent character invited local adaptation and negotiation that routinely broke with wider notions of Russian elder brotherhood.

[45] See, for example, Levina, *Chto chitat'*, 24; Shatagin and Osipov, *Velikaia pobeda*, 38. This formulation, as Anatol Lieven has noted, not only "reveals the closeness of the new Soviet-Russian relationship, but also the enduring elements of distance": Lieven, "The Weakness of Russian Nationalism," 65.

[46] Brandenberger, "Stalin's Populism," 726–730. For an excellent examination of this process during the war, see Reese, *Why Stalin's Soldiers Fought*, 14–20, chaps. 5–6, 8, and passim.

[47] The international context is considered in Chapter 2. On the Stalinist leadership's persistent anxiety over the way its policies were perceived in the republics as well as in the "European mirror," see Weiner, "Nature, Nurture, and Memory," 1122–1123.

Elder Brother, Loyal Friend

In the republics, too, Stalin's toast competed with a host of alternative official statements regarding the nature of wartime patriotism. As early as January 1944, Stalin provided a prototypical statement of sorts on non-Russian participation in the war. The occasion was a Politburo discussion about Oleksandr Dovzhenko's screenplay for the war film *Ukraine in Flames*. Among the problems with the script were several characters' fairly explicit rejection of class struggle and their promotion of a Ukrainian-centered patriotism.[48] Stalin lambasted Dovzhenko for failing to represent the class nature of the Great Patriotic War, for ignoring the fact that this was a struggle between ideological systems, and for criticizing the policies of the 1930s. Most egregious, however, was that Dovzhenko had implied that Ukrainians were fighting first and foremost for the Ukrainian nation. To this, Stalin responded,

> It is clear how untenable and incorrect such views are. If Dovzhenko wanted to tell the truth, he would have to say, no matter where the Soviet government sends you: to the north, south, west, east, remember that you are defending our Soviet Union, our common motherland, in collaboration with all the fraternal Soviet peoples, for defending the Union of Soviet Socialist Republics means also to defend and protect Soviet Ukraine. Ukraine as an independent state will be well preserved, will get stronger and flourish only within the Soviet Union as a whole.

The Ukrainian people, Stalin went on, understood something that Dovzhenko did not:

> All the peoples [*narody*] of the Soviet Union fight for Ukraine. During this fight, the areas of Ukraine that had been captured by the enemy during the early part of the war are now liberated. This was made possible thanks to the combat partnership of Russians and Ukrainians, Georgians and Belarusians, Armenians and Azeris, Kazakhs and Moldavians, Turkmen and Uzbeks, all peoples of the Soviet Union.[49]

Stalin concluded: "If one judges by Dovzhenko's screenplay, it is not representatives of all nations of the USSR that are fighting in the Great Patriotic War, but only Ukrainians." Tellingly, it was not the trope of the Russian elder brother and liberator that Stalin called on to remedy the script but pan-Sovietism. Soviet patriotism, the Soviet leader reminded, had no place for either the glorification of a unique

[48] RGASPI 558/11/1126/1–17, publ. as "Doklad I. V. Stalina," 384–393; RGASPI 17/125/293/20–35. See also Liber, *Alexander Dovzhenko*, 196–206; Yekelchyk, *Stalin's Empire of Memory*, 54–62.

[49] "Doklad I. V. Stalina," 384–393.

prerevolutionary past or the celebration of "narrow national limitations" in the present.[50]

The pan-Soviet/internationalist orientation of Stalin's critique set the tone for the war myth's subsequent elaboration among many non-Russian party organizations.[51] At minimum, this amounted to promoting a "loyal" ethnonational community's involvement in the war and wartime "friendship" with the Russian people – a Russocentric formula insofar as Russians were the common denominator in "Kazakh–Russian friendship," "Ukrainian–Russian friendship," and so on. However, while accounts of the distant past, the 1917 Revolution, and the early history of the USSR placed Russians squarely in the lead by virtue of their historical, cultural, and numerical significance, it was often lateral rather than vertical ties that suffused the prevailing victory myth.[52] As a party lecturer in the Yakut ASSR put it in September 1947, the Yakut contribution to victory over Germany was rooted in the "great friendship between the Yakut and Russian peoples," "tempered in the fire and labor of the Great Patriotic War." It was mutual respect, rather than subordination to the Russian people, that undergirded this friendship, while the lecturer attributed leadership to the Bolshevik Party and "the brilliant leadership of Stalin."[53] As Ronald Suny observes, where "brotherhood" indicates a vertical, hierarchical relationship between elder and younger siblings, "friendship" implies more or less equal status among peoples: "Friends after all are equivalent to one another; their relationship is about trust, devotion, dependability, affection, and reciprocity."[54]

Even in the formerly occupied western regions late in the war, it was frequently the "Soviet component," to borrow Amir Weiner's phrase, and not Russian salvation, that informed the war narrative's official manifestations.[55] This was partly due to concerns within the Central

[50] "Doklad I. V. Stalina," 391.

[51] For example: TsGAIPD RT 15/5/1143/51–55, 57–69. See also the reprimand issued by the Tatar obkom first secretary Z. I. Muratov during a meeting in which "nationalist" deviations are equated with fascism: TsGAIPD RT 15/5/1143/70–78. More generally, see Weiner, *Making Sense of War*, 331–363.

[52] One notable exception was Aleksandrov's 1943 response to a public lecture during a rally in Kiev in which the Ukrainian people expressed gratitude to the Russian people following liberation. The lecture not only asserted Russian–Ukrainian cooperation in the defeat of Germany, but equality in the prerevolutionary era as well. To this Aleksandrov remarked that "everyone recognizes that the Russian people are the elder brother in the family of nations of the Soviet Union ... Ukraine can be free only in union with the Russian people." RGASPI 17/125/190/25–42.

[53] RGASPI 17/125/507/239–247, publ. in Khlevniuk, *Sovetskaia natsional'naia*, 864–868, qt. 864.

[54] Suny, "The Contradictions of Identity," 26.

[55] Weiner, *Making Sense of War*, 356.

Committee that communities in formerly occupied territories might perceive the Soviet state as a tool of Russian domination. In 1945, the Agitprop deputy head, M. T. Iovchuk, together with his associate, E. N. Gorodetskii, wrote to Georgii Malenkov regarding "the state of political work among the population of the western regions of the Byelorussian Soviet Socialist Republic." The authors complained that the Party was not carrying out enough agitational work in areas where the Nazis had previously organized mass propaganda campaigns aimed at inciting ethnonational antagonism toward Soviet authority. It was these efforts that had supposedly contributed to the lasting presence of hostile Polish, Belarusian, and Ukrainian nationalists. The letter called for the immediate publication in local newspapers of "articles promoting the role of the Soviet state and the Party of Lenin and Stalin during the Great Patriotic War."[56]

In response, the Central Committee intensified mass political work in the western borderlands, which included a two-month crash course to prepare party cadres in Ukraine, Latvia, Lithuania, Estonia, Moldavia, and elsewhere.[57] Given claims over the anti-Russian character of "local" nationalism in these areas, the CC opted to underscore all-union friendship bonds rather than Russian guidance in the ensuing propaganda offensive. In the language of one CC resolution directed at western Ukraine, "Party organizations . . . must convey to the population that only the Soviet state, based on the friendship of the peoples, can provide workers of the western regions of Ukraine with genuine freedom, material well-being, and rapid cultural recovery."[58] There was also a renewed emphasis on class. Indeed, CC authorities saw class rhetoric as an antidote to the idealization of prerevolutionary national histories, something that would become more pronounced under the Zhdanovshchina.[59]

The minimization of the Russian liberation theme in favor of all-union "friendship" and class struggle, however, did not negate hierarchical notions of wartime heroism. As Weiner and others have argued, Russians continued to provide the greatest number of publicized Heroes of the Soviet Union, while the press ceased identifying the ethnicities of deported peoples and Jewish heroes, effectively erasing the latter's unique contribution.[60] However, the language of late-wartime dispatches and Central Committee resolutions routinely

[56] RGASPI 17/125/311/1–8. [57] For example, *KPSS v rezoliutsiiakh*, 7:533–536.
[58] *KPSS v rezoliutsiiakh*, 7:537–538, qt. 529.
[59] As shall be discussed, this applied to the RSFSR as well. On the postwar return of ideological rigor more generally, see Zubkova, *Russia after the War*, 117–129, and passim.
[60] Weiner, *Making Sense of War*, 191–236.

obscured the Russian wartime guidance theme, while signaling an overriding commitment to all-union bonds and the greater Soviet imagined community.

Shortly after Victory Day (May 9), Georgii Aleksandrov, the Agitprop chief, prepared a summary document on the war's significance as it stood circa mid-May 1945. The document – a draft resolution justifying the policies of the 1930s through the prism of the war experience – targeted local party organizations primarily in the Ukrainian SSR, which had suffered disproportionately during collectivization and where armed resistance to Soviet authority persisted. The draft urged that the party leadership "every day explain to the working people" the link between Stalin's foresight during the previous decade and victory: "The [CC CPSU] and comrade Stalin warned that the coming war will be severe, prolonged and bloody, and stressed the need in this context to prepare all peoples of the country for the upcoming war." According to the document, Germany's defeat was to be cast as the result of the combined efforts of the whole Soviet people, for its "willingness to make sacrifices," "selfless work in the name of victory," and "ability to provide the country with more metal, aircraft, guns, shells, tanks, cars, fabrics, ... cotton, bread, beets, potatoes, and other types of industrial and agricultural products."[61] Although the document predated Stalin's toast honoring the Russian people by less than two weeks, it was more anticipatory of a subsequent toast he delivered in late June in recognition of the "little screws" [*vintikami*] running "the great machine of state," the "simple, ordinary, modest people," "without whom, all of us marshals or commanding officers of the fronts or armies wouldn't be worth ... a damn."[62]

Like Stalin's later summation speech, his "little screws" toast linked up with late-wartime threads emphasizing all-Soviet heroism and sacrifice, threads that did not so much fuse with Stalin's victory toast exalting the Russian people, as circumvent it. However, Stalinist authorities never renounced the victory toast to the Russian people. As with the ethnic Russian core, non-Russian mobilization involved the coexistence of the two dominant paradigms, which remained in constant tension within the wider ideological ecosystem. It was left to local officialdom to negotiate the precise form this centrally conceived discursive tension would take in the republics.

[61] RGASPI 17/125/311/51–60. On the perception during the 1930s of the war's inevitability, see Weiner, 136.
[62] Stalin, *Sochineniia*, 15:206.

Negotiating Russian Elder Brotherhood at the Periphery

If postwar Kazakhstan is any indication, the developing war myth provided a means of combatting perceived local nationalist tendencies through the idiom of friendship rather than Russian elder brotherhood. Here, the Russocentric deluge that accompanied Stalin's toast appears not to have necessitated a shift toward a more Russian-dominated victory narrative. At the same time, postwar ideological campaigns placed elements within the Kazakh party bureau and scholarly community under particularly severe scrutiny for ideological errors, which included the promotion of supposedly anti-Russian interpretations of the past and insufficient deference to Russians in the present.[63] Such accusations and denunciations, and calls for all-union intervention into republican affairs, culminated only in 1952,[64] with the suppression of a historical work by the widely respected Kazakh academician E. B. Bekmakhanov, and his ultimate arrest and imprisonment.[65] Authorities' sensitivity to the slightest deviation from ideological norms in Kazakhstan makes for a revealing case study of the Stalinist victory myth's agitational role in a non-Russian republican context.

In June 1945, a letter by Konstantin Nefedov, the editor of *Kazakhstanskaia Pravda*, began making the rounds among Moscow authorities. In the letter, Nefedov complained to the high-ranking Malenkov that not enough had been done to publicize the bourgeois-nationalist errors found in the first edition of the once lauded *History of the Kazakh SSR*. Edited by Pankratova and the head of Agitprop for the Kazakh Party Central Committee M. A. Abdykalykov, the book had come under fire in mid-1944 for supposedly denigrating the historically progressive role of the Russian people. Although the book's faults were widely discussed and the matter was considered closed, Nefedov now asserted that Abdykalykov, together with other leading party figures in the republic, was actively suppressing details of the book's shortcomings.

[63] For an overview, see Blitstein, "Stalin's Nations," 63–71.

[64] Within the republic, denunciations persisted after 1952. That year, the bard Mukhtar Auezov actually fled to Moscow to escape prosecution by Kazakh authorities. See Kaziev, "Natsional'naia politika, 32–33.

[65] Controversy centered on Bekmakhanov's coverage of Kenesary Kasymov's resistance to Russian imperial expansion. Critics asserted that Bekmakhanov had "idealized" Kenesary as a "progressive" force, when in fact Kenesary was "neither revolutionary nor progressive," but led a "reactionary movement that dragged the Kazakh people backward, strengthening patriarchal feudalism ... [and] alienating Kazakhstan from Russia and the great Russian people." T. Shoinbaev, Kh. Aidarova, A. Iakunin, "Za marksistsko-leninskoe osveshchenie voprosov istorii Kazakhstana," *Pravda*, Dec. 26, 1950, 2–3. See also K. Sharapov, "E. Bekmakhanov," 109–114. In fact, Bekmakhanov had gone out of his way not to portray Kenesary as anti-Russian.

While the earlier debate over *History of the Kazakh SSR* centered on its account of Russian–Kazakh relations primarily during the nineteenth century, Nefedov's letter focused on enforcing Russian primacy in a Soviet context. During party meetings and discussions, Nefedov claimed, "it is not stated that Soviet Kazakhstan owes its present to the great Russian people, to the brotherhood of the peoples of the Soviet Union. And if it is said, then, in general terms, it is unconvincing."[66]

Notably, Nefedov complained that party officials were ignoring the role of Russians during the war: "Here there is a tendency . . . to inordinately exalt the historical role of the Kazakh people, particularly in the [Great] Patriotic War, while remaining silent or trying to silence the role of the great Russian people."[67] He went on to recount the mistreatment of a surviving member of the twenty-eight Panfilov-Guardsmen at the hands of the republican government. It was well known within the republic that two surviving Panfilovtsy resided within the Kazakh SSR. One of these, an ethnic Russian named Vasil'ev, was invited to Alma-Ata to attend a gala event. However, his clothing and boots were in such poor condition that Nefedov's editorial office, with little to no help from the local party organization, struggled to acquire decent attire on Vasil'ev's behalf. In the end, the office was only able to provide Vasil'ev with suitable boots. By contrast, according to Nefedov, when multiple ethnic-Kazakh Heroes of the Soviet Union visited for a similar event months later, Kazakh party and government agencies provided the men and their families, "not a few of whom were drunk," with 50,000 rubles worth of new clothing and shoes "[s]imply because [they were] Kazakhs." Hence, a component within republican officialdom was supposedly seeking at every turn to elevate the remembrance of Kazakh wartime heroism at Russians' expense. Nefedov called for Central Committee intervention "to fix the situation that has arisen."[68]

Nefedov, an ethnic Russian, clearly believed that accusations about the lack of attention accorded Russian wartime leadership in the republic would provoke the outrage of the center, and he looked to direct that outrage at his rivals, including Abdykalykov. This was a fairly standard tactic. As one historian has noted, the late-Stalinist "anti-nationalist campaign in Kazakhstan was not the result of pressure by all-union government bodies, but rather of the local initiative of 'internationalists' from among the creative and scientific intelligentsia, who were settling accounts with long-time enemies." Significantly, the all-union center

[66] RGASPI 17/125/340/81.

[67] Someone had highlighted the phrase "exalt the historical role of the Kazakh people," but stopped short of the mention of the war and the Russian people. RGASPI 17/125/340/78.

[68] RGASPI 17/125/340/78–85.

frequently acted "to prevent such local 'initiatives.'"[69] Although the Central Committee did launch an investigation in the summer of 1945, beginning a years-long cycle of personnel shakeups and public condemnations over suspected bourgeois-nationalist tendencies, it finessed the issue of Russian leadership in the war.

As in other republics, the Central Committee investigation in Kazakhstan uncovered instances of overzealous celebration of figures and events from the prerevolutionary past. This risked undermining the official line, which held that the process of unification with the Russian people was benevolent and progressive. To remedy these persistent deviations, central authorities renewed their call for a shift in focus among the republic's scholars, ideologists, and creative intelligentsia, away from distinct national histories toward a focus on the shared Soviet experience.[70]

Consonant with Nefedov's accusations, the report generated by the Central Committee investigative team also faulted republican portrayals of Soviet-era accomplishments, which included examples of authors writing Russians out of the war in favor of exclusively Kazakh narratives. The chief offender in this regard was the manuscript for "My Frontline Friends" [*Moi frontovye druz'ia*] by the Kazakh Hero of the Soviet Union Malik Gabdullin. Drawn from the author's firsthand experiences as part of the famed 8th Panfilov Rifle Division during the defense of Moscow,[71] the work was accused of promoting an "anti-Russian spirit." Gabdullin glorified the Kazakh battalion commander Momysh-uly and depicted harsh frontline measures of discipline, including summary executions of traitors and cowards. However, the CC report noted incredulously, "all these cowards, violators of discipline, traitors to the Motherland, turn out to be Russians." Hence, Gabdullin had provided a "deliberately perverted description of the role of the Russian soldier at war" and "described events in such a way that only Kazakhs fought heroically outside Moscow." To make matters worse, after a local party official earmarked the manuscript for further review, Abdykalykov reproached the official, an ethnic Russian, remarking, "Don't be so stubborn, and don't forget where you live and work."[72]

[69] Kaziev, "Natsional'naia politika, 33.

[70] See RGASPI 17/125/570/2–13, publ. in Khlevniuk, *Sovetskaia natsional'naia*, 162–170; "O podgotovke 2-go izdaniia 'Istorii Kazakhskoi SSR'," 49–51; *KPSS v rezoliutsiiakh*, 7:518. On a similar process unfolding in the Ukrainian SSR, see Yekelchyk, "Celebrating the Soviet Present"; Weiner, *Making Sense of War*, 331–363.

[71] The larger division is not to be confused with the twenty-eight Panfilov-Guardsmen, who were members of the division's 1075 Rifle Regiment.

[72] RGASPI 17/125/311/131–143, publ. in Gatagova, *TsK VKP(b)*, 990–997, qt. 994. Although the report highlighted the issue of ethnicity, Gabdullin was clearly transgressing other aspects of official war memory, including strictures regarding portrayals of Soviet soldiers as "positive heroes." See Clark, *The Soviet Novel*, 189–209.

The team assigned to assess ideological shortcomings in the republic thus took aim at republican-level portrayals of the war from an unabashedly Russocentric perspective. The direct subordination of Russian wartime heroism to that of another, non-Russian variety was flatly denounced. Nevertheless, the critique of Gabdullin's manuscript and several other works remained very much in line with Stalin's earlier pronouncement on Dovzhenko's *Ukraine in Flames*. There was nothing in the report noting the absence of Russian wartime *guidance* or deeming Russians *more* innately heroic than other peoples of the Union.[73] On the contrary, the report summarized its review of works on the Soviet era by chiding the Kazakh party organization in rote terms for failing to "reflect the heroic character of the Soviet people, their struggle for the freedom and independence of their socialist Motherland, [and] the friendship of the peoples of the USSR."[74]

Subsequent Central Committee reports connected to the investigation of the summer of 1945 were even more circumspect regarding depictions of Russian wartime centrality. One follow-up report sent by the ethnic Russian First Secretary of the Kazakh SSR, G. A. Borkov, to Malenkov, downgraded Gabdullin's violation from propagating an "anti-Russian" war narrative to "incorrectly treating the image of a Soviet officer," with no comment on the portrayal more generally of the Russian people at war. This was accompanied in the report by assurances that the republic's party organization was at work addressing its prior ideological errors, promoting Soviet-oriented themes – mainly the war – and carrying out additional measures aimed at encouraging all-union friendship rooted in the shared experience of the war. For example, the party organization had established a program to foster exchanges between Kazakh veterans of the Panfilov Rifle Division and residents of the USSR's Hero Cities.[75]

Borkov's report was not silent on the issue of Russian guidance. "Kazakh newspapers," the report pointed out, "have started to publish more articles on the friendship between the Russian and Kazakh peoples, the role of the Russian people in the creation of the Soviet state, the formation of the Kazakh Republic, and so on." Elsewhere, Borkov advocated the study of the "Russian people's fraternal assistance to the Kazakh people in their political, cultural, and economic development."[76]

[73] By contrast, the CC critique of Gabdullin has been cited as demonstrating that "recognizing the supremacy of the 'Great Russian People'" was a core aspect of the war's representation among non-Russians. This, however, conflates the issue of the war with the report's broader concern over prerevolutionary events and personalities. Cf. Schechter, "The Language of the Sword," 15–16.

[74] Gatagova, *TsK VKP(b)*, 994.

[75] RGASPI 17/125/311/108–130, esp. 109, 118, 120, 122, 130.

[76] RGASPI 17/125/311/130.

However, Borkov's summary, as well as later communications with the Central Committee, appeared unconcerned with the issue of Russian guidance during the war. As the war victory was fast becoming the paramount mobilizational theme among the republic's agitators,[77] the line on Russian wartime leadership was, at best, inconsistent. At least in this significant case, criticisms centered not on insufficient deference to Russians but on tone and the need to provide positive portrayals of Red Army soldiers and their experiences during demobilization. As one Kazakh control committee report noted, several short stories dealing with the return of Kazakh veterans to their villages were guilty of "libel against the Soviet people" for emphasizing the infidelity of the soldiers' spouses while their husbands were at the front.[78]

By June 1946, with the onset of the Zhdanovshchina, the Kazakh party organization could confidently outline its revamped ideological priorities.[79] During a July conference in Alma-Ata on propaganda work within the republic, Abdykalykov called for a major overhaul of every aspect of mass political work, which henceforth was to center on Soviet-era achievements.[80] The war was of paramount importance for the new Soviet orientation. "We must put an end," he declared, "to the situation in which all the activities of [party and state] institutions focused mainly on topics of the distant past of the Kazakh people." Rather, it was time to "require of them the complete and deep development of modern themes ... to show throughout [the republic] the extent of the heroic deeds of the people of Kazakhstan at the front and in the rear during the Great Patriotic War." Instead of the culmination of some age-old struggle between Germanic and Slavic civilizations, Abdykalykov stressed the contemporary nature of the war's origins and credited the "conditions of socialism" and the established Soviet system for making victory possible. In this vein, Abdykalykov reprimanded republican propagandists who had erroneously traced fascism's origins to reactionary movements of

[77] One 1946 report recorded no fewer than 221 party study circles focusing on the topic of the war. By comparison, during the same period there were just sixty-two such circles across the republic dedicated to examining the *Short Course of the History of the VKP(b)*. Both the Kazakh- and Russian-language editions of Stalin's *On the Great Patriotic War* similarly outnumbered the *Short Course*'s print run. See APRK 708/9/1334/91; RGASPI 17/125/311/120.

[78] RGASPI 17/125/570/2–13, publ. in Khlevniuk, *Sovetskaia natsional'naia*, 162–170, esp. 165–166. For an interesting look at the issue of wartime infidelity in postwar fiction, which highlights its "liberationist" elements, see Kirschenbaum, *The Legacy of the Siege*, 107–110.

[79] June 1946 is an earlier date from traditional accounts, which incorporates the campaign's vector in non-Russian republics and the Ukrainian SSR in particular. See Yekelchyk, "Celebrating the Soviet Present," 255–275; Hahn, *Postwar Soviet Politics*, 48.

[80] APRK 708/10/1358/12, 21, 26.

previous centuries. On the contrary, Abdykalykov, following Stalin, urged that fascism was "the product of modern imperialism, and fascists – the most reactionary element of monopoly capitalism." In other words, the war against fascism was first and foremost a clash of ideological systems. As such, the war's memory was near and dear to all Soviet national communities, non-Slavs included.[81]

The other speakers at the conference, mainly members of the Kazakh party establishment, reiterated the new, Soviet-centered focus in ideological work. The editor of a local newspaper, one Taikumanov, urged propagandists "to create new works that reflect our great Soviet era – the era of world-historic victories, the grand era of construction in the years of Stalin's five-year plans."[82] N. Stepanov, the Agitprop deputy, called for greater emphasis on the unshakable cohesion of the Soviet people at war, which Stepanov tied to ideological adherence and patriotic devotion to the socialist motherland.[83] The concluding speaker, named Maslin, argued that the war theme must reflect the new era in social relations. Victory, according to Maslin, had strengthened not only friendship between ethnonational groups, but especially the attachment of those groups to the larger, supranational body:

> If the wars of the past always led to a sharp increase in antagonism between the people and the state, the [Great] Patriotic War has shown that the interests of our people and those of the Soviet state have become even more inseparable . . . If the wars of the past have led to the aggravation of ethnic strife, and sometimes to the disintegration of multinational states, as a result of the Great Patriotic War our multinational Soviet state became even stronger. The friendship of the peoples of the Soviet Union is the greatest and indestructible foundation of our state.

While victory in the war had piqued the national consciousness and pride of every Soviet nation, its overriding significance, in Maslin's view, was "an even greater commitment to the multinational state."[84] Hence, what began as the Central Committee's involvement in the affairs of the Kazakh party organization for local nationalist tendencies and insufficient deference to the Russian people, resulted in a decidedly pan-Soviet conception of victory. Although republican officials, including Abdykalykov, would continue to run afoul of central authorities, subsequent violations would center on portrayals of prerevolutionary events and not republic-level representations of the Great Patriotic War.[85]

The case of the Kazakh SSR demonstrates how inconsistently the CC enforced any doctrine of Russian leadership – that is, if such an informal

[81] APRK 708/10/1358/26, 29. [82] APRK 708/10/1358/53.
[83] APRK 708/10/1358/148. [84] APRK 708/10/1358/167–169.
[85] Kaziev, "Natsional'naia politika, 29–33; Blitstein, "Stalin's Nations," 63–71.

doctrine even existed.[86] In the aftermath of repeated disciplinary measures affirming Kazakhstan's "voluntary" and "progressive" union with Russia before the Revolution, there remained a concerted effort among influential republican authorities to cast victory in the war as the shared achievement of all Soviet peoples. Even during the early 1950s, as Russian chauvinism soared to new heights, Kazakh cultural officials confidently asserted the supranational, all-Soviet framing of victory.

This was the line taken in January 1953, for example, during a series of meetings on museum work in the republic. The sessions were held to address the poor state of the republic's museums, especially the lack of exhibits reflecting the Soviet period. The Soviet era, one museum director noted, "concerns us more than all the history from primitive times up to the Revolution." Where museums had developed Soviet displays, these were often sloppily put together and blended with exhibits from other time periods. One regional museum's lead exhibit on the Great Patriotic War, for example, inexplicably consisted of a mock-up of the 1760 taking of Berlin by Russian soldiers during the Seven Years' War. This revealed not only an inattention to historical detail but, more disconcertingly, a potential failure among rural museum administrators to comprehend the vital ideological distinction between Russian and Soviet military feats.[87]

Despite the lack of success in portraying Soviet events in the republic's museums, discussants were clear on the war's significance in future museum work. The acting museum director for the Dzhambul region, one Esmurzaev, outlined the revised thematic plan for museums in the coming year, which included the fixture "Kazakhstan in the Great Patriotic War 1941–1945." In addition to providing an overview of the main events of the war, the exhibit would highlight the Kazakh people's unflagging response to the Party's call to take up arms in defense of the common socialist motherland. Esmurzaev and his colleagues made no mention of Russian leadership or even friendship in the war, but rather stressed ways the war theme could complement "our country's ideology of equality of all races and nations . . . the great sense of Soviet patriotism, [and] deep love and devotion to the great Party of Lenin and Stalin."[88]

And yet, we have seen that elements within the republican party committee and local intelligentsia, such as Nefedov, the Russian editor of *Kazakhstanskaia Pravda*, called on central authorities to enforce the notion of Russian wartime guidance in republic-level representations,

[86] On the "doctrine of Russian leadership," see Barghoorn, *Soviet Russian Nationalism*, chap. 2.
[87] The transcript incorrectly gives the year 1770. See TsGARK 1890/1/105/30.
[88] TsGARK 1890/1/105/30–32, 80–85, 90.

a plea the Central Committee ultimately ignored. Indeed, the impetus for many of the controversies over local nationalism within the republic emanated from republican officials themselves.[89] Thus, while the question of Russian wartime leadership became a key wedge issue for settling local disputes and a perceived means of displaying loyalty and deference to Moscow, it does not appear to have been a Central Committee priority.

Although processes in other republics varied, developments in Kazakhstan were hardly anomalous. Serhy Yekelchyk has demonstrated convincingly that local bureaucrats in the Ukrainian SSR – often ethnic Russians, but not always – could be greater "chauvinists" than their Russian counterparts at the all-union level.[90] Indeed, non-Russian party officials often pushed the war myth in a more Russocentric direction than central authorities intended. Yekelchyk, for example, contrasts the Dovzhenko Affair, in which the issue of the Russian elder brother did not play a role, with a similar event several months later involving the Ukrainian poet Maksym Rylsky. In March 1944, Fedir Ienevych, the head of the Ukrainian Institute of Marx, Engels, and Lenin, issued a report criticizing a 1943 lecture on Ukrainian history by Rylsky. Rylsky's speech had praised Ukrainians' "uninterrupted" historical contributions from the earliest times up to the present war with Germany. Ienevych's report condemned Rylsky for excessively glorifying prerevolutionary Ukrainian culture and for ignoring the guiding role of the Russian people, an accusation that extended to the present war: "It was necessary to stress in this speech . . . the most important, decisive role that the great Russian people played in liberating Ukraine from the German imperialists."[91]

Unlike the controversy over *Ukraine in Flames*, which featured Stalin's personal involvement, Ienevych's criticism of Rylsky did not occasion a more general denunciation. Ienevych was in fact fired in 1947, and he attempted to redeem himself by relaunching his assault on Rylsky's speech that year. This resulted in a resolution by the Ukrainian CC retroactively denouncing Rylsky's "nationalistic mistakes" and his treatment of "the history of Ukraine in isolation from the history of other peoples." However, Rylsky's inattention to Russian wartime liberation, a deviation in the eyes of the Ukrainian authority Ienevych, did not play any role in the affair's subsequent trajectory. Instead, criticisms fixed squarely on the prerevolutionary past.[92]

[89] Kaziev, "Natsional'naia politika, 33.
[90] Yekelchyk, *Stalin's Empire of Memory*, 34 and passim; Yekelchyk, "Stalinist Patriotism," 56.
[91] TsDAHO 1/70/266/1, cited in Yekelchyk, *Stalin's Empire of Memory*, 56.
[92] Yekelchyk, 54–57, qt. 77–78.

The Russian people's often-nebulous place in the emerging central victory myth thus lent a great deal of variability to republican representations of wartime ethnic relations. Where republican party leaders sometimes favored the pan-Soviet/internationalist variant of the victory myth, others sought to curry favor with and exhibit deference to the Kremlin through the promotion of Russian-dominated accounts of the war and liberation. This dynamic helps explain why several notable depictions of the war as a predominantly Russian event emerged during the final months of Stalin's life from non-Russian elites. In early 1953, the ethnic Azeri party boss of Azerbaijan, Mir Dzhafar Abbasovich Bagirov, submitted a chronicle of Russian greatness to the journal *Kommunist* that included the following synopsis of the war:

> The friendship of the peoples of our country, forged in the struggle for the victory of socialism, in the struggle for communism, rallied to their elder brother, the great Russian people, with particular force during the difficult years of the Great Patriotic War. ... The Great Patriotic War clearly confirmed that only by rallying around its elder brother, the Russian people, only with them, only under their leadership, are the peoples of our country invincible ... Noting the decisive role of the Russian people in achieving victory in the Great Patriotic War, comrade Stalin said at the reception of the commanders of the Red Army on May 24, 1945: [full text of Stalin's toast] ... The Russian people deservedly enjoy the title of first among equals, by rights they are the elder brother in the family of peoples of the Soviet Union.[93]

As with Nefedov's letter of complaint, such examples speak to the complicated and inconsistent way ethnic hierarchy, and particularly the ascendant place of Russians, was understood and enforced in the late-Stalinist USSR. More to the point, they demonstrate that Russocentrism connected to the war experience could at times manifest in non-Russian centers with perhaps greater ease than it could in all-union or major Russian centers.

"Our Russia Is No Longer the Same"

How were Russians to interpret their historical trajectory and wartime role in light of victory? We have seen that postwar ideologists – mining the discordant messages of wartime propaganda and later statements by Stalin, Zhdanov, and others – offered a wide spectrum of possible roles for Russians and their heroic past in narratives of the war. Stalin's toast, references to the great ancestors, and other allusions to Russian wartime centrality were not requisite components of the victory narrative, but

[93] Bagirov, "Starshii brat," 84–85.

variables that ideological producers could embrace or ignore depending on their predilections. Nevertheless, while the Central Committee tolerated a heterodox approach to the theme of Russian wartime leadership, the pervasiveness of late-Stalinist Russocentrism assured Russians a leading status in representations more generally. Public commemorations after the war, such as the 110th anniversary of Pushkin's death and the 800-year jubilee marking the founding of Moscow, both in 1947, only heightened the status of Russians and their unique history within the Soviet family of nations. The relationship between Stalinist war memory and the public celebration of Russian national history and culture is discussed in greater detail in the next chapter. It is useful here to consider some trends in postwar patriotic culture that most directly reflected official thinking on the Russian Question vis-à-vis the war. In this regard, too, the ambiguities emanating from the leadership and ideological establishment appear to have enabled both Russocentric and pan-Soviet ideological paradigms. The tension between these contrasting variants of the war myth at once reproduced the hierarchical heroism and primordialism of Stalin's victory toast while also assuring the preservation of a late-Stalinist line that implored Russians, like their non-Russian comrades, to glorify the Soviet present and a shared, supranational sense of identity.[94]

A vignette widely promoted after the war from Boris Gorbatov's serialized story *Aleksei Kulikov, Soldier* exemplified this Soviet emphasis among Russians. At the front, the titular hero discusses the matter of a particular traitor with his comrade Dubiaga. Dubiaga, treating the traitor's behavior lightly, remarks, "This is Russia, you know. Russia will remain Russia . . . All of Russia was once under the Tatars. Let it be under the Germans, and . . . ." Kulikov interrupts his friend:

> I do not want just any Russia . . . I'm not in agreement with any old Russia. I need the Russia where, as before, I am the master of my land, where there are collective farms, and where, if my wife gives birth, there is a hospital, and a school to teach my son. It's *Soviet* Russia I want, you understand? I don't want any other one, and there will never be another.[95]

Dubiaga, ashamed by this reprimand, eventually tries to flee to the Germans, but is shot by Kulikov as a traitor. Even more than Tvardovskii's popular depiction of the archetypical Russian soldier, the protagonist Vasilii Terkin, official treatments would home in on

[94] By contrast, Serhy Yekelchyk, among others, suggests that this "Soviet" emphasis applied primarily to non-Russians. See Yekelchyk, "Celebrating the Soviet Present," 255–275.
[95] Gorbatov, *Sobranie sochinenii*, 3:63–64 (italics added).

Kulikov's exchange with Dubiaga to delineate the permitted bounds of postwar Russocentrism connected to the war's memory.[96]

In theory, if not always in practice, the Zhdanovshchina's ideological reorientation toward the Soviet present applied in equal measure to the state's Russian-speaking core. In an April 1946 prelude to Zhdanov's assertion that "We are no longer the Russians we were before 1917," Zhdanov and Aleksandrov jointly instructed party secretaries A. A. Kuznetsov and G. M. Popov on "serious shortcomings" in Agitprop work. The instructions noted that "[i]n literature and the arts there is a tendency to move away from contemporary issues toward a one-sided fascination with historical themes." This accusation applied to Russian and non-Russian film, literature, music, but also the central press. The letter accused *Pravda* of "poorly covering issues of party life" and of "insufficient" coverage of "current topical issues" and Soviet themes.[97] In connection with these instructions, the CC instructed local agitators to deepen their coverage of class struggle alongside the theme of the war. The directive called for future party historical work to center on the lives of workers and peasants under tsarism, the nature of capitalism, the origins of the Bolshevik Party, the construction of the Soviet state, and the "reasons for the Soviet people's victory in the Great Patriotic War."[98]

Similarly, a 1947 internal primer entitled "Political Literacy for Communists" outlined how party activists should navigate political topics in light of postwar developments. While the most authoritative text on the 1941–5 conflict, *On the Great Patriotic War*, consisted of a collection of Stalin's wartime statements and correspondences with little further elaboration, "Political Literacy" gave a concise analysis of the war's key moments and broader significance.[99] Noteworthy for the utter absence of any reference to Russian wartime leadership or martial pedigree, "Political Literacy" located the war's origins in the decades-long "struggle against hostile capitalist forces" who "throughout the existence of the

[96] The postwar editions of the standard high school history textbook, for instance, discussed how Gorbatov's story reflected "the fundamental features of the Soviet people" during the war: "[l]oyalty to the Soviet homeland, readiness to give one's life for the achievements of the Great October Revolution, conscious service to the cause of socialism, loyalty to the Soviet people and to the Great Party of Lenin-Stalin." Pankratova, *Istoriia SSSR* (1952), 394. Henry C. Cassidy recognized the novella's appearance as much more than a typical work of wartime fiction; it was "a significant statement of policy, written for a public purpose." Cassidy, *Moscow Dateline*, 351–352. *Vasilii Terkin* remained popular, of course, and garnered Tvardovskii a Stalin Prize in January 1946.

[97] RGASPI 77/3/24/18–43. See also, Orlov, "Natsional'nyi i internatsional'nyi komponenty," 415.

[98] RGASPI 17/125/311/153–156.

[99] Stalin, *O Velikoi Otechestvennoi voiny*.

Soviet state strove to eliminate the Soviet system, to disrupt the building of socialism, to destroy the world's first socialist state." The document attributed Germany's defeat to exclusively postrevolutionary sources. It also accorded the supranational Soviet people a status long reserved for Russians alone: protector of world civilization.[100]

The same year, Agitprop produced a major draft plan entitled "Propaganda Measures Concerning the Idea of Soviet Patriotism among the Population." Coauthored by Aleksandrov, Fedoseev, and Kovalev, the plan contained several references to the Russian people's past scientific and cultural achievements and their role "in selfless struggle" against foreign invaders.[101] One leading historian has cited this plan as evidence of the overwhelmingly Russocentric ideological milieu.[102] However, the document is also significant for the way it attempted to reconcile the two dominant paradigms. Rather than present competing Russocentric and pan-Soviet readings of victory, it segmented these themes, confining the Russocentric paradigm to prerevolutionary achievements and early Soviet development, while framing the war effort in exclusively pan-Soviet terms. According to "Propaganda Measures," it was only by "ushering in a new epoch in the history of mankind" that the Soviet people were able to "save world civilization from the fascist barbarians." "[I]t is necessary," the authors urged, "to strongly emphasize that there is currently no other people that could have rendered such great services to humanity as did the Soviet people." For it, "under the leadership of the Bolshevik Party, built socialism, the most perfect social system"; "established a multinational state on the basis of equality and friendship"; and "defeated the army of German and Japanese imperialism, overturning and trampling upon German military doctrine."[103] The plan thus sectioned off prewar Russocentrism from the pan-Soviet internationalism embodied by the war victory. Such a compartmentalized approach to ideological harmonization would become a normal feature of patriotic discourse in the years after Stalin's death.

Where internal commentaries like "Political Literacy" and "Propaganda Measures" generally held up the war victory as the achievement of the socialist system and supra-ethnic Soviet people, and jettisoned explicit mention of Russian war leadership, other works, especially those intended for mass consumption, embraced elements of the Russocentric

[100] RGASPI 17/125/503/53–103, qts. 60–61, 103. [101] RGASPI 17/125/503/40–48.
[102] See especially Brandenberger, *National Bolshevism*, 193–194.
[103] RGASPI 17/125/503/41.

paradigm.[104] At the same time that the Central Committee was seeking to reel in Russocentric excesses in party work, the postwar editions of leading school texts on the history of the USSR appeared in print. These included Pankratova's tenth grade high school primer and Shestakov's revised *Short Course* in history, both of which featured coverage of the war that would remain essentially unchanged in all subsequent editions through Stalin's death. As with "Political Literacy" and "Propaganda Measures," the textbooks omitted discussion of Stalin's victory toast and some of the war's other Russocentric landmarks.[105] Both works likewise painted an inclusive, multiethnic picture of the war effort and highlighted the modern, Soviet nature of victory (the Soviet system, Communist Party organization, etc.). The model wartime patriots were not primarily military commanders from the distant past, but rather those who "reflected the features of the Soviet person born of the socialist system."[106] Pankratova continued to list the Jewish identity of the hero Solomon Gorelik, even in the book's later editions, in marked contrast to postwar representations more generally.[107] Russocentric flourishes remained, however. Shestakov devoted a sentence to the Russian people's leading role during the war while Pankratova went further. In addition to describing Soviet nations battling "under the leadership" of Russians, her book suggested that Nazi racial enmity was directed "above all [at] the great Russian people, who more than once in their history had opposed German aggressors."[108] Ultimately, the coexistence of party-generated texts that alternately downplayed and played up the theme of Russian wartime primacy speaks less to a clear Russocentric line on the war than a discursive tension between pan-Soviet and Russocentric patriotic currents.

Of course, the Zhdanovshchina's call for a more ideologically centered understanding of ethnic identity and Sovietness did little to prevent the campaign's devolution into a series of crude anti-Western and, by 1948–9, anti-Semitic persecutions that outlived Zhdanov himself. Broadly encompassing a campaign "against rootless cosmopolitanism," officials

[104] This is somewhat similar to what Brandenberger and Zelenov identified as a "bifurcation of party indoctrinational efforts" during the late 1930s in which propagandists "at the grass roots level" stressed Russocentric patriotism while "elite mobilizational efforts ... focused on ideologically orthodox themes." See Brandenberger and Zelenov, *Stalin's Master Narrative*, 23.

[105] Among other things, textbooks excised the phrase "Russia is vast" from Klochkov's battle cry during the feat of the twenty-eight Panfilov-Guardsmen, so that what remained was "There is nowhere to retreat. Moscow is at our backs." See, for example, Shestakov, *Istoriia SSSR*, (1945), 266. Pankratova's history recited Stalin's "great ancestors" speech where Shestakov's ignored it. Pankratova, *Istoriia SSSR* (1952), 372.

[106] Pankratova, 394.

[107] See Pankratova, *Istoriia SSSR*, 402–403; Shestakov, *Istoriia SSSR*, 267–268.

[108] Pankratova, *Istoriia SSSR*, 366, 403.

targeted cultural figures and academics for supposedly "groveling" at the feet of Western counterparts and for paying insufficient deference to the Russian foundations of postwar science and culture. Among the campaign's numerous victims during its anti-Semitic phase were surviving leaders of the Jewish Anti-Fascist Committee and Isaak Mints, the former head of the Commission on the History of the Great Patriotic War and author of one of the war's first official histories.[109] Although Mints survived, he was subjected to repeated public humiliations and lost his post at both Moscow State University and the Institute of History of the Academy of Sciences. He also had to abandon plans to publish a major volume on the war's history based on research conducted by his commission.[110]

How to square the victory myth's discursive tension, which tolerated a more inclusive, all-Soviet conception of patriotic identity, with the anticosmopolitan campaign of the late 1940s and early 1950s that was so clearly rooted in the xenophobia and anti-Semitism of certain Russian nationalist currents? It could be, as some have suggested, that the concepts "Soviet" and "Russian" became so enmeshed during the postwar era that there was little way to assert the pan-Soviet nuances of the war myth in the face of broader, Russocentric trends in public culture.[111] However, this interpretation discounts not only the variability of postwar victory narratives, but also the degree to which the fight against cosmopolitanism was routinely couched as a defense of pan-Soviet, as opposed to Russian, patriotic values. That is to say, the pan-Soviet paradigm could be every bit as insular and chauvinistic when wielded against otherness as the narrower, Russian variety.

[109] See especially Dobrenko, *Late Stalinism*, esp. 392–448; Kostyrchenko, *Tainaia politika*, passim; Slezkine, *The Jewish Century*, chap. 4; Rubenstein, *The Last Days of Stalin*, 62–63. See also the wide-ranging documentary study centering on the persecution of Leningrad philologists, Druzhinin, *Ideologiia i filologiia*.

[110] See Hellbeck, *Stalingrad*, 436–440.

[111] Allensworth describes the campaign "to unmask the Zionists and rootless cosmopolitans in the bosom of Mother Russia," pointing to a Russocentric article, "typical for the time," entitled "Hold Aloft the Banner of Russian Patriotism." This is indeed the translation as cited from Adam Ulam's biography of Stalin. However, the correct translation reads, "Hold Aloft the Banner of *Soviet* Patriotism." The article is in fact careful to flesh out the concept of Soviet patriotism as distinct from its Russian predecessor. Cf. Allensworth, *The Russian Question*, 156; Ulam, *Stalin*, 680. The original article is Golovenchenko, "Vysoko derzhat'," 39–48. Ola Hnatiuk argues correctly that the postwar leadership's anti-Semitic campaign was part of the broader attack on bourgeois nationalism. However, she posits that the campaign "strove to suppress minority nationalism by crediting the victory over Nazism to the Russian people alone," a contention strongly at odds with the evidence presented here. See Hnatiuk, "How the Soviet Union Suppressed the Holocaust."

Although anticosmopolitan accusations leveled at members of the intelligentsia often cited inadequate praise of prerevolutionary Russian achievements in the arts and sciences, such explicit Russocentrism did not typically extend beyond 1917.[112] When it did, more often than not, there were attempts to distinguish between "negative" (archaic, ethnonational) and "positive" (Soviet, supranational) patriotisms, a differentiation that was especially acute with regard to the war. It was in the context of the anticosmopolitan campaign that the historian Evgenii Tarle came under fire for failing to recognize those differences in his own writings. During a meeting on "the fight against bourgeois cosmopolitanism in the historical profession" in the Leningrad branch of the Institute of History, one of Tarle's colleagues reminded participants that cosmopolitanism in historical work embodied "two biases": "either historians underestimate Russia's role in world history [or] ignore the leap that our country has made as a result of the Great October Socialist Revolution." In Tarle's case, accusations contended that, although he had successfully "resurrected remarkable figures like Kutuzov, Ushakov, and others," in such works "the line between Old and Soviet Russia is often not drawn. No distinction has been made between the foreign policy of Old and Soviet Russia, between the old [military] and the Soviet army." Just as significant as recognizing past Russian contributions, Tarle's accuser concluded, the fight against cosmopolitanism involves a "struggle against the idealization of the past."[113]

A similarly "cosmopolitan" failure to distinguish between the "Old Russian" and Soviet patriotic ideals involved the husband-and-wife team of biologists Nina Kliueva and Grigorii Roskin, whose manuscript claiming a breakthrough treatment for cancer was published in the United States. Accused of broadcasting state secrets and dishonoring the motherland, "guided by considerations of personal fame and cheap popularity abroad," an Honor Court tried the two scientists in June 1947. The Central Committee followed the case with great interest. Both internal party reports and the transcript of the trial condemned the two scientists in decidedly pan-Soviet language. "How could there be people in our Soviet society," asked one report, "who are capable of national self-abasement, of kneeling before servants of foreign capital?" After all,

112 Aleksandrov, for instance, lost his post at Agitprop for his survey *The History of Western European Philosophy* because it omitted discussion on Russian philosophy and its global contributions. See Gorlizki and Khlevniuk, *Cold Peace*, 35–36.

113 ARAN 1577/2/211/64.

the Great October Socialist Revolution liberated the peoples of Russia from the economic and spiritual enslavement of foreign capital. ... Having created a powerful socialist industry and an advanced system of collective farming, the Soviet state has achieved economic independence. Having carried out the cultural revolution and having created our own Soviet state, our people have broken the material and spiritual dependence upon the bourgeois West. The Soviet Union has become the mainstay of world civilization and progress. In the Great Patriotic War the socialist system demonstrated its strength and superiority over the capitalist system. Given the Soviet Union's world-historical role, how can there be within the pores of the mighty Soviet body such groveling and lack of faith in the strength of our people?

The answer to the latter question, according to this and related pieces covering the trial, was the pernicious remnants of prerevolutionary Russia: "The roots of these kinds of antipatriotic sentiments and activities ... are to be found in the vestiges of the accursed past of tsarist Russia" and "its centuries-old backwardness."[114] Kliueva and Roskin were thus relics of a bygone era of Russian history; the Honor Court castigated them precisely for their insufficient Sovietness. One of the trial's most striking exchanges came when the head of the cancer biochemistry laboratory of the Academy of Medical Sciences, B. I. Zbarskii, berated the two defendants for misunderstanding the transcendent nature of Soviet patriotism. Taking aim at Roskin, Zbarskii – himself a Jew – conveyed his personal offense: "You insulted the patriotic feelings of a non-Russian by placing national patriotism at odds with Soviet patriotism. All of our nationalities – Georgians, Armenians, Jews – have a single patriotism: Soviet. You bring shame upon us all."[115]

At the time of the trial, it was still possible for an Agitprop report to describe Jewish writings on the war as "overwhelmingly imbued with the ideals of Soviet patriotism" and "reflective of the Stalinist notion of the friendship of the peoples."[116] From 1948, however, spurred on by the creation of the state of Israel (and Golda Meir's rapturous reception in Moscow), the anticosmopolitan campaign took a markedly anti-Semitic turn.[117] Authorities singled out Jews, whom they increasingly deemed incapable of subordinating their Jewish loyalties and identifications to those of Soviet authority. Yet even in its rabid anti-Semitism and frequent

[114] Nadzhafov and Belousova, *Stalin i kosmopolitizm*, 123–127.

[115] Gorinov, *Moskva poslevoennaia*, 231–234, qt. 233. [116] RGASPI 17/125/459/32–35.

[117] Slezkine aptly summarizes this anti-Semitic shift, noting the convergence of two trends, "the ethnicization of the Soviet state and the nationalization of ethnic Jews," which "kept reinforcing each other" until, for Stalin, the Jews as an ethnic group became "congenitally and irredeemably alien." Slezkine, *The Jewish Century*, 297–298. See also Rubenstein, *The Last Days of Stalin*, 60–95; Azadovskii and Egorov, "From Anti-Westernism to Anti-Semitism," 66–80. For Meir's own account of her reception, see Meir, *My Life*, 250.

references to Russian achievements, the later anticosmopolitan campaign remained generally compatible with the pan-Soviet/internationalist model of official war memory. While Jewish critics were censured for misrepresenting the "national character of the Soviet Russian man," such condemnations typically set apart the patriotism of the Soviet people during the war.[118] War-themed works by Jewish academics and writers throughout 1949 came under fire not for failing to promote the leading role of Russians but mostly for insufficient criticism of the policies of the United States and Great Britain during the war.[119]

In certain respects, the pervasive Russian chauvinism and anti-Semitism of the era helped shore up the pan-Soviet paradigm. Paradoxical as it might seem, by widening the range of possible outlets for Russocentric expression, while enabling a spectrum of possible readings of the war, the anticosmopolitan campaign effectively channeled notions of Russian primacy away from the war theme and into contained spaces of pre-Soviet arts, sciences, and revolutionary activism. Stalin's toast, for example, made a rather dramatic comeback during the later stages of the anticosmopolitan campaign. In line with broader trends, however, it served to highlight a vague notion of Russian historical exceptionalism that had little directly to do with the war. In April 1949, the deputy director of the Institute of History of the Academy of Sciences, V. I. Shunkov, attacked several Jewish historians affiliated with the organization for trying to silence "the historical role of the great Russian people who are 'the most outstanding nation of all the nations that make up the Soviet Union' (from the speech of Stalin of 24 May 1945)." This direct quote from Stalin's toast preceded a discussion on insufficient attention to prerevolutionary Russian achievements and the transformed Soviet Russian person with no mention of the war or the toast's connection to it.[120]

Another example comes from a 1949 report by M. S. Ivanov "On the Struggle against Cosmopolitanism in Historical Sciences." Largely directed against Mints and his associates in the Institute of History, the speaker accused several Jewish scholars of belittling "the importance of the Russian people, to whom Com[rade] Stalin gave a high estimation,

[118] The quote is from one of the touchstones of the anti-Semitic campaign, which targeted a group of Jewish theater critics. Regarding wartime patriotism, they were accused of forgetting that it was inspired, first of all, by "socialist construction." "Ob odnoi antipatrioticheskoi gruppe teatral'nykh kritikov," *Pravda*, Jan. 28, 1949, 3. For other examples of the war theme as a pan-Soviet (rather than Russocentric) critique of cosmopolitanism, see N. M. Gribachev, "Protiv kosmopolitizma i formalizma v poezii," *Pravda*, Feb. 16, 1949, 3; RGASPI 17/132/221/33–35, publ. in Nadzhafov and Belousova, *Stalin i kosmopolitizm*, 368–370.

[119] See the various examples under ARAN 1577/2/211/2–88; ARAN 1577/2/212/22–110.

[120] ARAN 1577/2/212/21–37, qt. 22.

pointing out that the great Russian people have such enduring qualities as a clear mind, staunch character." Ivanov's paraphrase of Stalin's toast initiated a critique of historical works that "deny the identity and importance of Russian culture, science, and art." Although chiding Mints for not depicting the "leading role" of the "Russian working class in the struggle for the October Socialist Revolution and the construction of socialism," Ivanov's insistence on highlighting the singular role of Russians did not extend to works covering the Civil or Great Patriotic wars. For Ivanov, these victories rested upon the leadership of the Party, the "liberating mission of the Red Army," and "the heroic role of the Soviet people," and not, as Stalin's toast in its original context would suggest, the leadership and primacy of the Russian nation.[121] Thus, the heightened Russocentrism and anti-Semitism of the late 1940s and early 1950s did not imply the Russification of the war's memory. On the contrary, it may have played a role in preserving its pan-Soviet orientation. At the very least, such examples attest the absence of a clear official line.

While many Soviet citizens embraced the Russocentric variant of the war's memory, there is evidence of veterans, members of the intelligentsia, and rank-and-file party officials who looked back on the war as something that transcended ethnonational categories. For them, the war's representation offered a genuine opportunity to reconfigure the friendship of the peoples and ground it in the evocative imagery of shared struggle and victory over a common enemy. This was the line taken in December 1947, for example, during a discussion among political lecturers of the remote Kolyma region of the RSFSR. When it came to the proposed lecture "On the Friendship of the Peoples of the USSR," one of the speakers recommended that the lecture "elaborate further ... the leading role of the Russian nation as the elder brother in the family of Soviet peoples." However, a party secretary by the name of Dakhno advised instead "to include a clause stating that all the peoples of our country heroically fought on the fronts of the [Great] Patriotic War, evidenced by the fact that all the peoples [*narody*] of the USSR are represented among the heroes of the Soviet Union." After all, Dakhno persisted, "there were [a]mong the twenty-eight Panfilov-Guardsmen representatives of many nationalities."[122]

The party bureau formally agreed to include both proposals in the official lecture: Russians' overall elder brother status on the one hand and the uniquely multinational nature of the war victory on the other. As this discussion indicates, one way of resolving the tension between

[121] ARAN 1577/2/211/2–5ob. [122] RGASPI 17/125/592/283.

Russocentric and pan-Soviet readings of the war was to limit the Russian leadership theme to the realms of prerevolutionary and early Soviet experiences while advancing the theme of victory as the shared feat of every Soviet nation. Even among the gold and tin miners of remote Kolyma, the theme of the war offered a means of tempering notions of Russian primacy and Russian-led hierarchy. Although such a segmented approach to Soviet patriotism would gain momentum only after Stalin's death, its presence amid the late-Stalinist Russocentric deluge is noteworthy indeed.

Conclusion

The concept of a Russian-led hierarchy of peoples was a fluid and often inconsistent feature of late Stalinism. In an era defined by primordial national hierarchies,[123] the victory myth's discursive tension offered a more flexible model of patriotic identity, one that authorities could wield as evidence of lateral, multiethnic solidarity. However, contradictory public pronouncements and the ambiguities emanating from the central ideological establishment invited local initiative. So long as republican ideological producers and creative intelligentsia did not directly subordinate the wartime heroism of Russians to that of non-Russians, they were granted relative freedom to produce narratives of the war that fell within the fuzzy permitted bounds of Soviet patriotism. Often these hewed to the pan-Soviet understanding of victory. But ideologists and cultural agents in the republics sometimes played up the Russocentric version of the war myth, whether as a means of settling local political squabbles or of assuring the center of regional loyalty. Such cultural agents could link the framework of Russian guidance to the war by way of Stalin's toast. That this was, in my reading, an internally inconsistent and contested phenomenon indicates a late-Stalinist leadership reticent to impose a singular, Russocentric meaning on the war's memory. It also highlights the durability of the pan-Soviet/internationalist mode of patriotism at a time when notions of Russian primacy were otherwise ubiquitous.

Given the vagaries of the Russian Question in official war memory, it is little wonder that Stalin's toast to the Russian people elicited some vexed reactions at the time.[124] There are, moreover, a number of apocryphal tales about the episode. According to Zhdanov's son, when Stalin announced that he would like to raise a toast to the health of the Russian

[123] Martin, *Affirmative Action Empire*, 448.
[124] For example: TsKhDOPIM 3/61/46/135–136.

people, those present in the hall, apparently confused, responded with the words, "to the Soviet people!" Slightly miffed by this alteration, Stalin then repeated the toast as he had initially stated it, carefully enunciating the leading status of the Russian nation above all others.[125] There is no evidence to corroborate this account by the younger Zhdanov, which he claimed to have heard from his father. Nonetheless, by suggesting a dissonant rather than harmonious relationship between Stalin's Russocentrism and an internationalist ethos tied to the war effort, such apocryphal tales speak precisely to the toast's ambiguous connection to the early war myth. As the next chapter will explore with regard to Soviet commemorative culture, even before Stalin's death and the onset of destalinization, the leadership recognized the limits of the Russocentric paradigm as a vehicle for social cohesion and mobilization – especially at a time of ideological Cold War.

[125] Zhdanov, *Vzgliad v proshloe*, 135.

2 Victory Days

The War Theme in the Stalinist Commemorative Landscape

> Everyone in the street wore some medal, or ribbon, or decoration reminiscent of the war. The city boiled with activity . . . This is a big year for celebration in Moscow. The lights on the buildings, and on the Kremlin, and on the bridges were left up, because rain could not hurt them, and they too would be needed again on the seventh of November.
>
> – John Steinbeck, on Moscow's 800-year jubilee in 1947[1]

> We have nothing to say about Russia. We talk about the Soviet Union, about Moscow, but where is Russia, where are the Russian people?
>
> – Moscow Party Secretary Georgii Popov, 1947[2]

In 1948, Soviet citizens went to work on Victory Day (May 9) for the first time since the war's conclusion. "It's Victory Day, and everyone is working," grumbled A. I. Dmitriev, a young factory employee from Perm. "The holiday was canceled by decree. That is to say, the holiday will remain, only now it's a workday, unlike before when no one had to work on this day." Three years later, the same man noted gloomily in his diary: "Today is 'Victory Day,' but this feels like no kind of holiday. Just a typical weekday – and cold."[3] Dmitriev was lamenting not only the loss of a day off work – the result of a December 1947 decree of the Presidium of the Supreme Soviet – but also the Soviet state's abandonment of much of the pomp that had surrounded the announcement of victory in 1945. The spontaneous, nationwide celebration sparked by news of Germany's capitulation in the early hours of May 9 (May 8 in Berlin) preceded an organized victory parade in Red Square the following month.[4] The June parade included a memorable entrance by Zhukov astride a white horse and the spectacle of waves of Red Army soldiers tossing Nazi banners at the base of Lenin's Mausoleum (Figure 2.1).[5]

[1] Steinbeck, *A Russian Journal*, 191, 204. [2] OKhDOPIM 3/67/12/2–4.
[3] Dmitriev, *Dnevnik rabochego*, www.permgani.ru/diary/1948.html#161.
[4] GARF R-7523/36/335/169.
[5] This scene was immortalized in an iconic series of photos and paintings. See, most famously, Mykhailo Khmelko's oil painting, *Triumph of the Victorious Motherland* (1949).

Figure 2.1 Moscow Victory Parade, June 24, 1945 (Heritage Images/ Hulton Archive via Getty Images).

One witness to the festivities recalled the tremendous joy that overcame veterans of the 1st Ukrainian Front as they prepared to participate in the parade and encountered civilian passersby:

> The most exciting and memorable moment of this encounter with the victors was that almost everyone cried. Women. Children. Even the assembled ranks of the victorious heroes! They wept from the most acute excitement, from delight, from joy! As a young boy, I believed that people cried from pain, resentment, grief. And that men just don't cry. But I learned only then, on that unforgettable day, that even men cry from joy, from happiness.[6]

The pageantry surrounding victory proved fleeting, however. The next year, authorities curtailed Victory Day's celebration in favor of smaller-scale, locally managed commemorations. The transition to work-place celebrations by 1948 was another step in the direction of quasi-normalcy that would define the May Ninth holiday into the 1960s.[7]

The evolution of Victory Day was but one symptom of a late-Stalinist commemorative agenda that was simultaneously "amnesiac" and

[6] Gorinov, *Moskva poslevoennaia*, 55.
[7] Rolf, *Soviet Mass Festivals*, 182; Gill, *Symbols and Legitimacy*, 152–153.

war-obsessed.[8] This agenda promoted endless discussions linked to large-scale war memorial complexes in Moscow and Soviet Hero Cities only to abandon most of the major projects. It sanctioned the release of significant works of literature and film dealing with the war, such as Aleksandr Fadeev's novel *The Young Guard* and the cinematic productions *The Third Blow* (1948), *The Battle of Stalingrad* (1949), and *The Fall of Berlin* (1949). However, these were increasingly bound to narrow ideological strictures or Stalin's cult, factors that precipitated the war theme's decline in popular culture. As charted by Denise Youngblood, filmmakers produced nine war films in 1946, five in 1949, and none by 1951.[9] The rhetoric of celebration and remembrance was ubiquitous during Victory Day anniversaries, even while its status was relegated, as the worker Dmitriev noted dejectedly, to that of a "working holiday."[10] From the leadership's perspective, May Ninth was no longer a time for the Soviet people to rest on their collective laurels. Rather, state commemorations sought to channel the war's memory into the task of rebuilding the devastated country, all the while suppressing potentially destabilizing popular recollections of the brutal costs and compromises required to achieve victory.[11]

This chapter examines victory in the war as an object of commemoration in late-Stalinist Moscow with an eye toward those paradoxical features of postwar commemorative culture.[12] In particular, the analysis

[8] On the state's "amnesiac agenda," see Kirschenbaum, *The Legacy of the Siege*, 117.

[9] Youngblood, *Russian War Films*, 89. For an analysis of postwar cinema's singular focus on the Stalin cult, see Youngblood, 95–102. On *The Young Guard* and its impact, Juliane Fürst writes that Fadeev "sanitized" the novel "by removing non-Soviet traces from their lives" and sought to "define and instil a particularly Soviet brand of patriotism able to subsume any other patriotic feelings that might flourish in the post-war period." She continues to note that the novel rendered impossible any "distinction between one's home and the Soviet system." See Fürst, *Stalin's Last Generation*, 137–166, qt. 143. Museum work on the war in and around Moscow focused squarely on the Soviet character of victory throughout the late-Stalinist period, although local museums were able to promote particularistic heroic narratives for a time. See, for example, *Tsentral'nyi Muzei Krasnoi Armii* (1946, 1949); *Kratkii putevoditel' po zalam ekspozitsii*; *Dokumenty voinskoi slavy*; *Ekskursii, lektsii, konsul'tatsii*; *Tematika ekskursii dlia soldat* (1951, 1953); *Polozhenie o tsentral'nom muzee sovetskoi armii*; *Znamia Pobedy*.

[10] Stalin also insinuated a moratorium on the publication of war memoirs, arguing, according to one source, that "it was too early to be writing memoirs so soon after these great events, at a time when passions were still too much aroused." A. M. Vasilevskii, quoted in Tumarkin, *The Living & the Dead*, 104.

[11] War invalids-turned-beggars were systematically cleared from public view in urban centers, although there is disagreement over the timing and nature of this phenomenon. See Edele, *Soviet Veterans*, 93–94. On the suppression of traumatic war narratives, see Fürst, *Stalin's Last Generation*, 156–158; Tumarkin, *The Living & the Dead*, 103–104.

[12] Evgeny Dobrenko has produced a magisterial analysis of late Stalinism that similarly highlights the era's paradoxical features and the war's role therein. His monograph was

attempts to square a persistent, all-Soviet variant of the war narrative with the simultaneous public veneration of key events and personalities from the prerevolutionary Russian past. Rather than a "national Bolshevik" symbiosis, which seamlessly linked the war and the celebration of tsarist and other prerevolutionary accomplishments in a patriotic "double axis," the chapter argues that postwar Soviet patriotism is better understood as an assemblage of disparate and contradictory, and at times compartmentalized, themes and images.[13] Where the celebration of the Russian national past functioned to redirect and contain nationalistic impulses lest they disrupt the hierarchical integrity of the friendship of the peoples, representations of the war as a pan-Soviet event provided an alternative means of social mobilization, one that offset appeals to ethnic difference with a vision of a close-knit Soviet people.[14]

The relationship between the 1945 victory and the wider sense of Russian historical exceptionalism was especially pronounced in commemorations of the late 1940s due to a spate of important anniversaries marking key moments in Russian and Soviet history. Ultimately the chapter finds that late-Stalinist authorities were often unable or unwilling to merge the two ideological paradigms into a coherent, Russified whole. Alongside narratives depicting 1945 as the culmination of a thousand-year, Russian triumphalist through line, the victory myth's discursive tension enabled the notion of a supranational Soviet people spurred on by a patriotism without precedent, an idea that would outlive Stalin.

Threads of War Memory in Postwar Moscow

In the lead-up to the thirtieth anniversary of Victory Day in 1975, a veteran by the name of B. S. Viskov recalled his experience producing the winning design for a temporary triumphal arch in Berlin, one of the first Soviet victory monuments ever built. "To my great surprise and joy, my project (the Arch of Victory) was approved and adopted by the Military Council of the Front." Viskov, who submitted his proposal as the war still raged, said he chose the form of an arch because it resembled the shape of the Cyrillic letter "P" for the Russian "*pobeda*" or "victory." The proposed arch was to be adorned with banners and capped with an

published as the present manuscript was being finalized; hence, I have not been able to engage with it as fully as it deserves. See Dobrenko, *Late Stalinism*, esp. 1–86.

[13] Cf. Brandenberger, *National Bolshevism*, esp. 196, 198, 220; Maddox, *Saving Stalin's Imperial City*, 174–181.

[14] On this tension, see also Liuks, "Evreiskii vopros v politike Stalina," 45; Livshin and Orlov, "Propaganda i politicheskaia sotsializatsiia," 104.

embossed Order of Victory. "Suddenly," Viskov recalled, "there was a problem: I had never actually seen an Order of Victory." After informing his superiors, Viskov claims he was brought before Zhukov personally, who granted access to his own copy of the medal so that Viskov could finalize his design. By May 1945, a hastily erected version of Viskov's Arch of Victory stood above Frankfurter Strasse, soon renamed Stalinallee.[15]

The year 1945 saw similar makeshift structures erected in Leningrad, Baku, and elsewhere, while larger-scale memorials appeared in Vienna, Budapest, Warsaw, Kaliningrad, Bucharest, and Berlin's Tiergarten. However, the relative swiftness with which Soviet war monuments began to dot Central and Eastern European cityscapes belied what was, in its early development, a highly contested process.[16] Some of the tensions that would animate central discussions over the war's memorialization were already present in Viskov's arch. An essentially "Soviet" vision, the chosen Order of Victory motif utilized the image of the Kremlin's fifteenth-century Spasskaia Tower, the centerpiece of the Order. Of course, the party leadership repurposed Kremlin imagery – Spasskaia Tower included – to signify Soviet political power. In Catherine Merridale's words, they "taught the old walls to speak Bolshevik Russian."[17] Nevertheless, associations with the pre-Soviet era were unavoidable and even embraced by many within the Party who sought to play up patriotic links with the past. Not only Kremlin imagery, but the form of the triumphal arch could be read multiple ways. Whatever its resemblance to the Russian letter "P," it had a time-honored pedigree and also offered a practical and cheap solution to commemoration. The Leningrad architect A. S. Nikol'skii claimed he needed only two or three

[15] B. S. Viskov, "Pervaia arka Pobedy," *Moskovskii khudozhnik*, Feb. 21, 1975, cited in Malinina, "Khudozhestvennyi obraz," 122. Grosse Frankfurter Strasse was subsequently renamed Stalinallee, then Karl-Marx-Allee.

[16] Within the USSR, contestations erupted between center and periphery, nation and state, Russian and non-Russian, conventional soldier and partisan, veteran and noncombatant. On the various fault lines created by the war's official representation, see, for example, Kirschenbaum, *The Legacy of the Siege*, passim; Weiner, "Nature, Nurture, and Memory," 1114–1155; Weiner, "The Making of a Dominant Myth," 638–660. Also, for an interesting look at the struggle between professional writers, on the one hand, and veterans, on the other, over the right to publicly tell the story of the war, see Schechter, "The Language of the Sword," 1–44. For more on these tensions, see Hellbeck, *Stalingrad*, 432–436. On the relationship of partisans to the larger war myth, see Slepyan, *Stalin's Guerrillas*, 287–295.

[17] Merridale goes on to write, "In their hands, the Kremlin became Red Russia's fortress, the silhouette with five bright-lit electric stars that was, and probably remains, the world's shorthand for Soviet power." Merridale, *Red Fortress*, 306. The regime replaced the double-headed eagle that stood atop Spasskaia Tower with a red star and covered over religious iconography on the tower's exterior.

days to erect a twenty-meter-high arch.[18] Still, many criticized the use of the arch in war commemoration because of its non-proletarian lineage.[19]

In recent years, scholars have explored political contests over the war's public remembrance in the context of Leningrad and other Soviet cities, where local impulses to remember clashed with a centralizing Kremlin vision bent on eradicating particularistic heroic narratives.[20] Among examples from the RSFSR, these particularistic variants of the war myth have in common not only the assertion of local or urban identities, but also a sense of Russian national continuity with the past. For many citizens and authorities alike, the continued existence of prerevolutionary structures symbolized the failure of Germany's stated goal to wipe the Soviet Union from the face of the earth. As such, preservationist movements in Leningrad and elsewhere, spurred on by government legislation in 1947 and 1948 granting protections to historical architectural monuments, often conflated the restoration of prerevolutionary structures with the memorialization of the 1941–5 war.[21]

Even where city commemorations employed ostensibly Soviet imagery, these remained vulnerable to reinterpretation at the local level. Leningrad triumphal arches featured images of Lenin and Stalin and scale models of Soviet military hardware. This did not prevent one of the city's leading architects from ascribing to these monuments a Russian imperial pedigree. As he observed approvingly in a city architectural journal in 1946, these structures recalled the Narva Triumphal Gate that had been built in 1814 to honor returning tsarist soldiers.[22] In the city of Sevastopol, then still part of the RSFSR, city architects undermined the goals of central authorities who envisaged the rebuilt city as an open-air museum of the Great Patriotic War. While Moscow mandated that planners imbed the Soviet victory in the cityscape through novel architectural forms and Stalin monuments, Sevastopol designers were, according to Karl Qualls, at pains to highlight continuity with the city's Russian imperial roots, "not just the most recent conflict."[23] All-union architects similarly approached

[18] See "Iz dnevnika A. S. Nikol'skogo," publ. in Afanas'ev, *Iz istorii*, 16.

[19] See the comments of Il'in, RGALI 674/2/185/33–33ob.

[20] On this issue more generally with regard to Leningrad, see Peri, *The War Within*, 245–252; Maddox, *Saving Stalin's Imperial City*; Kirschenbaum, *The Legacy of the Siege*, 113–150.

[21] Maddox, *Saving Stalin's Imperial City*, 68–97, 176–181, 197; Donovan, *Chronicles in Stone*, 31–56; Bittner, *The Many Lives of Khrushchev's Thaw*, 146–150. Lisa Kirschenbaum writes that the very act of rebuilding and beautifying the city paradoxically "allowed Leningraders to preserve the familiar places in which they had led their prewar lives and survived the blockade." Kirschenbaum, *The Legacy of the Siege*, 117.

[22] Kirschenbaum, *The Legacy of the Siege*, 113–114.

[23] Ultimately, Sevastopol residents maintained aspects of the city's pre-socialist identity in its reconstruction, in part, Qualls writes, because the leadership in Moscow recognized

the ruined center of Stalingrad as a blank slate upon which to project the war's official memory, only to be thwarted by bureaucratic infighting and changing priorities at the top.[24]

In these analyses of local memory, Moscow, as the seat of all-union power and the showcase socialist city, typically embodied an all-Soviet template against which localities struggled to carve out particularistic spaces.[25] Yet initial Moscow-based efforts to commemorate the war mirrored the wider split between the local and the all-union. As with "cultural agents" in Russian localities and non-Russian republics, who, in Yekelchyk's words, "defined their difference and protected their cultural domain," key figures at the very heart of the body politic emphasized Moscow's role as the capital of Russia (RSFSR) or as the bearer of a historical conception of Russian nationhood.[26] The compulsion to cast the war along an essentially Russian continuum thus had less to do with physical, cultural, or political aloofness from Moscow than congenital tensions within the victory myth itself.[27] In this light, the Kremlin's later attacks on particularistic war narratives were not merely a matter of bringing far flung localities to heel politically; these efforts aimed to mediate and subsume a range of interests under an overarching "patriotic culture of the whole."[28]

Tensions and contestations at the political heart of the Soviet Union are nowhere more evident than in the postwar campaign to establish a central victory monument in the capital. The city leadership under Georgii Popov, the head of both the Moscow Party and City Executive committees, was cognizant of a very real popular yearning for city-level commemorations of the war. The various summary reports on the political mood of

that "the stability and happiness of the population ... would reflect well on the central regime." Qualls, *From Ruins to Reconstruction*, 1–10, 46–84, qt. 47.

[24] Day, "The Rise and Fall of Stalinist Architecture," 172–192.

[25] For a good example, see Qualls, *From Ruins to Reconstruction*. To a greater extent than Leningrad and other RSFSR cities, the all-union government treated prerevolutionary monuments in Moscow with little regard until the late 1930s. Most famously, the nineteenth-century Cathedral of Christ the Savior, built to memorialize the expulsion of Napoleon's forces from Russia, was demolished in December 1931 to make space for the planned Palace of Soviets. See Colton, *Moscow*, 260–270, 351–352.

[26] The role of cultural agents in a non-Russian republican context has been traced by Yekelchyk, who demonstrates how they vacillated between "promoting the national patrimony and denouncing it as nationalistic deviation." In the case of Ukraine, they often "acted as classic indigenous elites who defined their difference ... without challenging (and, in fact, facilitating and justifying) imperial domination itself." Yekelchyk, "Stalinist Patriotism," 56. In the case of Moscow, G. M. Popov, the head of the Moscow Party Committee, frequently played this role.

[27] This differs somewhat from Weiner, who distinguishes between the "dominant myth" of the center and local visions, which depended in part on a locality's distance from Moscow. See Weiner, *Making Sense of War*, 62.

[28] This term is from Bodnar, *Remaking America*, 13–14.

Moscow residents that crossed Popov's desk indicate as much. According to one such report, among the most persistent questions addressed to city officials during public meetings concerned the construction of a war memorial in the capital.[29] This sentiment pervaded Moscow officialdom as well. Within a year of the war's conclusion, S. V. Kol'tsov, the head sculptor of the Moscow Artists' Union, warned that the prolonged absence of a Moscow war monument was contributing to a "pathological lack of patriotism," not only in the city, but in the country as a whole. It was time, Kol'tsov asserted, to erect a definitive "Victory Monument" at "the very heart of victory – Moscow," as a centerpiece for all-union commemoration. "We know that in Berlin ... Leningrad, Sofia ... in dozens of other cities and hundreds of villages such monuments or the like have been constructed ... Is Moscow really such an inconsequential point on the globe in the total victory over the forces of fascism that it does not deserve this distinction?" Kol'tsov urged Moscow architectural agencies to come together to carry out this "concrete task – the commemoration of our country's victory in Moscow."[30]

A key step in this direction came in June 1946, when Moscow hosted the largest ever Stalin-era discussion on the design and construction of war memorials.[31] Organized by the board of the Union of Architects, and including the most important artistic organizations, the conference aimed to resolve architectural issues that had arisen over the course of the war. The organizers devoted a whole session specifically to the question of the war's memorialization and publicly exhibited the most significant war memorial designs to emerge between 1942 and 1945.[32] An expert committee reviewed and debated the merits of the exhibited war memorial designs and attempted to chart an appropriate path forward. The conference devoted separate sessions to prerevolutionary structures and

[29] OKhDOPIM 3/61/46/135–136.

[30] RGALI 674/2/185/67–68. For his part, Kol'tsov favored building a grand triumphal arch on Red Square, possibly inspired by L. Pavlov's 1942 plan for an "Arch of Heroes." For another critique of the piecemeal, disorganized way memorials were planned, see comments by D. E. Arkin in Malinina, "Iz istorii," 258–259. For Arkin, the various draft projects produced by Moscow designers between 1942 and 1945 offered the best available template for future memorial construction. This is indicated in his earlier correspondence with Czechoslovak officials regarding monuments to the Red Army: RGALI 674/2/114/32.

[31] For the transcript of the conference sessions examined here, see RGALI 674/2/185/7–72ob.

[32] For images and descriptions of many of the most important designs discussed at the conference, see Afanas'ev, *Iz istorii sovetskoi arkhitektury*, 31–33, 66–72; Arkin, "Monumenty geroiam Velikoi Otechestvennoi voiny," 3–11; Novikov, "Proekty pamiatnikov geroiam," 22–27.

their restoration and to monuments dating from the revolution and Civil War eras respectively.[33]

The session on Great Patriotic War memorials witnessed a familiar split over the issue of historical heritage and its relationship to the Soviet victory. While discussants tended to highlight the war's unprecedented and ideological nature, and the uniquely Soviet provenance of victory, others looked to anchor the war in motifs from the Russian past. Among the participants representing the former view was M. A. Il'in. A specialist in late medieval Muscovite architecture, Il'in had been arrested during the 1930s for protesting the demolition of historical structures in Moscow. In March 1934, prosecutors sentenced Il'in to a three-year period of exile in Kazakhstan for purportedly "being, in his convictions, a [Russian] nationalist," and for having "actively opposed measures taken by the Soviet government to demolish unnecessary monuments of antiquity (churches, old country estates, chapels, monasteries)."[34] Il'in now stressed the need to separate the war's monumental commemoration from "problematic" historical models. He pointed in particular to plans involving the use of traditional monumental forms, which he worried very closely resembled tsarist-era prototypes. He noted that although Leningrad was outpacing Moscow in building memorials to the war, Leningraders' use of triumphal arches was ideologically fraught and demonstrated that "[t]o move away from traditional forms was proving quite difficult." While not advocating a specific memorial design, Il'in argued emphatically against monumental forms used in tsarist times. For Il'in, monuments to the Great Patriotic War "must become ours, Soviet, modern, and not cause unnecessary associations." The "great human dignity and heroic feats displayed by our people in the war against fascism," he concluded, "must convey a sense of our *modernity*."[35]

The most vocal contribution from the other end of the spectrum came from the architect A. E. Popov-Shaman, a leading figure within the Moscow department of the Union of Architects and a member of the planning administration for the construction of the Palace of Soviets. Responding to various calls for an entirely unprecedented "Soviet" style of war commemoration, Popov-Shaman reminded the audience that socialist realism "involves above all a unity between content – that which is socialist, new, [and] unique to our system – and a national form bearing all the wealth of centuries of national culture, [and] the

33 RGALI 674/2/185/2–5.

34 See Goncharov and Nekhotin, *Prosim osvobodit'*, 128–132, 183–185.

35 RGALI 674/2/185/24–35ob (emphasis added). Il'in made several references to an obelisk design proposal by I. Mel'chanov and S. Nanush'ian. This design is reproduced in Afanas'ev, *Iz istorii*, 160.

infinite riches of this national culture." Although acknowledging that war memorials must show "our Soviet culture," Popov-Shaman contended that an excessive focus on the present ignored heroic imagery that could be borrowed from the distant Russian past. As an example, he pointed to the motif of the Kremlin, not as some Sovietized symbol of the heart of the socialist motherland, but as a reminder of the primordial Russian roots that undergirded that motherland. Invoking medieval imagery, the architect submitted that

> [w]hen you look upon the Kremlin, a picture instantly comes to mind of a mighty militia of Russian heroes, giants in shining gilded helmets . . . on a green hill above the Moscow River, leaning on their damask-steel swords, guarding the peace of the motherland of free humanity in stoic splendor, warning that "those who come to us with the sword shall also perish by the sword."

Popov-Shaman then connected the Russian past and present via the figure of Stalin, noting:

> In our day, the image of the Kremlin has become a hundred times more precious for the *Russian person*. Within its walls, the brain of our country lives, works, [and] thinks about the fate of our people and the fate of all of progressive mankind . . . Here the wise leader [*vozhd'*], the father and friend of our great people, lives and works.

But memorial planners need not focus on the Kremlin exclusively. There were, in Popov-Shaman's view, countless other examples of heroic architecture in major urban centers like Leningrad and "the cradle of Russian statehood," Kiev, as well as the ancient towns of Vladimir and Suzdal. The "enormous wealth" of "memorial-monuments of Russian national architecture" to be found in these and other locales needed, Popov-Shaman argued, to be applied more directly into the style of socialist realism and, by extension, memorials to the war.[36]

If the discussion among these leading Moscow architects is any indication, the pan-Soviet and Russocentric patriotic threads of the war years extended unalloyed into postwar official thinking on commemoration. The contending ideological paradigms presented at the conference remained generally distinct from one another, and only Popov-Shaman advanced something approximating a Russian-Soviet amalgam in his reference to Stalin. This is not surprising given the vagaries and inconsistencies of postwar texts and pronouncements on the war examined in the previous chapter. But even guiding principles on urban

[36] RGALI 674/2/185/50–51ob (emphasis added).

reconstruction and memorialization did little to bridge this divide.[37] As summarized shortly after the war by a N. Ia. Kolli, a leading architectural theorist who participated in the conference, the relationship between new construction, including war monuments, and cultural heritage – that is, between the pre-Soviet past and the Soviet present – was highly ambivalent:

> The most important task in the reconstruction of our cities is a careful and loving attitude to the historically developed appearance of the city, the use of the most positive and progressive elements of the old layout and architecture in the restoration project, and their organic incorporation into the new face of cities. . . . At the same time, building a modern Soviet city requires us to consider not only the growth of the city over the past two centuries, but, especially, the huge changes that have taken place during the years of Soviet power ... as well as those requirements demanded of a city center by our Soviet way of life.[38]

The tension between the "form" of cultural heritage and the "content" of socialist development was, of course, nothing new. However, that tension was heightened in the case of early war memorialization, as planners drew upon what amounted to contrasting patriotic templates with little clear instruction on how or whether to reconcile them.[39] As they had late in the war, pan-Soviet/internationalist and Russocentric modes of war memory coexisted in uneasy tension rather than fuse into a coherent synergy.

The extent to which the conference impacted the subsequent trajectory of the nascent victory monument project is unclear. Deeper organizational issues, and not divided conceptions over the war's meaning, were primarily to blame for the project's postponement at the local level. Shortly after the architectural conference, during a party meeting on commemorations, the Moscow party boss, Georgii Popov, provided a rather pessimistic assessment of the very ability of local organs to effectively manage such a project. Popov noted that because monument construction in the city had stalled – partly due to Moscow's reliance upon inefficient bronze casting work outside the city – the list of projects awaiting realization had swollen to an unmanageable size. It was unlikely, therefore, that simply delegating projects to artistic bodies would produce

[37] The idea for embedding the war's memory into urban landscapes originated during the second half of the war. See RGASPI 17/125/299/80–120. For a case study exploring the limits of these efforts in Sevastopol, see Qualls, *From Ruins to Reconstruction*.

[38] Kolli and Kastel', "Arkhitekturnye voprosy," 12–13.

[39] Early postwar planning for the "blank slate" that was destroyed Stalingrad seems to confirm an official preference for symbols of an exclusively postrevolutionary character, including monuments to the recent victory and state administrative buildings. Among architects, there was a "romance of the blank slate," that was only complicated by the need to preserve and incorporate monuments of the distant Russian past. Day, "The Rise and Fall of Stalinist Architecture," 173–177.

results: "I know from experience that issuing construction orders ... results in no monuments." Popov lambasted government artistic agencies, suggesting that they were only qualified to "convene designers, organize a [design] competition, pay money, commission a project, and then no one ever builds this project." Popov contended that under current conditions the only way to reliably erect a monument was to appeal directly to the Central Committee with a detailed proposal in hand.[40]

In the meantime, Popov was satisfied to postpone the issue of a major monument until Moscow's artistic agencies had recovered sufficiently and proposed handing off responsibility entirely to the Central Committee.[41] Other representatives present at the meeting worried that such a delay risked damaging the local Party Committee's image. In the words of one speaker, "We simply need to do something ... Many people from the families of those killed come to us and point out that we have no kind of [historical] memory ... [A]fter ten years, [Moscow] will have become wealthier, we will have reliable workshops, but if we act now we will give the impression that something is being done." Popov demurred: "Let us not be swayed by the point of view that we can [only] raise patriotism, love for the Motherland through monuments to the dead." Here, Popov confronted one of the other major tensions of the war's memory, that between the triumph of victory and the tragedy of mass death. In line with the late-Stalinist culture of victory, Popov naturally advocated the triumphant over the tragic.[42] "After all," he continued, "we have the Bolshevik Party, which can lead the country and raise patriotism. We have a leader, C[omrade] Stalin, which they don't have in other countries. One shouldn't be so mechanistic." Popov directed the committee to focus on the development of modest forms of memorialization in factories, metro stations, housing blocks, and parks, something that was, in the short term, "a clearer, more concrete task."[43]

As Moscow officials pivoted to the management of smaller-scale commemorations, the victory monument project passed to all-union authorities. In June 1947, a Politburo commission chaired by Zhdanov charged G. A. Simonov, the head of the Council of Ministers' Committee for Architectural Affairs, to assess the feasibility of building the victory monument in Red Square, long its preferred venue. Simonov formed an

[40] Gorinov, *Moskva poslevoennaia*, 163. For similar complaints connected to Stalingrad's reconstruction, see Day, "The Rise and Fall of Stalinist Architecture," 184–185.

[41] This far-ranging discussion took place under the aegis of a holiday for tank operators, but the subject of war memorials featured prominently.

[42] On the tension between the war and victory in the war, see Dobrenko, *Late Stalinism*, 36–37.

[43] Gorinov, *Moskva poslevoennaia*, 163–165. On the Soviet culture of victory, see Edele, "The Soviet Culture of Victory," 780–798.

expert panel of architects and sculptors to weigh in on the project.[44] The resulting discussions conducted by the expert panel reveal an astonishing disregard for Red Square's historical architecture in relation to the projected monument. A. V. Shchusev, for instance, described the nineteenth-century GUM building along the northeastern edge of Red Square as an "unpleasant stain" that needed to be destroyed to create space for the victory monument. B. M. Iofan proposed demolishing the Russian revivalist building that housed the Historical Museum at the square's northwestern entrance. D. N. Chechulin concurred with the general thrust of these proposals, noting that if the museum building, which he called "definitely rubbish," were destroyed and GUM partially dismantled, then "we would have opened the beautiful square to the city." The panel members even entertained the idea of dismantling sections of the Kremlin abutting Red Square to clear the way for a "Pergamon Altar" victory memorial behind Lenin's Mausoleum. Chechulin expressed modest reservations about this, noting that "in this case, nothing will remain of the Kremlin." However, the demolition of a stretch of the Kremlin does not appear to have been a disqualifying proposition. Chechulin remained open to the idea, pointing out that a similar design proposal already existed that involved comparable demolition, adding that it was "well-realized" in conception.[45]

If organizational dysfunction – not to mention anticipated CC resistance – was the primary factor preventing local Moscow bodies from carrying out the project, all-union authorities would go on to cite the prohibitive cost. But as the formal conclusions that Simonov passed to the Politburo commission demonstrate, cost was subordinate to ideological considerations. It was not the cost of building the monument per se, but rather the cost associated with rendering the monument sufficiently freed of prerevolutionary associations. The expert panel concluded that, without significant demolition or the removal of buildings, Red Square would be an unrealistic site for the memorial. In the words of the panel's final report, the location presented

> a critical ideological and artistic challenge since Red Square is filled with architectural structures of various eras; in particular, the architecturally unsuccessful

[44] Regarding Red Square as the building site, see, for instance, RGASPI 17/125/572/34–55. The expert panel was a who's who of Soviet designers, including the architects G. A. Simonov, A. V. Shchusev, B. M. Iofan, A. G. Mordvinov, D. N. Chechulin, and the sculptors Mukhina and Merkurov.

[45] Iastrebov, "Pokushenie," 12. This was almost certainly a reference to G. R. Mushegian's 1944 design for a multiethnic-themed step pyramid monument, which called for the removal of those buildings "that have lost their importance for Moscow." See RGASPI 17/125/369/1–5.

building of the Historical Museum is at the entrance to the square, and the square's eastern side is occupied by the conspicuous historical and architectural monument of Saint Basil's Cathedral, which is in the immediate vicinity of the monument to Minin and Pozharskii.[46]

The existence of these prerevolutionary relics, particularly Saint Basil's, which had survived earlier calls for its demolition and remained protected by the diminished state heritage register, rendered the square's eastern flank unsuitable for a victory memorial complex precisely because these structures were reminiscent "of the past epoch of Russia."[47] The blurring of the present and the past – even the military-patriotic past embodied by the Minin and Pozharskii monument – was deemed to significantly "decrease the ideological ... possibilities of the [war] memorial." The most feasible location, by contrast, was on the site of the Historical Museum, the destruction of which the report sanctioned. But "given the great ideological and artistic importance of the victory monument," Simonov's conclusions underscored the immense work and associated costs involved to simply lay the project's groundwork.[48]

Simonov's report offers the best explanation for the memorial's indefinite postponement: it was simply inappropriate, in this instance, to so blatantly couple imagery of the Russian past with an all-union symbol of the Soviet state's greatest military feat. Given that these decisions were taken only a few months before Moscow's 800-year jubilee, during which organizers selectively promoted the city's cultural heritage and architectural landmarks, it is unlikely that such a demolition project would have received a green light. But without demolition, there could be no victory monument. The project's termination thus followed from the ambivalent nature of Stalinist war memory, which tolerated the continued presence of the pan-Soviet paradigm, rather than official concern for the protection of prerevolutionary symbols and a headlong drive to link those symbols to the memory of victory in 1945.

Notably, during the late 1960s, planners successfully established an all-union war memorial – the Tomb of the Unknown Soldier – in Alexander Gardens along the western wall of the Kremlin. However, not only did the location of Alexander Gardens avoid many of the problematic historical associations that plagued the earlier project, but the

[46] "Monument Pobedy na meste Istoricheskogo muzeia," 154–156.

[47] Purportedly, Stalin had removed a scale model of Saint Basil's Cathedral from a mockup of Red Square to "see how Red Square would look without it," prompting V. N. Semenov, the head of the Architectural Planning Department, to grab Stalin's arm. Colton, *Moscow*, 277.

[48] "Monument Pobedy na meste Istoricheskogo muzeia," 154–156. For a slightly different interpretation of this affair, see Colton, 352–353.

ideological contexts differed vastly. Where the late-Stalinist leadership maintained the war myth's discursive tension in part by refusing to embrace an exclusively Russocentric understanding of the war, by the mid-1960s, as subsequent chapters will show, the war myth had taken on an overwhelmingly pan-Soviet hue. There was little risk, in other words, that Russian historical imagery would overwhelm the later memorial's pan-Soviet internationalism.

Stalinist planners did not abandon the idea for a victory monument in the center of the city, however. In May 1948, the Council of Ministers adopted a resolution on "streamlining the process for building monuments in Moscow," which catalogued high-priority building projects. It listed Moscow's victory monument as number seven and provisionally slated it for construction in 1950 despite no approved design.[49] By then, however, Stalin had lost interest in carrying out bombastic public remembrances of the war, favoring instead more practical building projects, which included urban housing.[50] As with the long-languishing Palace of Soviets, even subtle changes in building priorities at the top could delay a project for years, even decades.[51] Boris Iofan, a central figure in both the Palace of Soviets and the victory monument projects, suggested to Stalin on multiple occasions that the Palace also serve as an all-union monument to victory in the war.[52] Although this would have avoided costly renovations to Red Square, the idea was never taken seriously. And in any case, consolidating the two projects would have resulted in the same abortive outcome.

Whatever the specific reasons for the project's postponement, late-Stalinist discussions concerning the victory monument are illuminating. Proposals advanced by some Moscow-based architects to couch the victory monument in Russian historical imagery contrasted markedly with the priorities of all-union planners, who appeared primarily concerned with maintaining the monument's Soviet integrity. Many decades later, encouraged by Gorbachev's call to fill in the "blank spots" of Soviet history, a senior archival official, A. Iastrebov, surveyed the discussions concerning a victory memorial complex in Red Square:

[49] RGASPI 17/125/637/79–83.

[50] Kirschenbaum, *The Legacy of the Siege*, 115–116; Schleifman, "Moscow's Victory Park," 10; Tumarkin, *The Living & the Dead*, 98, 100–104. On the shift in priorities away from purely symbolic monuments toward housing and other, more practical building priorities, see Day, "The Rise and Fall of Stalinist Architecture," 185–186; Colton, *Moscow*, 351–356.

[51] For the argument that Stalin lost interest in the Palace of Soviets, see Hoisington, "Ever Higher," 65–67. For more on the Palace's fate and Stalin's disengagement, see Colton, *Moscow*, 352–353, 364–367.

[52] See, for example, RGASPI 558/11/737/67.

> It's hard to believe what's been read: recognized masters of Soviet architecture vying with each other to repudiate the historical significance of the buildings in Red Square, ready to carry out all sorts of barbarism. Fortunately, the Victory Monument in Red Square never saw the light of day . . . Let the lessons of the past teach us to be wiser today.[53]

From Iastrebov's perspective, writing in the late 1980s, the postwar regime was guilty of unfathomable hostility to Russia's cultural heritage. Of course, this was not entirely true. At the same time that the country's top planners and political leaders contemplated razing parts of Red Square for the sake of a monument to victory, the leadership approved restoration projects and measures highlighting Moscow's history in advance of the city's 800-year anniversary. Significantly, it was at this time that Stalin ordered the construction of a monument to Iurii Dolgorukii, by tradition Moscow's founder, near the city center.[54] It was also at this time that the Council of Ministers approved a law "[o]n the improvement of the protection of cultural monuments," which declared all "[a]rchitectural monuments located on the territory of the USSR that have scientific, artistic, or historical value" to be "inviolable national property" and "under state protection."[55] The limitations on late-Stalinist Russocentrism involved not the abandonment of prerevolutionary imagery and architecture, but, where expedient, the capacity to dissociate markers to victory in the war from parallel public symbols of the Russian past.

The victory myth's discursive tension extended to localities in fits and starts, but pervaded much of the country by the late 1940s. Even in Leningrad, the end of the decade witnessed the rejection of particularistic heroic narratives in favor of a vision of an undifferentiated citizenry united by its superior social system and the leadership of the Party and Stalin.[56] This central conception coexisted with, but stood above, narratives of titular republican heroism, which authorities also reinforced and homogenized in the process of the war's memorialization.[57] Although many citizens no doubt continued to conceive of the recent war as the latest in a centuries-long string of Russian victories, authorities never explicitly endorsed such a direct link between past and present at the all-union level and increasingly resisted it in localities. With surprisingly few exceptions,

[53] Iastrebov, "Pokushenie," 12.
[54] Colton, *Moscow*, 324, 352. This monument replaced, of all things, an obelisk to the 1918 Soviet constitution and subsequent Liberty statue.
[55] Anderson, "The USSR's 1948 Instructions," 64.
[56] This is well observed in Maddox, *Saving Stalin's Imperial City*, 184–186.
[57] On Ukraine, see, for example, Amar, *The Paradox of Ukrainian Lviv*, 282–317; Weiner, "The Making of a Dominant Myth," 638–660. On Central Asia, see Shin, "Red Army Propaganda," 39–63; Carmack, "History and Hero-Making," 95–112.

the party leadership was careful not to anchor the war's commemoration overtly in either continuity with the Russian past or deference to the primordial Russian nation in the present.

Commemoration as Mobilization

Why would the Stalinist leadership favor an ambiguous, rather than decisively Russocentric, interpretation of victory, one that sometimes cordoned off Russia's prerevolutionary heroic mythology from the memory of 1941–5? Leaving aside the obvious ideological implications – Soviet history is replete with ideological retreats and compromises – two factors peculiar to the late 1940s stand out: Stalin's anxiety over the growth of Russian nationalism and the escalating Cold War. As David Brandenberger has shown, by 1949 Stalin perceived localism in terms of ethnonational zeal. The Leningrad leadership's celebration of the war's local dimensions appears to have fueled concerns in the center over the possible formation of a separate Russian Communist Party organization. This fear, in turn, was likely an important factor in the decision to launch the notorious purge of that city's leadership in the aftermath of Zhdanov's death known as the Leningrad Affair.[58] Indeed, that event involved a direct assault on Leningraders' earlier efforts to link 1945 with the city's local experiences and history. It saw authorities dismantle the various triumphal arches, close the widely visited Museum of the Defense of Leningrad, scrap plans to erect a major city war memorial, and limit discussions and publications that highlighted the unique role of Leningrad in the defeat of Germany.[59]

Popov's own downfall in Moscow shortly after the Leningrad purge was tied to accusations that he attempted to use his control of the city's party committee to "usurp the role of the ministries, the government, and the Central Committee." However, unlike his Leningrad compatriots, Stalin never saw Popov's leadership in Moscow as a potential base for the formation of a Russian Communist Party.[60] It would be a stretch to claim that Popov's handling of the war's commemoration had anything to do with this; the differences between the Leningrad and Moscow cases are numerous. Nevertheless, Popov's use of the war in his own public rhetoric

[58] Brandenberger, "Stalin, the Leningrad Affair," 241–255. See also Liuks, "Evreiskii vopros v politike Stalina," 52; Dzeniskevich, *Blokada i politika*, 12; Hahn, *Postwar Soviet Politics*, 9–20, 122–123. For a contrasting interpretation, see Bidlack, "Ideological or Political Origins," 90–95.

[59] Peri, *The War Within*, 245–252; Maddox, *Saving Stalin's Imperial City*, 170–193; Kirschenbaum, *The Legacy of the Siege*, 142–147.

[60] Also, unlike his Leningrad comrades, Popov survived his ouster. On this affair, see Gorlizki and Khlevniuk, *Cold Peace*, 89–92, qt. 90–91.

demonstrated a keen sense of the fluid permissible boundaries of Stalinist Russocentrism. An unabashed Russophile who did not hesitate to quote Stalin's victory toast in formal addresses, Popov regularly moderated his Russocentrism when it came to the substantial issues of industrial productivity and geopolitics, matters that evidently did not warrant Russocentric sloganeering. In one 1947 speech, for example, Popov shifted from praising the Russian people as the "most outstanding" Soviet nation to a discussion on the bellicosity of Great Britain, the United States, and other "reactionary elements." In stark contrast to the speech's nationalistic preamble, Popov reminded his audience that the Soviet Union as a whole "was the decisive force in the struggle against the German and Japanese aggressors" and that the "source of the power of our state is the leading role of the Bolshevik Party." It was the Party rather than the Russian people that "led the peoples of Russia in October 1917 to overthrow the power of the imperialists." It was the Party, and not any leading national community, that "played the decisive role in achieving victory in the Great Patriotic War."[61]

Even at the height of Stalinist Russocentrism, the discursive tension of the war's memory enabled alternating, context-specific conceptions of patriotic identity. In the case of Popov's speech, Russocentric allusions to the war offered a means of eliciting a sense of enthusiasm among the predominantly ethnic Russian attendees. But when it came to fears about the USSR's Cold War enemies and related concerns about economic recovery, Popov steered his speech in a decidedly pan-Soviet direction, coloring his ruminations on the war in ideological and internationalist terms. Such vacillations were hardly a coincidence. It was not only apprehension over Russian national assertiveness at home that necessitated Soviet patriotism's malleability, but also the leadership's need to present an undifferentiated "Soviet" front in the unfolding ideological confrontation with the West.

Scholars have long identified the emergence of the Cold War as a catalyst for the pervasive Russocentrism of the era.[62] As during the Soviet–German war, the argument runs, Cold War hostilities necessitated a broad-based patriotic agenda, one that paired popular imagery of the Russian past with an emphasis on Russian primacy in the present so as to boost the state's ability to mobilize society. Indeed, Russian achievements in the arts and sciences featured heavily in the cultural contest of the early Cold War. Stalin, moreover, sometimes saw it as advantageous

[61] Gorinov, *Moskva poslevoennaia*, 206–212.
[62] For example, Gruner, "Russia's Battle against the Foreign," 114; Anderson, *States and Nationalism*, 19.

to highlight the USSR's ethnonational diversity. Constitutional changes late in the war, for example, presented the country as a collection of ostensibly independent national states managing their own foreign affairs, "thus permitting the Soviet Union to masquerade as a confederation under international law and a federation under internal law." Hence, at Stalin's urging, the USSR later received three seats in the UN General Assembly: the USSR as a whole and both the Byelorussian and Ukrainian SSRs.[63]

However, far from imbuing the war's public memory with an exclusively Russocentric character, the Cold War reinforced the victory myth's discursive tension. In its pan-Soviet orientation, the war narrative functioned to rein in and moderate Russocentric excess that was being misconstrued by hostile ideological rivals. Early Soviet victory narratives developed first and foremost as rebuttals to the war myths promoted by the USSR's wartime allies. Of particular concern was the way Western narratives often credited Soviet successes to Hitler's mistakes or the fabled Russian winter, mud, and snow, as well as the use of Soviet fighters as cannon fodder motivated by nothing more than fear of their own government. These interpretations were based largely on the testimony, diaries, and memoirs of high-ranking German military officers, such as Franz Halder, the former head of the German Army General Staff, who became a consultant for the US Army Historical Division after the war. As a result, many early Western interpretations of the war on the Eastern Front reflected a fundamentally German version of events. The Historical Division even commissioned a research team that was known informally as the "Halder Group."[64]

Equally pernicious from Stalin's perspective were foreign accounts that praised Soviet wartime achievements as valiant demonstrations of the Russian people's patriotic spirit in spite of the foibles and incompetence of the Communist Party leadership. In a postwar statement that was endlessly rebroadcast in Soviet media, the journalist Ralph Parker described how the British and Americans "propagated the comforting 'theory' that the Russian people were defending not the Soviet regime but their fatherland, independent of its social structure, that the Red Army's successes were due to ... the innate virtues of the Russian man." The statement went on to claim that, "as the war progressed, it became clear even to those whose eyes were clouded by prejudice that neither the Communist Party nor the Soviet people as whole were in

[63] Molotov, *O preobrazovanii Narkomata Oborony i Narkomindela*, 5–26; Aspaturian, "The Union Republics and Soviet Diplomacy," 383–411, qt. 386.
[64] Smelser and Davies II, *The Myth of the Eastern Front*, 64–89.

any way willing to abandon their principles, but on the contrary considered their victories to be an endorsement of the correctness of these principles."[65] The need to assert the "Soviet" bases of victory in an atmosphere of ideological Cold War compelled the USSR's mythmakers to frame victory over Nazi Germany as a triumph of the Soviet system and supranational community. Rather than reinforce the tropes of Russian wartime primacy and historical pedigree, which were hardly in question among Western commentators, this tendency usually involved their suppression at the level of central commemorations.

As early as May 1945, the leadership indicated that official war memory would play a central role in combatting ideological challenges from abroad and in legitimizing the Soviet system on the international stage. Mere days after Germany's capitulation, Georgii Aleksandrov, the Agitprop head, together with the-then Deputy Foreign Minister Andrei Vyshinksii, fielded questions on revised thematic priorities during a meeting of the All-Union Lecture Bureau. "It is the unanimous opinion," one speaker announced on behalf of those present, "that the proportion of military topics be drastically reduced." Vyshinskii disagreed, countering that the war should not receive an insignificant place but rather should acquire "a different character" and "we should ... change the direction a bit ... especially since the end of the war in Europe does not end our military trials and peril." Aleksandrov elaborated, arguing that postwar lectures on military themes, and in particular those covering the recent war, needed to more fully emphasize geopolitical dimensions and ideological implications. Coverage of the war, he went on, must be able to respond to assertions in the Western media about the war's significance. Vyshinskii concurred, adding, "In the end, [the USSR and USA] have two opposing systems that do not interfere with one another but only under certain conditions. We should not demobilize our society and it would be wrong to lessen the taste for and interest in military history and affairs."[66]

Lecture Bureau officials developed this line over the course of the next several months. As one high-ranking member of the organization reiterated in a subsequent meeting, not only should lecturers maintain their prior output on military subjects, but they must approach the topic of the war from the standpoint of geopolitical "counter-propaganda":

> [N]ow there is a struggle, perhaps not clearly expressed, but all the same it is a struggle over the interpretation of victory, over which countries participated in the war, and to what extent ... In this regard, we must demonstrate the role of the

[65] Parker, *Conspiracy against Peace*, 91–94. [66] GARF R-9548/1/11/2–20.

Red Army, the role of our Soviet Union ... [as] the decisive factor in achieving this victory.

Other representatives present at the session echoed these concerns, arguing that the need to rebut "the polemical views of foreign scholars" should take precedence over other facets of the war theme.[67] While British and American narratives of the war inflated their own contributions, and occasionally highlighted traditional Russian patriotism or the harshness of the Russian winter, it was the duty of the Lecture Bureau to remind the Soviet people and the world of the singular role of the USSR, which alone possessed the political leadership, socioeconomic system, and ideology that made victory possible.[68]

Fashioned as a response to competing national war myths, the revised framework stressed supranational unity and cohesion over internal ethnic diversity and hierarchy, a shift that necessarily minimized the centrality of the Russian people and their heroic progenitors. In part, this change reflected a gnawing sense within Agitprop that Russocentric variations of the war myth held a limited appeal internationally.[69] But it also stemmed from the fact that British and American commentators rarely disputed the issue of Russian primacy, indeed they underscored it, portraying "Russian" and "Soviet" patriotisms as indistinguishable. Soviet efforts to counter Western "falsifications" about the war on the Eastern Front thus entailed a departure from anything resembling prerevolutionary patriotic templates. By August 1945, even a suggestion within the Lecture Bureau to continue according a central place to "our great commanders, Peter I, Suvorov, Kutuzov, Bagration, Ushakov, Nakhimov, and others" received pushback. Responding to this proposal, Major General N. A. Talenskii, the editor-in-chief of the journal *Military Thought*, argued for lecturers to move away from coverage of individual heroism, past and present, toward the "military-scientific essence" of Germany's defeat. Talenskii offered an implicit call to position the war narrative onto a squarely Soviet footing by deemphasizing heroic models based on prerevolutionary precedents.[70] By early 1946, the Lecture Bureau's coverage of the war reflected this pan-Soviet/internationalist line as its members structured their war narratives as refutations of foreign interpretations.[71]

67 GARF R-9548/1/12/39, 50–51.
68 For an Agitprop analysis of an American scholar's reference to "factors of a Russian patriotic character," see RGASPI 17/125/594/12–13, 35.
69 Liuks, "Evreiskii vopros v politike Stalina," 45
70 GARF R-9548/1/11/33–88, qt. 42–49.
71 See, for example, GARF R-9548/1/30/161–175ob, esp. 168ob–169ob.

That such adjustments were part of a more sweeping policy change is evident from Stalin's own public statements beginning in mid-February 1946.[72] His widely publicized speech of February 9, 1946, on the "summation" of the war, for instance, came in response to foreign claims that Soviet hegemony masked traditional Russian geopolitical objectives abroad and imperial dominance at home. He directed his comments not only at Soviet citizens but at "prominent foreign journalists" who had suggested "that the Soviet multinational state is an 'artificial and short-lived structure'" that would collapse under the weight of a major war. Stalin specifically addressed the implication that the Soviet Union was in effect a type of old-world empire, a major affront to the USSR's image at a time of renewed global decolonization. On the contrary, he declared,

> [W]e can say that the war refuted these statements of the foreign press and proved them to have been devoid of all foundation. The war proved that the Soviet multinational state system successfully passed the test, grew stronger than ever during the war, and turned out to be quite a viable state system. These gentlemen failed to realize that the analogy of Austria-Hungary was unsound, because our multinational state grew up not on the bourgeois basis, which produces sentiments of national distrust and national enmity, but on the Soviet basis, which ... cultivates feelings of friendship and fraternal cooperation among the peoples of our state.

Stalin concluded by pointing to "the single collective body of Soviet people," a transcendent identity rooted in the shared experience of defending the homeland of socialism. All Soviet people, Communists and non-Communists, "fought side by side and shed their blood on the various fronts for the sake of the freedom and greatness of our Motherland, and side by side they hammered out and forged our country's victory over her enemies." Whatever social, political, or ethnic distinctions characterized society before the war, in the wake of Germany's defeat, Stalin intimated, "we are now living in different times."[73]

Though not an outright repudiation of his victory toast, the address nevertheless represented a departure from his 1945 elevation of one nation above all others. Stalin's notion of a "single collective body of Soviet people," constituents of which had "fought side by side," was an extension of the pan-Soviet internationalism that grew out of postwar geopolitical concerns. It is no coincidence that while war commemoration

[72] This statement broke not only with Stalin's victory toast but with a speech he had given earlier in 1946 in which he praised the Russian "elder brother" during the war. See his address of Feb. 2, 1946, quoted in Brandenberger, "Sovetskii patriotizm," 23.

[73] Stalin, *Rech'*, 10–11, 23–24.

inside the USSR was relatively understated in the immediate postwar period, Soviet architects were carrying out expansive memorial projects abroad. Indeed, most of the first large-scale monumental structures commemorating the Soviet victory appeared not within the borders of the USSR but in Central and Eastern Europe, where the outward projection of an indivisible Soviet people served clear geopolitical ends.[74] In important respects, the roots of the Soviet war cult of the 1960s to the 1980s can be found in late-Stalinist commemorative practices, which often asserted an image of the victorious Soviet people as an undifferentiated entity on a larger European and world stage.[75]

Soviet monitors of foreign media continued to feed this sensitivity to "false" portrayals of the Soviet war effort throughout the late 1940s. Reviewing an article in January 1948 on wartime propaganda by the American scholar Paul Myron Anthony Linebarger, one monitor within the Agitprop department lambasted the publication's generally "anti-Soviet tone." However, the author of the report noted approvingly that Linebarger was "forced to admit the bold execution of Soviet propaganda," which channeled "Revolutionary Communist themes" in a patriotic direction.[76] Of particular concern for such monitors were diasporic publications that threatened to influence ethnonational counterparts residing within the Soviet Union, especially communities newly Sovietized or repatriated. The recently established Communist Information Bureau (Cominform) perceived some of the greatest threats to be emanating from the Armenian Revolutionary Federation (Dashnaktsutyun), then based in Lebanon, and similar organizations abroad associated with the Baltic republics. According to Cominform head B. N. Ponomarev, these groups were leading the anti-repatriation campaigns and spreading slander about conditions of immigrants who chose to return to their homeland in the Soviet Union after the war.[77]

Cominform and the Agitprop department responded by organizing a major campaign in 1948 to combat Western "falsifications" of the history of the war. As part of this effort, Cominform published an apologia

[74] In 1945 alone, large-scale Soviet war memorials were constructed in Vienna, Budapest, Warsaw, Kaliningrad, and Bucharest. Similar memorial complexes only later appeared in Volgograd (1967), Brest (1971), Kursk (1973), Leningrad (1975), Sevastopol (1977), and Kiev (1981). On Central and Eastern European Soviet war memorials and their primarily geopolitical function, see Fowkes, "Soviet War Memorials," 11–32; Fowkes, "The Role of Monumental Sculpture," 65–84. For an important examination of the ways the memory of the Soviet victory and liberation fostered an "empire of friends" between Soviet and Czechoslovak citizens in the postwar era, see Applebaum, *Empire of Friends*, 81–108.

[75] Weiner, "Nature, Nurture, and Memory," qt. 1126. The Treptower complex in Berlin is somewhat unique in that it employed many historical-Russocentric elements. This is discussed in the next chapter.

[76] RGASPI 17/125/594/12–42. [77] RGASPI 17/125/594/68, 70–78.

entitled *Falsifiers of History*, which it translated into numerous languages and disseminated abroad.[78] Ostensibly a response to a US State Department publication of documents from the German Foreign Office, which indicated cozy prewar relations between the Stalin and Hitler regimes, *Falsifiers* centered on justifying the Molotov-Ribbentrop pact, exposing German aggression and perfidy in 1941, and celebrating aspects of Soviet relations with the Western Allies.[79] Despite a print run of fifty thousand volumes in the USA alone, Ponomarev noted disappointedly to Zhdanov in April 1948 that "almost 99% of the [US] population is completely unaware of the publication."[80]

Following the relative failure of *Falsifiers of History*, the Agitprop leadership looked for ways to improve countermeasures abroad. On March 3, 1948, the department hosted a gathering of roughly three hundred officials, academics, and cultural figures. According to the meeting report, Ilya Ehrenburg was particularly outspoken during the session, recommending a move away from rote Soviet phraseology and toward the employment of contemporary literary styles, "which are more familiar and intelligible to the average American, Englishman, and Frenchman." He went on to state that it was necessary "to restore the wartime practice of translating into foreign languages the most interesting and relevant [Soviet] articles in major [international] newspapers."[81] The precise degree to which these suggestions influenced subsequent developments is unclear. The sum of the discussions and the reports generated as part of this effort called for a renewed propaganda counteroffensive to generally promote "comprehensive information for foreign societies on the social, economic, and cultural achievements of the peoples of the USSR."[82] It soon became apparent to the Cominform and Agitprop leadership that the theme of the war, and Victory Day in particular, offered the most viable centerpiece to this global media blitz.

The following month, Ponomarev and Mikhail Suslov, the new head of the Central Committee's Agitprop department, ordered Soviet news agencies to prepare to issue a whole series of articles and open letters on the war via foreign media outlets. These publications were to "promote the advantages of the Soviet social system" and coincide with V-E Day (May 8) celebrations abroad.[83] Ponomarev prepared a model text to be published in the British press from "the people of Stalingrad" appealing to the "working people of Coventry," a city destroyed during the Blitz:

[78] *Fal'sifikatory istorii.*
[79] The State Department publication was Sontag and Beddie, *Nazi-Soviet Relations*.
[80] RGASPI 17/125/594/62–63, 87–93. [81] RGASPI 17/125/594/47–51.
[82] RGASPI 17/125/594/47–61, 103–110, qt. 103. [83] RGASPI 17/125/594/65–67.

The time is near when a majestic ensemble of new buildings will be erected along the streets of Stalingrad, which will be a worthy monument to those heroes – Soviet soldiers who . . . defended the city . . . Now, as during the war, Stalingraders live united with the aspirations of ordinary people in all countries . . . That is why they, like all Soviet citizens, are so outraged by the unbridled way military history is now stirred up by the dark forces of reaction, by the merchants and agents of death in America and Europe . . . We, Stalingraders, are convinced that the ordinary people of your country will not allow these forces to destroy the friendship between our peoples, a friendship sealed in blood.[84]

Ponomarev and Suslov ordered the production of similarly internationalist collective statements in response to the "fascist slander" of organizations representing diasporic communities.[85] In May 1948, the Agitprop department drafted an open letter to the Armenian diaspora on behalf of repatriates already residing in the Armenian SSR. The letter noted the respect the Soviet state had for Armenia's traditions and historical heritage, and highlighted the creation of the Armenian Committee for the Protection of Historical Monuments. However, the main thrust of the letter drew attention to the benefits of life as part of a common Soviet political community. Rather than the age-old benevolence and guidance of the Russian people, the letter's authors cited "the life-giving nectar of Soviet reality" in the present. Only the Soviet system guaranteed industrial and technological advances to citizens regardless of national distinction. More importantly, Soviet citizenship offered the chance to become a "Soviet person imbued with a sense of friendship, humanity, mutual aid, national brotherhood, love, respect, self-sacrifice, and, highest among these, patriotism." These "lofty" traits were not innate to any one dominant ethnonational community but were "conceived in revolution and strengthened in the process of socialist construction and the Great Patriotic War."[86]

The pan-Soviet orientation of the victory narrative advanced through the campaign to combat Western "falsifications" helps contextualize domestic commemorative processes like the annual Victory Day anniversary.[87] As with the promotion of the victory myth abroad, the commemorative discourse of May Ninth routinely projected a flattened

[84] RGASPI 17/125/594/80–84.
[85] The reference to "fascist slander" is from Ponomarev: RGASPI 17/125/594/68.
[86] RGASPI 17/125/594/154–155, 158–177, qts. 159, 172–173. For a similar response to the Latvian diaspora, see ll. 70–78.
[87] Like Stalinist public festivals more generally, the holiday was designed from the ground up "to provide a template for ideal Soviet identities and behaviors." Petrone, *Life Has Become More Joyous, Comrades*, 203. Of course, as diaries of the era attest, the reception of Victory Day anniversaries of the mid to late 1940s varied widely. See, for example, Mikhaleva, *Gde vy, moi rodnye*, 454–455; Mechtova, "Dnevnik"; Rivkina, "Dnevnik." On public festivals and celebrations of the Stalinist 1930s, see Rolf, *Soviet Mass Festivals*,

image of the Soviet people as an undifferentiated whole and often involved the – at first glance puzzling – curtailment of Russian national themes and images. Notably, the lead Victory Day articles in *Pravda* from 1946 through 1950 conspicuously avoided any allusion to the Russian people, their heroic forebears, or Stalin's toast to their health. This was broadly in line with the aforementioned demands of combatting foreign falsifications. Just as important, however, was the fact that the pan-Soviet /internationalist conception of victory offered a presumably more effective means of mobilizing the multiethnic labor force for the anticipated war to come. Indeed, economic recovery and labor mobilization became core messages of domestic Victory Day anniversaries throughout the late 1940s.[88]

At precisely the time that Soviet authorities were launching a major V-E Day propaganda offensive abroad, the state compelled Soviet citizens to return to work on Victory Day. The exasperation of many workers aside, the May Ninth holiday's new "working" status was hardly an abrupt symbolic shift.[89] In 1948 – as in 1946 and 1947 – the week surrounding May Ninth was replete with veterans' talks, film festivals, museum exhibitions, victory concerts, cemetery visits, artillery salutes, and fireworks. More importantly, amid the festivities there was an ever-present emphasis on the mobilization of labor as "a kind of ritualistic replay" of the war against Nazi Germany.[90] *Pravda*'s lead Victory Day article in 1946 described the anniversary as channeling the might of the Soviet people "toward a single goal – the fulfillment and over-fulfillment of the five-year plan of economic reconstruction and development." The

esp. 106–154; Petrone, *Life Has Become More Joyous, Comrades*. On festivals during the initial years of Bolshevik rule, see von Geldern, *Bolshevik Festivals*.

88 Both Nina Tumarkin and, more recently, Steven Maddox have connected the war's commemoration to mobilization. Maddox, in particular, notes that war commemoration provided a means of mobilizing society for the task of restoring the economy and the ideological confrontation of the Cold War. But whereas Maddox observes the effects of this phenomenon from the perspective of postwar Leningrad, arguing that the Cold War led to a more prevalent official Russocentrism, the present discussion focuses on the sources of the drive to homogenize the war's remembrance. From this standpoint, the perceived disrupting effects of the Russocentric paradigm played a much greater role. Central authorities deliberately looked to minimize the Russocentrism of the war's memory in favor of the Soviet whole, even while embarking on the focused restoration and protection of tsarist and medieval architecture. Maddox, *Saving Stalin's Imperial City*, 146, 170–193; Tumarkin, *The Living & the Dead*, 103–105.

89 The formal decree can be found under GARF R-7523/36/335/169. In compensation, January 1 was turned into a non-working holiday. The symbolism of Victory Day's "demotion" is emphasized by Nina Tumarkin. See Tumarkin, *The Living & the Dead*, 103–105, 110. On the war as a "subordinate theme," see also Gill, *Symbols and Legitimacy*, 153. See also Kirschenbaum, *The Legacy of the Siege*, 113–150. For a contrasting view, see Gabowitsch, "Victory Day before Brezhnev."

90 See, for example, "Den' velikoi pobedy," 3–6; Lenoe, *Closer to the Masses*, qt. 37.

article linked the objectives of the postwar five-year plan with those of the war: "Heroes of the new five-year plan are now devoting their strength to the same great cause for which heroes of the [Great] Patriotic War performed their immortal exploits."[91] Even before May Ninth became a working holiday, there were pervasive calls to commemorate victory through campaigns of "socialist competition" in the workplace.[92] The planners of Moscow's one-year anniversary celebrations, for instance, scheduled many of the city's commemorative activities on May 8, a day ahead of the then-non-working Victory Day holiday, since these were to revolve around mobilizing particular industries and institutions. For organizers in 1946 and 1947, taking the day off work on Victory Day had already become anathema to its mobilizational raison d'être.[93]

Thus, despite the day off work on May 9, 1946, the party secretary of Alma-Ata boasted to his superiors that "[i]n honor of our victory, workers implemented vast projects aimed at the improvement of the economy of the city – paving streets, repairing homes, planting trees." He went on to cite the celebration of victory as the primary factor in "the mobilization of workers for the fulfillment and over-fulfilment of social obligations." The same month, the foreman of a candy factory in the Kazakh SSR, which was fulfilling its quotas at a rate of 160 percent, tied his factory's increased productivity to the remembrance of victory. In his words, "[t]he defeat of Nazi Germany [and] the Japanese samurai, and the transition to peaceful construction, inspire us to ever greater feats of labor." Victory Day anniversaries provided the necessary incentive for his factory "to consolidate production successes and further improve productivity."[94] By the time Victory Day became a working holiday, a group of miners accurately referred to a "glorious annual tradition" of socialist competition connected to May Ninth.[95] In the case of one Moscow metallurgical plant, the first "working" Victory Day in 1948 saw the plant's employees sign an agreement of socialist competition in which workers pledged to "conduct work during the month of May at 105 percent"; "to maintain a clean place of work"; and "reduce defective goods by five percent."[96]

[91] "Prazdnik Pobedy," *Pravda*, May 9, 1946, 1. The link between Victory Day and labor mobilization was greatly expanded the following year. See "Den' velikoi pobedy," 3–6.

[92] For excellent background on socialist competition and its emergence as a fixture of industrial culture in the USSR, see Siegelbaum, *Stakhanovism*, 40–53, qt. 40. See also Lenoe, *Closer to the Masses*, esp. chap. 7; Kotkin, *Magnetic Mountain*, 204.

[93] OKhDOPIM 3/63/39/105–107. [94] APRK 708/9/1334/43–45.

[95] "Ot shakhterov kombinata 'Cheliabinskugol'' predsedateliu Soveta Ministrov Soiuza SSR tovarishchu Stalinu I. V.," *Pravda*, May 9, 1951, 1.

[96] GARF R-7676/13/393/1–66, qt. 1-2ob. For other examples, see GARF 7913/13/366/1–17; 7913/13/367/1–159; 7913/13/368/1–169.

The mobilizing language of Victory Day commemorations recast the war as a conflict left partly unfinished. Hitler may be defeated, but would-be Hitlers from the capitalist West continued to lurk. Just as the five-year plans of the 1930s readied the country for war, the postwar labor front was vital to winning the conflict to come. "Today the Soviet people are celebrating Victory Day in an atmosphere of intense struggle to fulfill the postwar five-year plan in four years," claimed the lead article in *Pravda* on May 9, 1949. "But, while busy building communism, the Soviet people have not for a moment forgotten that instigators of a new war are encroaching upon the peace that was won at the cost of so many lost lives." These "capitalist bosses" were "following in the footsteps of the utterly defeated German fascists." However, "as during the war against the arch-enemy of mankind, fascism," the Soviet people, "inspired by the ideals of Leninism," now directed their labor toward rooting out this renewed threat.[97] The Great Patriotic War as a parable for structuring the Soviet people's response to the emerging Cold War is perhaps best captured in a 1948 propaganda poster by V. I. Govorkov. In the poster, a Red Army veteran holding an official history of the Great Patriotic War is chiding a top-hatted industrialist clinching an atomic bomb. "No more mischief [*Ne balui*]!" warns the soldier, lest the Soviet Union be forced to save the world a second time from the fascist menace (Figure 2.2). The conflation of the two conflicts as a single ideological struggle resonated with Soviet citizens. As one woman reflected in her diary in 1947, it was the Soviet government's commitment to the universal ideals of international brotherhood, the elimination of war, and the dignity of every human being that separated it from "a Hitler or a Truman."[98]

Although the forward-looking tropes of "overcoming postwar difficulties," "fulfilling the new five-year plan," and "bringing closer to us the cherished goal of mankind – communism," transcended ethno-territorial borders and minimized notions of Russian primacy, the Russocentric paradigm endured in central representations throughout 1946.[99] References to the "great ancestors" dotted newspapers while a well-known 1946 propaganda poster promoting reconstruction confidently linked the image of a Russian war veteran and engineer with the ghostly presence of the medieval founder of Moscow. "Glory to the Russian people," proclaimed the poster's text, "a hero people, a creator

[97] "Den' nashei velikoi pobedy," *Pravda*, May 9, 1949, 1.
[98] Malakhieva-Mirovich, *Maiatnik zhizni moei*, 702–704.
[99] The first two quotes are from "Prazdnik Pobedy," *Pravda*, May 9, 1947, 1; the latter from GARF R-7676/13/393/1ob.

Figure 2.2 "No more mischief!" (Universal History Archive/Universal Images Group via Getty Images), 1948.

people."[100] In a Victory Day editorial that same year, Isaak Mints noted the motivational role played by images of the Russian past for Soviet soldiers at the front. "Making their way to the center of Germany," Mints wrote, "Soviet troops launched an offensive in areas conquered by the guardsmen of Peter I and soldiers of the young Suvorov." These historical sites "inspired Soviet soldiers on to new heroic feats, culminating in the titanic Battle for Berlin and the hoisting of the Victory Banner over the Reichstag."[101] Although the striking imagery of this vignette was a minor component of the narrative as a whole, the notion of soldiers inspired by Russian imperial victories and "progressive" historical personalities persisted so long as the victory myth remained defined by a tension between contrasting pan-Soviet and Russocentric paradigms.[102]

[100] Brandenberger, *National Bolshevism*, 195.
[101] I. Mints, "Narod-pobeditel'," *Pravda*, May 9, 1946, 2. [102] Mints, 2.

Nevertheless, Russocentrism had less and less bearing on the victory myth as the decade wore on. Even chauvinistic attitudes among officials do not appear to have impacted the war's official interpretation beyond several isolated episodes. One of the better-documented cases involved the suppression of G. A. Deborin's 1948 monograph *International Relations during the Great Patriotic War*. In a letter to Agitprop officials, the head of the Main Political Directorate of the Armed Forces, F. F. Kuznetsov, complained that the book "diminished the historical role of the USSR in the Great Patriotic War" and "placed America, Britain, and France on equal footing with the Soviet Union in terms of their contribution to victory over Nazi Germany." Kuznetsov added that Deborin "underestimates the role of the Russian people in the Great Patriotic War."[103] Even before Agitprop formally intervened, Deborin, who was aware of Kuznetsov's accusations, issued a formal statement in which he acknowledged the book was "wholly flawed." Among its mistakes, Deborin admitted, was that the book did "not demonstrate American imperialists' extreme hatred for the USSR and the great Russian nation." "It was necessary," Deborin continued, "to talk in detail about the role of the Soviet social and political system, the role of Soviet patriotism, the friendship of the peoples . . . [and] the role of the great Russian nation."[104]

Both Kuznetsov's initial complaint and Deborin's self-critical statement made their way to the Agitprop leadership. The organization's deputy chief, Dmitrii Shepilov, drafted the detailed final report on the matter that arrived on Suslov's desk. Shepilov ultimately recommended that the book be taken out of its limited circulation and destroyed but not for all the same reasons Kuznetsov had mentioned. Shepilov agreed that the most egregious feature of the book was the exaggerated importance that it accorded Britain and the United States in Germany's defeat. He also noted the book's inadequate analysis of the war's origins, which failed to highlight the "connection with the general crisis of capitalism and the world's division into two systems." Yet Shepilov excised all references to the Russian nation from the report, emphasizing instead the book's failures from a purely ideological and pan-Soviet perspective. In spite of the overtly Russocentric sentiments emanating from figures such as Kuznetsov, the case of Deborin's monograph corroborates the tendency among the leadership to moderate rather than encourage Russocentric currents insofar as they risked overwhelming the victory myth's discursive tension.

[103] Nadzhafov and Belousova, *Stalin i kosmopolitizm*, 470.
[104] Nadzhafov and Belousova, 470–471.

Often recognized as an impetus for the continued promotion of state Russocentrism, Cold War tensions had a more complex impact on the war's official representation. Intended as both a weapon against the war narratives advanced in the capitalist West and as a mobilizing myth to spur economic reconstruction and foster ideological conformity, late-Stalinist war memory regularly privileged a de-ethnicized conception of the Soviet people and minimized overtly Russocentric themes linked to the war victory. As the leadership was well aware, the USSR's appeal as a beacon of socialism after 1945 hinged on its defeat of Nazism and had little to do with assertions of Russian exceptionalism, even in a revolutionary guise.[105] Explanations for victory that highlighted the pre-Soviet military pedigree and Russian national primacy risked undermining many of the USSR's ideological claims abroad.[106] As with ideologists who persisted in articulating the war's pan-Soviet character after May 1945, the public celebration of victory during the late 1940s reinforced an ideological line that did not fit neatly with the message of Stalin's toast. But if the Russocentric currents of postwar Soviet society did not define the prevailing victory myth, they found ample expression in other commemorative outlets.

Moscow's 800-Year Jubilee

In a January 1947 statement to Moscow-region secretaries, Georgii Popov, the aforementioned head of the Moscow Party Committee, complained that not enough was being done to highlight the uniquely Russian character of the RSFSR. As part of his diatribe, Popov pointed to the lack of public discussion regarding the Russian people's unique contribution to victory in the war and the dearth of references to Stalin's famed toast honoring that contribution:

> But Russia's role, the role of the Russian people . . . in destroying the enemy, in ensuring victory! They are not even using those utterances of C[omrade] Stalin, where he speaks about the Russian people, remember, at the reception in the Kremlin in honor of the Victory Parade [*sic*]. This material is not even used by our propagandists, by some of our comrades who are leading the preparations. It's not right. . . . We have nothing to say about Russia. We talk about the Soviet Union, about Moscow, but where is Russia, where are the Russian people?[107]

[105] Liuks, "Evreiskii vopros v politike Stalina," 45; Livshin and Orlov, "Propaganda i politicheskaia sotsializatsiia," 101, 104.
[106] See, for example, the published declaration collectively authored by European communist parties: "Deklaratsii o mezhdunarodnom polozhenii, priniatoi uchastnikami soveshchaniia predstavitelei riada Kompartii evropy," *Pravda*, Oct. 5, 1947, 2.
[107] OKhDOPIM 3/67/12/2–4.

Popov was certainly not alone in his drive to advance the victory myth's Russocentric paradigm. As discussed previously, many local architects and city planners looked back on the war as the culmination of a thousand years of Russian triumphs. No less a figure than Eisenstein was at work on the script for the film *Moscow 800*, a never-completed project that linked the eras of the Mongol Yoke, Ivan the Terrible, 1812, the Bolshevik Revolution, and victory in the Great Patriotic War.[108] The desire among a large swath of Russian speakers, including many party officials, to glorify Russia's military legacy did not end with failed war memorial designs or unfinished film scripts. To what extent did efforts to magnify the victory myth's Russocentric aspect shape the war's late-Stalinist remembrance?

In fact, official war memory continued to operate as a tension between two distinct ideological paradigms amid such challenges. The year 1947 saw several key anniversaries linked to prerevolutionary figures and events. It also marked thirty years since the Bolshevik Revolution. As this section details with regard to the celebration of Moscow's 800-year jubilee, the promotion of Russian national history and culture that pervaded postwar Soviet society interacted with concurrent representations of the war in complex and dynamic, though often discordant, ways. By maintaining a robust, pan-Soviet model of war memory alongside Russocentric narratives and historical commemorations, late-Stalinist patriotic discourse simultaneously promoted homogenizing (lateral) and variegating (hierarchical) conceptions of Soviet collective identity. Although inconsistent, this process increasingly siphoned Russocentric cultural energy away from the war theme and into carefully managed spaces of prerevolutionary cultural, scientific, and military triumphalism.

Planning for Moscow's 800-year jubilee began in early 1946 and picked up in May 1947.[109] Popov played a central role in every aspect of the multiday festivities. These included public lectures, walking tours, museum exhibitions, sporting events, concerts, fireworks, the production of commemorative texts and films, and other celebratory fare highlighting eight centuries of Moscow's greatness. Arguably the climax of the event was to be the laying of foundation stones for a monument to Iurii Dolgoruki and eight "wedding-cake" skyscrapers, seven of which would come to dominate the Moscow cityscape.[110] The fact that a projected

108 The film, was intended to commemorate the 800-year anniversary of the founding of Moscow. See Clark, *Moscow*, 345–346; Clark, "Eisenstein's Two Projects," 184–200.

109 OKhDOPIM 3/63/15/33; 3/67/2/10–11.

110 See "Zakladka mnogoetazhnykh zdanii," *Pravda*, Sep. 8, 1947; "Zakladka pamiatnika Iuriiu Dolgorukomu," *Pravda*, Sep. 8, 1947. For good overviews of the festivities, see

sculptural depiction of an armor-clad Iurii Dolgoruki on horseback was sited in place of an obelisk dating from the revolution seems a powerful symbolic statement. Regardless of the modernizing orientation of the newly planned high-rises, one literary scholar has noted a "Russian nationalist tinge" to official Soviet rhetoric associated with the anniversary date. "The capital," she goes on, "functioned less as a symbol of modernization than as a symbol of continuity in the Russian nation."[111]

However, the work of the Committee on Preparations for the 800th Anniversary of Moscow, chaired by Popov, suggests a more fragmented approach to the city's historical trajectory. This is nowhere more evident than in early planning deliberations over the appropriate timing for the celebrations. Given that there was no precise date for the city's founding, the Committee settled on September 7, 1947, because it fell on a non-working Sunday and, more importantly, because September was sandwiched between Victory Day and the thirtieth anniversary of the October Revolution in November. Zhdanov personally scribbled instructions on draft plans for the revolution's commemorations ordering that Moscow's 800th anniversary celebrations be fully completed in advance of the revolutionary holiday.[112] Popov elaborated on this, noting during one of the planning sessions that hosting Moscow's anniversary well before November 7 would provide a thematic "boundary [*rubezh*]" between the two jubilees that would enable the latter to emphasize exclusively Soviet achievements.[113] This decision was made despite evidence that Moscow residents preferred holding the 800th anniversary after November 7 for fear that it would overwhelm the revolutionary date.[114] Thus, Russian national fervor provoked by the September celebrations would, in theory, be confined to a period of weeks between September and November.

However, in Popov's hands, the 800-year jubilee was itself designed to steer national pride in a decidedly Soviet direction. Given Popov's adamant calls only a few months earlier for a greater focus on discernably Russian achievements, this is noteworthy indeed, and likely reflected Politburo interventions. Upon reviewing proposals ranging from restoration projects to the production of films and lectures covering Moscow's history, Popov and the Moscow party secretary for propaganda, N. N. Danilov, noted "shortcomings" in organizational work during

Clark, "Eisenstein's Two Projects," 188–190; Brandenberger, *National Bolshevism*, 216–217.

111 Clark, "Eisenstein's Two Projects," 188. On this trend during the prewar decade, see Clark, *Moscow, the Fourth Rome*.

112 RGASPI 17/125/503/124. 113 Gorinov, *Moskva poslevoennaia*, 221–229, qt. 228.

114 Gorinov, 245–246.

a May 1947 session. Public lecturers, he complained, were focusing "mainly on the distant history of Moscow," and only a handful had properly "interpreted the theme '800 years of Moscow' to mean the life of our capital in Soviet times." Out of nineteen lecture venues, Danilov protested, a full six of them were being devoted to lectures on purely historical subject matter. Speaking on behalf of the Moscow Party Committee, Danilov ordered the heads of district party organizations to more closely monitor Agitprop work under their purview because "there is a serious mistake when there is more said about the 770-year period [before the revolution] and hardly anything about Moscow during the Soviet era." Danilov then proceeded to criticize several specific proposals in which there was a "gravitation toward the distant past."[115]

Popov continued this line of criticism, noting "a historical bias" in current planning. The Moscow party leader specified that the Soviet era was to be the centerpiece of the celebrations, while the prerevolutionary era was a mere "auxiliary" theme. "[T]he real history of Moscow," he argued, "is that moment ... when, under the leadership of Lenin and Stalin, Moscow began to transform and became the capital, not of a [Russian] empire, but of the socialist state of workers and peasants." The objective was not to celebrate past achievements for their own sake, "like putting figurines atop a chest of drawers," but rather to do so in a way that highlighted "our modern tasks," which included "strengthening the Soviet patriotism of our people," "rallying our people around our Party, around our government, around our leader, C[omrade] Stalin," and "above all the construction of socialism" and the "building of communism." We must properly grasp this," Popov urged, "otherwise all our work will drag us into deep history."[116]

Popov and Danilov outlined appropriate measures to assure that the Soviet significance of the anniversary was paramount. First, the balance of cultural productions was to favor the Soviet side of the revolutionary divide – even among Russocentric productions. Popov specifically ordered works featuring Moscow "during the Great Patriotic War and the era of socialist construction." Indeed, for every opera on Dmitrii Donskoi or performance of Prokof'ev's "Aleksandr Nevskii," there were any number of pieces devoted to Soviet Moscow. These often included Russocentric overtones. The anniversary film *Moscow – The Capital of the USSR*, for example, opens in 1918, before jumping ahead to the German invasion in 1941 and Stalin's great ancestors speech. But the overriding message remained the Soviet essence of victory. Another documentary film released for the celebrations, *The Heart of the Motherland*, offers

[115] Gorinov, *Moskva poslevoennaia*, 222. [116] Gorinov, 226.

a sketch of the prerevolutionary era up through the growth of capitalism. This then serves to contrast the period preceding 1917 with, in the narrator's words, "the new era in the history of humanity" ushered in by the Bolshevik Revolution. Drawing contrasts, rather than parallels, with the 770 years before 1917 was a central part of the festivities. In one planned exhibit, organizers built a mockup of a tsarist-era school house in order to demonstrate the radical progress achieved in just a few decades of Soviet rule.[117] In this vein, the decision was taken to prominently display Zhdanov's reminder amid the many slogans on posters and banners during the festivities that "We are no longer the Russians we were before 1917."[118]

However, Soviet-centered productions also aimed to capture the city's pan-Soviet and internationalist ethos. The writer Roman Fatuev penned a series of commemorative essays that highlighted Moscow's status as a pan-ethnic hub. As the backdrop for exploring this theme, Fatuev naturally turned to the city's defense during the Battle of Moscow in late 1941, where, according to the author, a laterally arrayed community of Soviet peoples arose as one to defend the city: "shoulder to shoulder at the approaches to the capital, the sons of Russia, Ukraine, Belarus, Central Asia, [and] the Caucasus steadfastly defended every frontier, every inch of soil." Fatuev surveyed the feats of more than a dozen non-Russian heroes, with a particular emphasis on soldiers from the North Caucasus. Fatuev argued that while the names of fallen Russian heroes, like Zoia Kosmodem'ianskaia, Liza Chaikina, and Viktor Talalikhin, readily come to mind in discussions of the war, it was every bit as vital to honor Moscow's 800th anniversary by recalling the names of non-Russian heroes, which Fatuev listed at length. In Fatuev's telling, the various ethnicities who defended Moscow were more than just the sum of their parts. In fact, the war transformed the Soviet people into a monolith bound not only by a common socialist homeland, but by blood. "It was at Moscow," Fatuev emphasized, "that the blood of all the sons of the great Soviet country intermingled."[119]

In addition to a heavy emphasis on Soviet themes, the anniversary's organizers sought to compartmentalize the Russian national past as much as possible. In several cases, Danilov and Popov actively discouraged the production of epic dramas that attempted to portray all 800 years of Moscow's history as a linear narrative since they feared that the historical might drown out the more important Soviet aspects. Instead, they

117 See comments by Mart'ianov in Gorinov, 225, and discussions under OKhDOPIM 3/67/197/78–80.

118 As observed in Brandenberger, *National Bolshevism*, 217.

119 TsMAMLS 159/1/84/1–5.

advocated works "dedicated to individual historical problems, to individual epochs," which highlighted issues of relevance to Soviet society but without straining to cut across 1917.[120] This apparently had the intended effect. Some party officials later complained of an absence of connections with historical themes. In late August, for example, during a final meeting of the anniversary committee, one unidentified member expressed consternation. After reviewing a list of planned performances that included "Ivan the Terrible" and the opera "Dmitrii Donskoi" alongside stage productions of "The Young Guard" and other Soviet-oriented works, the agitated figure asked, "Where is the connection between the [Soviet-themed] productions and the historical holiday?" He went on to note the "crude" public portrayal of "Rus', the time of Aleksandr Nevskii, the period of Suvorov, and [18]12": "Where is all this reflected, in which things?" The representative criticized another of the committee's members responsible for cultural matters, complaining that "[h]e shows socialist Moscow, but what about historical Moscow?" What was needed, in the speaker's view, was to clearly portray the exploits of great figures from the past, the "revolutionary transition," and "socialist Moscow, all together" as a unified narrative. This provoked a stern rebuke from Popov, who reminded his colleague that "out of 800 years, the most important thing we have is the [final] thirty-year period. Therefore, theaters are doing the correct thing in paying more attention to the modern theme. [T]he historical aspect must be present, but it cannot be dominant."[121]

Finally, in order to assure the proper celebration of Moscow's history, Popov sanctioned the creation of an authoritative text that "would define our relationship to the 800th anniversary." Popov suggested that this take the form of a collective letter to Stalin on behalf of the "workers of Moscow." The text would be available to planners before the anniversary in order to serve as a thematic template on how to balance the "tribute to history" with "talk about socialist construction, about the unfolding thirty years [of Soviet rule]."[122] Addressed to the "great leader of the Communist Party and the Soviet people" on the occasion of the "800-year anniversary of the glorious capital of the Union of Soviet Socialist Republics," the letter's published version opened on a strikingly pan-Soviet note:

> The 800th anniversary of Moscow is a holiday of the whole Soviet people. For Russians and Ukrainians, Belarusians and Georgians, Azeris and Armenians, Kazakhs and Uzbeks, Latvians and Estonians, Turkmen and Tajiks, Lithuanians

[120] Gorinov, *Moskva poslevoennaia*, 222. [121] Gorinov, 243–244.
[122] Gorinov, 227, 248.

and Karelians, Moldavians and Kyrgyz, for all people populating our great motherland, united in a single and harmonious family, Moscow is as close and dear as a beloved mother ... To every end of the Soviet land, the shining stars of the Kremlin radiate, the symbol of the might and glory of our socialist homeland, the symbol of the unity and friendship of its peoples.

While emphasizing Moscow's place as "the center of the most progressive ideas of the great Lenin and Stalin," the letter did not ignore the city's history. After a brief run-through of military successes against Polish-Lithuanian and French invaders, it moved on to the great breaks and transitions that had occurred since the revolution. The only explicit mention of continuity with the prerevolutionary era emphasized in the letter were "the revolutionary traditions of the Moscow workers ... [E]verything else has become new!" It was precisely in the context of the "new," Soviet character of Moscow that the letter surveyed victory in the Great Patriotic War. Positioned at the opposite end of the text from the accounts of military feats in 1612 and 1812, even Stalin's Red Square invocation of the great ancestors was left unmentioned in the discussion of the war – although historical antecedents remained implicit. The letter grounded the 1941 defense of Moscow in expressly pan-Soviet/internationalist terms. As important as modern industry, party leadership, and Stalin's genius was the fact that, on the field of battle, "Ukrainians, Belarusians, Kazakhs, Georgians, and sons of every nation of the great Soviet Union fought shoulder-to-shoulder with the sons of Moscow."[123]

However, an even more authoritative commentary eclipsed the letter in the form of a greeting by Stalin, published on the front page of the same issue of *Pravda*. Stalin reiterated Moscow's role in liberating the Motherland "three times from foreign oppression," from the Mongols, Polish-Lithuanians, and Napoleon. Yet Stalin's greeting carefully distinguished between these "historical contributions," which were outlined in a single paragraph, and the remainder of the piece, which focused on those aspects of Soviet Moscow that separated it from previous incarnations.[124] In this sense, it mirrored the collective letter from workers and the jubilee celebrations more broadly. Whatever Moscow's historical role, after 1917 the city became "the inspirer of the construction of the new Soviet democracy"; "the banner of the struggle of all working people in the world, all oppressed races and nations for liberation from the rule of plutocracy and imperialism"; and the "center of the organization of the friendship of the peoples and fraternal cooperation in our

[123] "Pis'mo ot trudiashchikhsia goroda Moskvy Velikomu vozhdiu sovetskogo naroda tovarishchu Stalinu," *Pravda*, Sep. 7, 1947, 2–3.

[124] Cf. Brandenberger, *National Bolshevism*, 216; Clark, "Eisenstein's Two Projects," 188.

multinational state." Unlike its prerevolutionary predecessor, Soviet Moscow "has eliminated slums and has given workers the chance to move from basements and shacks into apartments and houses." There was no mention of the Great Patriotic War and certainly not in connection with the string of prerevolutionary military victories over foreign invaders.[125]

Of course, none of this signified the repudiation of the Russocentric paradigm. Throughout the anniversary event, cultural works and public statements regularly presented Russian historical and Soviet-era achievements along a single continuum. Lower-level officials, in particular, were less circumspect in demarcating the Soviet and pre-Soviet eras than were Stalin's authoritative holiday greeting or the formal letter from the workers of Moscow.[126] The animated film *To You, Moscow* by the director Grigorii Lomidze, to take another example, achieved what Eisenstein never did with his script for *Moscow 800*. The film traces the historical development of Moscow along successive heroic defenses against foreign invaders. Interspersed with documentary footage highlighting Moscow in its modern, Soviet condition, and photographs featuring a range of non-Russian Soviet peoples, the "Soviet" message is nevertheless undercut by the heavy focus on historical continuity. The film opens with a close-up of the 1944 medal awarded to defenders of Moscow, which depicts a T-34 tank alongside the famed monument to Minin and Pozharskii on Red Square, and concludes with the Victory Day celebrations of May 9, 1945. Bookended in such a way, *To You, Moscow* effectively cast 1945 as the culmination of a teleology that began in the year 1147.

The ambiguities created by the simultaneous presence of Russocentric (in both the archaic and contemporary sense) and pan-Soviet patriotic vectors can be discerned not only in the jubilee's productions, but also to some extent in the anniversary's popular reception. Among the recollections of participants are some that do not at all dwell on the prerevolutionary legacy or the state's deep Russian roots. What most struck the writer and translator V. G. Malakhieva-Mirovich about her experience of the anniversary's celebration was, in fact, how little it recalled the past. "In general," she observed, "all of this night's festivities evoked in me not the history of Moscow and those things that 'flow together with the heart of the Russian,' ... but rather, for some reason, the war, the 'horrors of war.'" Of all the holiday imagery, Malakhieva-Mirovich noted

125 "Privetstvie tov. I. V. Stalina," *Pravda*, Sep. 7, 1947, 1.

126 See, for example, I. Vlasov, "Moskva – natsional'naia gordost' sovetskogo naroda," *Pravda*, Sep. 5, 1947, 3, in which the Great Patriotic War is listed as the third in a line of past military victories.

in particular the spotlights and the sounds of fireworks, which, she felt, played on the war's memory. Whilc making no mention of historical motifs, she did record prominent imagery associated with Soviet achievements and personalities. "My thoughts seldom involve politics, foreign or domestic," she wrote on encountering massive portraits of Lenin and Stalin near one of her favorite Moscow parks. "But as in the days of the war, so too in times of peace, I trust the will and the power of our ship's helmsmen who navigate us ... out of the youth of monarchism and capitalism," toward communism.[127] Malakhieva-Mirovich's contemporary emphasis is striking. Yet considering the fragmented and semi-compartmentalized mode of patriotic representations during the 800-year jubilee, which maintained a pan-Soviet sense of the war's significance in tandem with Russocentric depictions, her reaction should perhaps not come as a surprise.

But if the pan-Soviet/internationalist variant of the victory myth offered the Stalinist leadership the inclusive, postrevolutionary heroic mythology it had long sought, why bother maintaining a discursive tension with Russian national-patriotic and historical themes at all – unless it was part of a larger Russocentric ideological rubric? As alluded to throughout the chapter, despite Stalin's high regard for Russia's state-building traditions and "progressive" historical personalities, public celebrations of events like the 800th anniversary of Moscow masked tenacious Communist anxieties over the potential emergence of an anti-Soviet Russian nationalism. For this reason, the Russian national-patriotic currents unleashed in the fight against Nazi Germany were not nearly so easy to roll back. It could be argued that the persistence of Russocentric etatism in the postwar era signified less Stalin's love for all things Russian than a veiled Russophobia – that is, a healthy respect for the potentially disruptive might of Russian national self-assertion. Discursive tension, in this light, resulted precisely from authorities' efforts to contain those national-patriotic currents, to steer them in a Soviet direction, all in a manner that did not provoke their wrath.

Stalin's Last Years

Although the two dominant paradigms of Stalinist war memory advanced generally distinct patriotic lines, ideologists toward the end of the dictator's life often successfully reconciled Russocentrism and pan-Soviet internationalism through the medium of the late Stalin cult. At the same time that Stalin's toast made an abrupt return to Victory Day

[127] Malakhieva-Mirovich, *Maiatnik zhizni moei*, 701–702.

commemorative articles in May 1951, construction commenced on the new Komsomol'skaia metro station, which opened in January 1952.[128] Based on the vision of A. V. Shchusev, the station's interior was inspired by Stalin's "great ancestors" speech.[129] The main hall contained a series of mosaics by P. D. Korin that portrayed individual scenes of Nevskii, Donskoi, Minin and Pozharskii, Suvorov, and Kutuzov, culminating with the Red Army's capture of the Reichstag and the victory parade on Red Square. The latter panel featured Stalin, glimmering in the white generalissimo's uniform of his later cultic image, looking on as soldiers below piled German standards near the entrance to Lenin's Mausoleum. In the words of one of the project's lead architects, the station's décor sought to trace "the victories of Russian arms over foreign invaders, from the era of Aleksandr Nevskii up through the Soviet people's victory over the dark forces of fascism in 1945."[130] The narrative told through the mosaics cast Stalin almost as the latter-day embodiment of the great ancestors – a clear manifestation of the Russocentric paradigm.

The greater attention to the victory myth's Russocentric tendency during these years might have anticipated a more sweeping revision of the war narrative had Stalin lived. As noted in the previous chapter, the early 1950s also saw an uptick of Russocentric depictions of the war among non-Russian party organizations. Hence, where some propagandists sought to smooth over the contradictions of postwar ideology by fragmenting patriotic themes, this was not the only strategy utilized to this end. Stalin's cult, and particularly his image as war leader, offered a fulcrum for the diverse patriotic tendencies emanating from the war years. The cult could accommodate the competing vectors of the war's memory without being overwhelmed by them. It was "tailored to the totality of the population" and did not differentiate between "Caucasus mountaineers or Ivanovo textile workers ... Soviet citizens of Muslim background or those of Russian Orthodox heritage," as Jan Plamper observes in his comprehensive analysis of the cult.[131] An all-encompassing, supranational symbol of Soviet authority, Stalin's image as war leader effectively superseded the various Russocentric and pan-Soviet wartime currents, becoming not only the ultimate source of victory but its embodiment.

[128] "Geroicheskii podvig sovetskogo naroda," *Pravda*, May 9, 1951, 1. The next year there was a single reference to Russian wartime leadership, but not in the format of the toast: "Den' Pobedy," *Pravda*, May 9, 1952, 1.
[129] See comments by P. D. Korin under RGALI 2466/1/194/23. On historical imagery in the Moscow metro, see Bouvard, *Le Métro de Moscou*, esp. 212–216.
[130] Quote from the architect A. Zabolotnaia: RGALI 2466/1/194/19–20ob.
[131] Plamper, *The Stalin Cult*, esp. 217–218.

Thus, the augmentation of the Russocentric paradigm during Stalin's final years might best be explained as a symptom of the late-Stalin cult's evolution. Komsomol'skaia station's linkage of Aleksandr Nevskii's victory over the Teutonic Knights with the Stalin-led victory in 1945 was arguably less a commentary on the Great Patriotic War than a series of analogues for Stalin. After all, by this time it had become increasingly difficult to separate victory from the person of Stalin, a fact well attested by one of the last significant war memorials of the era: Yerevan's Victory Monument (1950). Consisting of a large granite pedestal emblazoned with an Order of Victory and Armenian national flourishes, the structure served as a base for the largest Stalin monument in the USSR.[132] The late cult transcended not only Soviet nations and national traditions but also, occasionally, the USSR as a whole, as witnessed in the closing scene of the 1949 film *The Fall of Berlin*. After descending from his plane to greet the victorious marshals and a multiethnic coterie of Red Army troops, he is rushed by cheering POWs and soldiers of British, French, and other nationalities, all chanting "Long live Stalin!" These late-cultic representations suggest that it hardly mattered whether Stalin's image as war leader edged along a Russocentric or pan-Soviet plane. These paradigms were beneath him and, as such, bridled to him (Figure 2.3). In only a few years' time, destalinization would again let loose the disparate patriotic currents long held at bay by discursive tension and the cult of Generalissimo Stalin.

Conclusion

Late-Stalinist commemorations reveal the early victory myth to be far more muddled, multivalent, and ambiguous than is usually acknowledged. With the onset of the Cold War and growing concerns over potential manifestations of localism and Russian nationalism in the Party's ranks, the leadership sought out supra-ethnic and postrevolutionary mobilizational themes that contrasted simultaneous appeals to Russocentric hierarchy and historical pedigree. This challenge was especially pressing during the late 1940s since the Russocentric paradigm played into emerging Western explanations for the Soviet victory. The celebration of the Russian national past continued to play an important role in late-Stalinist patriotic memory. But the public glorification of certain prerevolutionary events and personalities never hindered the victory myth's ability to accommodate a range of loyalties and identities. In some respects, historical commemorations channeled

132 Lehmann, "Apricot Socialism," 29–30.

Figure 2.3a Stalin's late cultic image. [2.3a] "Glory to the victorious people! Glory to the dear Stalin!" (Universal History Archive/Universal Images Group via Getty Images), early 1950s.

Russocentrism away from the war theme and into the contained arena of the invented pre-Soviet past. Ultimately, official war memory under Stalin did less to enshrine a singular, Russian-dominated ethnic hierarchy and master historical narrative than create alternative avenues of patriotic expression, including one that subordinated all ethnonational communities – Russians as well as non-Russians – to the paramount Soviet whole.

In a recent article, the scholar Vitalii Tikhonov examined efforts among Soviet historians to locate the prerevolutionary origins of the friendship

Figure 2.3b Stalin's late cultic image. [2.3b]: "Great Stalin, the banner of the friendship of the peoples of the USSR!" (V. B. Koretsky/Hulton Archive via Getty Images), 1950.

of the peoples doctrine. The article shows that among the major themes explored by members of the postwar historical establishment was the shared struggle against the Mongol invasion. Tikhonov notes in passing that "[i]t is obvious that the Mongol invasion was seen as a prototype for the Nazi invasion." He concludes by pondering the dearth of works among his sample that extended their analyses into the Soviet period. The author proposes that the Soviet period may have been too politically sensitive for historians to attempt to construct a post-1917 myth of common origin. He also suggests that recent history was less important, since defining the ancient past was "the essential prerequisite for constructing [Soviet] nationhood."[133] Although there is a great deal of truth to this, it nevertheless ignores the late-Stalinist myth of victory in the war. The question Tikhonov poses could be asked a different way: Why did narratives of the war often eschew prerevolutionary imagery and pedigree? The answer, this chapter has argued, is that the war victory in its pan-Soviet guise became, for the Stalinist leadership, the potential raw material for a uniquely Soviet myth of common origin, a lateral patriotic

[133] Tikhonov, "Stalinskaia premiia kak instrument," 177–185.

ideal and usable past unmoored from prerevolutionary developments. As we shall see in the next chapters, the search for a modern, Soviet foundation myth would come to preoccupy Stalin's successors as they simultaneously unraveled and sought to maintain aspects of the Stalinist myth of the Great Patriotic War.

3 Usable Pasts

The Crisis of Patriotism and the Origins of the War Cult

At present, these places are within living memory, and there will be eyewitnesses for a long time to come. But there will be a time when there are people who have not lived through the events of our day, and it is for them that these places must be immortalized.

– A. A. Zaplotynskii, letter to the CC CPSU[1]

You see, history is history . . . You can rename cities, factories, etc. But what about Stalingrad? This city is not so easy to rename.

– Political Instructor Lt. Col. Antonov, 1956[2]

For the veteran L. S. Daniliuk, the war's memory possessed all the raw material necessary to reconstitute a usable past in the post-Stalin era. "It seems to me," he wrote in a letter to the Presidium of the Central Committee, "that we are far from doing everything [we can], when, on the occasion of Victory Day over fascist Germany, we limit ourselves to articles in newspapers and discussions between agitators and workers." Greater attention to the war's public veneration, Daniliuk reasoned, would assure that all citizens, and particularly the youth, maintain a deep love and respect for the Soviet homeland. Daniliuk first addressed the status of the May Ninth anniversary. He argued that the celebration of Victory Day should achieve a level at least "equivalent" to that of the October Revolution. "It goes without saying," he added, that "this holiday should be a non-working day." Among Daniliuk's other suggestions was a grand Victory Park in the Soviet capital with a museum dedicated to the history of the war. The proposed park would not only chronicle the years 1941–5, but also the Russian Civil War and the many other "glorious deeds" achieved in the name of the "whole Soviet people." But the envisaged memorial park did not confine itself to the celebration of Soviet achievements. The letter went on to advise that the park "depict the role of Aleksandr Nevskii, Suvorov, and Kutuzov,"

[1] RGASPI 17/125/299/135. [2] Aimermakher, *Doklad N. S. Khrushcheva*, 543.

and other "outstanding commanders of Russia" from the prerevolutionary epoch.[3]

The timing of Daniliuk's proposal was not coincidental. Only a few months earlier, the Party's first secretary, Nikita Khrushchev, had taken the extraordinary step of denouncing aspects of Stalin's rule and public persona to a closed session of the Twentieth Party Congress.[4] Among the convulsions that accompanied news of Khrushchev's "Secret Speech" were nationalist-oriented street demonstrations in Georgia and mass protests in the satellites of Poland and Hungary.[5] In addition to these upheavals, many in the Party blamed Khrushchev's assault on Stalin's legacy for a spike in youth hooliganism, and feared that what had become a bourgeoning cultural "Thaw" might broaden its critique of Stalinism to encompass the Soviet system as a whole. Notable in this regard was the publication of Vladimir Dudintsev's damning portrait of the Stalinist bureaucratic establishment, *Not by Bread Alone*. Released to favorable reviews, the novel faced a conservative backlash by the end of the year over concerns that it hinted at deeper systemic failures and contradictions.[6] For Daniliuk and many others, the lackluster public commemoration of the war had been a missed opportunity. With Stalin no longer an acceptable symbol of all-Soviet loyalty, the war's remembrance – sanitized of the dictator's presence – appeared to offer a stable source of patriotic identity that could weather the uncertainties of destalinization.

[3] RGASPI 5/30/231/1–3.

[4] The party leadership's decision to initiate destalinization derived from political, ideological, economic, military-strategic, and moral factors. Most importantly, from the standpoint of 1953–6, Stalin's death saw the repudiation of his methods of political control and the accompanying release of hundreds of thousands of Gulag prisoners. This compelled the leadership to disassociate the Party from Stalin and launch a very public campaign to correct the country's course by reclaiming the legacy of the mythical Lenin. See Taubman, *Khrushchev*, 236–282, 508–513. In the years 1954 and 1955 alone, the number of Gulag returnees reached approximately 1.3 million. See Dobson, *Khrushchev's Cold Summer*, 50–53. For recent work on destalinization in non-Russian Soviet republics, see Wojnowski, *The Near Abroad*, esp. chaps. 1–2; Wojnowski, "De-Stalinization and the Failure of Soviet Identity Building in Kazakhstan," 999–1021; Hasanli, *Khrushchev's Thaw and National Identity*, 43–86.

[5] See, for example, Kozlov, *Mass Uprisings in the USSR*, 112–135; Gati, *Failed Illusions*; Persak, "The Polish-Soviet Confrontation," 1285–1310.

[6] In fact, the novel's condemnation enhanced its popularity among reform-minded citizens. On these issues more generally, see Bittner, *The Many Lives of Khrushchev's Thaw*, esp. chaps. 2 and 6; Fürst, *Stalin's Last Generation*, 181–188, 342–365; Hornsby, *Protest, Reform and Repression*; LaPierre, *Hooligans in Khrushchev's Russia*, esp. 129–131; Kozlov, "Naming the Social Evil," 80–98; Tsipursky, *Socialist Fun*, 101–133; Zubkova, *Russia after the War*, 193–195. On the novel as a perceived attack on the Soviet system, see Jones, *Myth, Memory, Trauma*, 58–59, 73–74.

The party leadership shared much of this assessment.[7] Even before the Twentieth Congress, there was a fairly consistent push from above to expand state war commemoration, as elements within the political and military establishments identified the war's memory as a potentially legitimating force. Already in June 1955, Georgii Zhukov, newly appointed as Defense Minister, had sent a letter of his own to the Central Committee, along with a draft resolution, that foreshadowed many of the points raised by Daniliuk. Zhukov complained that in the ten years since Germany's defeat "not a single significant monument has been created in our country" that could adequately "reflect the great feats of the Soviet people . . . in the fight against fascism." This was especially irksome given that in Eastern Europe and China "memorials to perished Soviet soldiers had been built, and broad public attention is given to the matter of educating the masses in a spirit of respect for the Soviet Liberator-Army." Zhukov proposed the development of large-scale war monuments and memorial complexes throughout the country, a project the Ministry of Culture dutifully endorsed. By the time Daniliuk had issued his letter, the Central Committee was already overseeing plans for an all-union victory memorial and formulating a special commission to explore the larger question of the war's "immortalization" [*uvekovechenie pamiati*] across the USSR.[8]

These early official efforts differed from Daniliuk's proposal in a crucial respect. Where Daniliuk looked to anchor the war's remembrance in a distinctly Russian historical framework – in the imagery of Nevskii, Suvorov, and Kutuzov – the victory myth that would coalesce in the years after Stalin's death broke with the earlier discursive tension to recast 1945 along exclusively pan-Soviet lines. Indeed, authorities conceived of the aforementioned measures on the war's immortalization as contributing to the development of postrevolutionary history more generally, as part of a "return to the Soviet present," rendering such primordial allusions all but obsolete.[9]

But the Khrushchev-era program to create a distinctly Soviet historical mythology was contested and had a number of unintended consequences.[10]

[7] The authors of the Secret Speech had included within the finished text an appeal to promote the war narrative "above all" for its "political, educational, and practical significance." See Aimermakher, *Doklad N. S. Khrushcheva*, 84.

[8] RGANI 4/16/39/97–115; 4/16/226/101–110; Tomilina, *Pamiatnik pobedy*, 58–59, 63–81.

[9] On the turn toward the Soviet present, see, for example, Donovan, "How Well Do You Know Your Krai," 465–467.

[10] David Brandenberger has recently emphasized the almost immediate stifling of Russocentrism after Stalin's death, pointing, for example, to early programmatic statements in party journals over the course of 1953–4 by the likes of P. N. Fedoseev that "obscured the assertion of Russocentrism . . . in order to emphasize the renewed meaning of the 'brotherhood of peoples' both at home, in the USSR, and throughout the world." He adds that "the new definition also significantly reduced the number of references to prerevolutionary cultural and political history, which were increasingly rooted in

The Twentieth Congress line quickly gave way to a more ambiguous official stance on Stalin's war record, complicating early efforts to develop a post-Stalin history of the war. Meanwhile, the project to eradicate Stalin's cult prompted a critical engagement with the Russian historical motifs that had been a staple of Stalinist patriotic culture. As Khrushchev picked up his assault on the personality cult in 1961, there emerged what this chapter identifies as a "crisis of patriotic identity," which centered on renewed friction between the pan-Soviet/internationalist and Russocentric paradigms. The more overt push to instill a pan-Soviet sense of allegiance raised concerns, particularly among Russophile intellectuals, about the preservation of unique ethnic identities, histories, and hierarchy. Ideologists attempted to forestall this crisis in part through the "doctrine of the Soviet people," a revival of the Stalinist formula of discursive tension in the sense that it created separate discursive spheres for the articulation of contrasting hierarchical and lateral patriotic ideals. Yet rather than maintain this tension within the victory myth itself, as Stalinist authorities had done, the doctrine utilized the war theme as a pan-Soviet mobilizing ideal, while cordoning off Russocentrism within prerevolutionary and early Soviet narratives. The war victory was not the only mythology the Soviet leadership sought to harness for this purpose; it would, however, prove the most durable.[11]

The Pan-Soviet Ascendancy

Shortly after Stalin's death, Anna Pankratova began reworking her account of the Russian people's thousand-year struggle for freedom and independence, *The Great Russian People*, for an anticipated third edition. According to Boris Belenkin's analysis of the unfinished manuscript, not only did Pankratova minimize references to Stalin and remove many of his direct quotes, but she made subtle changes indicating a more equitable partnership between Russians and non-Russians. While her previous edition credited the Russian people with the establishment of the USSR and Soviet system, the revision attributed to Russians merely the creation of the RSFSR, an institution that "served as a model of state construction" for other republics. The

the Soviet experience to illustrate patriotic archetypes." See Brandenberger, "Ideologicheskie istoki sovetskogo patriotizma," esp. 28–30. This is all true, of course. But where Brandenberger has highlighted the swiftness with which the shift occurred in major party journals, this chapter demonstrates the complexities involved in implementing the new line, particularly once destalinization commenced. I am grateful to the author for sharing the unpublished manuscript with me.

11 One additional source of legitimacy pursued by the regime in the wake of destalinization was in the realm of science, particularly successes in the space race. See, for example, Jenks, *The Cosmonaut Who Couldn't Stop Smiling*; Froggatt, "Science in Propaganda and Popular Culture," esp. 2–24.

new text's treatment of the war likewise shifted attention away from Stalin and toward the Soviet people as a whole. The final words attributed to the hero-martyr Zoia Kosmodem'ianskaia before her execution, for example, changed from "Fight! Do not be afraid! Stalin is with us!" to "It is happiness to die for your people! Fight! Do not be afraid!" And yet, Pankratova seemed content to accord the Russian people a dominant role in victory. The title of the chapter on the war remained, as it had been in the earlier version, unambiguous: "The Russian People at the Head of the Fighting Alliance of Peoples of the USSR during the Great Patriotic War."[12]

The manuscript was never completed. It was soon apparent to Pankratova that the text "was hopelessly out of date and could not be corrected, it was dead." Notably, Belenkin writes, this was not merely about eradicating the public veneration of Stalin, but stemmed from "the new ideological line's clear prohibition against the use of the phrase 'great Russian people.'"[13] Her opus shelved, Pankratova helped launch a more general historiographical departure from Stalinist Russocentric themes via her capacity as editor-in-chief of the journal *Voprosy istorii*. Within a year of Stalin's death, Pankratova and many of those under her aegis were treating the very notion of a Russian through line linking Soviet with pre-Soviet achievements as a vestige of an altogether different era.[14]

The pivot toward an exclusively pan-Soviet model of patriotism rooted in "post-October themes," to quote a leading ideologue and party secretary Dmitrii Shepilov, began in the months after Stalin's death.[15] It was

[12] Belenkin, "Ispravlennomu ne verit'," 122–126. The manuscript is by all accounts housed in the archive of the Moscow-based human rights organization Memorial. However, the author was not allowed access to it and several staff members were unable to locate it. I am indebted to David Brandenberger for pointing out its existence.

[13] Belenkin, "Ispravlennomu ne verit'," 127–128.

[14] See "O nekotorykh vazhneishikh zadachakh," 3–11; "Istoricheskaia nauka v SSSR," 193–213, qt. 209; Belenkin, "Ispravlennomu ne verit'," 127–128; Makhnyrev, "Izmenenie roli mesta istoricheskikh iubileev," 133–153; Donovan, "How Well Do You Know Your Krai," 466. This shift can be observed in revisions to Stalinist historical biographies. Compare Pashuto, *Aleksandr Nevskii*, 129–130, with his expanded version, finished in 1955. The latter excised the previous edition's claim that victory in 1945 represented a conclusive end to the "age-old struggle" between Slavs and Germans: Pashuto, *Geroicheskaia bor'ba russkogo naroda*, 259. On similar trends concerning official views of Ivan Groznyi, see Perrie, *The Cult of Ivan the Terrible*, 179–186. On more general historiographical trends, see Sidorova, *Ottepel' v istoricheskoi nauke*. For the new line on the war, see "O razrabotke istorii Velikoi Otechestvennoi voiny," 3–8. On historical revisionism in the aftermath of the Secret Speech, see Markwick, *Rewriting History*; Jones, *Myth, Memory, Trauma*, chap. 2; Gallagher, *The Soviet History of World War II*, 133–175. On Pankratova during this period, see Kan, "Anna Pankratova i 'Voprosy istorii,'" 85–100; Zelnik, *Perils of Pankratova*, 52–66.

[15] These early programmatic statements are discussed in Brandenberger, "Ideologicheskie istoki sovetskogo patriotizma," 28–29. The new "Soviet" orientation undergirded a simultaneous campaign to promote local patriotic identities and *kraevedenie* – the study and celebration of one's territory [*krai*], be it city, region, or republic. Although kraevedenie

one of the major projects to emerge from the landmark Twentieth Party Congress three years later. As outlined by Shepilov, in light of the Congress, historical research must now emphasize "new and contemporary history," the "historical experience of building socialism," the "history of the October socialist revolution, the history of the Civil and ... Great Patriotic wars."[16] Of course, the new pan-Soviet orientation was hardly a complete rupture with the Stalinist past – although this was how Khrushchev depicted it. Rather, the Congress saw the privileging of one variant of Stalinist patriotism over another, albeit with Stalin's personal role largely excised. In place of the bloated mobilizational paradigms and ideological tensions of the previous years, the post-Stalinist leadership initially heralded a single, dominant line that was both more idealistic and internationalist in character. The new patriotism's Stalinist trappings were evident enough that Khrushchev anticipated the bristling of his colleagues in his opening Congress report: those "individual comrades who believe that love for their homeland is allegedly contrary to ... socialist internationalism." In response, the Party's first secretary traced the concept's origins to Lenin and his oft-cited declaration, made during the opening months of the First World War, which distinguished between pride in progressive national tendencies (revolutionary movements, worker solidarity, etc.) and oppressive economic and political systems. Far from a Stalinist innovation, Khrushchev alleged, the reassertion of the principle of Soviet patriotism was fully in line with the "return to Leninism" ostensibly launched by the Congress.[17]

encouraged investigations into local history that often included the prerevolutionary era, its aims nevertheless supported the new Soviet emphasis. It was a means of channeling local histories and identities into the larger Soviet historical teleology. See, for example, Johnson, "Jubilation Deferred," 94–95. The 300th anniversary of the "reunification of Ukraine and Russian," which took place in 1954, is noteworthy in this regard. Yekelchyk describes this event as the "last Stalinist festival," by which he means that it promoted a Russocentric historical narrative. However, there was a movement among local party officials not to be "overly historical" with the celebrations, and instead stress the anniversary's contemporary relevance and postrevolutionary significance. See Dobczansky, "Rehabilitating a Mythology," 370–371; Yekelchyk, *Stalin's Empire of Memory*, 154–159. Of course, the way this Soviet focus was popularly understood was far more complex. See Kirschenbaum, *The Legacy of the Siege*, 161–179. The Kraevedenie campaign intensified in the 1960s. See Donovan, "How Well Do You Know Your Krai," 464–483. During the late 1950s, some of the luminaries of the later village prose movement, like Fedor Abramov, produced war stories that focused on the themes of the Russian peasantry and village life. As with the later movement, these stories were fully compatible with the war's pan-Soviet orientation. This is discussed in Chapter 6. For an excellent treatment of Abramov during these years, see Pinsky, "The Individual after Stalin," 89–98, 109–111.

16 Aimermakher, *Doklad N. S. Khrushcheva*, 331.

17 *XX s"ezd kommunisticheskoi partii*, 1:87, 90–91, 98, 101–102, 113–114. On the "return to Leninism" and its fate, see Hornsby, *Protest, Reform and Repression*, 23–53, 211, 263.

The nature and prominence of the war as a distinct theme within this broader turn to the socialist present has been the subject of some debate. Many scholars have stressed the air of hesitation and uncertainty that characterized the war's official representation. Nina Tumarkin, in particular, describes a post-Stalin myth of the war "in its formative stage," with certain storylines solidified, such as the steadfastness and unity of the Soviet people, and others, notably Stalin's role, "in flux." Meanwhile, Tumarkin points out, Victory Day retained its "working" status and domestic commemorations remained relatively sparse and understated.[18] All the while, the Thaw complicated official attempts to promote the war as an unambiguously heroic myth. Unlike Stalin-era depictions or later, neo-Stalinist productions of the 1970s, writers and poets working in the war genre during the Thaw offered unprecedented glimpses of frontline panic and defeatism, of incompetent officers, commissars, and "bureaucrats" who consistently threatened to derail the path to victory. The most prominent writers and editors publishing in this vein – Simonov, Ehrenburg, Tvardovskii – drew upon firsthand experience at the front to give authentic portrayals of the human toll required to achieve victory.[19] Likewise, filmmakers brought to the screen morally ambiguous tales of imperfect soldiers and citizens struggling to come to terms with the devastation of war, the most famous of which garnered attention in the West. These included Mikhail Kalatozov (*The Cranes are Flying* [1957]), Sergei Bondarchuk (*Fate of a Man* [1959]), Grigorii Chukhrai (*Ballad of a Soldier* [1959]), and Andrei Tarkovskii (*Ivan's Childhood* [1962]).[20]

Vasily Grossman's suppressed magnum opus, *Life and Fate*, set against the backdrop of the Battle of Stalingrad, deserves special mention. Written throughout the 1950s and submitted for publication in 1960, Suslov famously proclaimed the novel unpublishable "for another two to three hundred years." *Life and Fate* not only drew parallels between Stalinism and Nazism, but pointed to conflict between pan-Soviet/internationalist and Russocentric wartime

18 Tumarkin, *The Living & the Dead*, esp. 110.

19 See, for example, Simonov, "Panteleev," in Simonov, *Stikhotvoreniia i poemy*, 309–354, and his subsequent *Zhivye i mertvye* (*The Living & Dead*), in Simonov, *Sobranie sochinenii*, vol. 4 (all); Bylinov, "Rota ukhodit s pesnei"; Slutskii, "Posledneiiu ustalost'iu ustav," in *Sobranie sochinenii*, 1:93. On the matter of historical realism and an analysis of readers' responses, see Jones, *Myth, Memory, Trauma*, esp. 187–198.

20 Youngblood, *Russian War Films*, 107–141; Woll, *Real Images*. See also Khaniutin, *Preduprezhdenie proshlogo*, 215–283.

paradigms, as well as the state's elevation of the latter over the former. The novel captures a palpable sense among Russians that they had borne the brunt of Bolshevik rule and had suffered disproportionately at the hands of the friendship of the peoples. Before departing for the front, for instance, the military commanders Nyeudobnov and Novikov, together with the political commissar Getmanov, express a clear preference for ethnic Russian officers: "Couldn't we do without the Kalmyk?" Getmanov muses, as the men discuss the appointment of a new chief of staff. "That's how we all feel," Nyeudobnov adds. "But then Marxism's taught us to look at things differently." This launches Getmanov into tirade against the state's mistreatment of the Russian people. "We are, after all, defending Russia," Getmanov retorts sharply. "In the name of the friendship of nations we keep sacrificing the Russians ... The great Russian people's becoming a national minority itself. I'm all for the friendship of nations, but not on these terms. I'm sick of it!"[21]

Such a tension is likewise observed in the character of the true-believing commissar Nikolay Krymov. Assigned to oversee the unit defending house 6/1, Krymov notably expresses unease over the state's blatant embrace of prerevolutionary patriotic motifs. "Krymov was feeling confused," Grossman writes.

> He felt uncomfortable when political instructors praised Russian generals of past centuries. The way these generals were constantly mentioned in articles in *Red Star* grated on his revolutionary spirit. He couldn't see the point of introducing the Suvorov medal, the Kutuzov medal and the Bogdan Khmelnitsky medal. The Revolution was the Revolution; the only banner its army needed was the Red Flag.

Gradually, Krymov finds himself reconciling his revolutionary spirit to the nationalism on display: "Yes, yes! This war, and the patriotic spirit it aroused, was indeed a war for the Revolution. It had been no betrayal of the Revolution to speak of Suvorov in house 6/1." Ultimately, the novel proposes that among the war's most enduring legacies was the displacement of internationalist idealism by an overt sense of Russian national exceptionalism, ideas hardly consonant with the prevailing, post-Stalinist conception of victory. The novel remained unpublished in the Soviet Union until 1988.[22]

[21] Grossman, *Life and Fate*, 221.

[22] Grossman, 134, 426, 516. On the novel's own life and fate, see Popoff, *Vasily Grossman*, esp. 213–254; Finney, "Vasily Grossman," 312–328; Garrard and Garrard, *The Life and Fate of Vasily Grossman*, esp. chap.7; Ellis, *Vasiliy Grossman*.

But where a number of historians have stressed the tentative nature of official war memory during this period, others propose a more linear trajectory. Imbued with eschatological significance, the war's public manifestations, Amir Weiner argues, "seemed only to intensify as the Soviet Union moved away from both the October Revolution and the war itself."[23] More recent scholarship has considered regional and societal variation to explore the ways both tendencies operated at once. Neither silenced nor wholly embraced during the 1950s and early 1960s, the intensity of the war's commemoration depended on the particular community involved. Within the military, the Komsomol, among veterans and certain localities, there was a relatively rich commemorative discourse that long predated the more centralized and grandiose war cult of the Brezhnev years.[24]

In part, these contradictions can be explained by the Khrushchev-era subordination of the victory myth to the postrevolutionary usable past more generally. Officially, of course, late-socialist commemorations always presented the Great Patriotic War as ancillary to the Revolution. Under Brezhnev, however, this unequal relationship was less pronounced and significant, particularly after the fiftieth anniversary of the Revolution in 1967.[25] But the years after the Twentieth Congress witnessed an unmistakable preference for yoking 1945 to the larger Soviet metanarrative. This is not to say that commemorations avoided the theme of the war. Plans for the 1957 anniversary of the Bolshevik Revolution, for instance, called for singling out the Soviet Union as the "only force in the world capable of halting the invasion of the fascist hordes." And yet, the leadership was determined not to overly militarize the celebrations or turn them into a façade for propagandizing the 1945 victory. The plans even specified that the war theme should point to the possibility of "cooperation between states of differing socioeconomic systems." Thus, in the name of "peaceful coexistence," the Presidium rejected a proposal to hold a military parade on Red Square during the anniversary that was evocative of the parade that took place on November 7, 1941.[26]

23 Weiner, *Making Sense of War*, 380.

24 See, for example, Gabowitsch, "Victory Day before Brezhnev"; Garner, "The Myth of Stalingrad"; Davis, *Myth Making*; Gabowitsch, "Russia's Arlington," 93–94, esp. note 5; Amar, *The Paradox of Ukrainian Lviv*, 261–317; Palmer, "How Memory Was Made," 373–407; Edele, *Soviet Veterans*, 7–8, and passim; Kirschenbaum, *The Legacy of the Siege*, esp. 113–185.

25 Gajos, "Fading Red October," 107–125.

26 Unlike the 1941 parade, the 1957 proposal called to include soldiers from the various countries of the socialist bloc. Makhnyrev, "Rol' i mesto istoricheskikh iubileev," 140–143, 151–153; Fursenko, *Prezidium TsK KPSS*, 1:229.

Likewise, among those segments of society with an established pattern of commemorating victory, the new line shored up the war's pan-Soviet bent. Revised patriotic educational programs developed by mass youth organizations broke sharply with Stalin-era traditions, which had sometimes foregrounded the study of "[p]rominent Russian military leaders, Aleksandr Nevskii, Dmitrii Donskoi, Aleksandr Suvorov, Mikhail Kutuzov," and other protectors of "Russian soil," to quote one 1951 program.[27] Although the emphasis on Russian historical themes largely disappeared from Komsomol, Pioneer, and DOSAAF agendas by 1955, it was only with the Twentieth Congress that the leaderships of these organizations shifted to the near-exclusive promotion of themes "associated with the struggle for Soviet power."[28]

Initial activities proposed in the aftermath of the Congress were relatively modest, including visits to grave sites and the establishment of grave markers dedicated to "fighters of the Revolution" and others "who died courageously during the October uprising, [and] during the years of the Civil and Great Patriotic wars."[29] No less important was the "labor glory" of workers. As the Leningrad organization of the Komsomol reported, "Labor veterans tell young people about the plight of workers in tsarist Russia, about the glorious traditions of the factory, [they] instill a sense of love for their factory, paying particular attention to the heroics of the present day."[30] By the early 1960s, pilgrimages to what the Komsomol formally labeled "places of the revolutionary, military, and labor glory of the Soviet people" had become a mainstay of youth military-patriotic education. The scale of these activities had grown so vast that by 1965 the Komsomol Central Committee established a Central Staff to direct the newly introduced All-Union Tourist Campaign of the Youth to Places of the Revolutionary, Military, and Labor Glory of the Soviet People. In a little over its first year, the campaign had, according to an internal report, founded over twenty-seven thousand museum exhibits and nearly six thousand monuments, obelisks and commemorative plaques.[31]

[27] RGASPI M-1/47/329/18, 37–38. The reference to "Russian soil" is from *Ikh vospital komsomol*, 22, 26, 30, 69. As noted, such historical Russocentrism remained highly compartmentalized during the postwar period (e.g., Shtorm, *Flotovodets Ushakov*).

[28] RGASPI M-1/47/394/25–26; RGASPI M-1/47/415/13–25; RGASPI M-1/47/416/32–58. See also the letter by the Komsomol first secretary to the Party Central Committee, under RGANI 5/33/4/42–44, cited in Hornsby, "Soviet Youth on the March," 421–422. This letter, however, was not a significant inflection point, since it aped earlier elaborations in the realm of patriotic education. See Aimermakher, *Doklad N. S. Khrushcheva*, 325–342.

[29] RGASPI M-1/47/416/36. [30] RGASPI M-1/47/496/1–11, qt. 3.

[31] RGASPI M-1/38/38/1–2. For a detailed overview of the campaigns, see Hornsby, "Soviet Youth on the March," 418–445.

As in other spheres of patriotic mobilization at this time, Komsomol activities downplayed notions of Russian leadership in favor of a broadly inclusive vision of the Soviet community. Starting in 1957, the Komsomol organized increasingly elaborate relay events, during which small teams followed carefully planned routes using various modes of transport (motorcycle, horse, skis, etc.). Along the way, the groups visited memorial sites and met with veterans and others who regaled the participants with accounts of their involvement in the construction and defense of socialism.[32] One of the initial relays, which established a quite typical pattern, traced the path of the advancing 62nd Army (8th Guards Army) as it moved westward following the victory at Stalingrad. The route was selected in large part because the 62nd reflected the Soviet people as a whole. In the words of the proposal: "Here were workers from Moscow and Leningrad factories, kolkhozniki from Siberia and metallurgists ... from the Urals, cotton growers from Uzbekistan and miners from Donbass, Gorkii mechanical engineers and Kazakh herdsmen, Viatskie loggers and Taiga hunters, Volga oarsmen and Ivanova textile workers." Likewise, it was under the command of the 62nd at Stalingrad that the famed defense of the Pavlov House took place. Much like the mythical feat of the twenty-eight Panfilovtsy, the proposal recalled how the struggle to hold the Pavlov House "itself personified the great family of peoples of the Soviet Union, their eternal [and] indestructible friendship, unity." It then went on to detail the Russian, Ukrainian, Georgian, Tatar, Tajik, Jewish, Uzbek, Kazakh, and Abkhaz makeup of the garrison's soldiers.[33] In the spirit of Soviet internationalism, the automobiles and motorcycles involved in these events were "colorfully adorned with the various flags of the union republics."[34]

But these events rarely centered on the war alone; rather, they underscored larger Soviet-era themes. Even the relay tracing the 62nd Army's advance was more an exploration of Soviet achievements in general than the war per se. As the proposal described:

> [A]long the route of the relay, Komsomol organizations will conduct meetings between youths and participants in the Civil and Great Patriotic wars ... [T]hey organize lectures, reports, talks for the youth about the Soviet people's struggle to build socialism in our country and protect the Soviet state from internal and external enemies. [Youth organizations] widely propagandize the successes achieved by the Soviet people, under the leadership of the [CPSU], in raising the country's national economy and improving the welfare of working people. ... Komsomol organizations must work on the improvement of fraternal and

[32] RGASPI M-1/47/416/39–48. [33] RGASPI M-1/47/416/49–72, qt. 52, 56.
[34] RGASPI M-1/47/496/28.

individual graves of Soviet soldiers and partisans killed in the fight with the enemies of the Soviet state.[35]

These activities certainly reflected an increasing militarization of society; yet it was a militarism of the *socialist* homeland, absent any nod to "great" personalities and military victories of the Russian past. Where prerevolutionary military sites, such as Borodino or Kulikovo, appear in military-patriotic youth activities outside of specific anniversary dates, it is primarily in the context of the creation of monument registries or "inspections of the conditions and content" of historical structures.[36] A few reports describe these sites almost in terms of ancient archaeological ruins, as essentially irrelevant to Soviet political identity.[37] That is, they were accorded reverence as relics of cultural heritage to be studied and cherished, but stood apart from the dominant foundation mythology of state. Notably, and in line with earlier trends, exceptions to this pan-Soviet orientation before the late 1970s occurred predominantly outside the RSFSR.[38]

But the war's rather amorphous presence in the Soviet commemorative culture of the late 1950s was also linked to the vagaries of the Twentieth Congress line itself. The final draft of the Secret Speech focused heavily on 1941–5, having expanded the scope of Stalin's wartime crimes to include the deportations of suspect ethnic minorities. This violation of the Leninist principle of multiethnic friendship was all the more egregious, the report noted, because many ethnic groups – Kalmyks, Chechens, and Bashkirs, for example – had been uprooted during the second half of the war, after the tide had turned decisively in the Soviets' favor and hence served no strategic purpose.[39] The draft also made explicit the connection between the early defeats and the purges, ridiculed Stalin's claimed strategic innovation of "active defense," and further refined the sources of the war victory. In Khrushchev's words: "Not Stalin, but the Party as a whole, the Soviet government, our heroic army, its talented generals and valiant warriors, the whole Soviet people – that's who ensured victory in the Great Patriotic War."[40]

[35] RGASPI M-1/47/416/67. [36] RGASPI M-1/32/1193/38–49, 50–53.

[37] RGASPI M-1/32/1193/51. See, for example, references to the monument to Dmitrii Donskoi and other "ruined monuments" associated with Kulikovo Field.

[38] One Komsomol chapter in the southwestern Ukrainian city of Izmail, for example, published an open letter stating that it was the duty of the city's youth "to provide the will and strength to make our city the pride of Russian arms." RGASPI M-1/32/1196/13–14. For a similar case in the Belarusian city of Minsk, see RGASPI M-1/47/496/12, 14.

[39] Aimermakher, *Doklad N. S. Khrushcheva*, 93–94. [40] Aimermakher, 87.

Not coincidentally, once the Party began disseminating the contents of the Secret Speech, popular responses homed in on Stalin's role in the war. But while many commentators saw in Stalin's wartime behavior the cult of personality at its most destructive,[41] many others considered Stalin's war leadership to be beyond reproach. Even among respondents who accepted the report's general thrust, Stalin's role in the defeat of Germany was frequently cited as an unimpeachable, even redeeming, virtue.[42] Summary reports also indicate widespread confusion, even outrage, over the Central Committee's evident inability to halt Stalin's "incorrect actions" during the war, suggesting how easily criticism of Stalin's wartime failures could spiral into condemnation of the leadership as a whole.[43] Well before the upheavals in Poland and Hungary, such barometers were giving the leadership pause. To preserve the war myth as a source of party authority, some argued, a degree of moderation over Stalin's image was necessary, especially his role in the war.[44]

That moderation came in the form of a CC resolution in June 1956, the most prominent of several official correctives advocating a more "balanced" understanding of Stalin. Although the June Resolution's ambivalence satisfied neither Stalin's defenders nor his greatest critics, its particular vagueness on the issue of the war effectively left that sensitive aspect of the Stalinist past open to interpretation.[45] And in any case, the resolution assured, Stalin's ability to affect the course of the war, for better or worse, was beside the point. There had always been a "Leninist core of leaders" ready to intervene at such critical junctures. This message was played up in the process of editing the resolution for publication. According to editorial additions, "it was precisely during the war" that members of the Central Committee and military most forcefully asserted themselves "over certain areas of activity" in order to forestall the effects of the personality cult.[46] Such reticence with regard to the specific nature of Stalin's wartime leadership remained essentially unchanged until 1961, when Khrushchev relaunched his campaign against the personality cult. But merely highlighting the Party's management of the war effort while remaining more or less agnostic on Stalin as war leader created its

41 See, for example, comments by Parkhomenko and Luchaninov: Aimermakher, 463–464.
42 E.g., Aimermakher, 542.
43 See, for example, the summary report containing a list of questions submitted to Ukrainian party committees in April 1956: Aimermakher, 480.
44 For a detailed analysis of the responses to the Secret Speech, and the leadership's anxieties over those responses, see Jones, *Myth, Memory, Trauma*, 24–50.
45 On the Party's slow walk back from the line taken during the Secret Speech, see Jones, 50–96.
46 Artizov, *Reabilitatsiia*, 2:133–146, esp. 138–140.

own complications; not simply in terms of Stalin's faults or merits as generalissimo, but regarding his role as a conduit for Russia's primordial myth of war.

The Great Ancestors Reconsidered

Although direct references to Stalin mostly disappeared from military-patriotic commemorations, preexisting representations and historical treatments could not avoid the Stalin question.[47] Indeed, the Twentieth Congress line, refracted through the June Resolution, had the paradoxical effect of providing a degree of cover for Russocentric conceptions of the war. This might explain why, before 1961, when the Twenty-Second Congress nullified the June Resolution, the Central Committee went out of its way to physically alter Stalin-era war commemorations that played up the Russocentric myth in certain cases while ignoring others. In 1959, for example, the CC Cultural Department oversaw the removal of a nearly imperceptible inscription on the mosaic walls of the chamber within the Soldier-Liberator monument in Berlin's Treptower Park. The mosaic, created by the artist A. A. Gorpenko, was overwhelmingly internationalist in tone, portraying as it did representatives of the various Soviet nationalities paying homage to the Red Army dead. To the right of the scene, however, Gorpenko depicted a worker clutching a garland inscribed with the words "Glory to the heroes of Great Rus'." The Cultural Department deemed this offensive enough to demand the mosaic's alteration. After considering a number of "Soviet" variations, authorities ordered that the original dedication be replaced with "Glory to the Heroes of the Soviet Army," an alteration that proved technically difficult (Figure 3.1).[48]

And yet, other historical-Russocentric elements within the Treptower complex remained untouched. These included an inscription of Stalin's 1941 great ancestors speech on one of the sarcophagi and accompanying bas reliefs depicting Nevskii and Kutuzov (Figure 3.2).[49] The Komsomol'skaia metro station in Moscow is another such case where its Stalin motif likely protected the station's underlying Russocentrism

[47] From 1957, Stalin appears in a decidedly balanced light in youth-oriented texts on the need for authority and leadership in general. See Jones, *Myth, Memory, Trauma*, 101.

[48] RGASPI 5/36/111/24. To this day, the attentive observer can still make out the faint contours of the words "Great Rus'" where "Soviet Army" has been superimposed. For the original inscription, see Belopol'skii, *Pamiatnik voinam Sovetskoi Armii*, 46.

[49] On the history of the Trepower memorial, see Köpstein, *Die sowjetischen Ehrenmale in Berlin*, 83–170; Stangl, "The Soviet War Memorial," 213–236.

Figure 3.1 A. A. Gorpenko's modified mosaic with the garland ribbon inscription "Glory to the Heroes of the Soviet Army" (Sobotta/ullstein bild via Getty Images).

during the initial wave of destalinization.[50] Between the twentieth and twenty-second party congresses, in the absence of an unambiguous declaration on Stalin's part in the war, cultural authorities proceeded cautiously with regard to symbols linked directly to the personality cult. In cases where there was no direct Stalin connection, however, such as Gorpenko's mosaic, enforcing adherence to the pan-Soviet line was a more straightforward proposition.

The close link between the Stalin image and the Russocentric paradigm was particularly evident in the historical press, where historians' commitment to pan-Soviet internationalism paralleled the ebbs and flows of the destalinization process more generally.[51] By early 1956, the historiographical trend was highly critical of the continued adulation of great personalities and events from the prerevolutionary era. In January of that year, *Voprosy istorii* published the proceedings of a conference that addressed precisely this issue. The transcript's various allusions to the

[50] Bouvard, *Le Métro de Moscou*, 212–216. After 1961, P. D. Korin, the original creator of the mosaics, effaced Stalin's image and replaced the final panel depicting the Victory Parade with a mother-motherland image.

[51] On the "freezes" and "thaws" of destalinization, see Jones, *Myth, Memory, Trauma*, esp. 57–128; Markwick, "Thaws and Freezes in Soviet Historiography, 1953–64," 173–192.

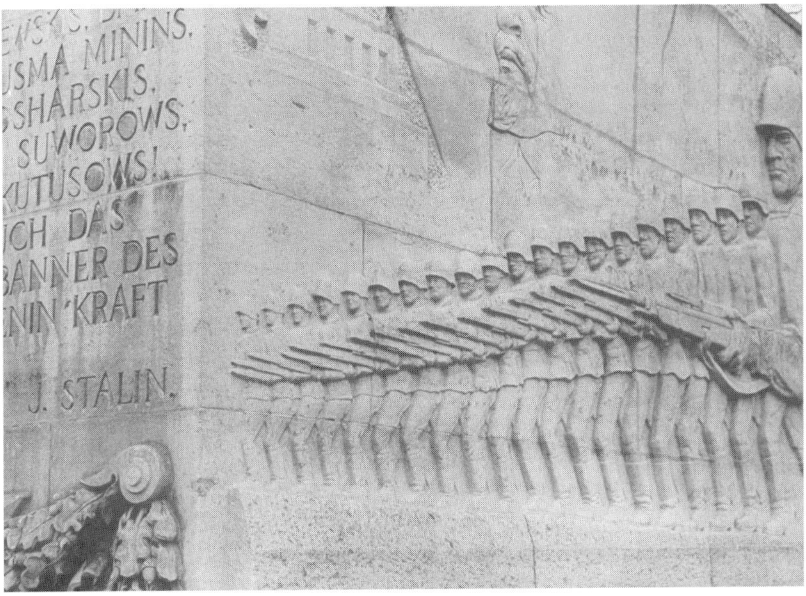

Figure 3.2 Treptower memorial sarcophagus with Stalin's "great ancestors" speech inscribed in German on the left (Robert Lackenbach/ The LIFE Images Collection via Getty Images).

problem of the "idealization of our great ancestors" was an obvious reference to Stalinist wartime appeals. The journal's summary of the conference aimed to contextualize such historical imagery, but without offending Russian national sensibilities:

Suvorov, Kutuzov, Nakhimov, and others were brilliant military leaders and naval commanders, but one should not attribute to them political views that were alien to them and to which they could by no means adhere. It is known that Suvorov commanded the soldiers who suppressed Pugachev's Rebellion. Suvorov participated in the wars of the Second Coalition against France. This coalition was of a counter-revolutionary nature.[52]

The journal went on to clarify that any reverence accorded these past military leaders derived from their objective talent and progressive traits, and had nothing to do with their Russian heritage. After all, the summary observed, the Soviet people also recognize the talent of the Prussian military theorist Carl von Clausewitz and certain "progressive moments

[52] "Istoricheskaia nauka v SSSR," 206, 210.

in the military history of Germany" despite the fact that a "reactionary military ideology" long dominated that country and continued to do so in the Federal Republic.[53] The published report thus equated the progressive qualities and significance of Clausewitz with those of Suvorov and the other great ancestors, parrying the idea that the latter's continued veneration was in any way due to his identity as a Russian.

As authorities began to soften the official stance on Stalin in the middle of the year, however, conservative historians mobilized in defense of certain Russocentric tropes.[54] During a conference hosted by the Institute of History that May, I. I. Simonov shot back at his reformist colleagues, arguing that the more critical approach toward heroic individuals from the Russian past represented a swing "from one extreme to another: from an anti-Marxist cult of the individual to an anarchical denial of the role of leaders."[55] As this reaction peaked in early 1957, an article in *Voprosy istorii*, which accused Pankratova and her former deputy E. N. Burdzhalov of seeking "to indiscriminately blacken the activities of I. V. Stalin," contended that the critique of Russian historical personalities had gone too far. The author alleged that Pankratova and Burdzhalov, "[h]aving correctly spoken out against 'jingoistic' [*kvasnogo* or 'beerhall'][56] patriotism," did not take seriously "the need for constant and systematic coverage of the genuine patriotic traditions of the peoples of Russia." This "one-sidedness" with regard to the Russian past in particular had "weakened the editorial staff's concern for conveying the patriotic acts of our heroic ancestors."[57] Despite Burdzhalov's dismissal from the journal in March 1957 and Pankratova's death that May, the defeat of Khrushchev's Stalinist political rivals within the leadership later that year undercut any attempt to revive the great ancestors theme and by extension the Russocentric paradigm of the previous era. But the way destalinization's "freezes" and "thaws" tracked with the revival or curtailment respectively of Russocentric imagery would help solidify the dictator's place as a defender of Russian national-patriotic culture in the neo-Stalinist imagination of later years.[58]

The ambiguous stance on Stalin's war record also impacted the production of authoritative new texts on party history and the war. The

[53] Ibid.

[54] While the specific context of Simonov's rebuttal was a paper criticizing Simonov and two of his associates for portraying Ivan Groznyi in a positive light during the war, the thrust of Simonov's response was not limited to Groznyi or other tsars, but addressed the depiction of past "heroes" more generally. Perrie, *The Cult of Ivan the Terrible*, 182–183.

[55] Kurmacheva, "Ob otsenke deiatel'nosti Ivana Groznogo," 196; Perrie, 183.

[56] On "kvasnyi patriotism" as "beerhall patriotism," see Jahn, *Patriotic Culture*, 29–30.

[57] "Za leninskuiu partiinost' v istoricheskoi nauke," 10, 16.

[58] *Politicheskii dnevnik*, 2:722.

historian Polly Jones describes a crisis within the institutions responsible for producing the first histories of the post-Twentieth Congress era, as the official stance on Stalin lurched from outright condemnation to partial defense and even qualified praise. Facing such unpredictable ideological conditions, authors and editorial teams were left to interpret the inconsistent messaging from above and work through the vagaries of party discourse to provide supposedly definitive treatments of historical matters.[59] It was this crisis that facilitated the retention of some of the more Russocentric features of the war narrative before the Twenty-Second Congress impelled a further crackdown on such trends.

A case in point is the 1959 *History of the Communist Party of the Soviet Union*, the replacement for Stalin's *Short Course*. For reasons that are not entirely clear, Boris Ponomarev, the head of the editorial commission, formally submitted the book for CC review only in late August or early September 1961, more than a year after its publication.[60] The new *History* covered events through the Twentieth Congress and therefore introduced a new chapter on the war. Ponomarev's main directive regarding the war chapter had been to counter the idea that victory rested solely with Stalin while keeping criticism of Stalin to a minimum and even allowing for limited praise of his war leadership.[61] In line with the ascendant pan-Soviet paradigm, the text jettisoned wartime Russocentric tropes and underscored multinational friendship, party leadership, and the Soviet system and ideology as the main sources of victory. However, the chapter went on to paraphrase Stalin's 1945 toast to the Russian people, noting their "leading role" in victory.[62] This was almost certainly an editorial improvisation. Shortly after Ponomarev submitted the book for retroactive approval, the CC ordered immediate revisions for a second edition to be published only a year later. A consequence of the more decisive condemnation of Stalin delivered during the Twenty-Second Party Congress, the new edition, released in 1962, not only denounced the myth of Stalin's military brilliance, but removed all references to Russian

[59] Jones, *Myth, Memory, Trauma*, 101–105.

[60] RGANI 5/30/349/1–15. Panas Fedenko, in his detailed reading of the *History*, has emphasized the exclusion of "nationalist Russian propaganda" as a highly distinctive feature of the text. Yet it is important to bear in mind that the Stalinist work it was replacing – the 1938 *Short Course* – also elided ideas of Russian primacy and primordialism, somewhat curiously given the otherwise pervasive celebration of the Russian people's history and status as first among equals. In this sense at least, there were clear elements of continuity between the Stalinist and post-Stalinist party histories. See Fedenko, *Khrushchev's New History*, 143; Brandenberger and Zelenov, *Stalin's Master Narrative*, 23; Brandenberger and Zelenov, "Stalin's Answer to the National Question," 878.

[61] RGANI 5/30/349/7.

[62] Ponomarev, *Istoriia Kommunisticheskoi partii*, 1st ed., 572–578

guidance during the war.[63] Although future editions would incorporate Russocentric themes into the coverage of the pre-1917 period, the doctrine of Russian leadership never again returned to the official party history's explication of the war victory.[64]

The lack of clarity over the issue of Russian wartime leadership was not the only signal to party authorities that a new authoritative history of the war was needed. More alarming still was a spate of histories published abroad, which continued to dredge up old tropes to explain Soviet wartime successes. In a review of recent "bourgeois" publications on the war, V. S. Rykalov, writing in *Voprosy istorii*, took aim at a number of French depictions of the Soviet-German front published between 1956 and 1962. Rykalov singled out the way authors such as Jacques Mordal and Augustin Guillaume interspersed discussions of military operations with "religious-philosophical arguments" about the traditional "Russian character" and the penchant for "Russian imperialism." The article alleged that the French writers were repeating the line of West German and British military historians who had long attributed victory to Soviet "numerical superiority," "the poor state of roads," and "climatic conditions." Emblematic of such falsifications, Rykalov asserted, was one author's particularly offensive chapter on the Battle of Moscow, which was titled, "The Counterattack of Santa Claus [*Ded Moroz*]."[65] It is little wonder, then, that initial discussions over the first official history of the war since Stalin's death prioritized the "modern" and "Soviet" condition of victory.[66]

In September 1957, the Presidium formally commissioned an authoritative history of the war that would serve as a replacement for Stalin's collection of wartime speeches, *On the Great Patriotic War*. The leadership placed Petr Pospelov at the head of the project for the multivolume history and embedded a new Department of the History of the Great Patriotic War, headed by Major-General Evgenii Boltin, within the Institute of Marxism-Leninism. Pospelov's commission published the first three volumes between May 1960 and August 1961, which together encompassed prewar developments up through the victory at Kursk.[67]

63 Ponomarev, 2nd ed., 593; Fedenko, *Khrushchev's New History*, 166–167, 171–172.
64 The book's sixth edition, for instance, emphasized the bravery and heroism of the Russian soldier in the Russo–Japanese and First World wars, as well as the sacrifices the Russian people made to help overcome the "backwardness of the national fringes." Ponomarev, 6th ed., 69, 156–160, 657.
65 Rykalov, "Istoricheskaia nauka za rubezhom," 156–158.
66 Mann, "Contested Memory," 199–200.
67 On the early development and work of the commission, see Mann, chap. 3. See also Boltin's summary of the early process: Boltin, "O khode raboty po sozdaniiu 'Istorii Velikoi Otechestvennoi voiny,' 109–113.

The commission's discussions of these volumes reveal little about official notions of the leading role of the Russian nation or Russocentric propaganda. Rather, meetings centered on periodization, the issues of Stalin and the early defeats, party leadership, and the nature of the war itself (imperialist or liberationist). As might be expected, the revamped, pan-Soviet version of the war generally won out in these meetings.[68] This included the promotion of a balanced view of Stalin, in which he – alongside German perfidy – was blamed for the early failures, while the system he established and his ultimate subordination to party constraints helped turn the tide of the disastrous summer of 1941. But the key sources of victory remained party leadership, the Soviet system, and the Soviet people's unwavering patriotism and faith in socialism.[69]

The absence of any deliberation over the role of Russian leadership can be explained by the fact that histories of the war tended to confine this topic to a concluding summary, typically labeled the "sources" or "lessons" of victory. In the case of the multivolume history, this summary was to occupy the entirety of the sixth and final volume of the series, which appeared in print only in January 1965, after Khrushchev's ouster and amid the partial rehabilitation of Stalin's image. For the three volumes released before the Twenty-Second Congress, the upshot was the sporadic reiteration of a number of Russocentric tropes as the members of the drafting commission attempted, for perhaps the first time since Stalin's death, to work through the contradictions of the competing Russocentric and pan-Soviet/internationalist variants of the war myth. The second volume, for instance, simply added "revolutionary" qualifiers to Stalin's Russocentric utterances. The volume quoted the great ancestors speech, noting the subsequent campaign to promote "the glorious pages of the history of the Russian people." However, the editors, led in this case by N. A. Fokin, affixed additional commentary, assuring that an alternative, socialist message was conveyed. In "paying tribute to the heroic past of our Motherland, [and] drawing historical parallels," cultural producers and Stalin himself

> emphasized with all their might that the enemy was now dealing with the *Soviet* people, with the new, *socialist* Russia, whose strength has increased tenfold since the Great October Revolution. The main thrust of journalism involved articles and essays ... that educated the Soviet people in the spirit of devotion to the *socialist* Fatherland, urging perseverance and fearlessness. The

68 RGASPI 71/22/13/1–40; RGASPI 71/22/14/27, 30–35, and passim; RGASPI 71/22/43/1–81; RGASPI 71/22/96/1–26.

69 For analysis of the creation and reception of the first volumes, see Mann, "Contested Memory," 150–341.

idea of defending the *Soviet* Motherland became the main theme of all [wartime] literature.[70]

Here, as elsewhere in the text, the pan-Soviet arguably takes precedence over the Russocentric. It was ultimately not Russia's venerable past that inspired victory but rather the drive to defend "the huge gains of socialism."[71] Yet by contextualizing historical-Russocentric appeals with adjoining passages emphasizing the revolutionary and supra-ethnic nature of victory, the *History* in effect presented two contending victory narratives alongside one another, which did little to resolve its ambiguities.

It was only in the context of the Twenty-Second Party Congress and introduction of the new (Third) Party Program in late 1961 that the drafting commission began to directly engage the question of wartime Russocentrism. Although the Congress is probably best known for Khrushchev's declaration that a communist society would, "in the main," be achieved by the year 1980, its most immediate consequence was the initiation of a more intense wave of destalinization.[72] This began with the late-night removal of Stalin's body from Lenin's Mausoleum and proceeded to target key remaining emblems of the personality cult, including those connected to Stalin's image as generalissimo. Most conspicuously, in November, the Supreme Soviet decreed the renaming of the city of Stalingrad to Volgograd.[73] By ending the official ambiguity over Stalin's wartime role as expressed in the June Resolution, it became possible to critique Stalin's appeals to Russian leadership and historical precedents. Indeed, following the Congress, Pospelov and Boltin cited the conditions set forth in the June Resolution as the main reason that Stalin's words and interpretations permeated the first three volumes. "Naturally," they reported, "the contents [of those volumes] could not reflect certain facts and material about the cult of personality . . . publicly announced at the Congress, but which, before then, the Soviet press could not openly cover."[74]

The first rumblings within the commission over the depiction of wartime ethnic relations grew out of a critical letter submitted by one of the commission's associates, Il'ia Starinov. A veteran of the Russian and

[70] Pospelov, *Istoriia Velikoi Otechestvennoi voiny*, 2:571–574 (emphasis added).
[71] Pospelov, 2:571–574.
[72] *XXII s"ezd kommunisticheskoi partii sovetskogo soiuza*, 1:167.
[73] It is a telling acknowledgment of the more decisive condemnation of the personality cult that residents of Stalingrad who opposed the name change tended to stress the name's evolution into a generic metonym for "heroic victory" rather than defend Stalin's war record or the city's connection to the person of Stalin. See Jones, *Myth, Memory, Trauma*, 113–118.
[74] RGANI 5/55/62/42.

Spanish civil wars, Starinov was a highly decorated partisan leader during World War II who had consulted on the initial volumes. Amid the renewed destalinization drive, however, Starinov, an ethnic Russian with ties to Ukraine, submitted a letter to the first secretary of the Ukrainian party committee in which he accused the editors not only of exaggerating the role of Stalin, but also of "political slander against the Ukrainian people." Starinov argued that photos used in the third volume, which purported to depict German soldiers leading an organized retreat of "the population of Ukraine," were highly misleading. Rather than fight the Germans, the photos purportedly showed Ukrainians "obediently carrying out the wishes of the occupiers." However, Starinov contended, the photos were in fact taken from a German propaganda film. In reality, he noted, there were no actual Germans present in the photo, only a single Russian Vlasovite. Starinov alleged that both Pospelov and Boltin had reviewed documents exposing the questionable nature of the photos but included them nonetheless. They were thereby guilty of falsifying the historical record through their insinuation that Ukrainians did not resist the German invaders.[75]

The Ideological Department found Starinov's claims credible enough that it ordered Pospelov to resolve the issue internally. Pospelov and Boltin reported back that the points raised in Starinov's letter could be chalked up to the rushed publication schedule and the ambiguous ideological conditions that predated the Twenty-Second Congress. Regarding the accusation of "slander against the Ukrainian people," the report asserted that researchers were never able to verify the photographs' provenance. The report also disputed allegations that the first volumes of the *History* cast Stalin in a positive light. In fact, the volumes criticized various aspects of Stalin's leadership, from prewar foreign policy to his responsibility for the failure of Soviet troops during particular engagements. In the main, the project heads asserted, the first three installments, together with the impending fourth volume, accomplished their most fundamental task: to "reveal the heroic feat of the Soviet people and its armed forces, who, under the leadership of the Communist Party, defeated the mighty enemy."[76]

But the increasing scrutiny in the wake of the Twenty-Second Congress prompted an internal debate over how best to address the Stalin question in the final two volumes. The solution offered during a commission conference "On the Liquidation of the Effects of the Cult of Personality in Coverage of the History of the Great Patriotic War," was to draw a greater contrast between Stalin's personal errors and the Party's

[75] RGANI 5/55/62/27–29. [76] RGANI 5/55/62/26, 40, 42–60.

collective successes. As Fokin argued, even Stalin's postwar acknowledgment of the Soviet government's "mistakes" was inaccurate since it implicated the government as a whole when in fact the mistakes were Stalin's alone. The members of the drafting commission agreed that the final volumes needed to root out the "gross errors" and "anti-Marxist" sentiment perpetuated in Stalin's speeches.[77] In practice, however, there was little agreement over which statements to remove. The fifth volume's lead editor, R. S. Roshchin, pointed to "diametrically opposed views" among the members of the drafting commission over precisely this issue.[78]

Nevertheless, Volume 5 of the *History*, which covered the war's conclusion, represented the least Russocentric installment yet published. Nearly every mention of "Russia" or "the Russian people" was in the context of foreign quotations, a rather common method of deflecting accusations of Russocentrism, while leaving it to the reader to determine whether or not this amounted to a tacit endorsement of the Russian nature of victory.[79] But the most overt Russocentric marker of the war's conclusion – Stalin's victory toast to the Russian people – remained outside the bounds of official patriotic expression. There were apparently clashes within the commission over whether or not to include the toast, although the archival record is incomplete. What is certain is that just before the commission submitted the manuscript to the printer in July 1962, one of its members made final edits by hand, striking through the entirety of Stalin's toast and substituting in its place the following, pan-Soviet alternative (Figure 3.3):

> The great victory over German imperialism is the fruit of the patriotic efforts of the peoples of the Soviet country – the sons of Russia, Ukraine, Belarus, Lithuania, Latvia and Estonia, Tajikistan, Azerbaijan, Uzbekistan, Georgia, Kazakhstan and Armenia, Kyrgyzstan, Turkmenistan and Moldova. Workers of all nations and nationalities united in fraternal union under the invincible banner of Lenin. The defeat of German imperialism was a historical inevitability, and not an accident, as those historians, philosophers and politicians now write in the West. Hitlerite Germany and its accomplices could not compete with the country of the Great October Revolution – a new type of state built on the principles of socialism.[80]

The removal of Stalin's toast was almost certainly due to its overt Russocentrism and not its reference to the Soviet government's wartime mistakes. The commission had already flagged an earlier internal summary document on the Kremlin reception, the marginalia of which

[77] RGASPI 71/22/108/27–30, 50–51. [78] RGASPI 71/22/44/7.
[79] For representative examples from just the first one hundred pages, see Pospelov, *Istoriia Velikoi Otechestvennoi voiny*, 5:13, 36–37, 56, 69, 72–73, 84, 90–91.
[80] RGASPI 71/22/765/13ob

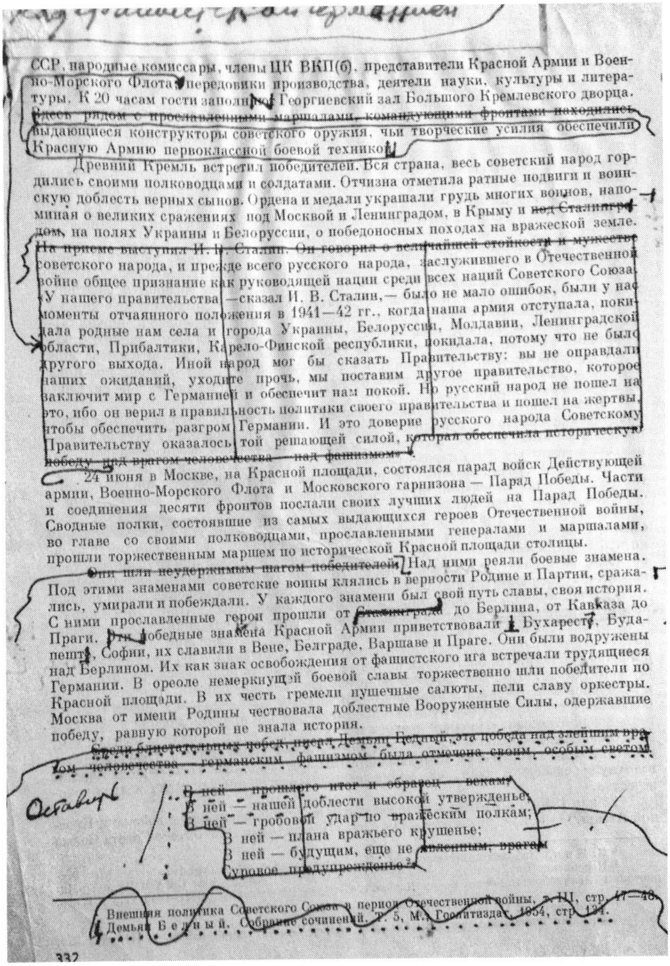
ССР, народные комиссары, члены ЦК ВКП(б), представители Красной Армии и Военно-Морского Флота, передовики производства, деятели науки, культуры и литературы. К 20 часам гости заполнили Георгиевский зал Большого Кремлевского дворца. Здесь рядом с прославленными маршалами, командующими фронтами находились выдающиеся конструкторы советского оружия, чьи творческие усилия обеспечили Красную Армию первоклассной боевой техникой.

Древний Кремль встретил победителей. Вся страна, весь советский народ гордились своими полководцами и солдатами. Отчизна отметила ратные подвиги и воинскую доблесть верных сынов. Ордена и медали украшали грудь многих воинов, напоминая о великих сражениях под Москвой и Ленинградом, в Крыму и под Сталинградом, на полях Украины и Белоруссии, о победоносных походах на вражеской земле. На приеме выступил И. В. Сталин. Он говорил о величайшей стойкости и мужестве советского народа, и прежде всего русского народа, заслужившего в Отечественной войне общее признание как руководящей нации среди всех наций Советского Союза. «У нашего правительства, — сказал И. В. Сталин, — было не мало ошибок, были у нас моменты отчаянного положения в 1941—42 гг., когда наша армия отступала, покидала родные нам села и города Украины, Белоруссии, Молдавии, Ленинградской области, Прибалтики, Карело-Финской республики, покидала, потому что не было другого выхода. Иной народ мог бы сказать Правительству: вы не оправдали наших ожиданий, уходите прочь, мы поставим другое правительство, которое заключит мир с Германией и обеспечит нам покой. Но русский народ не пошел на это, ибо он верил в правильность политики своего правительства и пошел на жертвы, чтобы обеспечить разгром Германии. И это доверие русского народа Советскому Правительству оказалось той решающей силой, которая обеспечила историческую победу над врагом человечества — над фашизмом».

24 июня в Москве, на Красной площади, состоялся парад войск Действующей армии, Военно-Морского Флота и Московского гарнизона — Парад Победы. Части и соединения десяти фронтов послали своих лучших людей на Парад Победы. Сводные полки, состоявшие из самых выдающихся героев Отечественной войны, во главе со своими полководцами, прославленными генералами и маршалами, прошли торжественным маршем по исторической Красной площади столицы. Они шли неудержимым шагом победителей. Над ними реяли боевые знамена. Под этими знаменами советские воины клялись в верности Родине и Партии, сражались, умирали и побеждали. У каждого знамени был свой путь славы, своя история. С ними прославленные герои прошли от Сталинграда до Берлина, от Кавказа до Праги. Эти победные знамена Красной Армии приветствовали Бухарест, Будапешт, Софии, их славили в Вене, Белграде, Варшаве и Праге. Они были водружены над Берлином. Их как знак освобождения от фашистского ига встречали трудящиеся Германии. В ореоле немеркнущей боевой славы торжественно шли победители по Красной площади. В их честь гремели пушечные салюты, пели славу оркестры. Москва от имени Родины чествовала доблестные Вооруженные Силы, одержавшие победу, равную которой не знала история.

Среди блистательных побед, пишет Демьян Бедный, эта победа над злейшим врагом человечества — германским фашизмом была отмечена своим, особым светом:

В ней — [illegible] итог и образец — векам;
В ней — нашей доблести высокой утвержденье;
В ней — гробовой удар по вражеским полкам;
В ней — плана вражьего крушенье;
В ней — будущим, еще не [illegible] врагам
Суровое предупрежденье.[2]

[1] Внешняя политика Советского Союза в период Отечественной войны, т. III, стр. 47—48.
[2] Демьян Бедный. Собрание сочинений, т. 5, М., Гослитиздат, 1954, стр. 134.

332

Figure 3.3a Draft from Volume 5 of the official history of the war with Stalin's toast removed and its replacement inserted (RGASPI 71/22/765/13ob.).

indicates that the problem lay directly with the reference to the leading role of Russians.[81]

[81] It is doubtful that the exclusion of Stalin's toast and its replacement with a pan-Soviet alternative came from the volume's lead editor, Roshchin, who was sympathetic to the Russocentric variant of the war narrative. More likely, this occurred under Boltin's initiative as he sought to fulfill the hardline shift in destalinization policy commenced

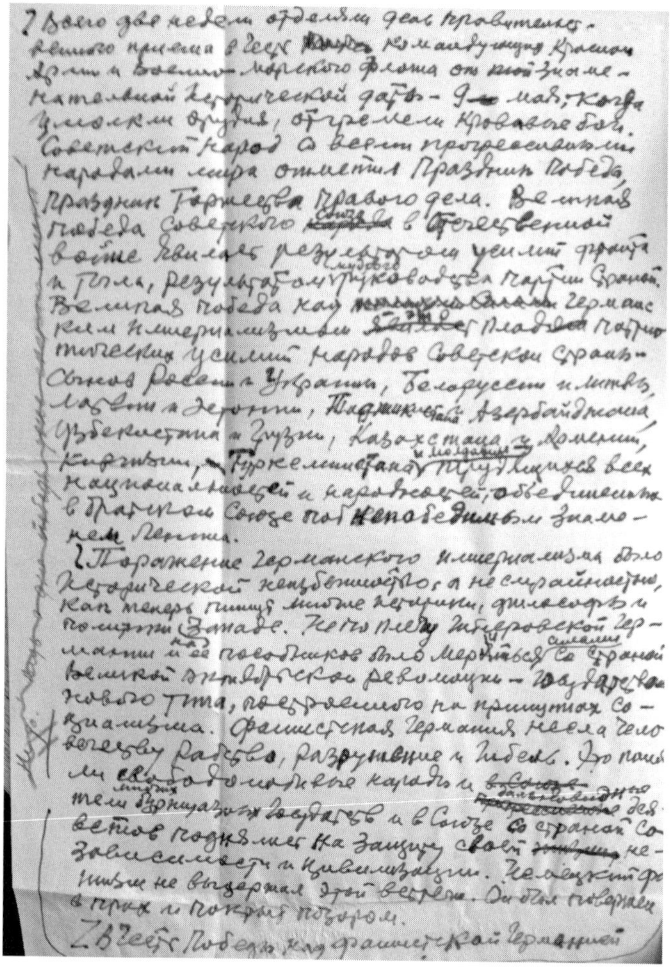

Figure 3.3b Draft from Volume 5 of the official history of the war with Stalin's toast removed and its replacement inserted (RGASPI 71/22/765/13ob.).

Until late 1962, the drafting commission did not openly cite Russocentrism per se as a function of Stalin's cult; more typical were vague references to "anti-Marxist" statements connected to the mobilization of the Soviet people.[82] However, in the immediate aftermath of the

by the Twenty-Second Congress. See the flagged wording next to a large exclamation point under RGASPI 71/22/723/6–7.

[82] For examples, see RGASPI 71/22/108/1–156 (all).

controversy surrounding Starinov's letter, and its accusation of "slander" against an ethnic minority, discussants began condemning chauvinistic depictions of wartime ethnic relations. The new tendency was on display during a meeting of December 28–29, 1962, when a researcher for the commission by the name of Prokof'ev detailed what he saw to be one of the fundamental challenges of the final volume: modulating the idea of national superiority. For Prokof'ev, the *History*'s promotion of a sense of Soviet superiority through phrases like "only our people, the hero people" posed unnecessary risks. On one hand, such sentiment seemed to deny the contributions of other countries in the anti-Hitler coalition, which could needlessly heighten Cold War tensions. But the larger point was the effect this might have within the USSR itself. Individual Soviet peoples might incorrectly equate the notion of the superiority of the Soviet Union on the international stage with a sense of the superiority of their particular nation or ethno-territorial republic. There could be little doubt as to which individual Soviet nation most concerned Prokof'ev. By way of an illustration, he pointed out a reference to "Soviet Russia" in the draft introduction of the forthcoming sixth volume: "Why 'Soviet Russia?' We must speak of the Soviet Union here. This infringes on the national feelings of Ukrainians and Belarusians" where occupation "was more difficult than in other republics." The *History*, Prokof'ev concluded, "must be careful about the national feelings of all peoples."[83]

The pendulum swing in this direction peaked in 1963 and early 1964, during late-stage preparations for the *History*'s sixth and final volume. As the definitive statement on the war's significance, the sixth volume had a unique function. In Boltin's words, "This is not a historical work in its purest form," but rather a "synthesis of results and lessons ... the final word, the conclusion to everything written in the first five volumes."[84] Given this objective, the tome represented the most ideologically significant installment of the *History*. As a full accounting of the "sources of victory" and the nature of wartime patriotism, it required that its authors attempt to resolve elements of ambiguity and contradiction for the reader.

The commission assigned M. G. Zhuravkov to address this matter in the volume's projected fourth chapter on ideology. In line with the predominant pan-Soviet paradigm, Zhuravkov and his associates looked to condemn manifestations of Russocentrism as both features of the Stalin cult and fodder for Western historians seeking to distort the nature of Soviet patriotism. As asserted in an initial draft, the challenge presented by foreign publications was the claim that "the ideology of our Party began to lose its socialist character and lean toward nationalism

[83] RGASPI 71/22/106/26–28, 47–68. [84] RGASPI 71/22/106/2.

during the Great Patriotic War." Zhuravkov's team pointed in particular to "bourgeois" representations of various Russocentric tropes: "the introduction, for example, of officer and general ranks, epaulets in the Red Army, the appeal to the courageous images of our people's great ancestors – Minin, Pozharskii, A[leksandr] Nevskii, Suvorov, Kutuzov." According to Zhuravkov, Western commentators exploited such wartime measures by suggesting that they were "an attempt to 'reinforce' socialist ideology with the revival of the 'vanished greatness' of Old Russia." Notes in the draft's margins ("Meaning Stalin!") suggest that the chapter further underscore the link between such Russocentric appeals and the Stalin cult.[85]

Along these lines, an early version of the chapter went so far as to describe the "serious damage to the understanding of the character of the Great Patriotic War caused by Stalin's appeal to the 'great ancestors.'" Although, "in [Stalin's] opinion," the intention was to "inspire the Soviet people," the drafters noted that "idealizing the activities of tsarist commanders" represented a fundamental break from properly Soviet notions of patriotism.[86] Such a critique, Zhuravkov's team clarified, was not meant to denigrate the heroic traditions of the Russian people, "which we all celebrate," but rather to bring into sharper relief the distinguishing features of Soviet patriotism: "a high communist ideology" and "loyalty to socialism as a new form of social organization." It was precisely the revolutionary character of Soviet patriotism that Western commentators had always ignored or belittled, preferring instead to advance the myth that the successes of the Red Army and Soviet people derived from the quasi-mystical "character of the Russian man." As Zhuravkov summarized:

> The denial of the qualitative originality of Soviet patriotism [and] references to the natural qualities of the Russian man as the main source of patriotic feelings are not only completely unscientific, but clearly hostile. These attempts were intended to hide from the common people of the capitalist world the truth about the genuine power of Soviet patriotism, to consciously belittle the spiritual power of socialism, to distort the essence of the question of the enormous moral and political advantages of the socialist system over the capitalist system.

The attention paid among Western observers to the "Russian" character, moreover, missed another fundamental point: "What has been stated about the Russian people fully applies to any other nation of the Soviet Union, because Soviet patriotism [and] love for a single socialist homeland is . . . integral to the spiritual image of every socialist nation."[87]

But the commission's more critical posture toward wartime Russocentrism and primordialism was internally contested. Most notably,

[85] RGASPI 71/22/820/13. [86] RGASPI 71/22/111/22. [87] RGASPI 71/22/820/.

Semen Roshchin, during one of the commission's final meetings before publication of Volume 6, criticized the seemingly anti-Russian tone of the chapter on ideology. Roshchin acknowledged that in some places "the line between prerevolutionary and Soviet patriotism[s] has been blurred" and that this needed to be remedied. However, equally problematic was the treatment of certain Russian historical themes. Roshchin singled out the draft's discussion of the great ancestors. "[T]hey put ['great ancestors'] in quotation marks," which, Roshchin complained, implied that the greatness of these figures was somehow ironic. "So, Aleksandr Nevskii, Dmitrii Donskoi, Minin and Pozharskii, Suvorov, [and] Kutuzov ... are not great ancestors? ... They will certainly need to remove these quote marks." He went on:

> Comrades, I think this is wrong. They are truly great ancestors and must be revered as great ancestors. This was especially true during the period of the Great Patriotic War ... Why do you all consider them generals of tsarism? I do not understand this. How were Aleksandr Nevskii and Dmitrii Donskoi tsarist commanders, what kind of tsarist commander was Minin, what kind of tsarist commander was Pozharskii?! This is ridiculous, it sounds wrong, how can this be?

Roshchin then pointed to several other sections in the manuscript, as well as to references and illustrations in previous volumes, which seemed to contradict the draft's skepticism toward Russia's heroic predecessors. "Bear in mind," Roshchin added, alluding to the apparent incongruities between the past and current volumes, "that the editorial staff evidently has no firm belief in the correctness of this wording ... So, the wording will need to be altered."[88]

Although Boltin reminded the meeting participants of the fundamental challenge emanating from "Western authors" who "question the superiority of Soviet [social] organization" and who seek to "prove that the victory of the Soviet Union was the result of a combination of random circumstances," Roshchin clearly swayed the members present. Boltin even conceded Roshchin's point: "As an old man, Suvorov – whom, by the way, I still consider our great ancestor [unnamed speaker interupts: "Despite the fact that he is a tsarist general?"] ... Despite the fact that he is a generalissimo, our great ancestor Suvorov said that victory is not achieved by sheer numbers." The closing statement of the meeting's chairman, P. P. Bogdanov, also supported Roshchin's argument. In seeking to correct some of the mistakes of the earlier volumes, the chairman observed, the drafters had overcorrected by lumping together every instance of Russocentrism with the Stalin cult.

[88] RGASPI 71/22/111/22–24.

The manuscript's characterization of certain key heroic personalities from the past, for example, as mere "generals of tsarism" was a symptom of this overcorrection:

> When one is angry with Stalin for some kind of error, one loses the accuracy of one's blow, and this should not be allowed. We are all indignant that great personalities are cited but folk traditions, traditions of national heroism are forgotten ... Suvorov, of course, should not be blamed for Stalin being a cultist. Because of Stalin, Suvorov was incorrectly depicted, and this has been pointed out.

With less than four months to finalize the manuscript for typesetting, the commission oversaw additional edits to address the concerns raised during the meeting.[89]

Released in early 1965, in time for the landmark twentieth anniversary of victory, the concluding volume of the *History* softened its hardline pan-Soviet orientation. The text presented the great ancestors theme as wholly distinct from Stalin and Stalinism. Rather, their "resurrection in our memory" was part of a more sweeping rediscovery among Soviet peoples "of heroic traditions" associated with past defenses of the homeland. Hence, the finished version severed what was initially conceived as a direct link between Stalin's cult and the excesses of the Russocentric paradigm. Moreover, although Stalin's toast was not revived, the published volume devoted two sentences to the doctrine of Russian leadership: one highlighted the Russian people's "leading role" in the context of the numbers of Heroes of the Soviet Union; the other referenced Nazi propaganda in the western republics, where efforts to sow discord between local populations and "the first among equals" were said to have failed. Heeding Roshchin's objections, the volume also eliminated the quotation marks that had previously accompanied the phrase "great ancestors."[90]

And yet, despite the somewhat diluted tone, the sixth volume as a whole leaned heavily toward the pan-Soviet interpretation of the war victory. It retained nearly all of Zhuravkov's commentary outlining the qualitative differences between Soviet and traditional Russian patriotisms. While citizens of the USSR will forever honor Russian heroic traditions, the published text asserted, "the Soviet people have their own traditions, which developed from the revolutionary struggle of the working class for Soviet power during the years of foreign intervention and the civil war. The basis of these traditions is devotion to the socialist

[89] RGASPI 71/22/111/127–34.
[90] Pospelov, *Istoriia Velikoi Otechestvennoi voiny*, 6:100, 153–155.

system ... and not the 'innate properties' of the Russian character."[91] The volume offered lengthy rebuttals to the arguments of "bourgeois ideologists" who contended that the Soviet victory was the result of "secondary factors and various accidents," "a fatal confluence of circumstances," "the severity of the Russian climate, weather conditions, and vast distances," or "the 'mystery' of the Russian soul."[92] It also played up the instrumental and pragmatic nature of historical-Russocentric appeals.[93] And aside from the two distinct mentions of Russian leadership noted previously, the sixth volume offered perhaps the most profuse articulation of lateral, pan-Soviet friendship bonds yet published. Where the Nazi leadership perceived the USSR as "a kind of 'ethnic conglomerate' deprived of internal unity," during the war "there emerged a higher level of fraternal cooperation" in which "each socialist republic made its valuable contribution to the rout of the enemy." According to the volume, the "friendship of Soviet peoples who built socialism" proved to be "the most important foundation ... of the popular defense of the socialist Fatherland."[94]

The official *History of the Great Patriotic War of the Soviet Union* thus reflected the tensions and contradictions long embedded within official war memory more generally. Over the course of the production of the six volumes, the editors pursued different avenues to reconcile these contradictions. These ranged from a qualified embrace of the Russocentric paradigm to a more critical stance that disavowed even the great ancestors as legitimate symbols of official patriotism. Mostly, the published *History* was the product of compromise between these two extremes. But with the Twenty-Second Congress, it was no longer possible for an official history to cast Stalin as a flawed but steadfast war leader, or to utilize his statements to perpetuate features of the Russocentric war myth. Countering the "Russian character" of wartime patriotism was all the more vital in the face of Western narratives that downplayed socialism and the Soviet system as the key factors in victory. Indeed, the balance struck between the Russocentric and pan-Soviet patriotic strands clearly relegated the former theme to a minor role in the narratives of the concluding volumes. Pospelov's formal address during the launch of the final volume was a remarkable endorsement of a purely pan-Soviet understanding of the war, one that framed Soviet patriotism as "essentially international" and a "refutation" of the idea of "higher" and "lower" peoples.[95] At the same time, the drafting commission was hardly

[91] Pospelov, 6:146–153 [92] Pospelov, 6:32, 153.
[93] For instance, the text highlights Stalin's use (and misuse) of Kutuzov in his own strategic thinking. Pospelov, 6:244.
[94] Pospelov, 6:99–101. [95] RGASPI 629/1/79/90–131.

unanimous over the question of Russian leadership or the use of certain historical patriotic tropes. The result of a contested process, the multivolume *History* articulated two distinct notions of the patriotic past – Soviet and socialist on one hand, Russocentric and primordial on the other – which did not so much synthesize as present competing victory narratives. Like the Stalinist work the multivolume *History* was replacing, readers were essentially free to pick and choose their preferred version.

Among the unused drafts for the ninth chapter of Volume 5 of the *History* was an alternative description of Stalin's toast to the Russian people. Rather than simply underscore the Russians' place as the "decisive force" in the war effort, as Stalin had done, the draft's author, T. I. Kirsanova, attempted to explain that Russians were the leading nation precisely because they refused to brandish their leading status. Stalin's toast, in this reading, recognized that Russians were the dominant force "because the patriotism of the Soviet-Russian people has nothing to do with highlighting their nation as 'chosen' [or] 'higher.'"[96] It was, somewhat paradoxically, the Russian people's ability to disappear within the larger Soviet body that garnered them deserved recognition as the leading nation. As Kirsanova and other representatives of the drafting commission reckoned with the Twenty-Second Congress line and its implications, the idea that Russians and other ethnonational communities should further subordinate their unique identities to the Soviet whole was gaining support within the ideological and political establishments.

"A New Historical Community of People"

During his speech introducing the new Party Program at the Twenty-Second Congress, Khrushchev offered a rather striking description of a Soviet imagined community bound by shared, postrevolutionary qualities:

> In the USSR, there has emerged a new historical community of people of different nationalities who share common characteristics – the Soviet people [*sovetskii narod*]. They have a common socialist Motherland – the USSR, a common economic base – the socialist economy, a common social class structure, a common worldview – Marxism-Leninism, a common purpose – the construction of communism, [and] many similarities in spiritual appearance, in psychology.[97]

Largely overshadowed in the flood of popular responses to the Congress proceedings,[98] Khrushchev's elaboration of the Soviet people as a "new

[96] RGASPI 71/22/723/1–9.
[97] RGANI 1/4/115/11; *XXII s"ezd kommunisticheskoi partii sovetskogo soiuza*, 1:153.
[98] Responses generally focused on Khrushchev's final defeat of his Presidium rivals – the "Anti-Party Group" – the removal of Stalin's body from Lenin's Mausoleum, and the

historical community" would transform the concept into a formal doctrine of state that political elites would replicate and embellish for decades.

The introduction of the "Soviet people doctrine" has long been the subject of scholarly debate.[99] Among the most significant recent interpretations is that offered by the political scientist Şener Aktürk. Aktürk contends that the increasing prevalence of "sovetskii narod discourse" between the 1960s and 1980s, alongside internal party efforts to eliminate key markers of sub-state ethnic identity, amounted to nothing less than an "all-Soviet nation-building project." The failure of this assimilationist endeavor was, in Aktürk's view, the result of multiculturalist opposition, both from within the Central Committee and from increasingly powerful elites in the union republics. Members of these factions objected to any attempt to do away with "line 5" of the internal passport, for instance, which indicated the holder's ethnic origin, on the grounds that such a measure amounted to the suppression of national cultures or, worse, their Russification. For Aktürk, however, the project's ultimate failure should not obscure the fact that "Soviet" reflected a legitimate sense of national identity, and "Soviet people" a multiethnic nation in the modern sociological sense.[100]

There can be little doubt that the doctrine represented an effort in the direction of greater assimilation. Indeed, it came on the heels of other homogenizing policies, most notably the 1958 education reforms, which retained a mandatory place for Russian language instruction in schools while rendering native language training optional. This was, in the words of one scholar, "*Soviet modernisation* through the medium of the Russian language."[101] It was with this objective in mind that the authors of the 1961 Party Program stressed that the borders between union republics were "losing their former significance."[102] Likewise, both the finished

declaration of Communism's impending arrival. See RGANI 1/4/167/4–44; RGANI 1/4/169/1–89; RGANI 1/4/170/1–44, 70–113.

99 For a sample of the vastly differing interpretations of the concept, which range from a deliberate screen for Russification to a serious attempt to construct a multiethnic "Soviet nation," see Dzyuba, *Internationalism or Russification*, 46–47, passim; Rakowska-Harmstone, "Chickens Coming Home to Roost," 519–548; Bilinsky, "The Concept of the Soviet People," 87–133; Szporluk, "The Fall of the Tsarist Empire," 82; Suny, "The Contradictions of Identity"; Aktürk, *Regimes of Ethnicity*, chap. 6; Whittington, "Making a Home for the Soviet People."

100 Indeed, the author argues that "Soviet nation" is a better approximation of the Russian *sovetskii narod*. Aktürk, *Regimes of Ethnicity*, esp. 197–228.

101 Lieven, "The Weakness of Russian Nationalism," qt. 65 (emphasis in original); Kaiser, *The Geography of Nationalism*, 26, 252, 289; Kreindler, "Soviet Language Planning," 46; Blitstein, "Stalin's Nations," 178–179.

102 *Programma Kommunisticheskoi partii*, 15, 113, 116.

Program and Khrushchev's Congress address referred to the "drawing together" or "rapprochement" [*sblizhenie*] of Soviet nations, while anticipating their "total unity."[103]

But despite the generally assimilationist vector of the first secretary's address and Party Program, both notably stopped short of invoking the Leninist concept of the "fusion" [*sliianie*] of nations, which implied the disappearance of national differences within a Soviet melting pot. They also validated institutionalized multiethnicity in places and encouraged the continued "blossoming" [*rastsvet*] of individual national cultures within the union. Additionally, both texts singled out the role of the "great Russian people" for their assistance in the realm of industrial development.[104] The simultaneous promotion of "blossoming," "drawing together," and even "fusion," was, of course, ideologically consistent – fusion being the synthetic outcome of the dialectical interaction of national "blossoming" (thesis) and international "drawing together" (antithesis).[105] But if assimilation, or "fusion," was the ultimate goal of the new doctrine, and if the USSR was now entering a higher stage of development marked by the full-scale construction of communism, why the continued emphasis on ethnonational diversity and the selective nods to Russian guidance? Was this an example of nationalist or multiculturalist pressure thwarting the designs of Khrushchev and his assimilationist supporters?

In fact, the campaign carried out under Khrushchev and, more fully, Brezhnev to promote the Soviet people as a "new historical community" was never precisely an effort to bring about assimilation in the sense of the theoretical "fusion" [*sliianie*] of peoples. True, there were perennial bids to eliminate passport ethnicity and create an all-encompassing "Soviet" category. But these efforts never rose to the level of serious policy debates. They remained the purview of mid-level academicians and ideologues, and sometimes made their way into the letters of confused citizens, desperate to make sense of official terminology about ethnonational processes in the USSR.[106] Nor is there evidence that either Khrushchev or Brezhnev personally supported such a measure.[107] And although late-socialist leaders sometimes referenced the eventual "fusion" of peoples, this remained a wholly abstract concept, unimaginable before the establishment of communism around the world. Unlike the union-wide

[103] *XXII s"ezd kommunisticheskoi partii sovetskogo soiuza*, 1:217.
[104] *Programma Kommunisticheskoi partii*, 16, 23, 112.
[105] On this process, see Rakowska-Harmstone, "Chickens Coming Home to Roost," 529.
[106] For examples between the late 1940s and 1960s, see RGASPI 599/1/19/1–24, 28–43; RGASPI 599/1/305/24–36; RGASPI 599/1/325/121–123.
[107] Andropov may have been different matter. See Aktürk, *Regimes of Ethnicity*, 219–223.

promotion of the Russian language, the removal of one's passport ethnicity was tantamount to a declaration that the fusion of nations, and hence global communism, was underway. "Even after communism is built in its foundations," Khrushchev himself warned during the Twenty-Second Congress, "it would be premature to declare any fusion of nations. As is well known, Lenin indicated that national and ethnic differences would exist long after the victory of socialism around the world."[108]

Rather than a purely assimilationist project, therefore, the Soviet people doctrine is better understood as an attempt to consolidate the pan-Soviet pole of a broader mobilizational repertoire that retained Russocentric elements – albeit not in connection with the victory myth. That is, it was a reconceptualization of discursive tension, but in a manner far more compartmentalized than under Stalin. While the Soviet people doctrine advanced a vision of a supra-ethnic "nation writ large," this was to coexist with, rather than supplant, alternative, hierarchical conceptions of the USSR and institutionalized multiethnicity.[109] This would explain the tension, apparent throughout the Program, between national "flourishing" on the one hand and "drawing together" and "total unity" on the other. During his introduction of the Program, Khrushchev himself alternated between familial and friendship metaphors, between national distinctiveness and social uniformity. Indeed, this tension appears in the very paragraph in which Khrushchev introduced the concept of the "new historical community":

> The Soviet system ... allowed the flourishing of all previously oppressed and disenfranchised peoples, who existed at different levels of historical development, from the patriarchal tribal system to the capitalist [system]. Previously backward peoples, with the help of those better developed, above all the great Russian people, traversed the capitalist path and rose to an advanced level. In the USSR, there has emerged a new historical community of people ...

But if Khrushchev celebrated ethnic diversity and particularism, including Russian guidance, on the path to revolution and socialist development, victory in the war was the "crucible" [*surovoe ispytanie*] of a decidedly monolithic and altogether "new" entity – the Soviet people.[110]

The Soviet people doctrine as a compartmentalized form of discursive tension stemmed directly from conclusions drawn during the Party Program's development between 1958 and 1961.[111] Given the highly

[108] *Programma Kommunisticheskoi partii*, 17; *XXII s"ezd kommunisticheskoi partii sovetskogo soiuza*, 1:217.
[109] Kumar, *Visions of Empire*, xiii–xiv.
[110] E.g., *XXII s"ezd kommunisticheskoi partii sovetskogo soiuza*, 1:252.
[111] According to Alexander Titov, party and state organizations received more than 170 thousand letters over the course of the public discussion phase. See Titov, "The 1961

deliberative nature of its formation and the direct involvement of Khrushchev, Suslov, Pospelov, Ponomarev, and others, the creation of the new Party Program offers perhaps the clearest look at official conceptions of Soviet patriotic identity in the early 1960s. It suggests that the rhetorical balance struck between assimilation and national flourishing, between the Soviet Union as a "nation writ large" and as a unique form of multinational federation, was not the result of internal conflict but rather an agreed upon framework for the expression of Soviet patriotism.

Discussions among the drafting commission's various working groups involved proposals ranging from the elimination of passport ethnicity and abolition of internal republican borders, to a more clearly articulated ethnic hierarchy. Rather than clash over issues of assimilation versus multiethnicity, the team of academicians assigned to focus on these issues, subgroup 18 ("on the question of national relations"), employed discursive tension. For instance, the group negotiated a number of proposals, mainly from representatives of non-Russian nationalities, to more clearly emphasize Russian leadership, both during the war and in more general terms. Z. I. Muratov, a high-ranking Tatar in the Central Committee, proposed a fuller acknowledgment of the Russian people's status as "first among equals." He suggested an initial passage highlighting "the great Russian people as the elder brother of the great family of socialist nations," which included their leading role "during the difficult years of the Great Patriotic War of the Soviet people." The group members demurred, permitting instead a single reference to the "great Russian people" in the context of industrial development, while identifying the war as a feat of the whole Soviet people.[112] All other calls to underscore Russian leadership or ethnic primacy were rejected outright. One delegate by the name of Bekmuratov, a Turkmen official from the Chardzhui City Party Committee, proposed a greater focus on "the historical merits of the great Russian people." The working group dismissed this proposal on the grounds that such a statement was already present in the context of industrialization and did not need to be repeated. The drafters also rejected the suggestion of an Azeri delegate to change the description of Russian from the "common" language to the "leading" language of the USSR since "leading" implied inequality and "exclusivity." Similarly, the drafting commission denied Ukrainian, Latvian, and Armenian proposals

Party Programme," 8–26. The language of the various drafts and expert commentary makes clear that Khrushchev's Congress speech on the "new historical community of people" grew out of these discussions. For examples, including one in which Khrushchev elected to remove material from the Program text and insert it instead in his Congress address, see RGASPI 586/1/186/76–90; RGASPI 586/1/201/35, 39–46.

112 RGASPI 586/1/206/2, 13; *Programma Kommunisticheskoi partii*, 16.

to define Russian as the "language of state." This, the editors noted, "went against the spirit of the Program" because it denied "the complete freedom of development" of ethnolinguistic processes in the country.[113]

But the team of specialists was equally unyielding over proposals to eliminate fundamental markers of sub-state ethnic identity in favor of an overarching "Soviet" category.[114] One quite typical suggestion submitted to the drafting commission was to state in the Program that the rapprochement of peoples "will inevitably lead to the formation of a single Soviet nation [*sovetskoi natsii*]." The subgroup's blanket justification for rejecting such proposals held that, "as Lenin teaches," such a process "will occur only after the victory of communism on a global scale."[115] Even in drafts of the Program dating from as early as 1958, the subgroup insisted that anything resembling the fusion of nations, including the elimination of passport ethnicity, should be dismissed on the grounds that such a process would occur "only after the establishment of a global communist economy."[116] The subgroup likewise resisted attempts to do away with the notion of Russian elder brotherhood entirely. While the Russian leadership doctrine was clearly not acceptable in the context of the war victory, the working group deemed it appropriate to stress the Russocentric nature of revolutionary activism and Soviet modernization. The drafters even rejected a call to remove, "out of considerations of tact," the word "great" from the phrase the "great Russian people," which applied, in this instance, to the development of modern industry in the republics. The editors insisted that the reference be retained since "the whole multinational [Communist] Party quite correctly recognizes the merits of the great Russian people."[117]

Throughout the Program's various drafts, the subgroup at once upheld the principle of institutionalized multiethnicity in specific contexts while favoring supra-ethnic uniformity in others. In a number of cases, the drafters rebuffed suggestions to qualify assimilationist overtones with reminders about the continued "flourishing" of nations and national particularity on the grounds that the Program devoted specific sections to these issues. One representative from the Armenian capital of Yerevan recommended supplementing the phrase "the further drawing together of nations and the achievement of their complete unity" with the concept of "flourishing," so that the draft would read: "the further flourishing

[113] RGASPI 586/1/288/48–51.
[114] According to a report of September 1961, the month before the Congress, a total of twelve people, out of several hundred, proposed eliminating line 5 from the passport. RGASPI 586/1/304/69.
[115] RGASPI 586/1/288/50. [116] RGASPI 586/1/186/4, 26–27, 78.
[117] RGASPI 586/1/288/46.

and drawing together of nations." The subgroup countered that the "flourishing of nations is repeatedly mentioned in Section 4" of the draft and therefore need not be repeated in the passage in question, which conveyed the idea of "total unity."[118] Conversely, the experts on the national question overruled several calls to balance the emphasis on national "flourishing" with additional assimilationist language. Such was the case with a rejected appeal by residents of the city of Ijevan, Armenia, to denote that "the time was already ripe for the elimination of borders between republics and even the national republics themselves."[119]

The drafters' evident commitment to compartmentalizing ideas of flourishing and drawing together confounded many readers of the early published draft. One Latvian respondent complained that the Program did not do enough to "answer the question about what role nationality plays in our time in the development of Soviet society [and] what kinds of national interests contradict proletarian internationalism." In response, the subgroup deflected: "The Program cannot provide answers to every specific question of practice." The main point, it asserted, was "the principle: do not ignore national characteristics, but do not inflate them either."[120]

Certainly, one of the reasons Khrushchev and the creators of the Party Program did not promote a fully assimilated "Soviet nation" as the exclusive form of patriotic identity was, as Aktürk observes, resistance from republican leaders. During the public discussion phase of the Program's development, Khrushchev personally intervened to remove language on "fusion" [*sliianie*] following concerns raised by several non-Russian party authorities.[121] There were fears, for instance, particularly among members of the Ukrainian intelligentsia, that the draft's assimilationist implications would "lead to the oblivion of their [Ukrainian] language and culture."[122] One letter from the Crimean city of Feodosia warned that many non-Russians would perceive the terms "drawing together" and "total unity" in the Program "as the absorption of all nations of the USSR by the Russian nation." The author went on:

> The danger is real because many people mistakenly consider the national question to be resolved. The facts suggest that in Ukraine the Russian language supersedes the Ukrainian language. If we embark on the path of building internationalism in the USSR by assessing everything national as nationalism but everything Russian

[118] RGASPI 586/1/288/47, 60. [119] RGASPI 586/1/288/50.
[120] RGASPI 586/1/288/54.
[121] RGASPI 586/1/201/35. See also Titov, "The 1961 Party Programme," 14–15.
[122] RGASPI 586/1/204/1–17, qt. 8–9; RGASPI 586/1/305/4.

as internationalism, then we will distort the Leninist doctrine of national development and place the USSR in the position of the [Third] Rome.[123]

Otto Kuusinen, the former Chairman of the Presidium of the recently absorbed Karelo-Finnish SSR, similarly urged moderation. "We know that since erasing national differences is such a distant goal of communism," Kuusinen wrote in a letter to Khrushchev, "it is probably better not to mention this in the Program."[124]

However, these letters of concern centered not only on fears over language rights or the creeping Russification of the state; there were also arguments that the promotion of a single Soviet nation would weaken some of the state's mobilization potential. For instance, Kuusinen claimed emphatically that an overemphasis on "fusion" in the Program text would undermine the Soviet Union's image as a beacon of national liberation in the Third World. Rather than "fusion," Kuusinen believed that the concept of "rapprochement of nations" would be more appealing globally. Peoples in the Third World, Kuusinen observed, would be unlikely to fight for national independence if the end goal was merely to be absorbed by a larger national or supranational body. By stressing rapprochement, on the other hand, "our Party's Program will have more influence among those many millions in Asia, Africa, and Latin America who are at this time fighting only for their national cause."[125] A similar argument about the threat assimilation posed to the state's ability to mobilize – especially in contexts where multiethnicity and ethnic particularism were more suitable – undergirded the various proposals of non-Russian party officials who called for a greater emphasis on Russian leadership. In these cases, the concern was not the threat posed to national cultures by state Russocentrism, but rather the danger to the principle of Russian elder brotherhood posed by full-bore assimilation. Conversely, some respondents feared that a narrowing gap between Soviet and Russian identities would damage the notion of a distinct, pan-Soviet identity. In the words of one letter writer from Ukraine, this was already a major problem among foreign observers: "Abroad they constantly write 'Russian' [and] 'Russia' instead of 'Soviet' [and] 'Soviet Union.' What to do about our diplomatic missions so that instead of writing 'Russia' they write 'Soviet Union.' It is a national shame . . . Our press should not repeat 'Russian' where 'Soviet' is stated."[126] In part buoyed by such arguments, the drafting commission – and by extension the party leadership – sought a patriotic framework which balanced,

[123] The author's name was rendered illegibly. RGASPI 586/1/305/156.
[124] RGASPI 586/1/214/2–7. [125] RGASPI 586/1/214/4–5.
[126] RGASPI 586/1/305/156.

through discursive tension, the hierarchical and lateral mobilizational models, just as many Stalin-era ideologists had done.

Although official representations had long tied the war to a supra-ethnic conception of the national community, the introduction of the Soviet people doctrine in late 1961 did not immediately underscore this connection. Indeed, the war is hardly mentioned in many of the first ideological tracts to elaborate on the Soviet people theme.[127] Over time, however, ideologues began to accord the war a special significance in the development of a "monolithic" Soviet society. P. K. Suzdalev, for example, argued that the Soviet people did not suddenly emerge during the course of the war since features of this emergent community already existed during the Civil War. However, in "the era of the Great Patriotic War, the character of the Soviet people was most vividly revealed." Maksim Kim, one of the foremost theorists of the Soviet people doctrine during the 1970s, put it in similar terms: "[T]he multinational Soviet people, a new historical community of people ... emerged from these harsh military trials morally stronger and monolithic, ideologically stable and devoted to the cause of communism."[128]

Although "monolithic unity" was the preferred configuration, the new framework enabled Soviet ideologists, where appropriate, to deploy the war's memory in the service of ethnonational diversity as well. Such a model of wartime patriotism, in which distinct Soviet peoples worked together to defeat a common enemy in a spirit of domestic internationalism, informed propaganda detailing, for example, the war's impact on decolonization and Third World liberation movements.[129] The war also frequently served as a shorthand justification for Soviet nationalities policy. To cite one illustrative example, shortly before his removal from power, Khrushchev lectured a visiting Iraqi military delegation on how best to deal with that country's Kurdish question by way of an analogy with the Soviet war effort. "Your state cannot be strong unless you solve the Kurdish problem," the First Secretary pontificated.

I know that you, as military men, ... think this way: once the sabre is in hand, you can single-handedly crush [your opponents]. But this overlooks the fact that for success against an external enemy, the unity of all the state's nationalities is required. ... You need to solve this issue in order to be strong. As I said, we [in

[127] See, in particular, Rogachev and Sverdlin, "Sovetskii narod – novaia istoricheskaia obshchnost' liudei," 11–20.

[128] The comments of Suzdalev and Kim are found in *Sovetskaia kul'tura v gody Velikoi Otechestvennoi voiny*, 262, 268–269.

[129] This argument was deployed by V. P. Sherstobitov, a theorist and close collaborator of Maksim Kim. See Sherstobitov, "Sotrudnichestvo sovetskikh narodov kak factor formirovaniia i razvitiia novoi istoricheskoi obshchnosti," 39–55.

the USSR] have a large number of nationalities. But in the Great Patriotic War all nationalities fought in harmony against and defeated the common enemy. In order for you to be strong, you need to correctly resolve the national issue. It all depends on your wisdom.[130]

Whether or not such remarks derived from genuine conviction, Khrushchev clearly understood the war victory to be a publicly convincing argument in support of Soviet multinational collaboration.

Under Brezhnev, the Soviet people doctrine became fully integrated with the war theme. His report on the twentieth anniversary of Victory Day in 1965, entitled "The Great Victory of the Soviet People," epitomized this connection. Brezhnev's address alternated from the multiethnic character of the struggle, where – in a major departure from the Stalin era – he listed republican contributions in accordance with the size of their populations,[131] to an emphasis on unity over diversity, the whole over its parts:

If there was a chief hero of the Great Patriotic War, that immortal hero was the entire close-knit family of peoples of our country, welded together by the indestructible bonds of fraternity. Russians, Ukrainians, Belarusians, Uzbeks, Kazakhs, Georgians, Azeris, Lithuanians, Moldavians, Latvians, Kyrgyz, Tajiks, Armenians, Turkmen, Estonians – in sum, the sons of all the peoples of the Soviet Union rose as one person to defend their country. The Leninist nationality policy of the Party withstood the test of war. Fascism failed to drive a wedge between socialist nations. Their fraternal union proved strong and viable and was one of the main sources of victory over the fascist aggressors.[132]

As a principal vehicle for the Soviet people doctrine, the war myth of the 1960s–80s was much more than an attempt to bolster party legitimacy; it served as a forum for projecting supra-ethnic unity and managing ethnic diversity.

Although Brezhnev's Victory Day address marked a more general elevation of the war theme in Soviet life, this was hardly an abrupt shift in patriotic politics. Like the Soviet people doctrine it embodied, the origins of the war cult are to be found in Khrushchev-era efforts both to fill the patriotic void left in the wake of Stalin's desacralization and to curate what Denis Kozlov has identified as a broader "historical turn" and "search for origins" in public discourse.[133]

[130] RGANI 52/1/566/46–54, publ. in Fursenko, *Prezidium TsK KPSS*, 3:951–955. Multiple sections of his memoirs, which he dictated from retirement and permitted to be smuggled abroad, similarly speak to the ways the war "convincingly confirmed" the "unity and monolithic solidity" of the Soviet multinational people: Khrushchev, *Memoirs of Nikita Khrushchev*, 1:275–76, 601.

[131] The list followed data from what was the most recent census in 1959. See *Chislennost' naseleniia SSSR*, www.demoscope.ru/weekly/ssp/ussr59_reg1.php.

[132] "Velikaia pobeda sovetskogo naroda," *Pravda*, May 9, 1965, 1–4.

[133] Kozlov, "The Historical Turn in Late Soviet Culture," 577–600.

The Crisis of Patriotism and Turn to the War

In January 1958, the CC Secretariat considered a proposal from the Stalingrad regional party committee regarding the fifteenth anniversary of the victory at Stalingrad. Among other things, the proposal called for establishing a monument to the Stalingrad battle and the participation in the festivities of Khrushchev and other high-level political representatives. According to minutes of the Secretariat meeting, the leadership approved most of the local commemorative measures, including the projected memorial complex. Yet Khrushchev adamantly opposed the involvement of any Presidium members in the celebration. "No one needs to go," he remarked. Then, almost as a concession, he added, "Send c[omrade] Chuikov."[134] Five years later, however, in 1963, Khrushchev not only found himself in the newly minted city of Volgograd, surveying the Stalingrad memorial's construction site with its lead artist, the sculptor Evgenii Vuchetich, but he was personally determining various elements of the design. Notably, it was Khrushchev who called for nearly doubling the height of the complex's planned central monument so that its grandiosity would surpass New York's Statue of Liberty.[135] What accounts for Khrushchev's about-face?

Khrushchev's initial reluctance to push ahead with the war's large-scale veneration is often cited as a feature that distinguished the Khrushchev years from the Brezhnev-era war cult.[136] Certainly, in the context of 1958, there is more than a grain of truth to this assertion. The ambiguous line on Stalin's war leadership, coupled with bureaucratic and financial constraints, stalled the initial wave of decrees on the war's "immortalization" that came in the wake of Stalin's death.[137] This is not to mention various other unresolved processes tied to the war's representation, such as the effort to create new official histories and the steady return of political prisoners and wartime deportees. For Khrushchev in 1958, the participation of the top party brass in the commemoration at Stalingrad represented an unnecessarily auspicious gesture vis-à-vis the war's memory at a time when so much remained "in flux."[138]

134 Fursenko, *Prezidium TsK KPSS*, 1:293; 2:1009–1010. Vasilii Ivanovich Chuikov commanded the 62nd Army during the Battle of Stalingrad.
135 Palmer, "How Memory Was Made," 394–395, 400–401.
136 Perhaps more than any other issue, historians have seized upon the status of Victory Day as evidence of the Khrushchev-era ambivalence over the war's public memory. In addition to works already cited, see, for example, Bonwetsch, "Ich habe an einem vollig anderen Krieg teilgenommen," 156–157; Figes, *The Whisperers*, 618–619; Youngblood, *Russian War Films*, 142–145; Wolfe, "Past as Present, Myth, or History," 259.
137 Indeed, the Stalin question was the central area of contention in advance of Victory Day's twentieth-anniversary commemoration.
138 Tumarkin is spot on here: Tumarkin, *The Living & the Dead*, 110.

However, from 1960, amid preparations for the Party Program, the leadership reexamined the notion of expanding the war's commemorative profile at the all-union level. In March of that year, at the urging of Khrushchev and Suslov, the Central Committee created a special commission to evaluate the state of soldiers' graves across the country. Headed by Leonid Brezhnev, the commission was given three months to complete its work, which it conducted in close collaboration with republican and regional party organizations.[139] It was not until July that the commission reported back to the Central Committee, concluding that the state of the memorialization of those killed in the war did "not correspond to the historic significance of the struggle of our people with German fascism." It went on: "Over the fifteen years that have passed since the day of victory ... there is not a single memorial constructed in the country that could, in a worthy manner, perpetuate the memory of soldiers and serve the cause of the education of our people, especially the youth, in glorious military traditions."[140]

The commission's resulting draft resolution, "On the immortalization of the world-historic victory of the Soviet people in the Great Patriotic War 1941–1945," offered a far more expansive vision of state war remembrance than the mere restoration of soldiers' graves. The document laid out a thirteen-point plan for rectifying the poor state of commemoration that reads like a schematic for the war cult to come. The first ten proposals all dealt with the establishment of war memorials across the Union, signaling the importance the Party would accord monumentalism in the context of the war's public memory. Point 11 proposed "[t]o establish annually on Victory Day – May 9 – a ubiquitous, nationwide holiday to the memory of the Soviet people killed in the struggle for the honor, freedom, and independence of our motherland." The resolution charged party-state organs from republican to city and district levels with "organizing on that day a collective march to memorial sites, fraternal graves" and the ceremonial laying of wreaths at those locations. In addition, the resolution instructed republican party organizations to "develop a ritual" to be carried out on Victory Day, presumably indicating republic-level standardization of the commemorative process. Point 12 addressed the development of educational practices among Soviet youth based on the theme of the war and proposed the mass dissemination of literature and art "that reflect the revolutionary and military traditions of the Soviet people ... in the struggle with the enemies of our motherland." These included, among other things, Great Patriotic War-themed "films and documentaries ... thematic albums, collections of reproductions of works

[139] Tomilina, *Pamiatnik pobedy*, 134–135. [140] RGASPI M-1/47/464/12–13.

of Soviet artists and sculptors, handbooks and guidebooks to places of historic battles [and] special radio and television productions."[141]

These measures, the resolution stipulated, were all to be carried out in time for the twentieth anniversary of Victory Day in 1965. Given such an agenda, it is probable that Khrushchev delayed the enactment of certain individual proposals, such as designating Victory Day a non-working state holiday, to coincide with this 1965 deadline. Unfortunately for Khrushchev, the seeds planted for the development of the war's all-union commemoration would blossom only after his ouster.

In one sense, the turn to the war that unfolded between 1960 and 1965 derived from various interrelated factors specific to the 1960s. These included not only the destabilization caused by Stalin's renunciation, but also global tectonic shifts in memory politics and generational pressures. Even if the USSR was not fully susceptible to all of the transnational pressures that affected the West – for example, the restructuring of the global economy – it could not avoid the shift in generation, and there was at least a familiarity in the country with the student movements and the events that contributed to the rise of Jewish memory – the capture and trial of Eichmann, the Auschwitz trials, and so on – which prompted the young in many countries to question and reproach the older generation's wartime activities. The expansion of the Soviet commemorative cult at precisely this time can be appreciated, in part, as a unique response to what was a pan-European process of national identity breakdown.[142]

It was during the first half of the 1960s that party authorities began addressing the growing rift between "fathers and sons," between the generation that had won the war and their children who appeared increasingly indifferent to the struggles and victories of their forebears. In the words of one Komsomol report, "This generation never heard the whistle of bombs and artillery barrages, they did not see the burning villages of the Smolensk region or the ruins of Volgograd, they could never know the hunger of a 900-day blockade."[143] The poet Egor Isaev, during a 1962 meeting on ideology and the arts, complained about the dismissive attitude he recently encountered during a visit with young Kiev-based poets and critics. According to Isaev, a few of the participants questioned the artistic merits of the war generation, whose output, they claimed, was forever tainted by Stalin's cult. "It all appeared very emotional, but was unconvincing and, to put it bluntly, blasphemous," Isaev asserted. "After all, this generation carried the whole war on its shoulders, [and] half of it

[141] RGASPI M-1/47/464/1–5.
[142] Knischewski and Spittler, "Memories," 239–254; Gillis, "Introduction," 13–19.
[143] RGASPI M-1/32/1193/103.

lies buried in the ground." To the charge that the wartime generation of writers and artists was corrupted by Stalin's cult, Isaev countered: "Their work began during the war. They believed in Stalin, but this was not their fault; this was their tragedy."[144]

A more pressing issue, perhaps, was the intermittent, conservative backlash to Thaw-related depictions of the war. During the early 1960s – and particularly after the publication of Solzhenitsyn's *One Day in the Life of Ivan Denisovich* – conservative critics and political authorities began openly questioning the "gloomy" and "pacifist" character of some of the most popular works set during the 1941–5 period.[145] In December 1962, the month after Solzhenitsyn's novella appeared in print, the ideological chief, Leonid Il'ichev, warned that the current obsession with the darker aspects of the Stalin era risked overshadowing the "great achievements" of the Soviet people.[146] A subsequent memorandum from the CC Ideological Department "on elevating the ideological and artistic level of cinema" was highly critical of "films on the military-patriotic theme [which] contain elements of pacifism, the desire to focus only on the horrors and suffering that war brings."[147] This was not an aversion to "realism" per se, as the artist P. D. Korin clarified. "[B]ut we are for inspired realism ... We have experienced enormous social shifts, we are correcting colossal social injustices, we have withstood the deadly and terrible battle with fascism, we were the first in space. Our time is a heroic time, and our art should reflect the heights of this era, it should be heroic."[148] Put simply, the first half of the decade witnessed the emergence of a very real concern among cultural and political authorities that the Thaw-era preoccupation with uncovering the universally tragic and human elements of the war might "overwhelm" the broader cultural agenda.[149]

It was in response to this perceived crisis of patriotic identity that schools, museums, and youth organizations mobilized to help mend the rift between generations and promote the war as a positive and redeeming narrative that could generate pride in the country and its leadership. This

144 Afiani, *Ideologicheskie komissii*, 346–347.

145 Denis Kozlov has shown how citizens mobilized personal war memories in opposition to *Denisovich*'s empathetic depiction of the titular protagonist, who was almost certainly meant to be a Vlasovite. "After unparalleled bloodshed," Kozlov writes, "it was only natural for those who had witnessed it to continue viewing yesterday's opponents on the same wartime terms." Kozlov, *The Readers of Novyi Mir*, 224–231, 226. See also Dobson, "Contesting the Paradigms of De-Stalinization," 580–600. On *Denisovich* and literary politics more generally, see Jones, *Myth, Memory, Trauma*, 144–157.

146 Jones, *Myth, Memory, Trauma*, qt. 150.

147 Afiani, *Ideologicheskie komissii*, 468.

148 Afiani, 482.

149 On the theme of the Terror in particular, see Jones, *Myth, Memory, Trauma*, 150–151.

campaign began in earnest by 1961, in time for the twentieth anniversary of the German invasion, and gradually accelerated in advance of the 1965 Victory Day jubilee.[150] As during the late 1950s, the Komsomol framed the steady uptick in commemorative work during these years as part of a more general exploration "of military and revolutionary glory." But the reports detailing these activities increasingly emphasized the popularity and efficacy of the Great Patriotic War theme above all others. After 1960, the "study of the historical and revolutionary past" often simply meant visits to soldiers' graves and World War II battle sites, meetings with war veterans, and the establishment of war monuments. Among local party authorities, there was evidently no better antidote to the perceived conflict between fathers and sons than the myth of victory in the war. Indeed, viewed from the perspective of the Komsomol, the milestone twentieth anniversary of victory in 1965 was less a break with the past than an expansion of well-established military-patriotic commemorative traditions.[151]

But it was not only generational pressures and the cultural politics of the Thaw that triggered the crisis of patriotic identity; just as significant were the tensions and contradictions of official patriotism as it had evolved since the war. Particularly in the wake of the Twenty-Second Congress and introduction of the Soviet people doctrine, open contestations over the nature of Soviet patriotism became more frequent, often centering on the pan-Soviet/Russocentric divide. The turn to the war, in this light, was an effort to reconcile the tensions embedded in Soviet patriotism, tensions that had become increasingly strained during the post-Stalin search for a usable past.

Certainly, for many sympathetic to what they perceived to be the resurrection of Russian national-patriotic culture under Stalin, pan-Soviet internationalism provided an insufficient basis for Soviet patriotic identity. This view was typified after the Twenty-Second Congress by the artist Il'ia Glazunov. During the December 1962 session with the Ideological Commission, Glazunov was outspoken over the need to root Soviet patriotism in the Russian national past. Citing "the miserable state of propaganda and educational organs dedicated to promoting patriotic

[150] Detailed documentation of these activities during the 1961–1965 period are available under RGASPI M-1/32/1193/1–300; RGASPI M-1/32/1194/1–306. Aspects of this campaign appear to have been genuinely popular. For example, in 1961, *Komsomol'skaia pravda* solicited veterans and civilians to submit recollections about "your most memorable day of the war." From the launch of this program until its conclusion in 1965, the editorial board received thousands of letters and memoirs that spoke directly to the first postwar generation. For background and documentation, see Petrova, *Samyi pamiatnyi den' voiny*.

[151] For example: RGASPI M-1/32/1193/217–218, and passim.

pride in the past and present," he claimed a "complete lack of propaganda about our Russian national traditions," which he saw as a violation of Leninist provisions on cultural heritage. Worse than this, Glazunov pointed to an active campaign to undercut the pursuit of national traditions. "I want to say that the patriotic picture is very sad in the field of the military past," Glazunov specified, before providing a list of destroyed tombs and sarcophagi of famed prerevolutionary commanders. Despite the fact that many of these structures were destroyed during Stalin's time, Glazunov underscored the present-day disregard for sites of Russian patriotic heritage. For instance, Glazunov noted the 1961 destruction of a twelfth-century church in the city of Vitebsk. "If we charged the Germans at the Nuremberg Trials with destroying monuments of the seventeenth and eighteenth centuries," Glazunov asked rhetorically, "then what will we do with the secretary of the executive committee [of Vitebsk] who still lives?" Glazunov's central concern was as follows: In the absence of a Russian national foundation, "on what will we cultivate patriotic pride, what will we love, what will we be proud of?" His address resonated with a number of the other speakers, including, most notably, the writer Vladimir Chivilikhin. However, Il'ichev, who chaired the meeting, found within it "excessive exaggerations" and deemed it "one-sided."[152]

By contrast, for many of those who embraced Khrushchev's agenda, the Twenty-Second Congress offered a welcome justification for a more sweeping condemnation of Stalin, one that deemed the co-optation of Russia's heroic past as antithetical to a postrevolutionary sense of identity.[153] Emblematic of this view was the prominent agrarian historian Sergei Dubrovskii of the Institute of History. In 1962, Dubrovskii, citing the recent Congress, called upon the leadership to remove remaining historical-Russocentric relics of the Stalin era. Stalin, Dubrovskii complained in a letter to *Izvestiia*, was clearly in violation of Lenin's 1918 decree on "Monumental Propaganda" when he sanctioned the creation of "monuments in honor of tsars and their servants, the renaming of streets, etc." Dubrovskii reserved particular scorn for Moscow's monument to Iurii Dolgorukii. Dubrovskii found the location of this "ugly monument" especially offensive since it had displaced the former Liberty Obelisk, a genuinely revolutionary monument erected to commemorate the 1918 Soviet constitution. Now, Dubrovskii grumbled, "there's a horse's tail dedicated to the memory of V. I. Lenin." For

[152] Afiani, *Ideologicheskie komissii TsK KPSS*, 327–28, 367.

[153] In addition to Dubrovskii, who is examined in greater detail, see also Ponomarev, "Zadachi istoricheskoi nauki," 3–37, esp. 17–18; "Vsesoiuznoe soveshchanie istorikov," 3–33, esp. 8–13.

Dubrovskii, the main problem was not the monument's location but Dolgorukii himself. Hardly the true founder of Moscow, Dolgorukii, the historian contended, had primarily distinguished himself with "predatory campaigns" and the "capture of prisoners, mainly women and children, who were then sold into slavery." Dubrovskii demanded the removal of the Dolgorukii monument and the restoration of the original obelisk. He also proposed an inscription on the obelisk, the text of which would be taken from the new Party Program.[154]

That September, Dubrovskii played a central role in an Institute of History conference honoring the 150th anniversary of the Battle of Borodino. Under the guidance of Ekaterina Furtseva, the Ministry of Culture closely managed the broader jubilee in order to steer the festivities away from anything resembling Russian nationalism.[155] During the conference, Dubrovskii took this role upon himself. His main address acknowledged that the anniversary was a chance for the country to celebrate "extraordinary examples of heroism, courage, and stamina." But he cautioned against drawing any direct links between the Russian past and Soviet present. Not only was this ideologically problematic but it played into the hands of Western propaganda. Dubrovskii first called on the historical community to combat the claims of foreign media outlets that "the foreign policy of Soviet Russia is a continuation of tsarist policies." The task of Soviet historians was not only to show how the people heroically opposed Napoleon's aggression, but to demonstrate that tsarist policy "was of a counterrevolutionary nature" and even to some extent justified the French mobilization for war against Russia.[156]

The "second slander of imperialist propaganda" Dubrovskii pointed to was the idea that the Soviet Army was a continuation of prerevolutionary military traditions. "No, comrades," Dubrovskii asserted, "the tsarist army has nothing in common with our Soviet Army":

> The tsarist army carried out a progressive act, it defeated Napoleon. This is indisputable. We are not nihilists, we value the national traditions of our people, but one has to draw a line. One must comprehend the different natures of tsarist battles, of tsarist commanders, and the battles of the Soviet Army. The battles of past militaries are often described as though they were battles of the Soviet Army and past commanders as though they were Soviet commanders.

Dubrovskii's third point expanded on this idea. It addressed the inevitable parallels observers of the anniversary would draw between the two patriotic wars. "We need to emphasize the fundamental difference

[154] Dubrovskii, "Pis'mo v redaktsiiu gazety 'Izvestiia,'" 341–342.
[155] APRF 3/50/597/104–105. More generally, Shein, *Voina 1812 goda*, 245.2–82.
[156] ARAN 1577/2/487/72–74.

between 1812 and 1941–1945. These are radical opposites. I'm talking about foreign policy, the nature of the army, even in military art." This was not to say that there was nothing to appreciate in the exploits of tsarist forces: "We carefully study all this inheritance and it is indisputable. But we must see the fundamental difference between the old days and our [Soviet] military art."[157]

Amid these growing ideological tensions, the Ideological Commission, again citing the Twenty-Second Congress, escalated Khrushchev's ongoing crackdown on "religious ideology," which, reports indicated, was mounting a return, particularly among the youth.[158] But this was not only a concern in the republics. As with the excessive glorification of "tsars and their servants," the Ideological Commission warned in October 1963 that religion in the USSR was fueling "bourgeois" propaganda highlighting a particular attachment among Russians ("the special and mysterious properties of the Russian soul, etc.") to the Church and religious belief.[159] Party authorities traced this revival of religious activity directly to the early years of the war:

> To a large extent, the revival of religious feelings and sentiments was caused by the hardships of the war that fell upon our country. The unsuccessful situation at the beginning of the Great Patriotic War, anxiety for the fate of loved ones, the plight of the population in the territories temporarily occupied by the enemy, all this led many people who did not have a solid scientific materialistic worldview to fall under religious influence.

This problem was exacerbated, another report detailed, "after the church declared its loyal attitude to the Soviet regime, and urged believers to defend their homeland from Hitler's invaders."[160] In order to counter the threat of religious ideology, the Ideological Commission recommended the expansion of "civic" or "socialist" rituals and holidays.[161] But whereas the earlier introduction of such practices failed to prevent the revival of religion ("It is no secret that at present the registration of births and marriages routinely takes place in an unsightly atmosphere"), the new wave of civic rituals needed to emphasize "the emotional factor." "Believers are always attracted by the emotional impact of religious rites," the report added. "The clergy and sectarians devote exceptional attention to the psychological moment. They strive to influence not so much the mind as the emotions of a person." It was the state's "inattention to the

[157] ARAN 1577/2/487/72–80. [158] E.g., RGANI 72/1/9/6–73.
[159] RGANI 72/1/9/37–39, 60–61, 72 [160] RGANI 72/1/15/341; RGANI 72/1/9/40.
[161] On the revival of civic rituals in the 1960s, see Smolkin, *A Sacred Space Is Never Empty*, 165–193; Whittington, "For the Soviet Person, New Rituals," 167–174; Sadomskaya, "New Soviet Rituals," 94–120; Lane, *The Rites of Rulers*.

emotional side of religion," the report noted, that gave religious practice its persistent appeal among Russians.[162]

By the end of 1963, preexisting military-patriotic rituals and "civic commemorations of soldiers, party workers, and activists who died in the struggle for Soviet power," had joined the new style of marriage and birth registrations, among other life events, in the pantheon of civic rituals.[163] Indeed, the Leningrad party secretary deemed commemorations of the war to be a particularly effective and "emotional" means of combatting religious belief among young and old alike.[164] The centrality of the war had been given a further boost in March of that year during a meeting of party and state leaders with Soviet writers and artists. At the meeting, Khrushchev vividly described witnessing the ceremonial laying of wreaths during a visit to the Soviet War Memorial in Berlin's Treptower Park. "These were touching moments," the first secretary recalled. "Hundreds of people came, the music sounded solemnly, everyone approached the monument in silence, no one could speak, the atmosphere itself affected people. The majestic sculpture excites a feeling of deep respect and appreciation for the heroic Soviet soldiers, a reverence for those who fell in the struggle against the dark forces of fascism" (Figure 3.4).[165] In response to Khrushchev's statement, the Komsomol further prioritized World War II monuments in its ideological work and anti-religious propaganda; crucially, it did so in a way that necessarily distanced the war victory from the prerevolutionary "Russian character."[166]

If Brezhnev's 1960 commission offered a template for a nationwide commemorative cult, then Il'ichev's address during the June 1963 Party Plenum signaled a major step toward its unveiling. Noting the increased tensions between generations and the gloomy tone of cultural productions set during the war, Il'ichev warned that the Party "cannot inspire new feats without respecting the feats already accomplished." The ideological chief spoke to the various calls by the likes of Glazunov for greater attention to the distant past. "Our duty is to maintain the pathos of

[162] RGANI 72/1/9/60–61.
[163] RGANI 72/1/15/118; Smolkin, *A Sacred Space Is Never Empty*, 182–183.
[164] RGANI 72/1/15/140–141. [165] RGASPI M-1/32/1193/23.
[166] RGASPI M-1/32/1223/81–101; RGASPI M-1/32/1193/22–34. Although patriotic rituals targeted religious belief while remaining generally compatible with ethnic identities, there was a clear apprehension among parts of the Komsomol leadership that the "civic" orientation would preclude the study and celebration of prerevolutionary Russian cultural artifacts, suggesting how closely religion could be tied to certain aspects of traditional Russian patriotism. See RGASPI M-1/32/1193/22–34. Cf. Whittington, "For the Soviet Person, New Rituals," 167–174. On the late-socialist compatibility between ethnic and Soviet identities in a non-Russian context, see, for example, Lehmann, "Apricot Socialism," 9–31; Suny, "The Contradictions of Identity," 17–36.

Figure 3.4 Khrushchev's 1963 visit to Berlin's Treptower Park Memorial, pictured here alongside the GDR's Walter Ulbricht and Poland's Wladislaw Gomulka (Vasily Yegorov/TASS via Getty Images).

today's struggle," he asserted, "in the name of [the generation] replacing us." Il'ichev went on to condemn "the remnants of a nationalistic, chauvinistic ideology," "the idealization of the past," and "national swagger" [*natsional'noe chvanstvo*], all of which "obscured the new, shared socialist traditions, common to all Soviet nations," who were on course to "achieve complete unity." It was in the context of such unity that Il'ichev invoked the war's memory: "For Soviet people, internationalism is not an abstract concept. Shoulder to shoulder, Soviet peoples of different nationalities constructed socialism [and] shed blood in the fight against fascism." But nearly the entire burden of preserving the war's patriotic memory, Il'ichev pointed out, fell on the shoulders of youth organizations. There was "no justification" for the wider public's continued "indifference [and] inattention to the memory of the heroes [of the war]." It was now time, Il'ichev proclaimed, "to establish the glorious tradition of a *nationwide* celebration of heroes who fell in the struggle for the freedom and honor of our Motherland," one of the few sections of his address that, according to the stenographic record, elicited both "stormy" and "prolonged" applause.[167]

Conclusion

Stalin's death and subsequent denunciation prompted a desperate search among the leadership for new sources of political legitimacy and patriotic identity. The call for a "return to Leninism," for a course correction following the years of the personality cult, led to a reconceptualization of Soviet patriotism as an expression of postrevolutionary loyalties, values, and idealism. However, the preference for "post-October" historical themes, together with the suppression of many of the most egregious aspects of Stalinist Russocentrism, clashed with a persistent Russocentric undercurrent in Soviet patriotic culture, which had its own adherents. These included Russian-speaking party officials and citizens more generally who continued to revere Stalin's war leadership and cherish what was perceived to be his resurrection of Russian national patriotism and its symbols. The unwillingness to decisively rid the war narrative of residual Stalinist elements in the late 1950s for fear of a potential backlash stalled initial efforts to exploit the war's memory on a grand scale. Hence, despite a clear desire on the part of the leadership to utilize the victory myth, the war's commemoration was confined to a patchwork of local and organizational rituals and practices, together with a steady stream of censored war memoirs and cultural productions, all of which – officially – subordinated the war to the larger Soviet metanarrative.

The Twenty-Second Party Congress brought increasing scrutiny to bear on Russocentric conceptions of the war and targeted the uncritical portrayal of a "single stream" uniting the heroic Russian past with the Soviet victory of 1945. Unlike the Stalinist version of discursive tension, the new doctrine of the Soviet people endorsed a purely pan-Soviet conception of the war and siloed ideas of Russian primacy in the imagery

[167] The other area of "story and prolonged applause" was the space race. *Plenum TsK KPSS (18–21 iiunia 1963 goda)*, 42–44 (emphasis added). See also the address of Sergei Pavlov, the Komsomol head: *Plenum*, 205–212.

of prerevolutionary and early Soviet "brotherhood." But while the Khrushchev leadership was successful in establishing a dominant pan-Soviet line on the war, the implementation of this line proved more difficult. Rather than resolve the tensions of official patriotism, the new line exposed and exacerbated them, something reflected in the creation of the multivolume history and in the seemingly incompatible conceptions of patriotism embodied by intellectuals like Il'ia Glazunov and Sergei Dubrovskii respectively.

Yet there was notable overlap between the paradigms these latter figures advocated. Each stressed the importance of patriotic "traditions" with which to inspire a popular sense of "love for the motherland," reverence for one's forebears, and disdain for one's enemies, among other heroic traits. The tension here was not over the centrality of these ideals, or the use of tradition as a vehicle for their promotion, but over their source – Soviet or Russian, postrevolutionary or primordial. Among the panoply of civic rituals to emerge in the early 1960s, only the war's commemoration could come close to bridging these gaps and masking their contradictions. The myth of the war victory overlapped with many Russian patriotic concerns while advancing a decidedly pan-Soviet vision of patriotic identity. In the republics, of course, the range of acceptable identities was more limited: it was not possible, for example, to advocate an exclusively Tajik-centered primordial identity outside the framework of prerevolutionary Russian guidance – that is, without falling afoul of central authorities. But at the all-union center, the expansion of the war cult, coupled with an official ambivalence over the Russian people's place within it, provided a new forum within which the pan-Soviet and Russocentric paradigms could compete with one another, not just to shape the war's memory, but to define what it meant to be Soviet.

4 Monumental Memory

Patriotic Identity in the High War Cult

> We are playing soccer with the skull of [Prince Petr] Bagration, [and] tossing out Suvorov's remains from his tomb . . . This is not a thing of the past, it is a struggle for the present.
>
> – Sergei Smirnov, 1966[1]

> There is nothing in this world as invisible as a monument . . . This can be no doubt explained. Anything that endures over time sacrifices its ability to make an impression.
>
> – Robert Musil, 1927[2]

In February 1965, a high-level ideological worker from Moscow by the name of Fedor Krotov descended upon the Kazakh capital of Alma-Ata. Krotov was part of a coterie of ideological officials dispatched to the republics to elicit recommendations on how to improve the state of political indoctrination in the country. More precisely, the objective had been to find ways to make political education engaging – exciting even. "Put yourselves in the place of the Central Committee," Krotov implored the gathered local party representatives. "[Y]ou need to make suggestions about how to instill fighting qualities, qualities of present-day revolutionaries, [the qualities] of a builder of communism, of a fighter."

Heeding Krotov's appeal, the assembled republican activists offered proposals mostly involving a greater emphasis on Marxist-Leninist classics. Then E. V. Raiskin, an agitator from a local factory cell, chimed in with an alternative proposition. "You said to imagine ourselves as Central Committee workers," Raiskin interjected.

> Well, I'd like to imagine myself in this role for a moment [laughter in the hall], and offer a proposal. Soon it's going to be Victory Day, the twentieth anniversary[.] I think it's time to incorporate that historic date into the network of party education and to give it maximum attention, to highlight military-political and economic

1 RGASPI M-1/32/1193/12. 2 Musil, "Monuments," 64, 66.

issues around this date. After all, this is a moment that will elevate the consciousness of our young people, and not only the young.

Raiskin went on to contrast the present dearth of commemorative imagery with the vivid portraits of heroes and other war-related paraphernalia that he used to encounter in his home village. "Why have we stopped producing these?" he asked. "That's all I wanted to say." Krotov did not comment on Raiskin's or any of the other speakers' suggestions; he simply listened and concluded with a promise to present the ideas to the Central Committee upon his return to the capital.[3]

Krotov's mission to Alma-Ata, and others like it, immediately preceded the Presidium's decision to elevate Victory Day to the status of an all-union, non-working holiday – which, in the eyes of many contemporary historians, signified the launch of the "full-blown" cult of the war.[4] Yet, despite the timing, it is not clear that feedback from the republics played any direct role in the decision. Plans involving the large-scale commemoration of the war (including the status of Victory Day) had been underway for many years. Krotov's discussion with party workers in Alma-Ata is significant, not because it prompted any initiatives in Moscow, but because it revealed the rather limited range of mobilizational tools at the Party's disposal. In this, the Brezhnev leadership faced many of the same dilemmas that had long vexed party ideologists: how to stimulate patriotism and enthusiasm around abstract ideological tenets and the vague promise of a communist future; how to extricate Soviet-era achievements as the basis of a usable past when so many of these remained inseparable from Stalin's name; how to bridle the ethnonational impulses of Russians and other Soviet peoples to the inclusive, supra-ethnic patriotism of the Soviet state.[5] From high-level deliberations in Moscow to factory-level agitators in the republics, the war victory stood out as an obvious instrument of social integration and mobilization; as a potential means of overcoming precisely these dilemmas.

This chapter considers the period of the war cult's maturation (1960s–80s) as the victory myth came to eclipse alternative modes of patriotic

[3] APRK 708/38/1284/4–56.

[4] RGANI 3/18/323/7; Tumarkin, *The Living & the Dead*, 124.

[5] On the social and cultural shifts of the late-socialist era, which added layers of complexity to these dilemmas and the political responses, see, for example, Gilburd, *To See Paris and Die*; Fürst and McLellan, *Dropping out of Socialism*; Fainberg and Kalinovsky, *Reconsidering Stagnation*; Tsipursky, *Socialist Fun*; Gorsuch and Koenker, *The Socialist Sixties*; Yurchak, *Everything Was Forever*; Fürst, "Where Did All the Normal People Go," 621–640; Chernyshova, *Soviet Consumer Culture*; Raleigh, *Soviet Baby Boomers*; Roth-Ey, *Moscow Prime Time*; Zhuk, *Rock and Roll in the Rocket City*. On little-explored, Brezhnev-era efforts within the Soviet literary establishment to reinvigorate popular enthusiasm for the Soviet project, see Jones, *Revolution Rekindled*, esp. 28–99.

expression. Indeed, it was precisely during these years that the war myth went beyond merely validating the original promise of the Bolshevik Revolution to "almost entirely overshadowing it," as Amir Weiner has argued.[6] The chapter views the war cult less as a break with the commemorative politics of the Khrushchev era than as their fulfillment. With good reason, recent scholarship has treated late socialism (1964–85) as a period distinct from the more turbulent Khrushchev years that preceded it.[7] Late-socialist war memory of course broke with the Thaw in key respects, not least of which was the former's prioritization of blandly "heroic" depictions of the country at war and the partial revival of Stalin's wartime image. Other notable contrasts include the late-socialist penchant for gigantomania and the rise of the cult of Brezhnev, itself rooted in his wartime service and the incipient myth of the 1943 battle for Malaia zemlia, an outpost near Novorossiisk where Brezhnev served as chief political officer.[8] In considering ways the war cult built upon Khrushchev-era initiatives, the chapter does not deny the various political, social, and cultural ruptures late socialism induced but rather seeks to bring to the fore often-neglected continuities in the Party's management of Soviet war memory after Stalin.

Indeed, the endeavor to reconcile the various patriotic strands unleashed by the dissolution of Stalin's cult did not abate with Khrushchev's ouster in October 1964. As the chapter argues, late-socialist war commemorations, in line with the Soviet people doctrine, continued to dilute particularistic depictions of the Russian nation at war while channeling Russocentrism toward the contained outlets of prerevolutionary and early Soviet history, culture, and modernization narratives. Hence, the Party sanctioned the creation of a mass Russian cultural organization, the All-Russian Society for the Preservation of Historical and Cultural Monuments (VOOPIiK), at the same time that it launched the commemorative cult of the war. Cultural nationalism provided a safety valve for Russophile activism as the leadership looked to the war cult to advance an exclusively internationalist model of Soviet patriotism.

But while authorities forced the most egregious claims about the Russocentric essence of victory underground, these ideas persisted at the margins of late-socialist culture, as well as outside the RSFSR, much as they had after the war. As the war cult grew in prominence, party-affiliated, Russophile intellectuals occasionally contested the internationalist orientation of the dominant victory myth. In response, the Party

[6] Weiner, *Making Sense of War*, 7.
[7] Klumbytė and Sharafutdinova, "Introduction: What Was Late Socialism?," 1–14.
[8] On the myth of Malaia zemlia and its place in the larger war cult, see Davis, *Myth Making*. For a recent, fascinating analysis of Brezhnev's connection to the war cult from the perspective of the USSR's Hero Cities, see Mijnssen, *Russia's Hero Cities*.

promoted the war victory in a way that maximally overlapped with certain Russophile concerns (patriotism, love of the homeland, respect for tradition, anti-Westernism, etc.) while simultaneously enforcing the victory myth's ideologically orthodox, pan-Soviet framing. Although the idea was to steer Russian nationalism in a Soviet and internationalist direction, "Russocentric nationalists" – as this chapter refers to them – often read these areas of overlap and ambiguity as implicit assertions of the Russocentric nature of the war. At the same time, the ostensibly pan-Soviet war cult fueled this ambiguity. The cult's ubiquity, rote rituals, and backward-looking orientation rendered official views about the war vulnerable to ethnonational redefinition from below. In the RSFSR, such ambiguity regarding the place of the Russian people – a defining feature of the war's memory – lent the Party an ample degree of plausible deniability as it aimed to project an image of lateral friendship while also harnessing a sense among Russians of their own nation's paramount wartime contribution.

The Twentieth Anniversary of Victory

Five days after Krotov's Alma-Ata meeting, on February 18, the Politburo tasked Suslov, Il'ichev, and party secretary Aleksandr Shelepin to finalize a resolution on the forthcoming Victory Day celebration.[9] The Presidium deliberated over the resulting draft between March 12 and 19, when it instructed the Secretariat to make further edits.[10] Finally, on March 30, 1965, the leadership issued a formal decree "On the celebration of the twentieth anniversary of the victory of the Soviet people in the Great Patriotic War." The six-page document overhauled the Victory Day jubilee in terms strikingly reminiscent of the report generated by Brezhnev's 1960 commission. It defined the holiday's overriding function as the "mobilization of the Soviet people to successfully implement the decisions of the twentieth and twenty-second congresses." To this end, the decree outlined union-wide measures to take place annually between May 3 and 9. These included the standard array of rituals already employed by patriotic youth organizations: meetings with veterans, the establishment and preservation of war memorials, the ceremonial laying of wreaths at gravesites, award presentations, excursions "to notable sites of battles and exploits." But the decree drastically expanded the scope of these activities. Such rites, the document stipulated, were to be conducted each year "in the capitals of the union republics, provincial, regional, and district centers, cities, industries, state and collective farms, institutes,

[9] RGANI 3/18/323/7. [10] RGANI 3/18/330/3.

military units, on ships and in military schools," among other venues. Naturally, it added, Victory Day "is henceforth declared a non-working day."[11]

The decree also detailed what was to be the proper framing of the war narrative during the jubilee period. Reflecting the residual potency of the Twenty-Second Congress line, the text offered a near-perfect encapsulation of the pan-Soviet/internationalist myth of the war. The Soviet people had "fought to defend the gains of socialism," had waged war in the spirit of "socialist patriotism ... proletarian internationalism, fraternity and friendship between peoples." Victory in 1945 demonstrated to the world "the superiority of the socialist social system over capitalism" and "created the conditions" for "the rise of national liberation movements in Asia, Africa, and Latin America." The decree placed the wartime contributions of the republics on equal footing with those of the RSFSR, with the emphasis tending toward social homogeneity rather than ethnic diversity. The finished draft mentioned neither Stalin nor the role of the Russian people, only the Communist Party – the "inspiration and organizer of victory" – which had "mobilized all the material and spiritual forces of Soviet society to defeat the enemy."[12]

While the Presidium decree denoted a certain high-level consensus about the war's status in society, its pan-Soviet framing obscured a persistent tension within the Party over the war's character. Among the prominent officials to serve on both Brezhnev's 1960 commission and his 1965 working group on the Victory Day jubilee was the former head of the Komsomol and KGB, Aleksandr Shelepin. Nikolai Mitrokhin has identified Shelepin as the country's most powerful pro-regime Russian nationalist and a key patron of nationalist figures throughout most of the 1960s. As Mitrokhin documents, until 1967, the so-called Shelepin group rivaled Brezhnev's Dnepropetrovsk faction for influence in state and party organs, and maintained the Komsomol – under Sergei Pavlov, himself a Russian nationalist sympathizer – as a conservative stronghold and bastion of Russian nationalist activism. By the beginning of 1965, the two factions held contrasting ideas about the implications of the war's memory. While Brezhnev and his supporters looked to extend the pan-Soviet victory myth of the Khrushchev years, such an "abstract and non-ethnic" conception of the war, Mitrokhin notes, alienated members of the Shelepin and Pavlov groups.[13]

The latter, by contrast, sought to leverage the war theme to promote their particular strain of Russocentric nationalism. This was not

[11] RGANI 3/18/333/81–84. [12] RGANI 3/18/333/79–82.
[13] Mitrokhin, *Russkaia partiia*, 277.

a separatist, but "nation-shaping" form of nationalism, which, as Brudny describes, "is articulated by representatives of the dominant nation who find the existing political, social, economic, and cultural realities of their own state in contradiction to their ideological principles." Unlike Stalinist Russocentrism, this brand of nationalism was unique to the late-socialist era. It was a direct reaction to both destalinization and Khrushchev's perceived antipathy for Russian-dominated hierarchy and prerevolutionary cultural heritage. Although Russocentric nationalists differed in opinion over Stalin's policies, they generally appealed to the Stalin-era Russocentric paradigm, as well as "memories of the last ten years of Stalin's rule, seeing in them the natural continuation of Russian history."[14]

This struggle was in full swing by February 1965, when a group of approximately fifteen party leaders, advisers, and speechwriters met outside Brezhnev's office on the fifth floor of the Central Committee building to begin work on the first secretary's report in honor of the twentieth anniversary jubilee. According to G. L. Smirnov's account of this and subsequent gatherings to draft the report, Brezhnev sought ways to render the Victory Day speech, and the holiday more generally, as inclusive as possible. But Shelepin regularly interfered in the process and attempted to steer the report in a "radical," pro-Stalinist direction. In the words of F. M. Burlatskii, the head speechwriter, Shelepin and his acolytes sought nothing less than "to shift the political rudder back to the former [Stalinist] era," entirely invalidating the Twenty-Second Congress line and abandoning the 1961 Party Program. Given Shelepin's ideological predilections, there can be little doubt that his program favored the Russocentric conceptualization of the war narrative.[15]

Ultimately, Brezhnev and his supporters in the Central Committee rejected the course proposed by Shelepin. The final report mentioned Stalin's name only once, as a concession to the Shelepin group, citing his capacity as the head of the State Defense Committee. But the address itself reiterated the pan-Soviet internationalism of the initial Presidium decree. It was, writes Burlatskii, a decisive continuation of the "principles, ideas, and attitudes" of the Khrushchev era, the long-term significance of which could hardly be overstated. In Burlatskii's assessment, this "historic decision ... predetermined the character of the Brezhnev era" as whole. However, Smirnov believes that the Shelepin group's activism "had a significant impact" on popular perceptions of both Stalin and the

[14] Mitrokhin, *Russkaia partiia*, 236–250, 269–299, qt. 250; Brudny, *Reinventing Russia*, 6, 61–63.

[15] Smirnov, *Uroki minuvshego*, 114–121; Burlatskii, *Vozhdi i sovetniki*, 282–287.

war. Regardless, from this point forward the Shelepin and Pavlov groups were unable to steer the war's memory in an explicitly Russocentric direction.[16]

Brezhnev's report, and the twentieth anniversary celebrations more generally, cut several ways. By all accounts, the holiday was a resounding success, particularly among veterans and members of the armed forces. KGB reports of the jubilee highlight overwhelming gratitude toward the Communist Party, the Soviet state, and Brezhnev personally for restoring the war's central place in public remembrance. The inclusion of Stalin's name was also broadly popular, although "individual servicemembers" are recorded to have "expressed their distaste for the report's mention of Stalin." Responses likewise admonished Khrushchev for failing to deliver such a celebration earlier. As one response put it, "There is a sense that the Central Committee and government want to act and achieve concrete things [in commemorating the war], and not make excuses or cite obstacles as Khrushchev did." Such indicators of the popular mood certainly reassured the leadership of the victory myth's potential as a source of legitimacy. Some respondents even stated as much, noting the way such a celebration of the war "will raise the authority of our Party and government." The expansion of the war cult over the course of the subsequent decade and a half, together with its balanced assessment of Stalin and glorification of Brezhnev, stemmed directly from these early, positive signals.[17]

Had the popularity of Victory Day's restoration helped resolve the crisis of patriotic identity of the early 1960s? Only temporarily. True, initial KGB reports give no indication that the holiday stoked a particularistic pride among Russians or, conversely, that its internationalist orientation triggered Russian national resentments. Indeed, the reports go out of their way to emphasize that veterans and others recalled the war against Germany as a victory of the "working class," as a great feat "of the whole Soviet people," as having been waged in defense of the shared socialist homeland (Figure 4.1).[18] However, Brezhnev's launch of the commemorative cult offered a new forum for all manner of public contest over the war. Not only did the war's new prominence exacerbate the ever-widening gulf between Russocentric and pan-Soviet conceptions of the war, but, for the liberal-reformist intelligentsia, it briefly gave new life to

[16] Mitrokhin, *Russkaia partiia*, 114; Burlatskii, *Vozhdi i sovetniki*, 290–291; Smirnov, *Uroki minuvshego*, 115–116.

[17] RGANI 5/30/462/38–43, 45, 59–64, qts. 38, 43, 45. Mark Edele concurs that the anniversary convinced the leadership that it was moving in the right direction. See Edele, *Soviet Veterans*, 9–10.

[18] RGANI 5/30/462/61–62, 64.

Figure 4.1 Veterans celebrate Victory Day in Moscow, 1976 (courtesy of Valery Shchekoldin).

the Thaw-inspired movement to redress lingering Stalin-era myths associated with victory, something that augured poorly for this faction's longer-term relations with the regime.

Konstantin Simonov, for one, used the occasion of the anniversary to affirm his commitment to historical truth, which he upheld in a commemorative speech and subsequent draft article as the foremost "duty of the writer." Simonov's speech was a rebuttal to an article published weeks earlier by Evgenii Vuchetich. In that article, the foremost sculptor of the war cult had articulated a rather slippery notion of "truth" when it came to representations of the war. Although the factual truth involved "cases of indiscretion, bewilderment, and sometimes even panic," Vuchetich asserted that the far more significant "truth of the phenomenon" was that the Red Army "broke the back of the fascist beast . . . then reached Berlin and hoisted the banner of our great victory over the Reichstag." It was the job of the artist to first recognize and then convey this latter, superior version of truth in depictions of the war.[19]

[19] E. Vuchetich, "Vnesem iasnost'," *Izvestiia*, Apr. 14, 1965; Lakshin, *Golosa i litsa*, 239–241. Vuchetich's article was itself a response to Tvardovskii's "Po sluchaiu iubileia," 3–19.

Simonov countered that Vuchetich's equivocal approach to truth was emblematic of the remnants of Stalinist mythmaking that persisted into the present day. For Simonov, the Victory Day anniversary was the ideal moment to root out such Stalinist distortions, starting with a full accounting of Stalin's culpability for the country's disastrous military setbacks in 1941. This was hardly an unpatriotic act. For "[o]nly by depicting the full measure of our misfortunes at the beginning of the war and the actual scale of our losses," he wrote, "can we reveal the true length of our journey to Berlin and the efforts required of the Party, the people, and the army during this endlessly long, difficult day." Two journals had already typeset Simonov's text when the hardline chief of the Main Political Directorate of the Soviet Army and Navy, Gen. Aleksei Epishev, forbade the article's publication and had the proofs confiscated.[20]

Clashes of this sort, between the advocates of historical truth and those who espoused what Vuchetich called the "truth of the phenomenon," endured into 1966, when the trial and sentencing of the writers Siniavskii and Daniel beckoned the end of the regime's limited toleration for Khrushchev-era revisionism.[21] This shift coincided with the rise of a number of ultra-conservative "neo-Stalinists" within party structures, including the notorious Sergei Trapeznikov, whom Brezhnev appointed to head the CC Department of Science.[22] The "embodiment of bureaucratic reaction against the Twentieth and Twenty-second Congresses," as one historian has labeled him, Trapeznikov, and such likeminded appointees as Vasilii Shauro (Department of Culture) and Vladimir Stepakov (Department of Propaganda), continued to advocate for a more sweeping rehabilitation of Stalin. In November 1965, Trapeznikov purportedly even called for the republication of the *Short Course* during a meeting on party history. As with Shelepin, these figures also campaigned on behalf of "radical nationalist intellectuals" to play a greater role in the work of popular mobilization.[23]

Amid this conservative pendulum swing, there was little appetite for myth-busting exposés of Soviet history by the liberal-reformist intelligentsia, especially when it came to the war. In early 1966, for instance, *Novyi mir* published an article by V. Kardin that challenged the historicity of the famed last stand of the twenty-eight Panfilov-Guardsmen, along with

[20] See RGANI 5/30/462/72–73; Simonov, "Uroki istorii i dolg pisatelia," 42–48; Bonwetsch, "The Purge of the Military," 409–410.

[21] Siniavskii and Daniel were imprisoned for publishing unflattering portraits of Soviet life abroad, which was deemed to have violated the law on "anti-Soviet agitation." Kozlov, *The Readers of Novyi Mir*, chap. 9; Caute, *Politics and the Novel*, chap. 23.

[22] Medvedev, *On Stalin and Stalinism*, 177.

[23] Markwick, *Rewriting History*, 200–201, qt. 200; Brudny, *Reinventing Russia*, qt. 63.

other "legends" associated with the Revolution and Civil War. For this assault on one of the most cherished tales of wartime heroism, the article, and the journal that published it, received a harsh rebuke from none other than Aleksander Krivitskii – the Panfilovtsy myth's originator – as well as admonitions by the country's military leadership and Brezhnev personally.[24] But even broadly patriotic works on the war that adhered to the Twenty-Second Congress line now came under fire for painting unflattering portraits of Stalin's war leadership. In perhaps the best-known episode, the historian A. M. Nekrich was denounced after the publication of his monograph, *June 22, 1941*, aroused the ire of neo-Stalinists within the leadership and historical establishment. Published in October 1965, Nekrich's book underscored the role of Stalin's purge of the officer corps and his general incompetence leading up to and during the war's outbreak as the key factors precipitating the early defeats. Although the book highlighted party leadership and the heroism and unity of the Soviet people, Nekrich was stripped of his party membership; he later emigrated to the United States.[25]

But debates sparked by the war cult's inauguration in 1965 were not confined to questions of historical truth and authenticity; the war's meaning for the broad sweep of Russian history was also contested. This debate was set off shortly after the Victory Day anniversary when an article entitled "Native Land: Reflections on a Letter" appeared in *Komsomol'skaia pravda*. The article's author, the journalist Vasilii Peskov, described receiving a letter from a mother distraught over a conversation she had with her son and her son's friend. When she emphasized the importance of the concept of Motherland to the boys, they gently mocked her, suggesting that absolute love for the Motherland is something "sentimental people invented." The mother pleaded with Peskov to address this matter, adding that "a sense of Motherland must live within every person."[26]

In response, Peskov issued an unabashedly Russocentric defense and elaboration of the concept of Motherland, stressing its eternal, primordial essence and drawing heavily from imagery of the war. Although claiming, "I am a Communist," Peskov criticized the Soviet state's one-sided preoccupation with modernity over and above historical rootedness.

[24] Kardin, "Legendy i fakty," 237–250. For a superb overview of the "Legends and Facts" controversy that explores Krivitskii's role in literary politics and the later perpetuation of the Panfilovtsy myth, see Kozlov, *The Readers of Novyi Mir*, 263–283.

[25] Nekrich, *1941, 22 iunia*; Martin, *Dissident Histories*, chap. 3; Markwick, *Rewriting History*, 209–219.

[26] V.M. Peskov, "Otechestvo. Razmyshleniia nad pis'mom," *Komsomol'skaia pravda*, Jun. 4, 1965, 4.

Motherland embodied both of these aspects: "It is a rocket aimed for the moon, and birds flying north above our homes ... [It is] the depth of centuries and also the present day." It was only with the outbreak of war in 1941 that the Communist Party recognized – if only momentarily – what Soviet citizens already knew: that a "people without such deep roots is an impoverished people, no matter how fast their planes ... no matter how tall their buildings." It should also come as no surprise, he went on, that "during the most difficult years of the war, we called out to our ancestors for help: 'Aleksandr Nevskii, Dmitrii Donskoi, Kuz'ma Minin, Dmitrii Pozharskii, Aleksandr Suvorov, Mikhail Kutuzov.'" The Great Patriotic War witnessed "the past become a weapon," Peskov reminded. "Nobody measured its strength. But we can say that it was no weaker than the famed Katiusha [rocket launcher]."[27]

Peskov's article provoked a number of critical reactions, the most notable of which came from three longtime party members and internationalist devotees, I. M. Danishevskii, S. A. Davydovskaia, and the historian S. M. Dubrovskii. The three Communists drafted an open letter, "On the Upbringing of Soviet Patriotism," conceived as a direct rejoinder to the ideas presented in Peskov's "Native Land," although they removed the names of Peskov and others on the advice of a colleague within the Komsomol organization.[28] Where Peskov's article articulated a Russocentric interpretation of the war, the open letter represented its diametrical opposite. To be sure, the letter acknowledged, the promotion of patriotism was vital in the ideological conditions of the Cold War. However, distinguishing between the "genuinely Soviet" variety on the one hand and "pre-Soviet ... Great Russian nationalist patriotism" on the other was every bit as important. This was not merely a question of ideological orthodoxy – although it was certainly that – but had practical implications as well. Russian national patriotism played into the hands of Western imperialists and émigré monarchists, and undermined domestic mobilization. "After all," the authors observed, "one cannot instill patriotism among the peoples of the Caucasus or Central Asia on the basis of Great Russian nationalism," which inherently "sows discord by juxtaposing one [Soviet] people against another."[29]

The authors took particular aim at the recent exaltation of the Russocentrism of the war years by various "wise men" in the Soviet press. For example, the letter asserted that the wartime emergence of the great ancestors theme was being falsely peddled as though it were a key weapon in the fight against the Germans. In fact, the recourse to this "primordial patriotism [*iskonnyi patriotizm*] inherited from tsarist

[27] Peskov, 4. [28] RGASPI M-1/32/1194/22–50. [29] RGASPI M-1/32/1194/25–36.

ideologues" was not only unnecessary "but sharply weakened our ideological position" and "contributed significantly to the reduction of the moral and political stamina of the people when confronted by Hitlerite propaganda." The authors implied that such propaganda was partly to blame for the many Soviet citizens who joined Vlasov's Russian Liberation Army, since such prerevolutionary messaging had more in common with the Vlasovites than the Soviet party-state. The letter offered several counterfactual examples, indicating the absurdity of the claim that the Party needed to rely on non-Marxist patriotic motifs. "What if, say, the French communists inspired themselves [during the war] with the image of their 'valiant ancestor,' the emperor Napoleon Bonaparte? And the antifascist German underground with the Prussian King Frederick II or Bismarck?" In fact, history teaches that "revolutionary" patriotism was more than sufficient to defeat the "fascist hordes":

> Let us recall the first years of Soviet Russia's existence. Hungry, impoverished, poorly armed, with neither experience nor any organization, the young Land of the Soviets triumphantly repulsed the combined forces of the domestic bourgeois-landlord counterrevolution ... Who would dispute that our strength was to be found precisely in those appeals, in those fiery revolutionary slogans that our country projected across the world, through the banner that we raised and under which we fought! But under this banner ... we were not inspired by images of shining princes and tsarist military leaders, even those of great talent.[30]

"Just imagine," the authors added, "if someone had tried to inspire the Soviet people with such noble 'ancestors' [at that time]!"[31]

The letter drew to a close with a concise summation of the authors' pan-Soviet conception of patriotism, which is worth quoting at length:

> In contrast to the "patriotism," which was known in the old days as "kvasnyi" ... we, the Soviet people, have our own, proletarian, socialist, common-to-all-the-peoples-of-our-country Soviet patriotism. It is based on the Marxist-Leninist understanding of the historical process, the proud traditions of the revolutionary liberation struggle of the working people of Great Russia and of all other nations and nationalities of our multinational homeland. This Soviet patriotism feeds on pride for the heroic pages of October and the Civil War, for victorious patriots, for the turbulent years of the Great Patriotic War ... for the creative genius of the people, for their courage in overcoming difficulties, in their historical achievements on the path to communism.[32]

Such a strictly Leninist interpretation was more or less consonant with the inclusive, supra-ethnic patriotism detailed in Brezhnev's twentieth

[30] A handwritten notation attempted to soften the language a bit by adding, "Of course, these personalities are important to study." RGANI M-1/32/1194/36.
[31] RGANI M-1/32/1194/34–37. [32] RGANI M-1/32/1194/47–49.

anniversary report – minus the latter's muted praise of Stalin. And yet, it was never published, although the underground *Politicheskii dnevnik* circulated key excerpts. The dissident Roy Medvedev, who was generally sympathetic, believed the authors' assertion that Russian nationalist themes in fact damaged the war effort to be too extreme.[33] Moreover, Russophiles in the party apparatus, and probably a great many Russian-speaking citizens, would have perceived the publication of such a letter to be an open declaration of war, which ran contrary to Brezhnev's preference for "stability." Nevertheless, as with other dismissed "policy papers," the letter's argument – a pushback against the Russocentric paradigm – would reverberate well after its formal rejection.[34]

Danishevskii, Dubrovskii, and Davydovskaia were hardly lone voices among the patriotic intelligentsia. In the wake of the twentieth anniversary, a number of Russian-speaking "cultural agents" in the republics, too, saw the preservation of the pan-Soviet/internationalist myth as vital to the USSR's cohesion. In late 1965, a group of Ukrainian writers and cinematographers submitted a letter to the Central Committee that made the rounds among the party leadership. The letter's authors traced competing lateral and hierarchical patriotic tendencies that, they claimed, originated during the war years. Soviet internationalism, the letter argued, grew out of wartime mobilization and the unprecedented degree of interethnic contact, as well as the spread of the Russian language as the dominant mode of "international communication." These phenomena represented the high point of the "friendship of the peoples" doctrine and contributed to a sense of a singular Soviet identity, "as if the normal geographical and ethnographic borders [of our country] had been erased."[35]

However, the war experience produced a second, more problematic tendency as well. Among other things, the authors asserted, the war witnessed mass repressions inflicted against suspect ethnic minorities. The wholesale deportation of supposedly disloyal Soviet nations gave rise to an inflated sense of one's ethnic particularity and difference vis-à-vis other Soviet peoples. For the Russians, this manifested as an extreme chauvinism and sense of ethnic supremacy. By war's end, the letter asserted,

[33] See *Politicheskii dnevnik*, 1:63–71.
[34] See most notably Zhdanov's so-called "theses" of 1944, which, though never published, reverberated in official culture. For an in-depth treatment of the various drafts of the theses, see Brandenberger and Dubrovskii, "Itogovyi partiinyi document," 148–163.
[35] RGANI 5/30/462/203–237.

one could overhear such conversations: "Only Russians can be trusted. The Russians endured all the hardships of the war both at the front and in the rear. It is not without reason that even Stalin was compelled to propose a toast to the Russian people." Behind all this was the notion: "How good it is when you are a true Great Russian and not a national minority" . . . And if before the war, we were unconcerned about our national origins, then after the war the question of nationality came to the fore, became natural, acquiring elements of suspicion and anxiety.[36]

At the time of the twentieth anniversary, according to the authors, this second, ethnocentric and chauvinistic tendency was again dominant, at least in the Ukrainian SSR, where the ostensibly progressive policy of continued national "flourishing" persisted unabated under the "nationally minded" party secretary Petro Shelest.[37] But the war's new prominence offered a chance to yet again bolster the tendency of a common, pan-Soviet identity. It was time, the authors contended, to do away with the longtime doctrine of national cultures, which held that they were "national [*natsional'naia*] in form, socialist in content," in favor of a definition that was "pan-national [*obshchenatsional'naia*] in form." "This very idea," they observed, "is contained in the [1961] CPSU Program." Such an embrace of the pan-Soviet tendency would enable the Party to clearly identify those "neonationalists" who "advocate the perpetuation of national differences" in the name of a heretical form of "national communism."[38]

It is certainly no coincidence that Peskov, the three longtime Bolsheviks, and the seven anonymous Ukrainian members of the cultural intelligentsia all refracted their concerns over the correct nature of Soviet patriotism through the prism of the war. With the twentieth anniversary of victory, the war narrative reemerged as a key site of contestation between the advocates of the pan-Soviet/internationalist and Russocentric paradigms respectively. For Russophile patriots like Peskov, the rhetoric of the war revealed the importance to the USSR's very survival of primordial Russian roots. However, this logic contained a fundamental flaw from the Politburo's perspective. To state openly that the Communist Party needed to rely on Russocentric nationalist tropes, an implicit acknowledgment of the inefficacy of Soviet-oriented patriotic themes, would have been a problematic core message of the fledgling war cult. The two letters examined here, by contrast, saw the appeal to Russian

[36] RGANI 5/30/462/204–215.

[37] For an elaboration of "national-mindedness" versus "nationalism" in the republics, see Smith, "The Battle for Language," 983–1002. On Shelest as "nationally minded," see Plokhy, *Lost Kingdom*, 238, 294.

[38] RGANI 5/30/462/230–234.

national sentiment, and corresponding growth of chauvinism and particularism, as distortions of true Soviet patriotism, which aspired to channel supranational unity out of ethnic diversity. It was pan-Soviet internationalism, the letters suggested, that triumphed over Germany in spite of, rather than because of, Stalin's appeal to Russocentrism. But such an openly antagonistic stance toward Russia's "deep history" had its own risks, particularly at a time when neo-Stalinists in the party apparatus were coming to see Russian nationalism as an effective tool of mobilization and were starting to actively cultivate nationalist support for the regime.[39]

Rather than openly endorse one side or the other as the dominant ideological paradigm, the Brezhnev leadership sought compromise by highlighting the ways the Great Patriotic War theme, even in its pan-Soviet guise, overlapped with Russocentric nationalist concerns. The development of the commemorative cult in the years after 1965 yet again cast the war as a supra-ethnic, socialist counterpoint to the variegated ethnic hierarchy promoted in many prerevolutionary and early Soviet narratives and commemorations. But this was never an explicit policy. To a much greater degree than before the twentieth anniversary, the war cult would deliberately play upon the ambiguities of Soviet patriotic identity. Like the turn to the war of the early 1960s, this aspect of Soviet patriotic memory first manifested among Soviet youth organizations, in the sharp uptick of military-patriotic indoctrination.

The Military-Patriotic Compromise

Both Brudny and Mitrokhin have demonstrated convincingly how, under the leadership of Sergei Pavlov (1959–68), the Komsomol took on an increasingly militant, anti-Western orientation during the second half of the 1960s, in part to insulate Soviet youth from the perceived encroachment of Western culture and ideas. Mitrokhin describes the ideology of the Pavlov group as a mélange of "romantic militarism," xenophobia, anti-Semitism, and ethnonationalism. Evidently as a means of disseminating this ideology, Pavlov oversaw the most radical expansion of military-patriotic education since Stalin's death.[40]

In December 1965, during the plenum of the Komsomol Central Committee, much of the organization's leadership signaled its support for this pivot toward Russocentric nationalism. For a number of the

[39] Brudny, *Reinventing Russia*, 61.
[40] Mitrokhin, *Russkaia partiia*, 249–250; Brudny, *Reinventing Russia*, 61–63; Brunstedt, "Building a Pan-Soviet Past," 163.

plenum's representatives, the intensified military-patriotic emphasis implied a strengthening of the Russocentric paradigm. This was the position of Sergei Narovchatov of the Moscow department of the RSFSR Writers' Union, who greeted the new line with a recitation of the wartime poetry of Pavel Kogan: "I am a patriot, / I am the Russian air, / I love the Russian land, / And where else do I find birch / Such as that which is at my side."[41] Valerii Ganichev, the deputy editor of the nationalist-aligned *Molodaia gvardiia*, recalled his exhilaration over the distinctly Russian flavor of the newly unveiled militarism during the plenum. Ganichev was especially struck by the words of the famed cosmonaut Iurii Gagarin. Gagarin purportedly became emotional before his address during a conversation about the Stalin-era destruction of the Cathedral of Christ the Savior in Moscow. The plenum's organizers had drafted a speech for the cosmonaut, but he decline to use it, and instead channeled his outrage into an impromptu proposal to restore the cathedral based solely on its role as a monument to the Patriotic War of 1812. "After all," Gagarin stated, "everyone still remembers the Great Patriotic War." The first human to venture into outer space apparently saw little need to distinguish between commemorations of the war against Napoleon and those marking the struggle against Hitler.[42]

Gagarin's open support for the cathedral's restoration, Ganichev writes, made a huge impression on those in the hall. In Ganichev's opinion, Gagarin was simply expressing the view held by the "broad masses." But among party ideologists, the cosmonaut's words "caused a panic." Similar proposals to incorporate architectural monuments of the Old Regime into the new military-patriotic curriculum raised alarms in certain quarters of the Komsomol as well. Notably, Marina Zhuravleva, a CC secretary within the organization, criticized the attempt to more fully embrace prerevolutionary iconography and personalities. In the aftermath of the 1965 plenum, Pavlov, likely in consultation with the Politburo, urged a middle course. The Komsomol first secretary directed the program's managers to continue the work of fostering an appreciation of prerevolutionary architecture in general, which he deemed "fruitful," but to "most importantly" focus on the modern military theme. This was, if not an implicit endorsement of compartmentalized discursive tension, then a step in that direction.[43]

As the military-patriotic program was put into effect over the course of 1966, Komsomol activities centered more directly on the theme of the Great Patriotic War.[44] But the degree to which the new focus could

[41] *Vernye podvigu ottsov*, 110. [42] Ganichev, "Molodaia gvardiia," 121–130.
[43] Ganichev, 129. [44] Ganichev, 129–131.

incorporate certain Russian national-patriotic elements remained an open question. Indeed, not all of the luminaries linked to the Komsomol's military-patriotic agenda shared the Russocentric outlook of the organization's hardliners. Significantly, Georgii Zhukov, whose memoirs caused a sensation upon publication in 1969, held a view of wartime patriotism at odds with the Russocentric nationalists in the Komsomol.[45] Ganichev was dismayed when, during a Komsomol delegation's visit with the retired marshal, Zhukov appeared to support the official Soviet explanation of victory. After presenting Zhukov with the poetry anthology *Oh, Russian Land*, the group engaged in a lengthy discussion about the war over brandy. Toward the end of the conversation, Ganichev posed a final question: "But all the same, Georgii Konstantinovich, why were we victorious?" This query apparently caused some discomfort in the room, and a member of the delegation, S. G. Arutiunian, immediately reprimanded him for the question's vagueness. "Of course, I knew from our textbooks," Ganichev mused, "that the main thing was the leadership and direction of the Party, the socialist economic system, the friendship of the peoples. And this is probably true to some extent." Ganichev evidently had hoped that his hero Zhukov might bolster the Russophile cause by ascribing some aspect of victory to the Russian nation and its pedigree. Zhukov was happy to answer, but not in the way Ganichev desired:

> The marshal paused, and, reassuring Arutiunian, said: "A good question, important. After all, at the beginning of the war we were weaker, and they were more experienced. We studied and learned a lot from German generals – Schlieffen, Clausewitz, Moltke. The Prussian officer is a genuine, centuries-old military pillar. The German army marched all over Europe: France, Belgium, Denmark, Norway, Greece, and Czechoslovakia. Everyone bowed before her. German technology was better in mass production – their tanks, planes, guns." The marshal was silent for a moment, his gaze seemed clouded, and he then said important, deeply felt words to us: "When war broke out, regular troops began to buckle, [but] it turned out that we had the best young soldier. Yes, we had the best, the most ideologically prepared . . . a sincere, young, ready-to-fight soldier!"

Somewhat surprised by Zhukov's response, Ganichev chalked up the marshal's ideological orthodoxy to criticism he received in 1957 about downplaying the political-ideological factor.[46]

Debates concerning the character of the new military-patriotic program – whether it should be rooted in the Russian martial longue durée or purely in the revolutionary transformations that came in the wake of 1917 – preoccupied Komsomol authorities throughout the year.[47]

[45] Zhukov, *Vospominaniia i razmyshleniia*. On the publication and reception of Zhukov's memoirs, see Roberts, *Stalin's General*, 296–304.
[46] Ganichev, "Molodaia gvardiia," 130–132. [47] See RGASPI M-1/32/1193–1194 (all).

A number of prominent writers, publishers, and academicians deliberated this issue during a conference on propagandizing military-patriotic subjects. The speakers at this meeting came down firmly on the side of promoting national-historical links across the revolutionary divide, and complained that the younger generation was not sufficiently imbued with "the entirety of our history." One of the attendees was Vasilii Peskov, the aforementioned author of "Native Land," who remarked pointedly that "[i]f a person does not grasp the meaning of [St. Basil's Cathedral], he will not respect the graves of the Heroes of Stalingrad." Reviakin, an instructor at a scientific institute, concurred, adding that, in his experience, party upbringing too often "contrasts the new with the old." Remedying this was crucial not only for Russian youths. Reviakin claimed that non-Russian students at his institution were especially appalled by the state's treatment of prerevolutionary Russian artifacts. "If you feel like that about your past," they would tell him, "how can you respect our history? Our national traditions?" Sergei Smirnov, the author of the popular *Brest Fortress* and a number of other war novels, acknowledged that it was important that revolutionary traditions break with certain, unnecessary connections with the past. However, he lamented, "we have also broken with world-class monuments." It was in precisely this context that Smirnov quipped: "We are playing soccer with the skull of Bagration, [we are] tossing out Suvorov's remains from his tomb." As with other disputes surrounding the role of prerevolutionary patriotic imagery, this was, Smirnov affirmed, "not a thing of the past, it is a struggle for the present."[48]

And yet, in the absence of a systematic program of indoctrination that could unite the old with the new, Smirnov held up the emerging war cult as the next best thing. "The education of the youth in the traditions of the Great Patriotic War," he noted, "this is the most intelligible thing that can be found now."

> It combines such good things as the campaign of the Red Pathfinders, the campaign of military glory ... Once again, I say that materials of the Great Patriotic War are the most effective. It is through them that our youth are taught how to respect history, monuments, how to honor heroism and love for their land.[49]

But the greater attention paid to the war theme over the past year was only a starting point. Smirnov pointed to the forthcoming twenty-fifth anniversary of the Battle of Moscow as a time to build upon these commemorative foundations, particularly in the realm of monument

[48] RGASPI M-1/32/1193/11–21. [49] RGANI M-1/32/1193/13–15.

construction. "I've traveled around the outskirts of Moscow," he noted of the city's dearth of memorial structures. "I can't express anything but shame, bitterness, and reproach."[50] For Smirnov, the most logical and efficient way to foster Soviet patriotism in lieu of a greater emphasis on Russia's prerevolutionary heritage was the further development of the cult of the Great Patriotic War.

Indeed, even where discussions tended to privilege the Russocentric paradigm, the war generally emerges as a pan-Soviet counterpoise, as an exclusive expression of the epoch of socialism.[51] In practice, moreover, the expansion of military-patriotic education commenced by the Komsomol plenum spurred initiatives recalling the immediate aftermath of the Twentieth Party Congress. They were pan-Soviet in orientation and yoked to the postrevolutionary metanarrative. For example, the year 1966 witnessed the enlargement of the All-Union Tourist Campaign of the Youth to Places of Revolutionary, Military, and Labor Glory. An internal report detailing the campaign's work that year, quoted at length here, reflected not only an increased militarism but also the decidedly pan-Soviet/internationalist nature of that militarism:

> Along with continual outings to places of historic battles of the Great Patriotic War, in a majority of the republics, districts and regions there is broad participation among young people in charting the path of the Red Army during the Civil War, in the study of the history of the creation and development of Soviet power. Massive paramilitary games, motorcycle relays, gatherings in places associated with the most significant events in the life of the Soviet state, the Party, and the Komsomol have become a tradition. A distinctive feature of this year's events was their pronounced military-patriotic orientation, which impelled tour groups and expeditions to prepare for the twenty-fifth anniversary of the defense of the hero-cities and victory at Moscow. Meetings with veterans of the Revolution, war, and labor, militia games, visits with famous military units, and the installation of monuments were essential elements. One specific assignment for [Moscow's] city and regional Komsomol organization was the charting of the boundary of the Battle of Moscow. Tens of thousands of young scouts learned the history of the battle, restored dugouts, pillboxes, [and] trenches, [they] put in order the graves of those killed near Moscow.[52]

The same year, Moscow hosted the All-Union Rally of Victors – the most elaborate event coordinated by the campaign. These rallies, which brought thousands of youths from across the USSR to the Hero Cities and other urban centers with links to the war, typically took place over the course of a week and involved games, excursions, and competitions designed to expose young people to the history of 1941–5. As with other major military-patriotic initiatives conducted by the Komsomol that year,

[50] Ibid. [51] RGANI M-1/32/1193/46. [52] RGASPI M-1/38/37/48–52.

preparations for and media coverage of the Moscow Victors' Rally reflected an exclusively postrevolutionary and pan-Soviet militarism – a departure from the Russocentric tone of the 1965 Komsomol plenum.[53]

In this sense especially, the patriotic ideology of the Pavlov group was not a marked break with the model established by the preceding two congresses and Party Program. The Russocentric appeals brought forth during the 1965 plenum helped propel the Komsomol in a more militant direction; but, under Pavlov, it was a militarism with a decidedly supra-ethnic and Soviet-centered character. The Brezhnev-Suslov faction of the leadership, after all, shared many of the concerns articulated during the plenum; for instance, that love for the Soviet homeland was declining among the country's youth, an issue exacerbated, as they saw it, by liberal-reformist efforts to debunk Stalin-era myths. As Brezhnev put it in a November 1966 tirade to his Politburo colleagues:

> In some of the writings in journals and our other publications, the [events] that are most sacred, most dear to the hearts of our people have been criticized. It seems that some of our writers (and their audiences) agree that allegedly ... there were no twenty-eight Panfilovtsy, that there were less of them, that this event was practically invented, that there was no [junior political officer] Klochko[v] and that he didn't call out: "there is nowhere to retreat – Moscow is at our backs[!]" They even agree on slanderous remarks against the October Revolution and other historical stages in the glorious history of our Party and Soviet people ... We really must introduce a new foundation for the system, a new foundation for the ideas of the Twenty-third Party Congress and for the history of our Motherland, and the history of the Great Patriotic War, and especially the whole history of our Party.[54]

Such concerns echoed those raised during the plenum by a number of senior members of the Pavlov group, including the first secretary of the Moscow city Komsomol organization, V. P. Trushin. "This is what worries me," Trushin noted in his address to the plenum. "The theme of the war is often represented only from the point of view of concentration camps and prisoners ... there is an obvious bias, a historical falsehood ... [to say] that the most active patriots during the war were those who found themselves in captivity."[55] The campaign for military-patriotic upbringing was an apparent compromise between the Russocentric nationalism emanating from power centers such as the Komsomol on one hand and the dominant pan-Soviet/internationalist

[53] For Palov's report to the Poliburo on the rally, see RASPI M-1/38/38/1–4. For press coverage, see *Komsomol'skaia pravda* issues from Aug. 31 to Sep. 13, 1966.

[54] "Dogovarivaiutsia do togo, chto ne bylo zalpa 'Avrory'," 112, 120.

[55] *Vernye podvigu ottsov*, 54. For similarly overlapping concerns, see the Fifteenth Komsomol Congress of May 1966: *XV s"ezd vsesoiuznogo leninskogo kommunisticheskogo soiuza molodezhi*.

line favored by Brezhnev and internationalist-minded patriots in the party apparatus.

By December 1966, Pavlov could articulate a clear sense of the direction, scope, and character of military-patriotic upbringing as it would be carried out for the foreseeable future. Writing in the Party's main ideological journal that month, Pavlov presented his vision for the program in the coming years. Unsurprisingly, his agenda homed in on topics common to *both* the plenum and Brezhnev's Politburo remarks, which necessarily excluded Russocentric themes:

> Young people show great interest in the history and theory of the communist movement. In this regard, during the coming academic year, we recommend a new program: "Conversations about the Party." It will consist of simple and spontaneous conversations with Old Communists, heroes of the Civil and Great Patriotic wars, senior workers. Mastering the rich historical experience of the country helps to ensure continuity between generations. The Komsomol organizations take great care in educating young people in the history of our state, the Communist Party, in the broad experience of building socialism in the USSR. Especially popular are the various trips to places of revolutionary, military, and labor glory.[56]

In short, such significant overlap existed between the pan-Soviet and Russocentric nationalist agendas that there was little need to steer the war narrative in a Russocentric direction. The victory myth, along with its commemorative edifice, was so appealing from the leadership's perspective precisely because it seemed to have the capacity to reconcile these competing tendencies, all without sacrificing the myth's fundamentally pan-Soviet/internationalist alignment (Figure 4.2).

Routinization of the 1970s

The rise of Russocentric nationalists and their supporters within the Party came to an end by the 1970s, something explored further in the next chapter. Suffice it to say that the crackdown on nationalism was, in part, connected to domestic commemorative politics: The impending celebrations of Lenin's 100th birthday (1970) and the fiftieth anniversary of the USSR's founding (1972) were important impetuses in the direction of the pan-Soviet model of patriotic identity. Mitrokhin observes that the previous such campaign to stifle "official" Russian nationalist expression occurred in 1967, during the run up to the fiftieth anniversary of the Bolshevik Revolution.[57] Unlike after the 1967 crackdown, Russocentric

[56] Quoted in *Politicheskii dnevnik*, 1:127–128. [57] Mitrokhin, *Russkaia partiia*, 118.

Figure 4.2 Young people meet with the Soviet cosmonauts Vladimir Komarov and Valery Bukovsky during the Komsomol congress of 1966 (Yevgeny Kassin/TASS via Getty Images).

nationalism did not return as a significant political force within the party apparatus following the anniversaries of the 1970s.

But the suppression of Russocentric nationalism was not only geared toward domestic audiences. The increased militarization of Soviet society during the second half of the 1960s, and the appearance of nationalist sympathizers within party and Komsomol ranks, had left the Soviet Union increasingly vulnerable to perceived ideological attacks from abroad. The late 1960s and 1970s witnessed a proliferation of texts designed to counter "bourgeois falsifications" about the fundamentally Russian character of the Soviet state.[58] By the early 1970s, the ideological establishment saw the main threat to be emanating from a number of professional historians in the United States and Great Britain. These included, most prominently, Richard Pipes, Frederick Barghoorn, and the British scholars Hugh Seton-Watson and Geoffrey Wheeler, among others. These bourgeois scholars, it was claimed, were perpetuating the ideas of former Vlasovites and retired Nazi generals. As summarized by

[58] See, for example, Bagramov, *Natsional'nyi vopros i burzhuaznaia ideologiia*; Modrzhinskaia, *Leninizm i sovremennaia ideologicheskaia bor'ba*; Tsamerian, *Teoreticheskie problemy*.

the academician I. P. Tsamerian: "They argue that the Soviet Union is not a federal, but unitary state, that allegedly the RSFSR and Russian nation occupy a privileged and dominant position in the Soviet Union . . . When it comes to the Soviet people and the events in the life of our multinational country, instead of 'Soviet citizens,' they deliberately write 'Russians.'" In the face of such direct challenges from "hundreds of specialists in anti-Soviet and anti-communist propaganda," the political leadership supercharged the Soviet people doctrine's pan-Soviet /internationalist pole.[59]

Following its introduction in 1961, political leaders and ideologists continued to develop the Soviet people doctrine and its framing of Soviet society as a "new historical community."[60] This occurred in fits and starts, but by 1971, when the Party hosted its Twenty-Fourth Congress, this idea had become a key feature of developed socialism.[61] In Brezhnev's 1971 formulation, the "new historical community of people" was forged "in the struggle for socialism, in the battles fought in its defense."[62] The concept even made its way into both the preamble and Article 70 of the Soviet constitution of 1977.[63] Deployed selectively so as not to antagonize skeptical non-Russian populations, who might view the doctrine as a screen for what was an essentially Russian imperial project, Yaroslav Bilinsky has proposed that it was also an effort to steal Russian nationalists' thunder.[64] Indeed, Russian nationalist activism briefly spiked in 1970 and 1979, following the release of census data that indicated falling birth rates among ethnic Russians vis-à-vis their Caucasian and Central Asian compatriots.[65] More so than in its 1960s manifestations, the Soviet people doctrine of the 1970s served to counteract attempts by Russians to "idealize the past and obscure the social contradictions in the history of their people."[66]

The weight accorded supra-ethnic unity at this time momentarily revived the idea of a singular "Soviet nation" [*sovetskaia natsiia*]. Although never acknowledged by the party leadership, ideologues under Brezhnev occasionally raised this possibility. In a review of the Soviet

59 Tsamerian, *Teoreticheskie problemy* 262–267.
60 For an excellent overview, see Aktürk, *Regimes of Ethnicity*, 197–228.
61 Simon, *Nationalism*, 307–314; Duncan, "Ideology and the National Question," 189; Hill, "The All-People's State," 111–112.
62 *XXIV s"ezd [KPSS]*, 101.
63 "Konstitutsiia (Osnovnoi Zakon) Soiuza Sovetskikh Sotsialisticheskikh Respublik," *Pravda*, Oct. 8, 1977, 3.
64 Bilinsky, "The Concept of the Soviet People," 133.
65 Brudny, *Reinventing Russia*, 144–147; Kaiser, *The Geography of Nationalism*, 394–99; Nahaylo and Swoboda, *Soviet Disunion*, 174–177.
66 Tsamerian, *Teoreticheskie problemy*, 268–269.

ideological literature, Tsamerian pointed to a number of individual "researchers who believe that [merger] is taking place" and who "come to the logical conclusion about the USSR becoming a single Soviet nation [*edinaia sovetskaia natsiia*]." However, such a view was a liability from an official standpoint, he wrote, "because the largest Soviet nation is the Russian socialist nation, and the Russian language serves as the language of interethnic communication." Therefore, "another conclusion follows: that this 'single Soviet nation' that speaks Russian is nothing more than an enlarged Russian Soviet nation." Hence, Tsamerian concluded, it was more appropriate, if not more "logical," to speak of "unity" and "solidarity" than merger or Soviet nationhood.[67]

Once again, the war provided the centerpiece of the Soviet people doctrine's laterally integrated pan-Soviet/internationalist pole. As Brezhnev reported to the Central Committee on the occasion of the fiftieth anniversary of the USSR's founding in December 1972, the "all-national pride of the Soviet person ... is more expansive and profound than the natural [sub-state] ethnic feelings of the individual peoples making up our country." Victory in the war, Brezhnev affirmed, was "the most convincing expression" of this ideal. Brezhnev's main address and the CC resolution on the thirtieth anniversary of victory in May 1975 struck a similar chord, with both texts attributing victory to supra-ethnic values such as "[d]edication to communist ideals." The Moscow Party Committee likewise orchestrated its May Ninth commemorations in a way that stressed universal themes tied exclusively with the socialist epoch (Figure 4.3).[68]

The strength of the pan-Soviet paradigm by the 1970s is further reflected in the virtual disappearance of wartime Russocentric tropes from central publications. This absence was not lost on members of the patriotic intelligentsia. During the Third RSFSR Writers' Congress in 1970, the children's author and historian Sergei Alekseev complained of the evident inability of the military-patriotic program to fully embrace the great ancestors theme. Citing recent criticism of patriotic children's literature for its overemphasis on the protagonists' deaths "in clashes with the enemy," Alekseev grumbled that patriotic upbringing had become overly restrictive. What was needed was a loosening of constraints, not

[67] Tsamerian, 247–248.
[68] See "O piatidesiatiletii Soiuza Sovetskikh Sotsialisticheskikh Respublik," *Pravda*, Dec. 22, 1972, 2–5; "Postanovlenie TsK KPSS 'O 30-letii Pobedy sovetskogo naroda v Velikoi Otechestvennoi voine 1941–1945 godov,'" *Pravda*, Feb. 9, 1975, 1–2; "Velikii podvig sovetskogo naroda," *Pravda*, May 9, 1975, 1–3. See also Pliashkevich, "Druzhba narodov SSSR," 3–11. On Moscow city commemorative planning for Victory Day in 1975, see, for instance, TsAOPIM 4/220/330/7–14, which highlighted the close link between the Revolution (Lenin's Mausoleum) and victory (Tomb of the Unknown Soldier).

Figure 4.3 Soviet poster commemorating the thirtieth anniversary of victory during the peak of the pan-Soviet/internationalist war cult in 1975 (courtesy of the Wende Museum).

just in the way stories were told, but in the historical material available to writers of the military-patriotic genre. "The history of our country and our peoples encompasses ten centuries," he declared. "This is a great story. [It's] the history not only of a people of toilers and creators, but also a history of the development and formation of the character of the Russian soldier." By tapping into the "exploits of grandfathers, great-grandfathers, and [more distant] ancestors," authors could reveal the "endless chain" of patriotism that united the past and the present. "It was not in vain," Alekseev added predictably, "that during the country's greatest trials the words resounded: 'Let the heroic image of our great ancestors inspire you in this war' [lists great ancestors]." But presently, "nothing was being done" on this topic – or "almost nothing," he corrected himself. Alekseev counted one and a half publications devoted to this theme over the past year; a half because that particular work was devoted exclusively to military affairs.[69]

Wartime Russocentric themes did not vanish entirely, however. The aforementioned publications devoted to countering "Western bourgeois slander" featured the great ancestors theme prominently – only now it was not to celebrate it but to explain it away. E. A. Bagramov, one of the leading Soviet authorities working in this genre and whose texts were frequently published abroad, put it this way:

> [I]n Western literature one comes across strange assertions to the effect that during the harsh years of war ... the Communist Party allegedly appealed not to the internationalism of the masses, but to the nationalism of the Russian people. To prove their point the authors refer to the fact that the Soviet leadership cited the names of outstanding Russian commanders of the past. They also maintain ... that during World War II the Russians supposedly fought not as much for the ideals of international communism as for their own ethnic territory. Yet the Communists appealed not to the nationalist, but to the *patriotic* feelings of the Russian people, to the best traditions of all the peoples of the USSR ... As for Soviet patriotism, it is of a truly international nature and does not oppose but unites nations.[70]

In other words, Nevskii, Donskoi, Kutuzov, and so on, were patriotic archetypes deployed not for their specific connection to the Russian nation but because they were effective vessels for socialist patriotic ideals, identifiable to all of the peoples of the USSR. Bagramov concluded his apologia with Egorov and Kantariia's hoisting of the Red Banner over the Reichstag. The image of the Russian and Georgian soldiers symbolized "the friendship of the Soviet peoples – a distinguishing feature of the Soviet way of life and, at the same time, one of the chief conditions of the victory over the Nazis." Thus, Bagramov, having indicated the instrumental nature of the great ancestors theme, shifted the focus to an undeniably Soviet source of victory, impossible in the prerevolutionary age, multiethnic friendship – a juxtaposition that further distanced the outcome of the war in 1945 from the Russocentric appeals of 1941. As with the larger war myth by this point, Stalin's toast to the Russian people was not even acknowledged as a legitimate topic requiring

[69] "III s"ezd pisatelei RSFSR," *Literaturnaia gazeta*, April 1, 1970, 10. A database search of the Soviet central press turned up only one reference to the great ancestors speech between 1961 and 1979: Alekseev's address during the writers' congress.

[70] Bagramov, *The CPSU's Nationalities Policy*, 55–56. This text was based on his earlier *Natsional'nyi vopros i burzhuaznaia ideologiia*.

contextualization. Rather, it was consigned, along with other "negative" features of Stalin's cult, to the proverbial dust heap.

And yet, the partial resurrection of the Soviet dictator as war leader from the mid-1960s created an additional silo for the Russocentrism of the war years: literary depictions of Stalin. Simonov's *The Living & the Dead*, published in 1959, had deliberately obscured Stalin's more blatant Russocentric pandering. For example, the character General Fedor Serpilin, who attended the Red Square parade of November 1941, was unable to recall precisely what Stalin said: only that the "Germans were near Moscow ... and that was the main thing."[71] By contrast, the great ancestors featured explicitly in later war novels, but mostly in the context of Stalin's personal foibles and office décor. In Bondarev's 1969 *Hot Snow*, Stalin summons Lieutenant-General Bessonov to his Kremlin office. When Bessonov arrives, he scans the space, which appeared "like a hall, a study, with portraits of Suvorov and Kutuzov on the walls, and a long meeting table ... with a topographic map on another huge table."[72] Stadniuk's three-volume *War*, which typified the dry "official" style of many war novels of the cult, contains a similar scene. Molotov enters Stalin's office and the two have a brief discussion about the various portraits on the walls. When Stalin asks Molotov which portraits they should hang next, Molotov answers, "Perhaps Timoshenko and Zhukov?" Stadniuk recounts the rest of the conversation: "'This is closer to the truth,' Stalin answered seriously. 'Maybe we'll hang portraits of Timoshenko and Zhukov after our victory. But now it is necessary to see portraits of Suvorov and Kutuzov here.' 'Yes, there is a reason for this,' agreed Molotov.'"[73]

In this way, war novelists perpetuated the great ancestors theme indirectly, through the rather neutral vessel of the "balanced" late-socialist version of Stalin at war. This practice persisted well into the 1980s and not only in war novels. Anatolii Rybakov's *Children of the Arbat*, published in 1987 under conditions of glasnost, depicted Stalin's personal obsession with state-building tsars like Peter the Great and Ivan Groznyi.[74] Of course, Rybakov was criticizing rather than fawning over this aspect of the dictator. But the frequent symbolic conflation of the person of Stalin with Russian national-patriotic imagery helped further

[71] Simonov, *Sobranie sochinenii*, 4:323–347, qt. 341. [72] Bondarev, *Goriachii sneg*, 76.

[73] Stadniuk, *Voina*, 278–287. The novel contains several other discussions of Russia's great ancestors outside the association with Stalin; yet these are almost always in the context of military lessons from the past rather than as part of a grand Russian ethno-historical myth of war – although the latter is certainly implied.

[74] Rybakov, *Deti Arbata*, 269–270. On this aspect of the novel, see also Perrie, "The Tsar, the Emperor, the Leader," 77–100.

the dictator's reputation as a staunch defender of Russian national identity throughout the late-socialist era.

During the high war cult of the 1970s, however, such historical-Russocentric themes did not typically extend beyond the confines of Stalin's office. Indeed, the broader abandonment of war-related Russocentrism was evident in the strikingly orthodox accounts of the war contained in the Russian nationalist press at the time. For its issue marking the USSR's fiftieth anniversary, *Nash sovremennik*, the premier nationalist journal of the 1970s, featured poetry and essays by non-Russian and non-Slavic authors.[75] Its main critical essay, however, was written by the Russian nationalist and long-time advocate of the Orthodox Church, Vladislav Shoshin. Consonant with the Soviet people doctrine, Shoshin characterized the early development of the "friendship of the peoples" in Russocentric fashion: "The noble example of the Russian people helped each nationality realize their place in the family of peoples of the Russian [*Rossiiskii*], and later Union, republics." Moreover, Shoshin cited Russian benevolence, rather than socialist "internationalism," as the inspiration behind Soviet aid to the Third World.

Shoshin's Russocentric worldview, however, did not extend to the war. The war years, Shoshin wrote in rather stock phraseology, "strengthened the unity of the fraternal peoples. The strength of socialist internationalism was tested in the fires of battle." The author then highlighted several literary accounts of shared multiethnic heroism, for example an Uzbek soldier saving a Russian girl and a Russian soldier rescuing his Uzbek comrade. "It is significant," Shoshin wrote, "that the first part of [Mukhtar] Auezov's novel *The Path of Abai* came out in Georgia in 1942," when the war was in full swing. Auezov's novel depicted the harsh, everyday life and social stratification of prerevolutionary Kazakhstan, and the constructive bonds that developed between the novel's protagonist and Russian revolutionaries in exile. That such a novel first appeared in Georgia was, for Shoshin, an indication of the transcendent, revolutionary values that bound every Soviet nation. Similarly, Shoshin went on to cite the work of war novelist Aleksandr Fadeev as evidence that Soviet literature not only reveals various nationalities fighting side by side, but also those non-ethnic, socialist principles around which the Soviet population rallied during the war. Fadeev, Shoshin wrote, portrayed youths of various nationalities during wartime, "however, the reader never senses a substantial difference in the ethnicities of the novel's heroes. This is not

[75] Brudny notes that between 1971 and the end of the Brezhnev period, the circulation of *Nash sovremennik* grew by 236 percent. Brudny, *Reinventing Russia*, 18.

the irrational passion of war; it is a manifestation of the solidarity of the Soviet people." In Shoshin's telling, ethnic distinctions were less significant than the Soviet identity that united all citizens. And although the war "strengthened the unity" of the Soviet people, it was communist ideology, not some contingent, fleeting "passion of war," much less Russians as the carrier of higher culture and patriotic traditions, that stood at the core of the Soviet imagined community.[76]

The pan-Soviet internationalism of the war effort was also on display in the journal's issue celebrating the thirtieth anniversary of victory. Yet again, the editorial board chose an author sympathetic to the nationalist cause to write the lead critical essay – in this case the Russophile literary critic Vladimir Korobov. Korobov's essay surveyed his favorite war novelists, among whom were Russocentric nationalists and neo-Stalinists like Mikhail Alekseev, Iurii Bondarev, Ivan Stadniuk, and others. But Korobov did not underscore these writers' balanced assessment of Stalin or the way they linked the war experience to the Russian identity of their protagonists. Rather, what most struck Korobov was how these authors' stories "affirm that which is most excellent in the Soviet person – a great love for the Motherland, a sense of responsibility for its fate and its future; [they] prove the strength and fortitude of our people." Bondarev's war novels, for instance, exposed the internal struggles of the Soviet soldier, "the daily, minute-by-minute, superhuman overcoming of troublesome thoughts [and] mental anxiety, where abstract philosophical and moral categories in war take a kind of very specific and visible form." Likewise, Korobov credited the work of Ivan Stadniuk for providing readers a realistic glimpse of both the decision-making that went on in the Kremlin (a veiled reference to Stalin) and the passion with which Soviet soldiers fought and died at the front. There was, in other words, little way to discern whether Korobov was praising the transcendent, ideological patriotism born of the 1917 revolution or the primordial variety rooted deep within the Russian historical experience.[77]

If these commemorative articles are any indication, the Soviet victory myth, even among the most extreme Russocentric nationalist outlets, retained its pan-Soviet gloss. Where the creation of organizations like VOOPIiK (discussed in the next chapter) provided an outlet for controlled explorations of prerevolutionary Russian history and culture, the military-patriotic compromise now extended beyond the Komsomol to facilitate proper engagement with the war theme among nationalists and

[76] Shoshin, "Velikaia letopis' druzhby," 97–101. For background on Shoshin, see Brudny, *Reinventing Russia*, 70–71.

[77] Korobov, "Kakie byli vremena!" 155–162.

internationalists alike. Seen from this vantage point, the expansion of the war cult was less an outgrowth of officially co-opted Russian nationalism than a way to contain that nationalism. Indeed, the suppression among Russians of a particularistic sense of their leadership during the war is evident not only in the texts and speeches of political leaders and ideologists, but in the various projects for the memorials that would become the war cult's most indelible feature.

Monuments to No Nation in Particular

The post-Stalin leadership had been fairly consistent in its evaluation of war memorials as a potentially effective tool of political indoctrination and mobilization. But financial obstacles and the memory politics of destalinization frequently undercut monument projects during the 1950s. The turn to the war of the early 1960s and Brezhnev's subsequent launch of the war cult returned the issue of war memorials to the fore. By the twentieth anniversary of victory, several major memorial projects conceived under Khrushchev were nearing completion. These included the Tomb of the Unknown Soldier in Alexander Gardens at the base of the Kremlin wall in Moscow (1967) and the Vuchetich-led Monument to the Heroes of Stalingrad in Volgograd (1967), with its enormous *Motherland Calls* central sculpture. By this time, Vuchetich was also overseeing Moscow's ill-fated Victory Monument project, sited on the city's Poklonnaia Hill, where planners had installed a foundation stone in 1958.[78]

Attention to the planning behind war memorials, even the "paper monuments" that never advanced to the construction stage, offers an important window into the war's public memory.[79] This is because of both the volume of documentation produced – it is not uncommon for memorial projects to take a decade or more to come to fruition – and, as Antony Kalashnikov has noted, the "future-oriented, posterity-focused" nature of the discourse surrounding monuments.[80] Implicitly or

[78] On Soviet war memorials and their significance for the war cult, see, for example, Cohen, *War Monuments*, 147–182; Gabowitsch, "Soviet War Memorials from Berlin to Pyongyang"; Gabowitsch, "Patron-Client Networks and the Making of Soviet War Memorials," 14–17; Konradova and Ryleva, "Geroi i Zhertvy," 241–261; Palmer, "How Memory Was Made," 373–407; Kirschenbaum, *The Legacy of the Siege*, 186–228; Fowkes, "Soviet War Memorials," 11–32; Fowkes, "The Role of Monumental Sculpture"; Schleifman, "Moscow's Victory Park"; Tumarkin, *The Living & the Dead*, 125–157.

[79] This might be why, as Catriona Kelly has recently observed, the relatively few studies of the war cult's creation have focused disproportionally on its monuments. Kelly, "The Motherland and the Fight with Fascism," 1–2.

[80] Kalashnikov, "Stalinist War Monuments," 2.

explicitly, discussions about memorials, especially those dedicated to foundational myths of state, are also discussions about national identity. As James Young writes, monuments constitute attempts "to create shared spaces that lend a common spatial frame to otherwise disparate experiences and understanding," thereby propagating "the illusion of common memory."[81]

What follows is not a comprehensive survey of Soviet war memorial planning – a nearly impossible task.[82] Rather, the discussion below will survey key instances where the tension between Russocentric and pan-Soviet models of war memory was particularly pointed. To be sure, the vast majority of built monuments were pan-Soviet in composition and tended to obscure particularistic expressions of Russian leadership in favor of the undifferentiated Soviet whole. This was especially true of central and RSFSR memorials. However, the handful of cases examined here demonstrate that, whatever the official line, many of the war cult's planners held to the Russocentric paradigm only to be thwarted by the intervention of central cultural authorities or the party leadership. Moreover, as with other forms of Soviet war memory, the question of Russian leadership and ethnic particularism in non-Russian contexts did not necessarily follow the pattern of the country's largest republic.

Shortly after the twentieth anniversary of Victory Day, the Komsomol Central Committee sent delegations to inspect the state of the country's war monuments. The sites selected represented a geographic cross section of the USSR: the Russian oblasts of Arkhangelsk, Smolensk, Moscow, Novgorod, Pskov, as well as various locales in the Byelorussian, Ukrainian, Uzbek, and Turkmen SSRs. The Komsomol brigades reported back that while the state of the country's monuments was poor everywhere, Moscow, "the great capital of our Motherland" and newly minted Hero City, stood out for the impoverished condition of its commemorative markers, especially along the 600 kilometers of former battlefront. This was all the more troublesome, the report contended, because many of the greatest acts of heroism took place along the sporadically marked front, including the last stand of the twenty-eight Panfilov-Guardsmen. Without appropriate memorial structures, the country's youth and foreign visitors could not appreciate the full extent of the Soviet people's heroism in the defense of Moscow. With the twenty-fifth anniversary of the Battle of Moscow approaching, the report called for the mobilization of the Komsomol to begin the work of

[81] Young, *The Texture of Memory*, 6.
[82] Although the scholar Mischa Gabowitsch is currently engaged in such a comprehensive effort.

establishing monuments in honor of the first significant defeat suffered by the Wehrmacht.[83]

The Komsomol-initiated monuments created for the 1966 celebrations consisted of simple pedestals topped with models of military hardware, including tanks, aircraft, artillery guns, and rocket installations. Additionally, the organization sponsored the construction of a boundary memorial consisting of three massive "hedgehog" anti-tank barriers, marking the farthest extent of the German advance toward the capital.[84] In the aftermath of the anniversary, however, planners grew more ambitious and attempted to unify the entire battlefront, from Kalinin in the northwest to Tula in the south, into a single "Boundary of Glory" complex: a vast network of monuments, museums, panoramas, and victory parks, united thematically and compositionally.[85] Although never implemented, the design proposals and resulting debate over the Boundary project reveal the Russocentric paradigm to be alive and well among Moscow's cultural establishment.

Moscow planning agencies hosted a closed design competition for the Boundary in September 1971. The call for proposals specified simply that designs should "reflect the leading role of the Communist Party," "the mass heroism of Soviet soldiers," and "the selfless labor of the residents of Moscow." The program provisionally designated a compositional fulcrum in the city of Zelenograd, forty kilometers to the north of the city center, where "the architectural-spatial solution must reach the greatest artistic expressiveness."[86] On September 15, following a public exhibition of the twelve approved submissions, the Moscow Department of the Union of Architects held a discussion on the proposals attended by the design teams and a variety of Moscow-based architects, veterans, and members of the press.[87] The transcript of the discussion was to form the basis of the competition jury's assessment several weeks later, and it was during this discussion that basic decisions were taken over the entries and the future of the project (Figure 4.4).[88]

Of particular note is the way that many of the discussants looked to root the memorial complex in the Russian national past. Several of the design collectives favored relocating the central monument from Zelenograd to

[83] RGASPI M-1/32/1193/38–49, qt. 39.
[84] Kozlov, *Velikaia Otechestvennaia voina 1941–1945*, 622–623; Shul'gina, "Monumenty na istoricheskikh rubezhakh," 24.
[85] In fact, several other such "boundaries" already existed, albeit on a smaller scale, including Leningrad's Greenbelt of Glory. See Kirschenbaum, *The Legacy of the Siege*, 189.
[86] RGALI 2466/4/157/7–19.
[87] A. Tatulov, "Tam, gde bylo srazhenie," *Pravda*, Sep. 4, 1971, 6.
[88] See especially the concluding statement by V. A. Nesterov: RGALI 2466/4/193/68.

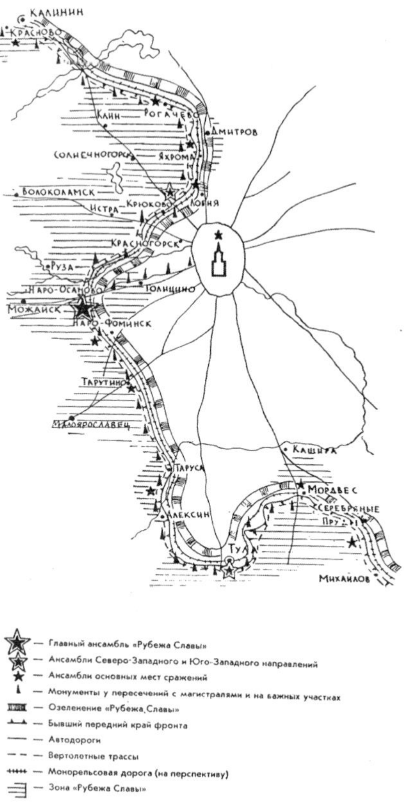

Figure 4.4 Draft of the projected "Boundary of Glory" memorial network (RGALI 2466/1/912/14).

a western location along the Mozhaisk Highway. The reason offered had less to do with highlighting battles fought in 1941 than with, as one speaker put it, uniting the "two patriotic wars: [18]12 and [19]41." The architect V. N. Simbirtsev, for example, proposed situating the main component of the Boundary on Moscow's Poklonnaia Hill, also the intended site for the all-union Victory Monument. In Simbirtsev's view, constructing the Boundary's center along the main western approach to the city, "where we, the Russian army, retreated in 1812 and then drove out Napoleon," could allow for the incorporation of the many monuments to the 1812 victory as well. Although Poklonnaia Hill was not connected to any battle of the Great Patriotic War and had clear prerevolutionary overtones, Colonel N. A. Ruban, a participant in the defense of the capital, argued that it was a relevant place to memorialize the Soviet victory, noting that it was directly past this site that many soldiers from Moscow came in 1941 before joining the battle. For these and several other discussants, a Mozhaisk-oriented central structure would resonate with veterans precisely because of its links with the past.[89]

Participants also debated the appropriate character of the individual monuments along the Boundary route. The speakers all agreed that the best monuments were those "imbued with the patriotism" and "the love for the Motherland that permeated the Russian and Soviet people during every stage of the war." Examples from the competition entries included non-ethnic, allegorical imagery, such as a classical Winged Victory and a Soviet mother-motherland sculpture set against a background of bayonet rods formed into an obelisk. However, traditional Russian and Slavic forms abounded as well. Simbirtsev, for one, reminded the audience that, historically, Russia has commemorated its great victories through the construction of Orthodox churches. He pointed to Vladimir Pokrovskii's church-monument near Leipzig commemorating the defeat of Napoleon at the Battle of the Nations and Russia's Kolomna Cathedral upon which it was based, deeming the latter "the greatest piece of Russian architecture." The figure of the mother-motherland was another point of debate. While motherland monuments were, strictly speaking, allegorical depictions of the Soviet socialist homeland, several discussants read into the form's ambiguity a more Russian meaning. Simbirtsev, remarking on a "very expressive" mother-motherland proposal, noted that it aroused in him a primordial, Russian sense of patriotism. The design, Simbirtsev gushed, recalled the words of Pushkin's notoriously nationalistic poem "To the Slanderers of Russia," which he then went on to recite, concluding with the verse, "Will the Russian land not rise?"[90]

Among the most controversial issues was the use in several of the proposals of the traditional Slavic kurgan (burial mound). The submission by Voenproekt-2 called for a series of burial mounds, each equipped with a spotlight that would light up the Boundary at night. For Simbirtsev, the problem had nothing to do with the Slavic origins of kurgany but rather their overly solemn tone. Burial mounds, Simbirtsev reminded, "are first

[89] RGALI 2466/4/193/8, 64.

[90] RGALI 2466/4/193/11–13, 16–19, 39. My reading of the use of the mother-motherland here is not to deny the deeply ingrained significance of the feminized motherland in Russian culture, only to take the designers at their word regarding its distinctly Soviet character. As Linda Edmondson argues, the concept of motherland is far more ambiguous than is often suggested. See the following and Edmondson, "Putting Mother Russia in a European Context," 53–64; cf. Hellberg-Hirn, *Soil and Soul*, 120–121.

and foremost tombs"; better "to convey a sense of victory." "It reminds me of death," added D. V. Genningson, "but the heroic glory of our people must be optimistic." Others disagreed that the kurgan detracted from a sense of victory. Rather, as the spokesman for the military advisory commission of the Union of Architects, A. M. Gorbachev, put it, the kurgan was a powerful reminder of the Russian past. These mounds, he observed, "stand guard for our Motherland, as Russian militiamen stood, as the Russian army stood, and ... as the Red Army stood."[91]

Of course, not all of the proposals employed such historical-Russocentric imagery, but generic Soviet forms received less attention during the proceedings. In the end, the jury found all of the projects wanting. Citing "excessive labor costs," "unrealistic scales," and "complexity in development," the jury report nevertheless suggested ways to improve the program in the future. Apparently swayed by the discussion, the jury recommended relocating the compositional center to a site along the Mozhaisk highway. The main reason was a desire to pin the heart of the Boundary of Glory to the Moscow-Smolensk-Berlin line. The center of the complex would then stand at the crossroads of two sacred axes: the north-south Boundary of Glory and the east-west Road to Berlin. But the report allowed that such a relocation had the potential benefit of "bringing together the great epics of the struggles waged by the peoples of Russia in the past and the USSR in our own time."[92]

The Russocentrism expressed during the Boundary discussion raises the question of the ability of monument planners to steer such projects in an overtly Russocentric direction – something at odds with the victory myth as officially conceived. Higher authorities would almost certainly have rejected any proposal to explicitly link 1945 with pre-Soviet Russian victories, and indeed a subsequent commission killed the Boundary project.[93] But the use of ambiguous forms such as mother-motherland monuments and burial mounds was fairly common in late-socialist war memorial design. A look at one of the touchstones during the Boundary deliberations, the central *Motherland Calls* sculpture from Volgograd's Monument to the Heroes of Stalingrad complex, offers a glimpse at the way planners of successful memorial projects understood and advanced these fraught symbols.

Already in March 1958, the board of the RSFSR Ministry of Culture noted with slight unease Vuchetich's choice of building location for the central sculptural composition atop Mamaev Kurgan, named for the Tatar

[91] RGALI 2466/4/193/14–16, 28, 39, 50, 64. [92] RGALI 2466/4/912/8–10, 14.
[93] RGALI 2466/4/912/8–9, 31. Initial reasons cited included "excessive labor costs," "hypertrophied scales," and "complexity in development."

commander whom Dmitrii Donskoi defeated during the Battle of Kulikovo Field. The sculptor Lev Kerbel' complained that appropriating the site, with its Russian historical associations, constituted a "deeply national [*natsional'nyi*] device." However, S. M. Orlova deemed the location entirely appropriate given its simplicity and compositional links with Vuchetich's earlier Treptower Park memorial in Berlin, which also employed a burial mound design.[94] By March 1961, Vuchetich had essentially determined the form the mother-motherland would take. Nevertheless, he fielded additional suggestions that month from the Artistic-Expert Council for Monumental Sculpture. It was during this meeting that the question of the monument's "national" character was ultimately decided.

The critic and art historian A. A. Fedorov-Davydov first drew attention to the issue of the motherland's Russianness during the session. Although generally positive about the design, Fedorov-Davydov questioned its classical connotations, particularly its evocation of the Nike of Samothrace: "The clothing may be reminiscent of the Nike, but I would like for there to be a hint of Russian dress. I would like to see more national clothing, so that it is a bit modernized." The sculptor M. G. Manizer, though concerned that the mother-motherland's raised sword might resemble a Christian cross from a certain vantage point, nevertheless concurred that "Russian elements should be introduced into the clothing." The painter Sergei Chirkov shared the view that Russian national dress should be incorporated: "This thing must be national. All masterpieces of world art, all realistic art, has always been a monument to the era, the people, the nation [*natsiia*]. And if we say this thing has an association with the Nike, let it be a Russian Nike. I would like to see the image of the Russian motherland expressed here."[95]

But while the discussants seemed eager to advance the memorial as a Russian national monument, their intention was very clearly to underscore the "Soviet" essence of the structure. This was made plain only after some prodding by Lev Kerbel', among the most powerful representatives of the cultural establishment at the meeting. In response to Fedorov-Davydov's call to drape the mother-motherland in Russian national dress, Kerbel' shot back: "I reject the idea ... Victory at Stalingrad is an international matter. To eliminate fascism and then dress the figure in national costume is wrong." This prompted a rather awkward rejoinder from Fedorov-Davydov:

> but if the clothes are made more modern, more national ... I agree that it's not necessary to specify what the clothes will consist of. But the fascination with antiquity consisted precisely in the fact that the designated Greek costume was

[94] GARF A-501/1/4093/5–6. [95] GARF A-501/1/4093/82–87, 92.

> so generalized, idealized, that it acquired the character of a world image, of internationalism ... No matter how symbolic we are with the image, the significance of the victory won by the Russian people in the fight against fascism ... was that the USSR defeated and saved the world from fascism.

"Then I don't understand you," Kerbel' responded, flummoxed. Fedorov-Davydov tried again:

> I want to say: if we claim to be ushering in a new era in monumental art, opening a new page, we must create new forms. In sculpture, we're doing what the Greeks did in their time ... I want this woman to resemble less an ancient statue and more a mother-motherland, which, with all its architectonics, would say that this motherland is my country during a particular era ... I want to see more of the contemporary and less of the antiquity.

Recognizing that Fedorov-Davydov had evidently used "Soviet" and "Russian" interchangeably, the painter B. V. Ioganson proposed that an even more "modern" and "national" form "would be a victorious soldier from Stalingrad." This was also the context of Chirkov's "Russian motherland" suggestion, which he intended to mean "Soviet": "I repeat, [the national] should not be expressed in costume, but we must reflect the *era in which this monument belongs*." Summarizing the emerging consensus over the sculpture's fundamental Sovietness, the meeting's final contributor, A. I. Lebedev, added, "I wish only one thing: that the face and clothing better reflect a modern, Soviet person. By no means does this imply that the artist should resort to ... a genre interpretation of costume. All of this must be universalized."[96]

Vuchetich ultimately retained the sculpture's Nike motif, a decision the expert committee formally approved the next year (Figure 4.5).[97] According to Scott Palmer's study of the Stalingrad memorial, Vuchetich favored the neoclassical idiom not only because it better reflected the universal character of the Soviet victory; the sculptor's ego played a role as well. The chosen form "invited admiration from the widest possible audience," Palmer writes, which "sustained Vuchetich's pretensions as crafting works of universal significance."[98] But the preference in the upper echelons of the Party and state for ambiguity over ethnonational particularism within the RSFSR should not be discounted. Indeed, the idea that major war memorial complexes within the Russian republic should express a vague notion of pan-ethnicity was evident in the monumental commemoration of one the Soviet Union's most important tales of multiethnic heroism, the feat of the twenty-eight Panfilov-Guardsmen.

[96] GARF A-501/1/4093/84–93 (emphasis added).

[97] Palmer, "How Memory Was Made," 396. [98] Palmer, 395–396.

Figure 4.5 Unveiling ceremony for the Stalingrad memorial complex on Mamaev Kurgan (Nikolai Surovtsev/TASS via Getty Images).

With the failure of Moscow's Boundary of Glory complex, individual monuments continued to appear along the former battlefront. Locals would later apply the label "Boundary of Glory" to these structures; however, there was little compositional coordination among them. Without doubt, the most important of these piecemeal monuments from the standpoint of late-socialist ritual was the Monument to the Twenty-Eight Panfilov Heroes at Dubosekovo, the site of the alleged 1941 engagement, which was inaugurated in May 1975. But the Dubosekovo memorial was not the only monument to the twenty-eight Panfilovtsy established at that time. The very same month, officials in Alma-Ata, the capital of the Kazakh SSR, unveiled the city's grand Memorial of Glory dedicated to the Panfilov heroes. An outgrowth of the renewed public emphasis on the Soviet people doctrine and, likely, a belated reaction to Kardin's "Legends and Facts" article, the myth of the twenty-eight Panfilovtsy received a major boost during the 1970s. But while commemorating the same multiethnic feat, the planning for the Dubosekovo and Alma-Ata monuments differed in telling respects.

Alma-Ata's monument to the twenty-eight heroes captured the balance struck in the original Panfilovtsy myth between a unified, supranational Soviet people on the one hand and a rigid ethnic hierarchy on the other. The memorial consisted of a central sculpture in the shape of a map of the USSR. Filling out the map were busts of soldierly representatives of each of the union's titular nationalities, differentiated by ethnically distinctive facial features. At the forefront of the monument, bursting forth from the map with arms stretched wide, was the political commissar Klochkov – the embodiment of the Russian nation and the obviously dominant national grouping. Behind the sculpture stood a mock-up of the walls of the Kremlin. In case the Russocentric overtones were not already clear, the memorial's inscription repeated in large gold letters Klochkov's battle cry, including its suggestion that the entity the Panfilovtsy defended was not necessarily the Soviet Union but "Russia."

The memorial's Russocentric elements were contested during the planning stage. Notably, the ethnic Russian first secretary of the Alma-Ata party committee, Fedor Mochalin, called for their removal on the grounds that Kazakh soldiers fought to defend not only Moscow (and presumably not only Russia) but the USSR as a whole. One of the two lead designers, the Belarusian sculptor A. F. Artimovich, complained that the monument's design had already run the gauntlet of institutional approval, and to do away with any of the individual aspects would amount to the "rejection of the entire plan." It was the city committee's ethnic Kazakh second secretary, Anet Bektemisov, who most vocally defended the Russocentric motif, including Klochkov's battle cry. Bektemisov fired back: "I believe that the fragment of the Kremlin wall is historically justified. The words of Commissar Klochkov, 'There is nowhere to retreat, Moscow is at our backs,' have gone down in history." Although, given Mochalin's reservations, the committee ordered a hastily drafted backup option, the organizers ultimately commissioned Artimovich and Andriushchenko's Russocentric map sculpture (Figure 4.6).[99]

Yet the Alma-Ata monument to the twenty-eight heroes was something of an exception to the way the tale of the Panfilovtsy had evolved by the 1970s, when its message of lateral wartime unity was in the ascendancy. Indeed, the Kazakh memorial's theme of multiethnic steadfastness under

[99] TsGAGA 116/1/284/1–5. See also TsGAGA 116/2/206 (all); 174/29/725/130–137; 174/29/777/226–227. The Alma-Ata project was spurred by local party organizations and veterans: "Uvekovechim pamiat' gvardeitsev-panfilovtsev. K 30-letiiu Velikoi Pobedy," *Vecherniaia Alma-Ata*, Dec. 14, 1974, 1.

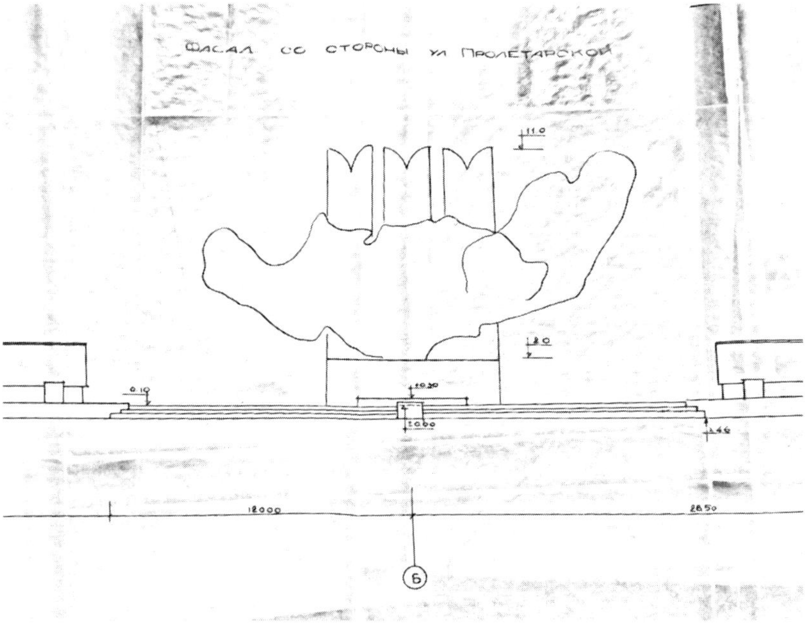

Figure 4.6 An early sketch of the Monument of Glory dedicated to the twenty-eight Panfilovtsy in the Kazakh capital of Alma-Ata (TsGAGA 116/2/206/69–70).

the leadership of the Great Russian people stood in stark contrast to the Dubosekovo complex. Developed by an artistic collective under the management of the sculptor A. G. Postol, the Dubosekovo memorial consisted of six massive granite sculptural representations of the defenders. However, unlike the Kazakh depiction, the Dubosekovo memorial did not highlight the ethnic identities of the men. During closed discussions about the memorial design, there was an explicit decision to downplay ethnonational variation and hierarchy in favor of pan-Soviet homogeneity. When two of the judges criticized the favored design's uniform depiction of the Panfilovtsy, the solution they offered was not to diversify the soldiers by national origin, but rather to give them different haircuts and clothing: "Someone," one of the judges said, "must be in a quilted jacket, someone [else] in an overcoat." Moreover, "the headgear can be diversified. There [should be] caps, helmets." This, the juror concluded, "could give multiple dimensions to the memorial." In line with this vision, the planners also omitted Klochkov's battle cry from the finished complex. Rather than Uzbek, Kyrgyz, and Kazakh soldiers,

Figure 4.7 Late-socialist military-patriotic event with part of the Monument to the Twenty-Eight Panfilov Heroes pictured in the background (courtesy of Valery Shchekoldin).

under the leadership of a Russian, the memorial presented the Panfilovtsy simply as generic heroes of Soviet origin (Figure 4.7).[100]

The ambiguity of the Dubosekovo monument was consistent with the war cult's pan-Soviet internationalism, which dominated central and RSFSR commemorations. Its inauguration attracted hundreds of guests from Central Asian republics, citizens who read into the memorial an inclusive, multiethnic significance that had little to do with the Russian elder brother trope.[101] The memorial regularly attracted Komsomol delegations from the republics and visitors from foreign Communist parties, who identified with its universal, heroic imagery.[102] At the same time, the memorial's ambiguity allowed for implicit ethnic Russian identification with the legacy of the Panfilovtsy. Moreover, where the

[100] See RGALI 3151/1/315/4–6.

[101] One particularly striking archival photo of the unveiling shows two Central Asian men, one a veteran and the other a young man, carrying a large painting through the procession that depicts Major-General Panfilov at the front flanked by two members of the twenty-eight. Panfilov appears to be preparing them for the impending fight to the death with the advancing German army. The soldier to Panfilov's right is Central Asian while to his left stands a Russian. TsMAMLS 192/1/626/1–27, esp. 24.

[102] On the site's appeal abroad, see RGASPI M-1/32/1193/38–39.

complex's physical "hardware," in Alexander Etkind's formulation, remained ambiguous, its associated "software," the manuals and guidebooks published to inform visitors about the complex, could be altered to suit current needs.[103] Indeed, an authoritative text by the Propaganda Department later affirmed that the six monumental figures "represent the soldiers of the six nationalities who together spilled their blood for the freedom and independence of the Motherland."[104] Like so many other components of the late-socialist war cult, the matrix of RSFSR monuments underscored, not the unique identity of the Russian elder brother, but the idea that victory belonged to no one nation in particular.

Russian National Redefinition in Moscow

While the promotion of ambiguity among the Union's ethnic Russian core had obvious advantages as a method of mobilization, there were potential drawbacks as well. In particular, the Party's attempt to shore up the pan-Soviet consistency of the war cult, while bringing Russocentric nationalists to heel by playing on their shared interest in military-patriotic themes, left the war's memory susceptible to Russian national-patriotic co-option from below. There is perhaps no better example of this late-socialist phenomenon than the Victory Monument project on Moscow's Poklonnaia Hill.

As depicted in *War and Peace*, upon arriving at the western gates of the city of Moscow in 1812, Napoleon marveled at the city's exotic splendor and "experienced that somewhat envious and restless curiosity which people experience at the sight of alien forms of life that know nothing of them."[105] Partly because of Tolstoy's colorful account, the elevation at the western edge of the city from which Napoleon gazed upon Moscow, Poklonnaia Hill, became a symbol of Russian arms and resilience. The territory around the hill provided a base of commemoration for Russia's war against the French and the post-Soviet political leadership claimed the site for the Russian Federation's national World War II memorial.[106]

[103] As Etkind writes, "The monumental hardware of cultural memory does not function unless it interacts with its discursive software." Etkind, *Warped Mourning*, 172–195, qt. 177.

[104] *Metodicheskoe posobie*, 17. [105] Tolstoy, *War and Peace*, 871.

[106] This section builds on important previous studies of the Poklonnaia Hill memorial. However, prior studies either focused on the post-Soviet period or did not have access to many Politburo and Secretariat documents from the Russian Presidential Archive (APRF). The latter were published in Tomilina, *Pamiatnik pobedy*, in 2004 and form the basis of the analysis here. See Krylova, "Dancing on the Graves of the Dead," 83–102; Forest and Johnson, "Unraveling the Threads of History: Soviet-Era Monuments and Post-Soviet National Identity in Moscow," 524–547; Smith, *Mythmaking in the New Russia*, 85–91; Schleifman, "Moscow's Victory Park," 5–34; Tumarkin, "The Story of a War Memorial," 125–146.

Yet the Soviet decision to erect Victory Monument on Poklonnaia Hill had nothing to do with the site's prerevolutionary Russian heritage. Rather, the project suggests how local authorities could co-opt memorials intended to advance a pan-Soviet vision and imbue these with a particularistic, Russian pedigree.

In 1955, in response to Zhukov's call for major memorial complexes in Moscow and other urban centers, the CC Secretariat assigned a special commission to determine a suitable building site in the Soviet capital. It was this commission that first suggested Poklonnaia Hill in both its 1956 report to the Central Committee and its program for an open design competition. According to these documents, the decision derived solely from Poklonnaia Hill's accessibility from a major traffic thoroughfare, the Moscow-Minsk highway.[107] Moreover, throughout the 1950s, the area around Poklonnaia Hill became the center of major urban development. This included, among other things, the improvement of transportation networks and the construction of luxury apartment buildings for party elites. One of these structures was built over a communal grave of Russian soldiers killed in 1812 and another over a Jewish cemetery.[108] Tumarkin points out that as part of the new construction works – and entirely unrelated to the potential Victory Monument – Poklonnaia Hill was largely razed for security purposes in 1957 so that potential snipers would not have vantage points from which to take aim at important political figures as they drove down the main boulevard. As debris from the renovations piled up, the new mound of earth gradually became known as Poklonnaia Hill.[109] Hence the commission selected Poklonnaia Hill simply because the area's renovation made possible a massive architectural undertaking.

But this decision, having nothing to do with an effort to link Russian victories of the past and present, opened up Poklonnaia Hill to local redefinition. In subsequent years, this part of Moscow gradually took on a more explicit symbolic connection to prerevolutionary military achievements. The main boulevard was given the distinguished title Kutuzov Prospect in 1957, and, in the 1960s, local planners established two monuments in the area that were associated with the war against Napoleon.[110] These actions were local attempts by city officials to ascribe the planned World War II memorial with the Russian military pedigree it

[107] Tomilina, *Pamiatnik pobedy*, 68–76. [108] Colton, *Moscow*, 338–339, 364.
[109] Tumarkin, *The Living & the Dead*, 215.
[110] Adrianov, "Triumfal'naia Arka meniaet adres," 10–11; Kurlat, and Sokolovskii, *S putevoditelem po Moskve*, 222. The Borodino panorama was conceived in the late-Stalin era. See Abrosimov, "Pamiatnik slavy i pobedy russkogo naroda," no. 1 (1952): 30–32.

formally lacked. In 1965, Moscow city and party officials requested to delay the deadline for Victory Monument until 1970, to allow for the installation on Kutuzov Prospect of a copy of Bove's nineteenth-century Triumphal Arch commemorating victory over Napoleon. In the words of the memo, the arch would have the power to unite "the historical events of the two Patriotic wars of 1812 and 1941–1945."[111]

However, before the mid-1980s, all-union authorities did not openly advance such an agenda, and any explicit connection between the two wars was dropped. Once the memorial's planners made the determined building site public, official publications attempted to sell the rather dubious idea that Poklonnaia Hill played an important role in the Great Patriotic War. As a 1980 Moscow guidebook describes it, "Poklonnaia Hill preserves the memory of the events of the Great Patriotic War. Here, in 1941, Moscow's auxiliary defensive line was created."[112] Rather than embrace the link between the two victories, the memorial's "software" presented the hill as a natural setting for commemorating the Soviet victory.[113]

But while the overt conflation of 1812 and 1945 was unintended from the perspective of the memorial's planners, the close proximity of symbols commemorating the two patriotic wars, together with the efforts of some local officials to play up their linkages, rendered Victory Monument vulnerable to further redefinition as the project dragged on. By the middle of the 1980s, the project's new lead designer, the first secretary of the USSR Union of Architects, Anatolii Polianskii, described the site for a Soviet television documentary as marking the culmination of a process that started well before 1917:

> The site selected for the construction of such an important complex unifies ... Kutuzov Prospect, which would appear to embody a military-patriotic theme: the monument to the defense of Moscow, then "The Battle of Borodino" [panorama], the monument to Kutuzov, the Triumphal Arch honoring the victory of 1812, and, finally, the composition-complex Victory of the Soviet People in the Great Patriotic War.[114]

Buttressed by gradual, local efforts to erode the distinction between "Soviet" and "Russian" conceptions of the war's legacy, post-Soviet planners would recognize Poklonnaia Hill as an unmistakably Russian lieu de mémoire. Stripped of most of its Soviet symbolism, and incorporating religious and Russian imperial iconography, Boris Yeltsin

111 Tomilina, *Pamiatnik pobedy*, 118–119.
112 Kurlat, and Sokolovskii, *S putevoditelem po Moskve*, 226.
113 For an inside account of the bureaucratic process by which the complex's central monument was determined, see Grishin, *Ot Khrushcheva do Gorbacheva*, 309–310.
114 TsMAMLS 236/1/35/8–22, qt. 8–9.

Figure 4.8 Aerial view of Moscow's Poklonnaia Hill during the opening of the Russian Federation's national war memorial on the site in 1995 (Alexander Nemyonov/TASS via Getty Images).

consecrated the national war memorial of the fledgling Russian Federation on the site in 1995. But the decision to situate the Russian national memorial on Poklonnaia Hill was less an extension of Soviet commemorative processes than a result of their unintended consequences (Figure 4.8).

Conclusion

Although the transformation of the war's collective memory into arguably the supreme myth of state during this period was broadly popular, its precise orientation was contested from the outset. Despite neo-Stalinist and Russophile attempts to recast the war along Russocentric lines, the Brezhnev leadership retained the Soviet people doctrine, including its placement of the victory myth at the pan-Soviet/internationalist pole of the mobilizational spectrum.

As fears over the decline in revolutionary fervor among the postwar generation came to a head during the latter half of the 1960s, the military-patriotic theme emerged as a potentially effective facilitator of ideological reengagement with the country's youth. The increased emphasis on martial culture and history was itself contested, with many Russocentric nationalist activists looking to anchor military-patriotic upbringing in explicitly Russian national themes. Rather than risk an open confrontation with these elements, however, the Brezhnev leadership expanded the commemorative cult of World War II as the centerpiece of military-patriotic education. This expansion stressed implicit points of overlap between the pan-Soviet model of patriotism and nationalist priorities, but without ceding control of the war narrative.

The war cult generally privileged a vague internationalism over explicit Russocentrism, bolstering its all-union appeal, even as non-Russian republican commemorations remained more or less free to highlight ethnic diversity and hierarchy. At the same time, the Russian people's ambiguous place within the victory myth created potential avenues for the development of a Russian national-patriotic conceptualization of the war, as exhibited by the evolving symbolism of Moscow's Poklonnaia Hill. However, the Russocentric nationalist exploitation of these avenues between the 1960s and 1980s remained a marginal tendency. Throughout the era, nationalist attempts to foster something akin to a Russocentric war memory would encounter fierce resistance from a political establishment committed to the myth's internationalist configuration – which is a story in and of itself.

5 Patriotic Wars

Late-Soviet War Memory and the Politics of Russian Nationalism

> We must preserve the connection between eras, allowing no one to break this eternal chain.
>
> – Sergei Semanov[1]

> Brezhnev himself ... complained at this meeting that whenever he turned on the television, he heard only the ringing of church bells and saw nothing but onion domes. "What's the matter, comrades?" he asked. "What time are we living in? Before the Revolution or after it?"
>
> – Alexander Yanov[2]

Buried in the pages of *Molodaia gvardiia*'s Victory Day issue in 1965 was an open letter by three prominent members of the cultural establishment, S. T. Konenkov, P. D. Korin, and L. M. Leonov. The letter acknowledged that the twentieth anniversary of victory in the Great Patriotic War was first and foremost a time to celebrate the heroism "of recent decades." However, its authors used the occasion to decry the state's wanton disregard for churches and other prerevolutionary cultural monuments. Victory Day was, for them, a particularly appropriate moment to raise this issue. After all, it was during the war that the state most forcefully appealed to Russia's history and patriotic traditions. The legendary battle cry of the commander of the twenty-eight Panfilovtsy, the letter reminded, had referred to Moscow as the capital of "Russia." It was precisely Moscow's "famous churches, historic buildings, the sacred remains of fortress walls, the scars of past interventions" that stiffened the resolve of the Panfilovtsy as they fought to the death in the face of overwhelming odds. In making this case, the letter cited Lenin on the protection of Russia's cultural heritage. As good Leninists, "[w]e need to educate our children in love and respect for their grandfathers and

[1] Semanov, *Serdtse rodiny*, 35.

[2] This anecdote is recounted in Yanov, *The Russian Challenge*, 113. Of course, Brezhnev is on record describing historical heritage "as an extraordinarily rich reservoir of experience, as material for reflections, for the critical analysis of our own decisions and actions." *Pamiatniki*, 11, cited in Kelly, "The Shock of the Old," 99.

great-grandfathers, to fill the soul of the child with a sense of patriotism, a sense of respect for the memory of our ancestors, [and] of the Russian past."[3]

The arguments put forth in the *Molodaia gvardiia* letter were not new. We have seen that movements to restore and protect prerevolutionary edifices in Leningrad and other cities emerged in response to the destruction brought about by the Soviet-German war.[4] Under the relative liberalization of the Khrushchev years, writers, academics, and other critics articulated similar preservationist impulses, and typically couched preservation in terms of furthering Soviet objectives. As the medievalist Dmitrii Likhachev argued in 1961, "It is impossible to nourish Soviet patriotism without nourishing pride in the great past of our people."[5] Even before Khrushchev's ouster, the state gave in to student demands for the formation of an independent club, Rodina, devoted to the study and protection of Russian cultural artifacts.[6]

However, the mid-to-late 1960s marked the beginning of this tendency's expansion and official endorsement. What had been mere grassroots opposition to the Khrushchev-era destruction of Orthodox churches and other monuments of prerevolutionary Russia, for example, achieved institutional recognition in 1965, with the creation of the historical preservation society VOOPIiK. Russian nationalists of various stripes, moreover, gained significant influence at this time through major literary journals, while the writers of the "village prose" movement [*derevenshchiki*], which glorified Russian peasant communities and often criticized collectivization and Soviet destruction of the countryside, increased in both output and popularity. Perhaps most shocking, elements within the Communist Party hierarchy, particularly the informal network known as the "Russian Party," appear to have backed this cultural renewal.[7]

Scholars have described these phenomena as symptomatic of an emergent Russian nationalism that blossomed between the late 1960s and

[3] Konenkov et al., "Beregite sviatyniu nashu!" 216–219.

[4] This is discussed in Chapter 2. See Maddox, *Saving Stalin's Imperial City*; Maddox, "These Monuments Must Be Protected!," 608–626; Qualls, *From Ruins to Reconstruction*; Kirschenbaum, *The Legacy of the Siege*.

[5] Likhachev, "Pamiatniki kul'tury – vsenarodnoe dostoianie," quoted in Donovan, "How Well Do You Know Your Krai," 470.

[6] Dunlop, *Faces*, 65–67.

[7] Kelly, "The Shock of the Old," 88–109; Donovan, *Chronicles in Stone*, esp. 31–105; Donovan, "The 'Old New Russian Town,'" 18–35; Donovan, "*Nestolichnaya kul'tura*"; O'Connor, *Intellectuals and Apparatchiks*, chap. 2; Mitrokhin, *Russkaia partiia*; Brudny, *Reinventing Russia*; Dunlop, *Faces*; Zaslavsky, *The Neo-Stalinist State*, chap. 5; Yanov, *The Russian Challenge*; Yanov, *The Russian New Right*.

early 1980s.[8] Encompassing a range of ideological viewpoints, both Soviet and anti-Soviet, neo-Stalinist and anti-Stalinist, conservative and Westernizing, this movement facilitated what one historian has called "the rediscovery of a 'Russia' separate from the Soviet Union," which would in turn become an important factor in the USSR's collapse.[9] Although authorities regularly silenced nationalists who challenged the legitimacy of the Party, the various pro-regime "Russocentric nationalists" identified in the previous chapter achieved formal recognition, even prominence, in official mouthpieces, as well as key posts in party and state organs. In addition to the Shelepin and Pavlov cliques that emerged out of the institution of the Komsomol, some of the most significant drivers of Russocentric nationalism throughout the Brezhnev era were the aforementioned VOOPIiK and the editorial boards and publishing houses of such "thick" journals as *Molodaia gvardiia* [*Young Guard*] and *Nash sovremennik* [*Our Contemporary*].[10] While the views and concerns among Russocentric nationalists varied, they shared two things in common. First, there was a philosophical orientation around the so-called "single-stream" [*edinyi potok*] thesis of Russian culture and history. Much like the Russocentric paradigm, this view emphasized continuity between the Russian past and Soviet present, often portraying the whole of Russian history as an unbroken continuum. The Bolshevik Revolution and the establishment of the Soviet state were merely the most recent expressions of what was a fundamentally Russian project.[11] The second shared trait of Russocentric nationalists was the ability to publicly moderate these single-stream views and frame their messages in terms consonant with regime priorities.

In his important study of the growth and development of Russian nationalism, Yitzhak Brudny explains the leeway afforded Russocentric nationalists during this period as a deliberate "politics of inclusion" designed to co-opt elements within the Russian nationalist intelligentsia. According to Brudny, this policy offered "a new basis of political legitimacy" and enabled the regime to "regain the Stalin-era ability to politically

[8] In late 1982, John Dunlop began his survey of Brezhnev-era trends by remarking that the Russian nationalist "thought and sentiment that has increasingly made its presence felt in the USSR since the mid-sixties … in one form or another, could become the ruling ideology of state once the various stages of the Brezhnev succession have come to an end." Dunlop, *Faces*, ix, 62. See also Brudny, *Reinventing Russia*, esp. 138–142.

[9] Hosking, *Rulers and Victims*, chaps. 9–11, qt. 338.

[10] The Russocentric nationalism discussed throughout this chapter is roughly the equivalent of the national Bolshevik strand of nationalism defined in Dunlop, *Faces*, 254–265. In contrast to separatist nationalism, these groups primarily advocated "nation-shaping" Russian nationalism – that is, nationalism which aims "to nationalize an existing polity" from within. See Brubaker, *Nationalism Reframed*, 79; Brudny, *Reinventing Russia*, 5–6.

[11] O'Connor, *Intellectuals and Apparatchiks*, 54–55.

mobilize the most important Soviet nationality, ethnic Russians"; to isolate the liberal-reformist intelligentsia; to garner support for investment in the agricultural sector; and to provide a conservative domestic counterweight to inevitable Western influences brought on by détente.[12] Largely absent from Brudny's analysis, however, is the role of the ubiquitous state cult of World War II, the grandest mobilizational campaign of the era. As we have seen, contrary to Russocentric nationalism, the late-socialist war cult tended to advance the internationalist pole of the doctrine of the Soviet people. What effect, if any, did Russocentric nationalism have on the Soviet myth of victory in the war? How, if at all, did these concurrent patriotic themes overlap? Did nationalists successfully revive the victory myth's Russocentric paradigm and produce something akin to a Russian national-patriotic variation of the war narrative?[13]

This chapter explores the relationship between Russocentric nationalism and official war memory during the zenith of inclusionary politics (1968–80s). It focuses on some of the most explicit nationalist writings in the official press and the involvement of nationalist enthusiasts in late-socialist memory politics – for example, their role in the 1980 anniversary of the Battle of Kulikovo Field – to determine the war's place in the pro-regime nationalist imagination. As this chapter argues, Russocentric nationalists reveled in prerevolutionary Russian themes but largely abstained from claiming the war as an unambiguously Russian achievement. That is to say that at the peak of official support for Russian nationalist expression and activism, the Russocentric paradigm did not extend to official representations of victory, even among this paradigm's most ardent supporters. It was only through marginal or unofficial channels that nationalist-oriented writers even attempted to articulate a single-stream reading of the war, suggesting that the official line, and resulting editorial restraint, continued to guard against the war myth's Russification. In an era defined by the growth of Russian national self-expression, the victory myth retained its role as social leveler and instrument of pan-Soviet identity and mobilization.

We have seen, however, that the victory myth's dominant pan-Soviet paradigm squared with a number of important nationalist priorities, including the promotion of loyalty to the motherland, military-patriotic preparedness, anti-Westernism, as well as the implicit rejection of the uniqueness of Jewish wartime suffering.[14] Over time, several prominent

[12] Brudny, *Reinventing Russia*, 3–4, 57–80.
[13] These questions are vital to comprehending late-socialist politics of patriotism since, as Mitrokhin suggests, Russian nationalists were instrumental in the war cult's development: Mitrokhin, *Russkaia partiia*, 114–116, 276–283, 291–293.
[14] Weiner, "In the Long Shadow of War," 455–456.

Russocentric writers and activists found ways to navigate the Soviet people doctrine by exploiting areas of ambiguity and overlap with the war's official memory. By the end of the 1970s, among nationalist intellectuals and their supporters, this patriotic parallelism had begun to redefine the nature of victory in subtle but not insignificant ways.

The chapter thus explores the outer parameters of the concept of inclusionary politics. The party leadership remained committed to the Soviet people doctrine, in which the war's memory continued to serve as the principal pan-Soviet/internationalist theme. Not only did this official stance clash with the spirit of Brezhnev's policy of nationalist "inclusion," but for Russocentric nationalists and their sympathizers, emboldened by inclusionary politics, it brought into sharp relief the limits of their own hierarchical primacy. Working within official parameters, these groups attempted to bridge the gulf between "Russian" and "Soviet" understandings of the war and its legacy, and, by extension, to collapse the segmented discursive tension that had come to define Soviet patriotism after Stalin. While these efforts ultimately failed, they demonstrate the persistence of the Russocentric variant of the war myth, which festered at the margins of official culture at a time when many of the constraints on nationalist expression were about to be lifted under the banner of glasnost.

Nationalist "Salvos" of the Late 1960s

According to Brudny, the years 1965 to 1970 represented the "first phase," but also the highpoint, of the politics of inclusion. It was during these years that Russian nationalists held the greatest sway within the party apparatus. Ranking party members, such as the head of the Central Committee Department of Culture, Vasilii Shauro, his deputy Iurii Melent'ev, and Vladimir Stepakov, the head of the Propaganda Department, actively protected Russocentric nationalists working in publishing houses and the Komsomol. This group appears to have succeeded in convincing Brezhnev and his chief ideologue, Suslov, that support for some nationalist causes, such as historical preservation, and the toleration of certain nationalist themes in public discourse, would enable the regime to more effectively carry out its policy goals and revive the declining mobilizational power of the Communist Party. By 1968, a group of writers known as Chalmaevists – so called for their ideological affinities with the critic Viktor Chalmaev – openly condemned what they saw as Western influences in Soviet society from an avowedly nationalist position.[15]

[15] Brudny, *Reinventing Russia*, 57–93.

How did this most radical phase of inclusionary politics impact and interact with the concurrent development of the war cult? There can be little doubt that the Russian nationalist element within the Party, and the writers and activists it supported, understood the war in Russocentric terms and hoped to shape the war's public memory along those lines. As the aforementioned open letter in *Molodaia gvardiia* attests, key nationalist-oriented intellectuals saw Khrushchev's fall as a sign that they were free to recast certain wartime markers, such as the Panfilovtsy legend, in order to legitimate their claim that victory was a fundamentally Russian achievement. There are striking examples from this period of Russocentric nationalists working to steer the war cult in a Russocentric direction. In June 1969, for instance, Vladimir Ivanov, VOOPIiK's first deputy chairman, proposed to the Komsomol leadership that VOOPIiK help plan the military-patriotic activities linked to the following year's Victory Day anniversary. As part of the Komsomol's regular pilgrimages to "sites of the revolutionary, combat, and labor glory of the Soviet people," Ivanov recommended that Komsomol members mark May Ninth by visiting important places associated with Nevskii, Suvorov, Kutuzov, Nakhimov, and Ushakov – all historical figures whose names adorned World War II military decorations. By paying homage to these figures, Ivanov argued, Komsomol members could better appreciate "how the combat traditions of the past helped the soldiers of the Soviet Army smash the fascist invaders."[16] Throughout the era, VOOPIiK representatives continued to cite the war's deleterious impact on Russian cultural monuments as part of its raison d'être.[17]

Despite these efforts, the war's public remembrance remained largely unaffected by the state's guarded endorsement of Russocentric nationalism during the late 1960s. Komsomol military-patriotic activities, as observed in Chapter 4, retained their pan-Soviet orientation and rarely indulged the Russian nationalist worldview held by some of the organization's leadership. Moreover, authorities closely monitored the activities of preservationist movements. As one political scientist has noted, VOOPIiK "was top-heavy with bureaucrats who had previously distinguished themselves by destroying churches rather than saving them."[18] Notable exceptions aside, there was very little effort during VOOPIiK's first decade to encroach upon Soviet-era pillars, especially victory in the war.[19] And although village prose writers like Vasilii Belov, Fedor Abramov,

[16] GARF A-639/1/236/2. [17] Donovan, *Chronicles in Stone*, 12–13, and passim.

[18] Dunlop, *Faces*, 69–70.

[19] Indeed, the organization was tightly controlled by party authorities; so tightly, in fact, that its members began issuing complaints about bureaucratic control almost immediately. See, for example, "Ne ochen' udachnoe nachalo," *Literaturnaia gazeta*, Oct. 30, 1965.

and Aleksei Leonov frequently wrote about the war, the genre did not present a coherent Russocentric, much less nationalist, counter narrative. These writers typically portrayed the difficulties of war on the home front from the perspective of the residents of a single village, foregrounding "daily life, with the emphasis on how much harder it is to survive during wartime when most of the men are away and the remaining villagers – women, old people, and children – must fuel the war effort." While this certainly undermined the rosy picture sometimes presented in state propaganda and socialist-realist novels, village prose war literature was broadly heroic, observes Kathleen Parthé, and rarely contested the pan-Soviet conception of victory directly.[20]

Only the Chalmaevists and their supporters operating within the Molodaia gvardiia publishing house were able to mount a sustained Russophile critique of Soviet patriotic politics in official media before nationalist expression came under tighter party scrutiny in the early 1970s.[21] This group deserves special attention, therefore, since its publications probed the limits of inclusionary politics. Considering the penchant of many of these writers for Russian military victories, one might expect the Great Patriotic War to feature prominently in Chalmaevist narratives. However, where Russocentric nationalists openly celebrated a single-stream historical narrative, their writings tended to adhere to the Soviet people doctrine's conception of the war as a pan-Soviet /internationalist achievement. Thus, despite offering a Russocentric interpretation of historical processes in general, when it came to the war in particular, Chalmaevists resorted to ambiguous language or conformed to the victory myth's official, internationalist reading. This strongly suggests that the military-patriotic compromise discussed in Chapter 4 successfully cordoned off the war theme from nationalist co-option, even while stressing points of overlap with nationalist concerns. The remainder of this section examines several of the group's most influential publications to shed light on what was a rather tenuous junction of permitted Russian nationalism and late-socialist representations of the war.

In 1968, Viktor Chalmaev launched the movement that bore his name with two essays described by John Dunlop as the "most sensational

For more on the limitations placed on VOOPIiK activities, see Brudny, *Reinventing Russia*, 69–70; Dunlop, *Faces*, 66–71, qt. 69.

20 Parthé, *Russian Village Prose*, qt. 51, 83–87. Parthé notes that editors and censors were particularly concerned with village prose writers' portrayals of the larger war effort, and often intervened to maintain the generally heroic contours of the victory myth. See Parthé, 172, n19.

21 Hosking, *Rulers and Victims*, 365; Brudny, *Reinventing Russia*, 93.

salvos" to appear in the radical nationalist press.[22] In both "Great Strivings" [*Velikie iskaniia*] and "Inevitability" [*Neizbezhnost'*], Chalmaev admonished the Westernizing tendencies he perceived to be emanating from the liberal-reformist wing of the intelligentsia. In particular, he alleged that certain Soviet writers and their supporters within the leadership had "consigned to oblivion" the "entire centuries-old prehistory of the spiritual life of Russians."[23] To prevent the moral degradation of Soviet society, it was necessary to recover Russia's "historical glory," including the place of the Orthodox Church, as a bulwark against "Western, individualistic philistinism."[24] Chalmaev did not reject 1917, which he acknowledged had paved the way for "the highest form of social and state organization – scientific communism," but aimed to directly anchor Soviet triumphs in the Russian past.[25]

It was precisely Russian military exploits that most fully revealed "the spirit of eternal, thousand-year-old Russia."[26] And yet, Chalmaev remained ambivalent over the relationship between Russia's past and the Great Patriotic War. He noted, for example, that "a soul devastated by lack of faith cannot become a Donskoi, a [Petr] Bagration, or a[n Aleksandr] Matrosov overnight" – the former two names representing pre-1917 military commanders, the latter a legendary infantryman who died in 1943 in a heroic action.[27] Chalmaev also alluded to the war through a discussion of Fedor Abramov's then-unfinished multivolume work tracing the plight of a single peasant family, *The Priaslins*. In both cases, Chalmaev deliberately avoided making any sweeping Russocentric claim on the broader war narrative by homing in on discrete matters – the heroism of a foot soldier like Matrosov or the resilience of a Russian family. The war in these cases served as a mere backdrop for the author to extol the positive qualities of individual Russians. "There is something traditionally Russian, cheerful in this peasant boy," Chalmaev wrote of one of Abramov's characters. Chalmaev, by way of Abramov, does imply that the fortitude required to endure the war's hardships was somehow linked to the eternal Russian spirit: "The Priaslin family, depleted in

[22] Dunlop, *Faces*, 218. The semi-official support for these publications is reflected primarily in the journal's increased print runs at the time and in Chalmaev's appointment as deputy editor of the journal *Nash sovremennik*. See Brudny, *Reinventing Russia*, 65–66.

[23] Chalmaev, "Neizbezhnost'," 266. [24] Chalmaev, "Velikie iskaniia," 282.

[25] Chalmaev, "Neizbezhnost'," 266.

[26] Chalmaev, Velikie iskaniia," qt. 274; Chalmaev, "Neizbezhnost'," 263–268.

[27] Unbeknownst to Chalmaev, Matrosov may not have been Russian at all, but an ethnic Tatar from Bashkortostan. See Belenkaja, "Verteidigung der Heimat." This would not have concerned Chalmaev, however, who was clearly expressing Russian multiethnic, imperial qualities. Petr Bagration, whom Chalmaev also mentions, was descended from Georgian royalty.

number, covered in wounds, exhausted [by the war] – this is Rus' in the flesh."[28] The scale, however, is always intimate; Chalmaev does not advance any single-stream argument about the war's significance aside from the long reach of its devastation.

Where Chalmaev directly engages the theme of the war, he jettisons his Russocentric framework altogether. He is careful, for example, to associate victory with the *Soviet* people and, rather than suggest an unambiguous connection with the pre-Soviet era, pairs the war with vaguely equivocal terms like "bygone days": "The neon-filled clouds are broken up by the rays of the sun, which emanate from bygone days, and from the Herculean feats of the Soviet people in the Great Patriotic War, to all other times."[29] Lest the reader confuse "Soviet" for "Russian," Chalmaev is careful to distinguish between the two, noting that those who glorify the words Rus' and Russia "as a kind of idealized, rural oasis" are "objectively dangerous to the notion of a truly Soviet motherland."[30] He concludes "Inevitability" by quoting at length a work by the Lithuanian poet Justinas Marcinkevicius about Germany's destruction of the poet's homeland during the war. His suggestion, of course, is that national identity, be it Lithuanian or Russian, is essential to a healthy society. And indeed, most Russocentric nationalists prided themselves on an innately Russian sense of compassion for other national groups.[31] However, in an essay that otherwise focuses on the particular role of Russians in past conflicts, it is noteworthy indeed that the author concludes by universalizing the experience of the Great Patriotic War across ethno-territorial boundaries.[32]

Chalmaev's pieces in *Molodaia gvardiia* are particularly significant for what they reveal about the relationship between Russocentric nationalism and the fledgling war cult. Chalmaev was writing in the aftermath of the landmark twentieth anniversary of Victory Day, yet observed that overt displays of Russian pride were simultaneously in decline. That is, he did not consider Brezhnev's fledgling embrace of the war's public memory to be a coup for Russian patriots. Rather, Chalmaev implied that the current political and cultural establishment was complicit in obscuring Russian exceptionalism. For instance, Chalmaev contrasted the present dearth of publications on prerevolutionary themes and events with those produced during Khrushchev's final years. Such works included Aleksei Cherkasov's 1963 *Intoxication* [*Khmel'*], which chronicles Siberian life from the nineteenth century through the 1917 Revolution, and

[28] Chalmaev, "Neizbezhnost'," 285. [29] Chalmaev, 262. [30] Chalmaev, 277.

[31] On this feature of Russian nationalism, see Hosking, *Rulers and Victims*, 363.

[32] Chalmaev, "Neizbezhnost'," 289. The Russian translation of the poem, published in 1964, is entitled "Krov' i pepel."

Vsevolod Ivanov’s *Black People* [*Chernye liudi*], set in the seventeenth century. The appearance of these historical novels, according to Chalmaev, represented “a new phase” in the Soviet state’s development of Russian national consciousness. However, for Chalmaev, this spate of publications was a momentary exception to a broader decline in official support for patriotic education among young people.[33] Chalmaev, therefore, suggests an official divide between the pan-Soviet patriotism associated with the Brezhnev war cult on the one hand and Russian prerevolutionary themes on the other, rather than some Russocentric conflation of the two. The task of bridging this discursive divide became one of the key goals of Chalmaev’s followers and Russocentric nationalists more generally.

The other landmark nationalist works of the late 1960s and early 1970s to appear in *Molodaia gvardiia* followed Chalmaev’s lead in both their approach to the war theme and their veiled opposition to pan-Soviet notions of patriotic identity. Mikhail Lobanov’s “Enlightened Philistinism” [*Prosveshchennoe meshchanstvo*] (1968) ostensibly took aim at encroaching Western industrial capitalism to argue for the importance of Russian cultural and spiritual identity in the face of currents that threatened to diminish one’s sense of ethnonational distinctiveness. For Lobanov, this “Americanism of the soul” had already taken root among elements within Soviet society: officials and members of the intelligentsia who portrayed national feeling as anachronistic. Although this most directly applied to liberal-reformist writers, it also implicated members of Brezhnev’s inner circle, later embodied by the figure of Alexander Yakovlev. By privileging the supranational and postrevolutionary over the national and transhistorical, these critics of Russia’s national reawakening, Lobanov warned, threatened to undermine the cohesion of the Soviet state and its foundation of Russian culture and traditions. “To integrate,” he writes,

> is to completely scrape away the wild remnant of the national, the *narodnyi*, to mix all in a general industrial dance, so that neither the spirit, nor memory of the past, nor language itself is left for these peoples . . . Never mind that from such integration among nations, . . . instead of colorful meadows dotted with flowers, there will stretch something like a bleak asphalt highway, that [this] leveling will give rise to a standardization that is disastrous for creativity.[34]

Although focusing on Western socioeconomic and cultural integration, Lobanov, to a greater degree than Chalmaev, offered an implied critique

[33] Chalmaev, “Neizbezhnost’,” 265.
[34] Lobanov, “Prosveshchennoe meshchanstvo,” 304.

of the Soviet people doctrine and the concept's alleged diminution of sub-state national (Russian) identity.

At the same time, Lobanov, like Chalmaev, stopped short of issuing a Russian national claim on victory in the war. The single passage alluding to the war is illustrative of the way Russocentric nationalist writers attempted to draw on the war's emotive capacity to convey Russocentric ideas without overtly contradicting the internationalist message of official war memory. In the case of "Enlightened Philistinism," Lobanov presented an anecdote about a trip he made with his uncle to a small village. During a visit with a local family, Lobanov became acquainted with a quiet *frontovik* who was highly decorated for his service. The veteran so struck the author with his humility that Lobanov recalled Tolstoy: "Lev Tolstoy knew his people. No wonder he so loved his [Captain] Tushin. Such people saved Russia. Is the embodiment of the historical and moral potential of the people [*narod*] not to be found in them? And is our faith and hope not to be found here?"[35] In Lobanov's telling, there is no question that the hero of Tolstoy's novel "saved Russia"; precisely whether the object of salvation during the Great Patriotic War for the humble *frontovik* was Russia or the Soviet Union is never specified.

As it so happens, the final significant Chalmaevist publication, Sergei Semanov's 1970 essay "On Relative and Eternal Values" [*O tsennostiakh otnositel'nykh i vechnykh*], addressed Lobanov's anecdote and made somewhat more explicit that which Lobanov had only implied. Both Lobanov and Chalmaev had come under fire in the liberal-reformist journal *Novyi mir* for promoting ideas deemed antithetical to Marxism-Leninism.[36] In the case of Lobanov's article, *Novyi mir* singled out the author's unfettered admiration for Tolstoy's Captain Tushin because of the fictional Tushin's status as a tsarist army officer. Semanov responded to the piece by arguing that Lobanov's praise for Captain Tushin had nothing to do with the character's privileged social status; rather, Lobanov had emphasized Tushin's distinct psychological makeup, which held great significance for the Soviet people. "Is there not," Semanov asked, "a Tushin among the Decembrists … [or] the Bolsheviks?"[37] Perhaps most egregious in Semanov's defense of Lobanov was the attempt to forge an unambiguous connection between the *frontovik* and Tushin. "This soldier," wrote Semanov, "and Tolstoy's Tushin were positioned

35 Lobanov, 306.
36 See Dement'ev, "O traditsiiakh i narodnosti," 215–235. According to Dunlop, Dement'ev's article was the journal's attempt to "prove its bona fides to the regime, as well as to assail a tendency which its editorial board found particularly dangerous and repugnant." Dunlop, *Faces*, 221.
37 Semanov, "O tsennostiakh," 310.

[by Lobanov] as mirror images, each with psychological traits quite typical of the Russian national character." Seemingly aware that he was violating some political taboo, Semanov immediately added, "Could one not argue this? What's so terrible here?"[38]

Semanov's article was something of an anomaly in the extent of its violation of the Soviet people doctrine – indeed it was the final straw that led to the removal of Anatolii Nikonov from his post as editor-in-chief of the journal *Molodaia gvardiia*. Semanov flouted the vagaries of language deployed by his fellow Chalmaevists, railing, for example, against those who favored a more classical Marxist-Leninist interpretation of the past: "[A]ll of those who want to see nothing of our [Russian] culture and folk life." But he went further. In his criticism of the Soviet people doctrine, which he, like many Russocentric nationalists, considered to be an effort to subsume Russian national identity "into a unified and monolithic whole," Semanov praised Stalin's handling of the Russian question and implicitly called for a return to Stalinist methods of rule.[39]

Semanov touched on the Great Patriotic War more than either Chalmaev or Lobanov and therefore offers perhaps the clearest picture of the war through the prism of Russocentric nationalism at its most irreverent. Significantly, Semanov repeated the patterns observed in the works of the earlier two authors. In his discussion of patriotic education, for instance, Semanov speaks of "the glory of Borodino and Stalingrad." Although Semanov isolates Stalingrad from the larger war narrative, assuring that no message is directly conveyed about the victory myth overall, his reference to Borodino was certainly consonant with his single-stream vision. The context in which Semanov linked Stalingrad and Borodino, however, reveals a great deal of ambiguity:

> We, Soviet citizens, are proud of the creations of the ancient masters of Novgorod and Yerevan, Kiev and Samarkand . . . the feat of the people who have mastered the huge spaces of Europe, Asia and America, by the glory of Borodino and Stalingrad, proud of the great Russian Revolution which has opened a new epoch in the fate of the homeland and the whole world. Yes, the whole world.[40]

Semanov rather benignly describes a motherland inhabited by "Soviet citizens" with an admittedly multiethnic, pre-Soviet heritage. Borodino,

[38] Semanov, 310.

[39] See Semanov, 317–319. As Yanov recognized, what Semanov put forth was quite different from the nostalgic desire among neo-Stalinists to preserve the myth of Stalin's wartime leadership. In fact, writes Yanov, "Semanov reminded people of precisely what needed to be forgotten." Yanov, *The Russian Challenge*, 117.

[40] Semanov, 317.

in this sense, served as a mere cultural landmark for territorial Russians, no different from Novgorodian architecture, or, for that matter, the ancient monuments of Samarkand for Uzbeks. After all, the regime continued to acknowledge prerevolutionary cultural heritage and "progressive" tendencies, albeit as relics of a prior era. By clarifying that the year 1917 ushered in a "new epoch" for the territory of the former Russian Empire and "the whole world," the passage's link between Borodino and Stalingrad was vague enough to merit multiple interpretations, including one more or less harmonious with the official line.

Yet where Semanov goes beyond such passing statements to address the war or the war's significance for contemporary Soviet society in any detail, he entirely eschews Russocentrism to stress supra-ethnic, lateral friendship bonds between Soviet nationalities. In describing his elation during the recent twenty-fifth anniversary of Victory Day, for example, Semanov notes that the war's memory was an ideal way to instill "a sense of continuity between generations in the construction and protection of the Motherland." Yet rather than defer to prerevolutionary Russian sources, Semanov, in accordance with the official line, insists that patriotism associated with the war theme is rooted not in "the distant past, nor customs and traditions arising from time immemorial, but rather [in] that which has been created over the past five decades, especially the great Revolution." Thus, Semanov largely adheres to the Soviet people doctrine's segmented conception of patriotism insofar as the war victory is concerned. His single stream abruptly branches into two when the focus turns to the experience of 1941–5 as a whole. The conditions that made victory possible in 1945 emerged from "our great Revolution" not "time immemorial." It was in this context, coincidently, that Semanov raised the issue of inter-ethnic unity, reminding the reader that "we must preserve and protect the solidarity of our multinational fatherland and the friendship of our peoples as the apple of our eye."[41]

The role of Stalin in the Chalmaevist conception of the war, while only hinted at, is significant. For many nationalists who were sympathetic to Chalmaevism, such as those of the Pavlov group, Stalin was often seen as a defender and mobilizer of Russian national consciousness. This was most directly a reaction to Khrushchev's destalinization campaign and its targeting of the Russocentric wartime line. The Chalmaevists and many of their supporters, after all, came to understand Stalin and the war through the lens of destalinization. Whereas Stalinist Russocentrism was quietly

[41] Semanov, "O tsennostiakh," 316–317.

denounced or explained away, many Russocentric nationalists and neo-Stalinists looked to embrace that which the arch-internationalist Khrushchev condemned. They saw in Stalin's wartime rhetoric and activities a true Russian national patriot whose role in victory had been unjustly diminished in official representations.

On at least one occasion, Chalmaevists were able to link Stalin, the war, and Russian national patriotism along a single axis. This was the 1969 ode to Stalin by the poet Feliks Chuev. Chuev suggested that Stalin led the country to victory by summoning a Russian national-patriotic spirit. His poem, published in *Molodaia gvardiia*, called for the creation of a war memorial in the form of a mausoleum to house Stalin's remains: "Let those who enter feel a debt / To the Motherland, to all that is Russian. / There, in the middle, is our Generalissimo / And his great Marshals."[42] Although a work of verse, the poem's Russocentrism and reverence for Stalin were exceptional even by *Molodaia gvardiia*'s standards. According to Semanov's recollections, the poem was one of the principal factors sparking the regime's anti-nationalist backlash of the early 1970s. In Semanov's words, "Since then, nothing similar to Chuev could be published, whether [authors themselves] were cautious, or editors were on guard, no one knows, and it doesn't matter. But these lines were not forgotten."[43] As a statement on the nature of the war, therefore, the poem was limited. Unlike some other Chalmaevist tendencies, Chuev's sentiments would not later return to the pages of the Russocentric nationalist press.

At its most extreme, therefore, the Russocentric nationalists of *Molodaia gvardiia* during the late 1960s made no serious attempt to incorporate the Great Patriotic War into their polemics. The victory myth largely retained its internationalist character as Chalmaevists, reluctantly perhaps, presented 1945 as the legacy of "that which has been created over the past five decades." There was a great deal of overlap between the party leadership and the Chalmaevists regarding the capacity of the war's memory to instill patriotism. However, where Russocentric nationalists referred to state policies and commemorations involving remembrance of the war, they portrayed these as largely antithetical to their single-stream project. Yet in viewing official war memory and historical Russocentrism as embodying discordant ideological currents, nationalists in fact had a great deal in common with the Brezhnev leadership.

[42] Mitrokhin notes that the poem became a rallying cry for the Pavlov group. See Mitrokhin, *Russkaia partiia*, 278.

[43] Semanov, *Andropov*, 294.

The *Molodaia Gvardiia* and Yakovlev Affairs

The nationalist writings in *Molodaia gvardiia* became the subject of an intense debate between the liberal and conservative wings of the intelligentsia. While the party leadership allowed this debate to take place, in 1969 it increased its involvement, first through a Central Committee resolution stating that cultural institution chiefs – including editorial heads of literary journals – would be held directly responsible for the content of their productions, and next through a party-backed, pseudonymous publication in *Literaturnaia gazeta* that was especially critical of the nationalism found in *Molodaia gvardiia*.[44] Neither document addressed the topic of the war directly. However, the *Literaturnaia gazeta* piece, which rather delicately censured Chalmaev and writers of his ilk for "showing the Russian national . . . character not in its contemporary, Soviet capacity, but rather as dominated by certain old-patriarchal traits," was published in the Victory Day issue, following two pages of articles commemorating the war.[45] The editors' decision to quite literally surround a message of opposition to the nationalist tendencies of *Molodaia gvardiia* with articles and iconography devoted to the celebration of victory appears deliberate. It is certainly possible that the use of Victory Day imagery aimed to render the anti-nationalist message more palatable to the paper's predominantly Russian-speaking audience. Regardless, the effect was to further dissociate the pan-Soviet/internationalist patriotism of victory from the Russocentric nationalism of the Chalmaevists. In this, *Literaturnaia gazeta*'s Victory Day issue embodied broader political processes. Increasingly, authorities and nationalist writers alike came to understand the pan-Soviet and Russocentric paradigms as counterpoising modes of patriotic expression.

A major reshuffling of the party apparatus and literary establishment followed. The shakeup began not with *Molodaia gvardiia* but with the decimation in early 1970 of the editorial staff of the liberal-reformist journal *Novyi mir* and the forced resignation of its editor-in-chief, Aleksandr Tvardovskii.[46] The purge appears to have stemmed from the leadership's concerns about a potentially united conservative bloc brought together by its collective outrage over *Novyi mir*'s criticism of Chalmaev and Lobanov.[47] In July 1969, the journal *Ogonek* published an

[44] Brudny, *Reinventing Russia*, 80–88. [45] Ivanov, "Natsional'nyi kharakter," 3–4.
[46] Most at fault, according to Yanov, was the critique found in Dement'ev, "O traditsiiakh i narodnosti." Yanov, *The Russian New Right*, 49–52.
[47] On the Brezhnev leadership's perception of the danger of this unified right, see Yanov, *The Russian Challenge*, 115–1 16.

open letter signed by eleven prominent defenders of the Chalmaevists.[48] For the Brezhnev leadership, the signatories represented a worrying alliance of Russocentric nationalists and neo-Stalinists. The letter accused *Novyi mir* of minimizing the importance of "the traditions of the Russian people and the past glory of Russian martial feats." Although acknowledging that Chalmaev had been excessive in his Russophilism, the spirit in which Chalmaev and his followers were writing was, the letter argued, fundamentally correct. *Molodaia gvardiia* had consistently worked to "develop in the youthful member of the Komsomol feelings of Soviet patriotism, selfless love for the socialist homeland, internationalism, and the desire to struggle relentlessly against hostile ideological influences."[49] Yet as Brudny points out, the purge of *Novyi mir* was politically expedient. It served to defuse conservative pressure and turn the tables on the nationalist press. For without *Novyi mir* as its foil, *Molodaia gvardiia*'s entire purpose from an official standpoint was in jeopardy.[50]

Indeed, shortly after the *Novyi mir* affair, authorities commenced a campaign to root out Chalmaevism once and for all. This was in no small part a response to Chuev's poem and Semanov's radical "On Relative and Eternal Values," the latter of which made its appearance in August 1970.[51] In December, with Brezhnev's direct involvement, the Central Committee Secretariat removed Anatolii Nikonov, *Molodaia gvardiia*'s chief editor, from his post. Closely connected to Nikonov's dismissal was the sacking of Chalmaev earlier in the year from the editorial board of the nationalist journal *Nash sovremennik* and the removal of a number of supporters of Russocentric nationalism – members of the Shelepin group – from thcir positions in the party apparatus.[52] Also at this time, a meeting took place between the deputy head of the Central Committee Cultural Department, Iurii Melent'ev, and Brezhnev. Melent'ev hoped he could convince the general secretary to sign off on a program of patriotic indoctrination for Soviet youth based on the nationalistic principles espoused by the Chalmaevists. According to Yanov's account of the meeting, Brezhnev responded coldly: "There is

48 In fact, Chalmaev and Lobanov had been the letter's main authors, along with several other Chalmaevists. Kozlov, *The Readers of Novyi Mir*, 306–308; Petelin, *Schast'e byt' samim soboi*, 194–195.

49 "Protiv chego vystupaet 'Novyi mir'?" 26–29.

50 Brudny, *Reinventing Russia*, 89–90.

51 The publication in *Sovetskaia Rossiia* of a positive review of the anti-Semitic, Stalinist novel *In the Name of the Father and the Son*, which the CC Secretariat had already formally rebuked, was an additional factor in the move against Russocentric nationalism. Brudny, 90. As observed in the previous chapter, the anniversaries of Lenin's birth and establishment of the USSR, in 1970 and 1972 respectively, also played a significant part. See Mitrokhin, *Russkaia partiia*, 118.

52 Mitrokhin, *Russkaia partiia*, 116–118.

no place for you even in the Party, let alone the Central Committee."[53] Melent'ev lost his Central Committee status the following year. Shelepin remained in the Politburo, in a weakened state, until he too was purged in 1975.[54] As a result of these moves, there no longer existed a support base for Russian nationalism in the Politburo or Central Committee Secretariat after 1970. Although Russocentric nationalist writers continued to operate, until the 1980s their ideas, in the words of Hosking, were "preached in a less systematic, more fragmentary way."[55]

The crackdown on Russocentric nationalism was connected to the movement's call for a return to Stalinist methods of rule, its endorsement of anti-Semitic and anti-intellectual currents, and political infighting between rival party factions, which saw the rise of the staunch anti-nationalist Alexander Yakovlev within the Propaganda Department. However, the struggle over the war's memory played a significant role as well. Although Chalmaevists stopped short of attempting a Russocentric variant of the war narrative, the vague parallels that hinted at a single stream linking 1945 with past Russian military victories apparently alarmed liberal-reformist and moderate elements of the party leadership and intelligentsia. The underground journal *Politicheskii dnevnik* noted "widespread objections and protests among the Soviet public," who resisted not only the positive light Semanov cast on Stalinist repressions, but also the insinuation that "Russians alone . . . apparently won the Great Patriotic War." While *Politicheskii dnevnik* may have exaggerated the level of protest, critics produced a number of rebuttals to the Chalmaevist position on the war. Emblematic of these was a manuscript by Raisa Lert submitted to the journal *Voprosy istorii*. Although never published, Lert's manuscript evidently reflected concerns within the leadership over the war's representation in the Russocentric nationalist press.[56]

Among other things, Lert objected to the organic linkage that Chalmaevists insinuated between Russian historical themes and Soviet-era patriotic culture. Russian chauvinism, she observed, was the inevitable consequence of the cacophonous wartime messaging: "The conditions of war with the fascist invaders made possible the forcible merger of communist ideology with the alien concept of national exclusivity."

[53] Quoted in Yanov, *The Russian Challenge*, 119–120.
[54] Although most of these prominent figures were simply reassigned, it was usually a shift away from party organs to less important state structures, or to the influential but politically marginal publishing sphere. See Mitrokhin, *Russkaia partiia*, 113–123.
[55] Hosking, *Rulers and Victims*, 365; Brudny, *Reinventing Russia*, 94–95; Mitrokhin, *Russkaia partiia*, 113–123.
[56] *Politicheskii dnevnik*, 2:712–713.

Thus, Stalin's rhetoric and policies had allowed chauvinism to "graft onto the healthy sense of national pride" that arose following Germany's invasion. Only after Stalin's death could the holdover Russocentrism of the 1930s and the war be discredited and removed from official commemorations. Now, Lert contended, the chauvinistic war narrative had made its return by way of the Chalmaevists. These writers, in other words, risked destabilizing the discursive tension maintained via the Soviet people doctrine. Why, Lert asked, should prerevolutionary military commanders continue "to be revered in a socialist country?" From Lert's perspective, the problem with Chalmaevism was precisely that it looked to prerevolutionary Russia not "as the subject of scientific research" but as the "sacred" past, "the genealogy" of the USSR. Thus, in Lert's telling, it was not only the Chalmaevists' endorsement of Stalin's Terror that violated patriotic norms, but equally their efforts to revive wartime Russocentric appeals as a core component of the victory myth.[57]

Lert's manuscript was unpublishable for a number of reasons; not least among these was her claim that Russian chauvinism was the sole outcome of wartime propaganda. Lert essentially ceded patriotic war memory to Russocentric nationalists without asserting the pan-Soviet /internationalist interpretation. Nevertheless, Lert held that the Chalmaevists' attempt to "locate the roots," as she put it, of Soviet patriotic identity "in remote antiquity" prompted the regime's continued assault on Russocentric nationalism during the early 1970s.[58] This official stance was codified in journal articles, an Academy of Social Sciences report, and a new Central Committee resolution.[59] Unlike Lert's critique, however, the official line held up the war narrative as the principal expression of the Party's opposition to Russian nationalist views.

Shortly after the purge of *Molodaia gvardiia*, for example, an authoritative article in *Kommunist*, which called out Chalmaev, Lobanov, and Semanov by name, contrasted the glorification of prerevolutionary traditions with the commemoration of truly Soviet achievements, especially victory in 1945. So as to not inflame nationalist sensibilities, the article affirmed the Soviet state's commitment to protecting Russian and non-Russian prerevolutionary cultural monuments: "We must not forget the important fact that in every Union Republic voluntary societies for the protection of historical and cultural monuments exist and are active." However, the author stressed, these prerevolutionary relics were of

[57] Lert, *Na tom stoiu*, 7–31. See also *Politicheskii dnevnik*, 2:713–738.
[58] Lert, *Na tom stoiu*, 31. [59] Brudny, *Reinventing Russia*, 94–95.

diminishing significance since "in the *Soviet era* . . . a qualitatively new, socialist culture has developed new traditions. And this – with all due respect to the values of the past – inspires in us a *singular* [*osobyi*] pride." These new values and traditions, the piece went on,

> most fully and visibly express the spiritual greatness of the *Soviet* people; the over one hundred nations and nationalities of the Soviet people, who built socialism and have entered into a period of full-scale construction of communism, are united in brotherly bonds of friendship, Soviet patriotism, and proletarian internationalism.

The article pointed to the many socialist-era memorials and rituals that "serve the cause of the *revolutionary* education of future generations" and commemorate the achievements of the Soviet people. Although Lenin, the Revolution, and Civil War all figured in the article's tribute to Soviet accomplishments, the commemoration of the Great Patriotic War provided the central focus:

> In recent years, places of pilgrimage have become genuine memorials to the heroism of the Soviet people, such as the Tomb of the Unknown Soldier at the Kremlin wall in Moscow, Mamaev Kurgan in Volgograd, Piskarevskoe Cemetery in Leningrad, and also monuments to the death of fascism – [the village of] Krasukha and Salaspils [concentration camp], Khatyn' and [the village of] Pirchiupis and others. Of great significance are the excursions by youth and other organizations to sites of the revolutionary, military and labor glory of the Soviet people.[60]

The author was careful to note that these new Soviet traditions were not "anational" [*beznatsional'nyi*]. Rather, Soviet patriotic culture reflected the "progressive" aspects of national feeling present among all Soviet nationalities. Nevertheless, it was certainly no coincidence that the article put forth the war cult as the embodiment of this socialist culture and, implicitly, as the antithesis to the brand of Russian national feeling promoted by the Chalmaevists. Throughout the 1970s, the Brezhnev leadership would continue to aggressively advance the war myth as an inclusive source of pan-Soviet identity, capable of channeling Russocentric nationalism's emphasis on love for the motherland, patriotism, and anti-Westernism in an internationalist direction.[61]

[60] Ivanov, "Sotsializm i kul'turnoe nasledie," 93–95 (emphases in original).

[61] Among the many examples, see "O piatidesiatiletii Soiuza Sovetskikh Sotsialisticheskikh Respublik," *Pravda*, Dec. 22, 1972, 2–5; "Postanovlenie TsK KPSS 'O 30-letii Pobedy sovetskogo naroda v Velikoi Otechestvennoi voine 1941–1945 godov,'" *Pravda*, Feb. 9, 1975, 1–2; "Velikii podvig sovetskogo naroda," *Pravda*, May 9, 1975, 1–3.

On the other hand, where the application of tighter restraints on nationalist trends devolved into outright provocation of nationalist sensibilities, as observed in the *Novyi mir* affair, the Politburo acted swiftly to placate the offended parties. The process of forging a supranational identity, and the associated diminution of sub-state ethnic loyalties, was intended to be gradual. If confronted with the choice of putting the brakes on this progression or facing widespread resistance from the Russian-speaking base, the Brezhnev leadership opted for the former. This, in some respects, explains the fate of the ardent internationalist and acting head of the Propaganda Department Alexander Yakovlev.[62] In the wake of the party crackdown on Russian nationalism, Yakovlev initiated a campaign of his own, the highpoint of which was the appearance in *Literaturnaia gazeta* of his article "Against Anti-Historicism," the most explicit lashing out at Russocentric nationalism from an orthodox Marxist-Leninist position yet published. Among other things, Yakovlev contrasted the internationalist patriotism of the Soviet people, which drew on "the genuinely democratic, revolutionary themes and traditions of national history," with idealized notions about the Russian national spirit and prerevolutionary rural life. Indeed, the crux of Yakovlev's polemic was an unambiguous assertion of the novelty of the Soviet people. Yakovlev took aim at those "zealots of the nationalist spirit," such as the Chalmaevists, "who seem to shy away from such words and concepts as 'Soviet' [and] 'socialist,'" and who "fail to recognize the undisputed fact that a new historical community of people has emerged within our country – the Soviet people." "We appreciate everything the geniuses of the past have done," Yakovlev concluded, "but the greatest pride is our present reality." For his vigorous attack on nationalism from a Marxist-Leninist stance, Yakovlev was demoted and sent to Canada as Soviet ambassador.[63]

The Yakovlev affair is often cited as evidence of the residual strength of Russian nationalism and its role as a parallel or co-opted ideology of state.[64] True, Yakovlev's banishment was clearly a response to the

[62] The then-head of the Molodaia gvardiia publishing house, V. N. Ganichev, has questioned the true extent of Yakovlev's internationalism, contending that it was an attempt to expunge from his record his prior association with the Shelepin group. See Mitrokhin, *Russkaia partiia*, 132–133.

[63] Iakovlev, "Protiv antiistorizma," 4–5. Despite the article's avowed hostility to Russian chauvinism, one recent interpretation has highlighted its implicit Russocentrism, in particular its reference to "stagnant traditions." See Davoliūtė, *The Making and Breaking of Soviet Lithuania*, 132–133. For Yakovlev's later reflections on the episode, see Iakovlev, *Omut pamiati*, 188–191, 202–203; Iakovlev, *Sumerki*, chaps. 9–10; "Fashizm prost, kak palka." For some differing views on the Yakovlev episode, see Mitrokhin, *Russkaia partiia*, 131–136; Brudny, *Reinventing Russia*, 94–102; Cherniaev, *Moia zhizn'*, 297–299; Yanov, *The Russian Challenge*, 120–123.

[64] Cohen, *Russian Imperialism*, 104–105.

unwelcome political pressure put on Brezhnev from Russian nationalist sympathizers, and possibly reflected Brezhnev's own plans to create a domestic conservative counterweight to the policy of détente on the international stage.[65] However, this explanation is incomplete. Alongside campaigns to combat non-Russian nationalism, the leadership continued to uphold the victory myth as a patriotic antidote to Russocentric nationalism, which was itself often rooted in the wartime experience.[66] Notably, although "Against Anti-Historicism" avoided any discussion of the Great Patriotic War, many of the responses to Yakovlev's article criticized a perceived hostility toward the war's veneration. Among the biggest critics of the article were leaders of non-Russian communist parties who, predictably perhaps, went out of their way to prove their subservience to the Russian elder brother. But within the RSFSR, a great deal of criticism was leveled by veterans.[67] According to the head of the Molodaia gvardiia publishing house, Valerii Ganichev, Yakovlev had delivered a public lecture at the USSR Academy of Sciences to regional and republican Komsomol secretaries that turned out to be an early draft of "Against Anti-Historicism." At the end of the lecture, Yakovlev purportedly condemned critics who "profess and praise the traditions of the past" and who write with "undue exaggeration of the successes of the Great Patriotic War." Whether or not this was an off-the-cuff remark, such an explosive statement did not make its way into the published version. Nonetheless, Brezhnev was particularly alarmed by the number of veterans' letters the Central Committee received expressing indignation over the fact that Yakovlev "wanted to erase the Great Patriotic War in addition to our history more generally." If Ganichev is correct, Yakovlev's dismissal may have been as much about his perceived mishandling of the victory myth as it was about offending Russian national sensibilities.[68]

Indeed, one of the most ardent responses to "Against Anti-Historicism" framed the debate over Russian nationalism largely as a struggle over the legacy of the war. Published in the nationalist samizdat journal *Veche* by the then-anonymous Vladimir Osipov, "The Struggle with So-Called Russophilism, or the Path of National Suicide" offered

[65] Mitrokhin, *Russkaia partiia*, 133–134; Brudny, *Reinventing Russia*, 99–102.

[66] The parallel anti-nationalist campaigns saw Petr Shelest and Vasilii Mzhavanadze, the first secretaries of the Ukrainian and Georgian communist parties respectively, lose their positions for their perceived support of local nationalism. Although corruption played a role in the Georgian case, local nationalism was probably the decisive factor. See Suny, *The Making of the Georgian Nation*, 306–307; Simon, *Nationalism*, 287–288.

[67] The novelist Mikhail Sholokhov, apparently prodded by the chief editor of the journal *Ogonek*, Anatolii Sofronov, also issued a devastating letter condemning Yakovlev's article. See "Fashizm prost, kak palka."

[68] Ganichev, "Molodaia gvardiia," 127–129.

the most explicit affirmation of the Russocentric victory narrative of the late-socialist era.[69] In Osipov's telling, the Soviet Union was victorious in the war not because of its ideology, fraternal bonds, or sociopolitical system; rather, it was due to the fortitude of the Russian people, often in spite of the Party and state. Osipov pointed out, for example, that Stalin broke up the Comintern not merely to strengthen the anti-Hitler alliance but also "because the communist parties rejected a nihilistic attitude toward their fatherlands." "Why," he asks,

> was an army [i.e., the Vlasovites] which fought on the side of the enemy in a patriotic war formed for the first time in Russian history in the [19]40s? Why could Stalin, the supreme commander, not trust his supposedly loyal generals and constantly shuffled military cadres, fearing treachery and conspiracy?[70]

The answer, of course, was that the Soviet regime had foolishly suppressed Russian national sentiment to the detriment of the state's ability to combat the enemy or even sustain loyalty. Only by eliminating the "anational" approach to mobilization was the Soviet Union victorious.

Contrary to the Chalmaevists writing in the official press, Osipov rejected the notion that the use of prerevolutionary imagery in wartime propaganda was an artificial process meant to convey socialist ideals. Instead, he argued, it was a practice designed to draw on the primordial Russian spirit:

> Why was it that during the same Patriotic War, when the country was in deadly peril and we needed to arouse extraordinary strength of spirit, "Soviet patriotism" (in the sense proposed by Comrade Yakovlev) proved inadequate, and it was necessary on short notice to recall the Church, Aleksandr Nevskii, Peter I, and Suvorov, i.e., princes, tsars, and reactionary military commanders? Why did the cult of the heroes of the civil war and class struggle prove insufficient? And in whom does the "anti-Russophile" Yakovlev place his hopes in the coming war [with China]?

For Osipov, present-day notions of a pan-Soviet patriotism and imagined community, which sought "the elimination of national particularities, [and] the total liquidation of the nation in general," were incapable of mobilizing Soviet society. This criticism did not apply to Yakovlev alone, but Brezhnev's ruling clique: "[b]ureaucratic supporters of the USSR, who are actually supporters of the (supposedly) anational character of the USSR." These proponents of an "anational" state, who act as though "[b]efore 1917, all is darkness and gloom[,] ... [as though] there is absolutely nothing positive in a thousand years of history," were

[69] Osipov, "Bor'ba s tak nazyvaemym rusofil'stvom," 19–57. On Russian nationalist samizdat during the Brezhnev era, see Mitrokhin, *Russkaia partiia*, 430–488.
[70] Osipov, "Bor'ba s tak nazyvaemym rusofil'stvom," 49–50.

attempting to obliterate the Russian national core of the greatest Soviet achievement – victory in the war.[71]

Thus, despite Yakovlev's avoidance of the war theme in print, his antinationalist polemic effectively relinquished patriotic memory of the war to the nationalist camp. In other words, as much as Yakovlev's removal placated Russocentric nationalists, it also signified an effort to preserve the patriotic formula of the Soviet people doctrine and reclaim the victory myth as a pan-Soviet source of patriotic mobilization. This would explain why the Brezhnev leadership, as it went ahead with the war cult's expansion in the aftermath of the Yakovlev affair, continued at every turn to resist the Russocentric variant of the war's memory. The victory myth's role in Soviet patriotism's discursive tension, as observed in the previous chapter, was reflected throughout the 1970s in both official commemorations and nationalist writings, where the Party doggedly opposed the nationalist tendency to cut across the revolutionary divide.[72] Observing this persistent facet of cultural politics, the Russophile literary critic Viktor Petelin noted in 1976 that "[i]t is good that Comrade Yakovlev was transferred to a different job, but the problem is that his 'spirit' remains, as well as his method of debate."[73] Some nationalist authors nevertheless found ways to reproduce the Russocentric paradigm of the war's memory at the margins of official culture.

The Patriotic Parallelism of Sergei Semanov

Chalmaevist tendencies did not altogether disappear in the 1970s. Albeit in a less systematic capacity, certain nationalist intellectuals attempted to carve out a Russocentric alternative to the pan-Soviet internationalism of the official war myth. Most tenacious in this regard was Sergei Semanov. Despite the party crackdown on nationalist expression, Semanov retained his position as editor of the biographical "Lives of Remarkable People" series and later became editor-in-chief of the journal *Chelovek i zakon*. At the same time, Semanov continued to publish in the nationalist press, his essays often grappling with the theme of the war. Published in 1977 with a print run of thirty-five thousand, the collection *Heart of the Motherland* [*Serdtse rodiny*] brought together the most significant of these essays. It is therefore best appreciated not as a one-time coup for Russocentric nationalism, but

[71] Osipov, 19–21, 48–50.

[72] In 1974, the same year that Solzhenitsyn was sent into exile, the KGB closed the underground journal *Veche* and arrested its editor, Vladimir Osipov. Brudny writes that this "eliminated the possibility of an 'independent from the state' Russian nationalist movement." Brudny, *Reinventing Russia*, 103.

[73] "Dukh ostaetsia, kak i metody polemiki," 88–89.

rather as evidence of a steady flow of nationalist expression – curtailed but not extinguished – that persisted after 1970.

Heart of the Motherland was a nostalgic ode to the city of Moscow told largely from the perspective of successive military conflicts. Indeed, war provided the overriding motif, bridging the pre-socialist and Soviet epochs. The defenders of Moscow before and after 1917, Semanov reminded, could summon age-old Russian military might in their rout of the enemy. In his discussion of the Great Patriotic War, Semanov focused in particular on Russocentric wartime propaganda. Soviet military orders named for Suvorov, Kutuzov, Nevskii, and so on, demonstrated that "[t]hese [pre-Soviet] commanders stood united in combat regiments alongside heroes of the Soviet epoch – Frunze and [Grigorii] Kotovskii, [Nikolai] Shchors and [Sergei] Lazo, [Valerii] Chkalov and Chapaev." In another example, Semanov recalled from his youth a giant outdoor mural erected in 1942:

> In one area, there were Russian knights in pointed helmets cutting down with [their] swords riders with crosses on their cloaks who were fleeing across the ice. In the center stood a knight; this was clearly Aleksandr Nevskii. And on the other side of the mural was our Red Army in broad, red-starred helmets attacking with bayonets at the ready ... On the top of the mural were the dates "1242–1942." And at the bottom a Slavonic epigraph in scarlet and white: "He who comes to us with the sword, will also perish by the sword. By this [motto] the Russian land stood and will continue to stand! [So stated] Aleksandr Nevskii." In such a way, the Soviet people marked the 700th anniversary of the Battle on the Ice.

Perhaps the most striking coupling of the Great Patriotic War and pre-Soviet Russia concerned the poet Aleksei Nedogonov:

> At the end of the Great Patriotic War, among the ranks of our troops who came to save Bulgaria from Hitlerism, was a young officer, [Aleksei Nedogonov,] a native of the Donbas working class who was raised and educated in the Soviet era. ... At the Shipka Pass he saw a church that had been built over a burial site for Russian soldiers who died the previous century while liberating this fraternal country from the yoke of the Janissaries. And that is when he, a soldier of the Great Patriotic [War], felt the connection between old and new: "A great church stood / In blush tones / ... Remove your cap, Stalingrader / Here lie our ancestors! ... Take off your cap Stalingrader." We must preserve the connection between eras, allowing no one to break this eternal chain.

Added to these Russocentric musings on the war, Semanov underscored the role of winter as a deciding factor in Russian and Soviet military history, from Karl XII of Sweden to Napoleon and others. The Nazis were the last in a long line of these would-be conquerors who were "completely swept away from the historical scene" after facing winter conditions. The defeat of the Nazis, Semanov contended, was already a foregone conclusion, "[b]efore the Battle of Moscow; [b]efore Stalingrad." This had nothing to do with the leadership of the Communist Party, the Soviet socioeconomic system, or even the heroism of the (predominantly Russian) Soviet people; rather, for Semanov, victory was determined by the most primeval of forces – Russia itself.[74]

However, Semanov offset his grand Russian war narrative in important respects. First, it should be reiterated that his nationalist single-stream depiction of the past was far less explicit in the original journal essays that comprised *Heart of the Motherland* than it was in their 1977 compilation. In effect, the book artificially grafted together what were loosely connected essays in such a way that a single-stream thesis could be much more clearly discerned. The first subsection of the book, for example, which initially comprised an independent article, dealt almost exclusively with prerevolutionary Moscow, including the 1812 war against Napoleon. The next subsection of the same chapter, originally part of a separate publication, focused principally on the Soviet era and the Great Patriotic War, with little reference to pre-Soviet Russia. But the effect when each formerly independent article was placed one after the other was to enunciate a Russian national-patriotic through line. In this sense, *Heart of the Motherland* was something of an anomaly. The Russocentrism of Semanov's narrative did not typify the nationalist press during the 1970s, which generally toed the official line regarding the Soviet people doctrine and the war's role therein.

Second, Semanov rather delicately wove a second, pan-Soviet/internationalist interpretation of the war into his text. Like the majority of the Russocentric nationalist writers of the Brezhnev era, Semanov sought to remain within the regime's good graces, often by expressing his ideas within the framework of the official ideology.[75] While Leninist slogans were sometimes inserted as mere window dressing, ideological orthodoxy comes to the fore whenever *Heart of the Motherland* deals substantively with the Great Patriotic War. For example, Semanov rebutted the idea that the war embodied a Russian primordial struggle:

> Bourgeois nationalists who fought against the Soviet system [during and immediately after the war] liked to say that they were fighting against Russians . . . This is a blatant lie, calculated to stir up the basest of racist instincts. Of course, Russian citizens of the Soviet Union were killed – many unfortunately . . . But former Vlasovites, policemen, drivers of gas vans and other traitors easily found refuge

[74] Semanov, *Serdtse rodiny*, 8–13, 16, 31–33, 35, 46, 50, 80–81. Although beyond the scope of the present discussion, Semanov's anti-Semitism was also present in *Heart of the Motherland*. For analysis, see Dunlop, *Faces*, 260–261.

[75] Dunlop, *Faces*, 43, 254–265. In Cosgrove's useful typology, Semanov represented a "Red Statist" orientation. See Cosgrove, *Russian Nationalism*, 36–39.

> with the fascists, even if their origins were as Russian as could be . . . No, the fascist nationalists fought not against the Russians; rather, they could not accept socialism, the Soviet social system, our labor morals, our workers' ideals. They therefore challenged not Russians, but the whole Soviet people.[76]

Indeed, the war is presented at various times as an event free of ethnic particularities, as one fought primarily "for the ideals of peace and socialism." Contrary to passages that alluded to an eternal struggle against foreign invaders, Semanov simultaneously regarded 1941–5 as a fundamental clash of social systems:

> The objectives of the fascist aggressors, of imperialism as a whole, were only too obvious. The progressive Soviet system, the workers' socialist state had been the object of impassioned and frank hatred. Our people prudently started to prepare for war ahead of time. It is difficult to determine what the fate of the world would have been if the Soviet leadership had held a different political line.[77]

Despite the implied praise for Stalin's foresight during the 1930s, through these and other passages, Semanov constructed a parallel narrative of the war. While the first hinted at specifically Russian aspects of the conflict, the other adhered completely to the official line that victory was the result of supra-ethnic, Soviet sources.

The parallel, pan-Soviet narrative is readily observed in Semanov's frequent attempts to distinguish between past and present. He notes, for example, that

> [i]n Soviet Russia, a new society was created, free from the power of money, from estate or national restrictions . . . The young Red Army, having learned all that was best from the old army, repeatedly and extensively developed and enriched this legacy, creating new Soviet army traditions and heroics. . . . In the Soviet Army, the complete triumph of Leninist internationalism, a profound respect for other peoples has been established. And this is our greatest asset. During the Great Patriotic War, Hitlerism brought our people untold misery and suffering. But what happened? The Soviet soldier always distinguished average Germans from the Nazis . . . Even in the midst of battle our society condemned some of the articles by the well-known journalist Ilya Ehrenburg in which the class distinction between the German people and the ruling elite was not always clear. So, years of trials have shown that the internationalism of the Soviet soldier is an attitude that has entered into the flesh and blood of our [Soviet] people.[78]

Often the two narratives brushed against each other, as when Semanov described the inspiration behind Aleksei Nedogonov's poem cited above. Despite the suggestion of continuity between past and present, Semanov explains the poem as a tale at once of "loyalty to the best traditions of [the poet's Russian] father and of the internationalism and patriotism that is

[76] Semanov, *Serdtse rodiny*, 80–81. [77] Semanov, 36–37. [78] Semanov, 31–32.

organic and natural to the Soviet man."[79] Such vacillations are evident throughout Semanov's work: in nearly every instance where a single-stream interpretation is implied, there is a parallel reference to Soviet patriotism's supranational, postrevolutionary character.

Semanov also qualified his Russocentrism in the same way party ideologists later clarified Stalin's – that is, he emphasized its purely instrumental nature, effectively hamstringing the broader nationalist implications of his argument. This is particularly true in Semanov's description of Soviet wartime propaganda, in which "the best artists of socialist realism began to draw inspiration from the [prerevolutionary] military past, the Homeland, and its people." Although films based on the lives of Nevskii, Suvorov, Minin, and Pozharskii made their way into Soviet cinemas, Semanov is at pains to stress that these were not meant as historical representations of the thirteenth, seventeenth, or eighteenth centuries, or as mere costume dramas "of the type so prevalent now in the bourgeois West (we'll mention here the Hollywood film 'Ben Hur' and countless subsequent vulgarities)." Rather, these films personified and made comprehensible universal themes about national cohesion and defense in an age of increasing international tension. "The film *Aleksandr Nevskii*," Semanov writes, "was not conceived as a picture of life in the thirteenth century . . . but rather [articulated ideas about] the need for popular unity in the face of enemy invasion . . . [and] about betrayal as the worst method of the enemy." Semanov goes on:

> The hero is a symbol of a larger phenomenon in the life of the people. We mention Aleksandr Nevskii and from this name emerges the Battle on the Ice, which stopped aggressors from the West. We mention Dmitrii Donskoi and this brings to mind the great era of the Kulikovo battle, which liberated our country from foreign yoke.[80]

In other words, Semanov was acknowledging that Soviet propaganda did not call upon some primordial Russian essence in the fight against Nazi Germany, but instead filled what were essentially empty vessels – Nevskii, Donskoi, Kutuzov – with universal tropes for the purpose of popular mobilization in wartime. By emphasizing the symbolic, constructed nature of contemporary portrayals of these prerevolutionary icons, Semanov underscored the very artificiality of his single-stream narrative.

The case of Semanov's *Heart of the Motherland* reveals the extent to which the most extreme Russocentric nationalists of the 1970s could approximate a Russocentric counter narrative of the war. On the one hand, there

[79] Semanov, 35. [80] Semanov, 94–97.

remained clear limitations on what Russophiles like Semanov could claim about the war. Semanov consistently obscured the connection between 1945 and the Russian single stream. Where he does stress Russocentrism, as in his discussion of wartime propaganda, this is paired with an extended passage on the constructed and pragmatic nature of this imagery. But although his constant fluctuations and qualifications enabled the text to pass the censors, such a technique offered readers the chance to decipher a Russocentric narrative on their own.

Semanov's nationalism would run afoul of the authorities by the early 1980s. Yet his practice of parallelism, which involved embedding the internationalist victory myth within a more sweeping Russian historical narrative, was increasingly tolerated during the USSR's final decade.[81] In November 1982, only days before Brezhnev's death, a nationalistic novel by Vladimir Chivilikhin entitled *Memory* [*Pamiat'*] received the USSR State Prize. The tome focused heavily on past Russian military exploits and, like *Heart of the Motherland*, hinted that there was a Russocentric underpinning to victory in the Great Patriotic War. Nevertheless, Chivilikhin was tactful in the way he applied his single stream to the events of 1941–5. In tracing Russia's historical evolution into a unified state, for instance, Chivilikhin writes:

> This was a consequence of the Kulikovo battle – the last encounter between the predatory Horde and the young Russia . . . The Patriotic Liberation War of 1612, the Patriotic Liberation War of 1812, *the unprecedented military and labor friendship of the peoples of our Motherland during the Great Patriotic War of 1941–1945* – all this and much else in the past and the present has roots in the battle on the Nepriadva [River].[82]

Perhaps unsurprisingly, the Great Patriotic War appears awkwardly out of place when crammed into the narrative of Russia's single stream. But so long as the war narrative preserved its ostensibly Soviet character, nationalist producers were increasingly free to fill in the edges of a larger Russian national story of war.[83]

[81] Semanov was removed from his post at *Chelovek i zakon* primarily for his perceived connection to anti-Soviet nationalists. See "Zapiska KGB SSSR v TsK KPSS ob antisovetskoi deiatel'nosti Ivanova," 108–110; "Zapiska otdela administrativnykh organov TsK KPSS," 110; "Zapiska KGB SSSR v TsK KPSS ob antisovetskoi deiatel'nosti S. N. Semanova," 110–111; "Chastnoe opredelenie," 86–87; "Radio Svoboda," 87–89; Mitrokhin, *Russkaia partiia*, 548–554; Brudny, *Reinventing Russia*, 118; Zubok, *Zhivago's Children*, 331.

[82] Chivilikhin, *Pamiat'*, 2:737 (emphasis added). Brudny is probably correct in suggesting that in awarding the USSR State Prize to Chivilikhin, Andropov sought to garner support for his succession to the post of general secretary. Brudny, *Reinventing Russia*, 123.

[83] For an argument that the Soviet myth of the war was a minor blip within a larger myth of Russian martial exceptionalism, see Carleton, *Russia: The Story of War*.

Kulikovo, 1980

The appearance of Chivilikhin's *Memory*, and the acclaim it received in official circles, was only possible in the context of 1980–2.[84] Brudny argues persuasively that these years witnessed a relaxation of ideological discipline connected to the volatile international situation in Poland and Afghanistan, and the worsening crisis in Soviet agricultural production. Russian national pride and privilege were stoked, Brudny writes, to facilitate ethnic Russian support for the regime at a time of external and internal political instability.[85] The year 1980 also happened to be the 600th anniversary of Dmitrii Donskoi's victory over the Mongols at the Battle of Kulikovo Field. The partial loosening of formal restrictions combined with the jubilee celebration of Kulikovo exploded in the pages of the nationalist press. Articles published at this time directly challenged the regime's stance on the Russian Orthodox Church and were more vocal than ever on the issue of historical preservation. The level of nationalist expression surrounding the Kulikovo date apparently shocked the regime, which had not crafted a coherent official response.[86]

As initially conceived, the Kulikovo commemoration followed the compartmentalized pattern of other state celebrations of prerevolutionary events. Whatever its role in co-opting Russian nationalist support for the regime, the anniversary aimed to siphon, contain, defuse, and ultimately rechannel what had become an unwieldy Russian nationalist current in a way that neither offended Russian national sensibilities nor relinquished ownership of the main source of supra-ethnic patriotic identity – memory of the World War II victory. As shall be discussed, however, the jubilee's orchestration reflected a significant shift in the Soviet Union's commemorative politics, a shift that portended a growing tension between Russian and Soviet identities at the dawn of what would be the USSR's final decade.

Instructions from central planners regarded the anniversary as a time to disseminate "historical knowledge" of Russian state building and of

[84] Chivilikhin's novel-essay *Pamiat'* was first published in serialized form in *Nash sovremennik* to commemorate the 600th anniversary of the Battle of Kulikovo Field. Only in 1982 and 1984 was it issued in two bound volumes. On the longer-term significance of this novel, see Kazarkin, "Pamiat' – Ekologiia kul'tury," 156–162; Weiner, *A Little Corner of Freedom*, 334–335.

[85] Brudny, *Reinventing Russia*, 116–117. This was also probably connected to Brezhnev's declining health. The general secretary's health was certainly a factor in the decline of détente and the decision to intervene in Afghanistan. See Zubok, *A Failed Empire*, 257, 263–264.

[86] Brudny, *Reinventing Russia*, 117, 294 n66; Cosgrove, *Russian Nationalism*, 43–50. On the nationalist responses to the Kulikovo anniversary, see Duncan, *Russian Messianism*, 77–81.

the "high moral and fighting spirit of Russian soldiers" and their inspirational leader Dmitrii Donskoi. As far as explicit connections to the Soviet era, commemorations were to elucidate the place and significance of "the Kulikovo theme" in the "patriotic consciousness" of "the Russian and Soviet people" today.[87] Boris Rybakov, who has been described as a Russian nationalist "super-patriot,"[88] clarified what this latter objective entailed in his official report on the anniversary:

> Six centuries separate us from this great historical event ... A new era in the history of the world was opened by the victory of the Great October Socialist Revolution. During the years of Soviet power, within an entirely novel, newly born socio-economic formation, there has emerged a new historical community of people – the Soviet people. The creation of a developed socialist society in the USSR has ensured ... the friendship of all the peoples of the USSR, and the flowering of Soviet patriotism. Describing Soviet patriotism, Leonid Brezhnev stated: "Perhaps there is no person who doesn't experience an intractable feeling of love and attachment to the land of his grandfathers and great-grandfathers, to his native culture, his language, his traditions and customs. But in a socialist society this feeling, the sense of patriotism, grows beyond the boundaries delineated by nationality and is filled with new content." The Kulikovo battle is one of those events that inspires in us a feeling of deep respect for our ancestors, a sense of pride in the patriotic feat they have performed.[89]

This report, which was read out before the Politburo and other leading party members during the main commemorative meeting in Moscow, indicates that, as with previous such events, the celebration of Kulikovo was not simply intended to venerate the distant Russian past but rather to delicately differentiate past from present.

For the most part, cultural productions linked to the anniversary either focused exclusively on Kulikovo and its prerevolutionary Russian significance,[90] or treated it as an accessible patriotic analogue that remained, by virtue of its sociopolitical context, aloof from properly Soviet notions of patriotism, homeland, and national identity.[91] Even the major nationalist journals and broadsheets limited their historical-Russocentric narratives. Valentin Rasputin hinted that victory at

87 Shkurko, "Voprosy muzeefikatsii pamiatnikov Kulikovskoi bitvy," 226–227.
88 For this assessment, see Klein, *Voskreshenie Peruna*, 70.
89 Rybakov, *Kulikovskaia bitva*, 5–6.
90 See, for instance, the short television documentaries, Ermilov, *Pole Kulikovo*, and Karpov, *Na pole Kulikovom*.
91 Commemorative articles and films often concluded by noting that Soviet citizens "have not forgotten that during the Great Patriotic War the image of Dmitrii Donskoi . . . roused Soviet fighters to perform feats in the name of defending the socialist Homeland." This formulation cast pre-Soviet "Russia" and the "USSR" as fundamentally distinct entities. See, for example, A. Preobrazhenskii, "Bessmertie podviga," *Sovetskaia kul'tura*, Sep. 5, 1980, 2–3.

Kulikovo in 1380 was tied to the Soviet Union's fate. He asked whether the Russian people might again be required "to defend the Russian land and Russian blood" at some future Kulikovo. Others noted the huge debt the West owed Russia for saving it from "both" the Mongols and the Wehrmacht.[92] More often, however, nationalist authors abided the Soviet people doctrine's discursive tension. In one quite typical Kulikovo anniversary article in the predominant nationalist journal of this period, *Nash sovremennik*, Iurii Seleznev emphasized the ideological factors that set the events of 1941–5 apart from Kulikovo:

> In the Great Patriotic War, the Hitlerite Nazis confronted true socialism and a true union of nations in the entity of our state – the USSR. The victory of our Motherland over fascism enabled many nations of Europe and Asia to form their own independent national and multinational states, and allowed others to begin socialist movements and national-liberation, anti-imperial struggles.[93]

Likewise, the author of *Nash sovremennik*'s main commemorative essay, the nationalist historian Vadim Kargalov, capped off his discussion of Kulikovo's influence on subsequent Russian military victories by reminding that the forthcoming anniversary was principally a chance "to better represent and appreciate those radical changes wrought by the Great October Socialist Revolution."[94] As before, the closer the single stream of Russian history approached the years 1941–5, the more it tended to dissipate.

There were two notable exceptions, however. For its anniversary issue, *Literaturnaia gazeta* published competing variants of the Kulikovo theme side by side. The first was written by the liberal-reformist Iurii Trifonov and offered an analysis of Kulikovo that stressed its purely historical significance. The second essay was the work of the Russocentric nationalist Egor Isaev. Isaev wrote that "[i]n our long-suffering and at times glorious history, there are, I believe, not one but three great fields [of battle]. These are Kulikovo Field, then Borodino, then, next to these, the Prokhorov Field near Belgorod," which was part of the 1943 Battle of Kursk. It was certainly not unheard of among Russocentric nationalists to draw parallels between a prerevolutionary victory and an individual battle from 1941–5. Isaev, however, went further than even the Chalmaevists in specifying that Prokhorov Field embodied World War II as a whole, that it

92 Rasputin, "Za Nepriadvoi lebedi krichali. K 600-letiiu bitvu na pole Kulikovom," *Sovetskaia kul'tura*, Jan. 4, 1980; Duncan, *Russian Messianism*, 79–80.
93 Seleznev, "'Chtoby starye rasskazyvali, a molodye pomnili!'" 179–180.
94 Kargalov, "Ratnaia slava Rossii," 172, 179. See also Kargalov, "Ot nepriadvy do ugry," 160–179.

"symbolizes all the fields of the heroic battles of the Great Patriotic War."[95] The decision to juxtapose these contrasting analyses of Kulikovo's relevance to Soviet society, presumably so that readers could pick the version that best suited their tastes, reflected a deepening Russian-Soviet divide in patriotic memory.

Nevertheless, while all-union party and state organs and publishing houses – including those under the purview of the RSRSR Writers Union – generally maintained the war's inclusive, pan-Soviet orientation amid a flurry of Russian nationalist expression, a more sweeping shift was taking place at the level of RSFSR patriotic politics. In the aftermath of the anti-nationalist campaign of the early 1970s, many of the avowed Russian nationalists who were removed from positions of all-union authority found refuge within RSFSR state structures.[96] Notably, the aforementioned Iurii Melent'ev, the former deputy head of the USSR Ministry of Culture, retained the post of Minister of Culture of the RSFSR from 1974 until 1990. Because the site of Kulikovo Field fell within RSFSR jurisdiction, Melent'ev and like-minded figures in the republic's Council of Ministers managed the day-to-day organization of anniversary projects both in Moscow and at Kulikovo itself. Unlike earlier state anniversaries, such as the founding of Moscow (1947) and Borodino battle (1962), therefore, the Kulikovo event was largely controlled by authorities sympathetic to Russocentric nationalism. As such, the event provides an important look at late-socialist "inclusionary politics" as they operated at the level of the Russian Republic.

The influence of Russocentric nationalism was reflected in both the exhibition "600 Years of the Kulikovo Battle," hosted by the State Historical Museum (GIM) in Moscow, and the emergence of VOOPIiK as a prime executor of patriotic education and republican commemorations. Melent'ev granted a great deal of leeway to the experts responsible for organizing GIM's Kulikovo exhibition.[97] Under Melent'ev's tutelage, the group, which consisted of a mix of Russophile historians and Slavicists from Moscow State University, looked to play up the connection between Kulikovo and the Soviet experience of 1941–5. Although primarily focused on artifacts from the fourteenth century and explanatory materials detailing the history of Kulikovo, the organizers devoted a section to the "Kulikovo Battle and the patriotic upbringing of the Soviet people during the Great Patriotic War." The section was, on its face, fully in line with

95 Iurii Trifonov, "Slavim cherez shest' vekov," *Literaturnaia gazeta*, Sep. 3, 1980, 6; Egor Isaev, "Za volnoi pamiati," *Literaturnaia gazeta*, Sep. 3, 1980, 6.

96 Mitrokhin, *Russkaia partiia*, 368–370.

97 See Melent'ev's statement on the museum exhibition: Melent'ev, "Pole sud'by narodnoi," 270–275.

patriotic discursive tension. The text introducing the exhibit emphasized the purely symbolic relationship between Kulikovo and the Soviet war effort. Yet the displays themselves bombarded the visitor with imagery emphasizing Russian historical exceptionalism and the Russian people's unique role in victory. Alongside Great Patriotic War military banners hung Kulikovo-themed wartime posters depicting the trope of medieval Russian warriors hovering above Soviet fighting men. Most prominent in this regard was Ivanov and Burov's "Better an Honorable Death Than a Shameful Life!" Stalin's great ancestors speech, or variations thereof, adorned most of the exhibited works.[98] As noted elsewhere, though censors did not prohibit references to wartime Russocentric propaganda, it was customary to qualify these references by emphasizing their pragmatic and instrumental nature. Within the GIM exhibit, however, wartime Russocentrism overwhelmed such distinctions. Melent'ev's subsequent statements on museum work related to the Kulikovo anniversary suggest that the blurring of the revolutionary divide was deliberate. The cultural minister described the exhibition as depicting the "eternal struggle" of Russians against "the dark forces of violence, injustice, [and] fascism."[99]

Melent'ev oversaw an even more significant development in the context of the 1980 anniversary. The Kulikovo jubilee stands out as a watershed for VOOPIiK's rising influence in the republic's commemorative politics.[100] Indeed, aided by Melent'ev and the head of VOOPIiK, Viacheslav Kochemasov, who was also a deputy chairman of the RSFSR Council of Ministers, the VOOPIiK Presidium conceived and developed many of the major initiatives for Kulikovo's commemoration. On March 1, 1979, VOOPIiK's Central Council issued the first resolution "On the restoration and improvement of historical and cultural monuments commemorating the events of the Kulikovo Battle at Kulikovo Field." Within six days, the RSFSR Council of Ministers had approved this resolution "in the main" and set in motion plans to restore existing commemorative structures at the battle site, including the nineteenth-century monumental column on the elevation known as Red Hill and the nearby memorial church of St. Sergius of Radonezh.[101] The seeming indifference exhibited by the Ministry of Culture of the USSR, which

[98] The organizers included A. S. Korkh, A. V. Uspenskaia, L. L. Savchenkova, E. G. Gorokhova, and the museum's deputy director A. I. Shkurko. For a detailed overview of the exhibit, see "Tematiko-ekspozitsionnyi plan iubileinoi vystavki," 278–280.

[99] Melent'ev, "Pole sud'by narodnoi," 270–275.

[100] The organization's petitions to the CPSU Central Committee apparently played a role in determining the scale of restoration projects and public events marking the anniversary date. See Romanova, *Proshedshikh dnei ocharovanie*, 131–134.

[101] GARF A-259/48/872/93–94.

the Deputy Chairman of the Tula regional Executive Committee accused of utter "inertia" in the fulfillment of its promised support for some of the restorations, only magnified the role of VOOPIiK in its collaboration with local and republican cultural authorities.[102]

Once planning commenced, Mikhail Suslov summoned Kochemasov, the VOOPIiK head, to the Secretariat to discuss the anniversary festivities. There was apparently some concern among leading members of the Central Committee that the anniversary at Kulikovo Field would draw Russian nationalists from across the republic and become, in effect, a venue for a mass nationalist gathering. Kochemasov countered that such reports on the character of the anniversary were grossly exaggerated. "We are in control of the situation," he assured the Party's ideological chief. "Well, alright. We agree under one condition," Suslov responded. "You personally must accept total responsibility for the character and order of the activities surrounding the anniversary."[103] With Secretariat approval, VOOPIiK, together with local and republican state organs, threw itself into the work of restoring the Kulikovo site and organizing commemorative events to coincide with the September 1980 jubilee.

Unlike many previous events in which VOOPIiK took part, there was, according to Kochemasov, a great deal of ambition among planners for the Kulikovo anniversary. "From the first organizational meeting," he recalls, "a completely different approach prevailed, namely the idea to initiate a mass-scale operation. To resurrect, restore all the monuments that are in one way or another connected to Dmitrii Donskoi's campaign." This was a daunting task. As with the Borodino battlefield of the early 1960s, the Soviet state's general disregard for Russian prerevolutionary battle sites had long been evident at Kulikovo Field. In the summer of 1979, representatives of VOOPIiK and the RSFSR Ministry of Culture traveled to survey the site and the adjacent village of Monastyrshchina, which contained relics and other historical links to the battle. Kochemasov's account of his group's arrival at Kulikovo is worth quoting at length:

> The picture that opened before us was much worse than we could have imagined. There were practically no roads. We could barely make it to Kulikovo Field ... There were, in fact, no houses. One was destroyed, another was boarded up, and there was desolation everywhere. Even within the church itself. We stood near the church and examined the ruins. We were silent. I did not want to talk. Bitter feelings arose. We agreed that we must put in order everything that we can: restore the church, establish a convenient road linked to the main Tula thoroughfare. And we determined that the main priority should be the objects on Kulikovo Field

[102] GARF A-259/48/872/68–74. [103] *Kak grazhdanin Rossii*, 106–107.

itself, as well as improvements to the area that would allow for the accommodation of tourists.[104]

Thanks to the support of the RSFSR ministries and Tula regional bodies, restoration projects were fully underway by late 1979.[105] These included the refurbishment of the ancient stone church at Monastyrshchina and the complete renovation of Red Hill and the surrounding structures. A network of footpaths was installed so that visitors could more easily navigate the area. In addition, the architect V. A. Shatokhin oversaw the first phase of a major tourist complex linking the adjacent village of Ivanovka with Red Hill.[106] Although work continued right up until the anniversary in September 1980, Kochemasov writes that one week before the jubilee, during his final inspection of the site, a "completely different picture" presented itself. In addition to the renovations, a new asphalt road enabled the arrival of a constant flow of tourists.[107]

From an ideological standpoint, the most important aspect of the planning involved the overhaul of the church of St. Sergius of Radonezh, which housed the Museum of the Battle of Kulikovo. While commemorative souvenirs and brochures produced for the anniversary tended to section off Kulikovo from Soviet-era achievements,[108] the VOOPIiK-linked artists, curators, and scholars tasked with developing the museum, like their GIM counterparts, tested the limits of the official call to show "the significance of the Kulikovo theme" for Soviet society. But in the case of St. Sergius, the intent appears far less deliberate. The final report on the museum's renovation notes that "exhibits dedicated to the Kulikovo Battle itself and its historical significance naturally occupied the bulk of the church." However, the altar room contained a final section covering the place of Kulikovo in the "patriotic consciousness of the people." Here, Great Patriotic War paraphernalia, including wartime posters and Red Army rifles, mingled haphazardly with medieval artifacts and iconography. Although later framed in terms of "demonstrating the effective continuity of military traditions," there was little to distinguish the character of the Great Patriotic War from victory over the Mongols in 1380.[109] Hence, where Boris Rybakov's official report offered a reading of the Kulikovo anniversary that was "national in form, socialist in content," under Melent'ev's management, GIM's Kulikovo exposition and the reconstituted St. Sergius museum inverted this formulation. Mirroring late-socialist cultural trends in other Soviet republics, the presentation of

[104] *Kak grazhdanin Rossii*, 106. [105] GARF A-259/48/872/11–12
[106] Shkurko, "Voprosy muzeefikatsii pamiatnikov Kulikovskoi bitvy," 225–233.
[107] *Kak grazhdanin Rossii*, 106. [108] See GARF A-259/48/872/16–17.
[109] Shkurko, "Voprosy muzeefikatsii pamiatnikov Kulikovskoi bitvy," 227, 232.

Kulikovo's connection to the Great Patriotic War was, in these instances, primarily "national in content."[110]

At the same time that Melent'ev and Kochemasov reported on the success of the event at Kulikovo, which purportedly saw tens of thousands of attendees and glowing reviews from cultural luminaries like Valentin Rasputin, party authorities moved swiftly to once again tighten the ideological reins.[111] *Pravda*'s subsequent reports on the anniversary offered strikingly orthodox readings of the event. The newspaper published a slightly modified version of Rybakov's report to close out its coverage of the Kulikovo theme on September 9.[112] Even within RSFSR institutions, a more disciplined ideological atmosphere prevailed. Tellingly, at the end of September, the RSFSR Council of Ministers rejected a request by Melent'ev to establish a state commission to oversee the further development of the Kulikovo site, deeming it "unnecessary" and advising that VOOPIiK assume this role.[113] By mid-1981, partly due to the unanticipated extent of nationalist assertiveness surrounding Kulikovo, the regime further reasserted its commitment to ideological orthodoxy. In addition to Sergei Semanov's sacking noted previously, there was a shake-up of the editorial board of *Nash sovremennik*, and *Literaturnaia Rossiia* printed a statement by Brezhnev highly critical of Russian nationalism in general.[114]

With the death of Mikhail Suslov, the Party's longtime chief ideologue, in January 1982, and his replacement by Andropov, the crackdown on Russian nationalism only gained momentum. To some extent, Suslov embodied a line of ideological continuity with late-Stalinist innovations in the concept of Soviet patriotism. This might explain the greater disregard Andropov initially exhibited toward Russian nationalist sensibilities and his forceful attack on nationalist trends in the cultural and political realms. Andropov's primary concern was not in enforcing a discursive tension between Russocentrism and pan-Soviet internationalism, as Suslov had done, but in crafting a single, overarching pan-Soviet

[110] This turn of phrase seems to accurately capture developments in non-Russian republics. See, for example, Herzog, "'National in Form and Socialist in Content' or Rather 'Socialist in Form,'" 115–140.

[111] See Melent'ev, "Pole sud'by narodnoi," 270–275; *Kak grazhdanin Rossii*, 106–107.

[112] See "Nemerknushchaia stranitsa istorii," *Pravda*, Sep. 9, 1980, 3. As with the 1947 anniversary of the founding of Moscow, the party newspaper had entirely jettisoned even remotely Russocentric forms of patriotic expression in time for the Bolshevik Revolution anniversary in November. See *Pravda*, Nov. 7, 1980, 1–4.

[113] GARF A-259/48/3348/18. A scaled-down commission was later approved to help conduct a formal reception at the site of Kulikovo in early 1981 with Tula oblast representatives. GARF A-259/48/3348/1–3.

[114] Cosgrove, *Russian Nationalism*, 50–51.

line.[115] A February 1982 article in *Pravda* even reengaged some of the more radical nationalist writings on Kulikovo, accusing, for example, the author Vadim Kozhinov of taking the battle out of its historical context. Rather than accurately depicting it as a struggle between Muscovy and "the Tatar-Mongols," Kozhinov "preached his thesis" that Kulikovo was a universal Russian struggle against "worldwide cosmopolitan aggression" and a sign "of the unshakeable magnanimity of Russians." It was, the author concluded, "idiotic, idealized history" to claim that "Rus' was born 'for the sake of universal human unity.'"[116] While directed at Kozhinov, these same criticisms could be applied to Melent'ev's own public statements on Kulikovo.

By the summer of 1982, even VOOPIiK was signaling its renewed adherence to the pan-Soviet/internationalist line. During its Fourth Congress in Novgorod, which stretched from June to July, there were numerous calls to refocus VOOPIiK's activities toward projects linked exclusively to the Soviet era. The architect and museum director, V. I. Baldin, declared that despite the society's important work over the past several years, it was now critical to "[p]ay particular attention to the revolutionary past and socialist development." The head of the cultural section of the Main Political Directorate of the Soviet Army and Navy, Major-General V. I. Anikovich, conveyed the thanks of soldiers and sailors for VOOPIiK's important work, particularly on "monuments embodying the outstanding events of the Great October Socialist Revolution, the Civil and Great Patriotic wars." He stressed, however, that the most important task VOOPIiK could perform in the future, and an area where the organization had often underperformed, was in the construction and preservation of monuments "dedicated to the heroic victory of the Soviet people in the Great Patriotic War." The upcoming fortieth anniversary of Victory Day, Anikovich concluded, offered an ideal moment for the society to demonstrate its commitment to "reflecting the heroic deeds of the *modern* Soviet soldier." One after the other, the congress participants emphasized that, while the preservation of Russian cultural monuments was well and good, a reorientation was necessary, one that, in the words of the academician Iu. A. Tikhonov, centered on "memorial sites associated with the history of Soviet society" and that reflected "the formation and development of the socialist state, the labor of the Soviet people, [and] their heroism on the fronts of . . . the Great Patriotic War."[117]

[115] On the immediate shift that accompanied Suslov's death at the level of cultural politics, see Cosgrove, 52.
[116] V. Kuleshov, "Tochnost' kriteriev," *Pravda*, Feb. 1, 1982, 7.
[117] GARF A-639/1/689/27–28, 37–42 (emphasis added), 55–56.

At the time of Brezhnev's death in November, and Andropov's own ascension to the post of general secretary, the instability aroused by the 1982 anti-nationalist campaign had compelled Andropov to moderate his approach. This probably explains Vladimir Chivilikhin's receipt of the USSR State Prize that month.[118] However, nationalists sought compromise as well. The journal *Nash sovremennik*, in its April edition, signaled the editors' intention to abandon their revived Russocentric stance, which had peaked in November 1981, in favor of an approach that fully complied with discursive tension. An essay by the historian Apollon Kuz'min offered a less-than-rhapsodic reading of Ilya Ehrenburg's wartime writings, which had conflated notions of Russianness and Sovietness. Kuz'min noted that "[n]either 1812 nor the 'ruins of the Kremlin in Novgorod,' nor the 'deeds of Peter [the Great]' have any relation to the socialist nature of Soviet patriotism."[119] Even this more modest take on the significance of wartime Russocentrism was insufficient, however. Iurii Surovtsev, a secretary with the USSR Writers' Union, lambasted Kuz'min's article for hewing too closely to the very nationalism it purported to criticize. Kuz'min, Surovtsev complained, was himself inflating the importance of national particularism and categorization in the USSR. "Is it not now time," Surovtsev asked, "as our society moves toward social homogeneity, to recognize the important category of a socialist nationality[?]"[120] Andropov's compromise with Russian nationalism, and his essential reiteration of patriotic discursive tension, clearly favored the internationalist pole of that tension. Shortly after Chivilikhin was awarded the USSR State Prize, Andropov removed the Russophile head of the Propaganda Department, Evgenii Tiazhel'nikov, and replaced him with the internationalist-minded Boris Stukalin. The June 1983 party plenum on ideology further reified Andropov's anti-nationalist formula.[121]

It was not Andropov but the new Politburo member in charge of ideology, Konstantin Chernenko, who delivered the main address during the plenum. Chernenko's own brief tenure as general secretary from February 1984 to March 1985, following Andropov's death, retained his predecessor's heavy emphasis on the pan-Soviet/internationalist paradigm, as well as the skeptical official posture toward Russocentrism.[122] In

[118] Brudny suggests that this was a tactical maneuver for Andropov to garner support for his succession. Brudny, *Reinventing Russia*, 123.
[119] See, in particular, Kuz'min, "Pisatel' i istoriia," 164–165. On the affair surrounding the November 1981 issue, see Cosgrove, *Russian Nationalism*, 47–52.
[120] Iu. Surovtsev, "Vospitanie slovom," *Pravda*, Aug. 17, 1982, 3.
[121] *KPSS v rezoliutsiiakh*, 14:417–433.
[122] On developments under Chernenko, see Cosgrove, *Russian Nationalism*, 75–81; Duncan, *Russian Messianism*, 110–114.

mid-1984, the CPSU Central Committee called on republican officials to deploy detachments of the Komsomol and other patriotic societies to help organize events and garner popular enthusiasm for the fortieth anniversary of Victory Day in May 1985.[123] For this endeavor, Melent'ev naturally turned to VOOPIiK.[124] Next to the Komsomol, VOOPIiK was perhaps the most active network involved in patriotic mobilization during the May Ninth anniversary in the RSFSR.[125] As detailed in September 1984 by the VOOPIiK council of the far eastern Amur oblast, its tasks were far ranging and not merely ancillary to official commemorations. The council outlined the following measures, which were similar to those issued in oblasts and major cities elsewhere:

> To deploy broad ideological, mass political work explaining the world-historic significance of the Victory of the Soviet people in the Great Patriotic War, the decisive contribution of the USSR to the defeat of fascist Germany . . . To reveal in depth the role of the CPSU as the organizer and inspirer of victory over the enemy, the mass heroism of the Soviet people, the soldiers of the army and navy, [and] workers at the home front. . . . To organize in clubs and cultural centers, at monuments and memorial sites, systematic lectures, reports, [and] speeches by war and labor veterans . . . To take part in socio-political readings . . . To put into exemplary condition historical monuments and memorial sites connected to the events of the Great Patriotic War. To play an active role in preparing rallies, laying wreaths at monuments and obelisks to soldiers who fell at the fronts of the Great Patriotic War . . . To instruct the youth section of [VOOPIiK] to organize work on the participation of young people in the All-Union Campaign to Places of Revolutionary and Military Glory, which is dedicated to the fortieth anniversary of the Victory of the Soviet people in the Great Patriotic War.[126]

In line with the society's Fourth Congress and the June 1983 party plenum on ideology, VOOPIiK authorities adhered to a strictly pan-Soviet understanding of victory. Likewise, if the summary reports produced in the aftermath of the anniversary are to be believed, the society's activists carried out their work with a singularly pan-Soviet focus, and only rarely allowed even oblique allusions to the war as part of a larger Russian continuum.[127]

[123] "Postanovlenie TsK KPSS o 40-letii pobedy sovetskogo naroda," in *KPSS v rezoliutsiiakh*, 14:586–589.
[124] GARF A-639/1/770/51–53.
[125] VOOPIiK activities during this anniversary are well documented. See GARF A-639/1/770–773 (all).
[126] GARF A-639/1/770/6–9.
[127] See GARF A-639/1/772/101A–205. One exceptional instance was *Komsomol'skaia pravda*'s coverage of the All-Union March of Victors, which took place in Tula near the site of Kulikovo Field. The article mentioned that Kulikovo "entered the history of the glorious pages of our homeland alongside the fields of Poltava, Borodino, Stalingrad, and the Kursk salient." V. Kiselev and S. Maslov, "Dorogami slavy," *Komsomol'skaia pravda*, May 12, 1985, 1, 3.

By the early 1980s, VOOPIiK had evolved from a politically impotent, if highly popular, organization devoted to the protection of prerevolutionary Russian cultural artifacts, into one of the main articulators of Soviet patriotism and official war memory. That the society's leaders and activists followed the internationalist framing of the war during the fortieth anniversary of Victory Day of course says more about official strictures on patriotic expression than about the actual conviction of VOOPIiK members or, for that matter, Russian-speaking society more broadly. As with Russocentric nationalists like Sergei Semanov, the organization's outward acts of Soviet allegiance maximally overlapped with nationalist concerns of superpower status and patriotic indoctrination, among other themes. Nationalist intellectuals and activists also embraced key Russocentric wartime markers, with the exception of Stalin's toast, which disappeared from even most nationalist writings. Although they did so within the officially prescribed formula, depicting, for example, the great ancestors theme as a highly pragmatic appeal to recognizable expressions of revolutionary heroism, such qualifications were often drowned out by otherwise indulgent paeans to Russian exceptionalism and military glory. Russocentric nationalists thus negotiated the Soviet people doctrine by way of a patriotic parallelism, privately conflating Soviet and Russian identities and histories while publicly compartmentalizing the Russian past and the Soviet present. Crucially, they did so just as a new, energetic general secretary was about to lift many of the constraints on public expression that had for so long preserved the sanctity of the pan-Soviet/internationalist model of the war's memory.

Conclusion

During the apex of official support for Russocentric nationalism, the victory myth retained its predominantly pan-Soviet character and the party leadership resisted overt attempts to "Russify" it in official outlets. Authorities enforced the Soviet people doctrine's fragmented conception of patriotism, which permitted the Russocentric paradigm in certain discursive spheres while preserving the war victory as an event with an exclusively Soviet provenance. Such an official view of the war narrative was intended to be neither offensive to Russocentric nationalists, who could read the Soviet victory as a Russian achievement so long as this was not openly advocated, nor Russocentric in a way that might disrupt the Soviet people doctrine's discursive tension. As it had in some respects since the Stalin era, the victory theme offered Soviet ideologists an evocative and inclusive myth of pan-Soviet origin, which had the potential to transcend, rather than reinforce, internal ethnonational divisions and hierarchy. In this sense, late-socialist war memory can be seen as a countermeasure to the increasing Russian national self-assertion, which, together with the nationalisms of non-Russian Soviet peoples, would later contribute to the Soviet Union's demise.

At the same time, working within this official schema, certain Russophile intellectuals and sympathetic organizations like VOOPIiK subverted the victory myth from below, as it were, by homing in on ambiguities in the war's public representation. Russocentric nationalists promoted those aspects of the war's memory that overlapped with their own predilections. They played up the Russocentric paradigm of the war years, even while stressing this line's pragmatic and artificial nature. Some defended Stalin's image as war leader while hinting that his most important contribution lay with his resurrection of distinctly Russian national-patriotic traditions. By the end of the 1970s, writers like Vladimir Chivilikhin and Sergei Semanov were situating the victory myth, complete with its internationalist gloss, within a broader Russian national mythology of war, effectively blurring the war's political and ideological particularities. For those willing to read between the lines, it was entirely possible to decipher an emergent Russocentric myth of the war at the margins of Soviet Russian cultural production.

The official crackdown on nationalist expression that came in the wake of the Kulikovo anniversary put an end to nationalist efforts to collapse the discursive tension of the Soviet people doctrine. However, it could not fully expunge the Russocentric conception of the war held by many nationalists and probably a considerable swath of Soviet society. In 1984, during an interview about his novel *Memory*, Chivilikhin encapsulated his views on patriotism, which he rooted deep within the Russian historical experience:

> Memory is one of the most powerful weapons on earth. Russian military art has almost no analogues in the world. Not a single nation in its history has produced as many great military leaders as Russia. The warrior Sviatoslav, Aleksandr Nevskii, Dmitrii Donskoi, Peter I, Suvorov, Kutuzov, Brusilov, Frunze, Zhukov. And these are only the most famous, the list goes on. Russian arms crushed the hordes of Mamai, the troops of Polish barons, Swedes, Turks, crusaders and Teutonic Knights, Napoleon's army, stunned by the Battle of Borodino, found an inglorious end among the snowy Russian fields. In Russia, the armored fascist hordes were crushed ... In order to defeat Russia, it is necessary to defeat all of its people. And this is impossible. Our land has always scorched the feet of conquerors!

It was within this decidedly Russian historical framework that Chivilikhin turned to the approaching Victory Day jubilee. "Forty years of the Victory of our people in the Great Patriotic War will be celebrated next year.

Forty years from the day of the triumph of our unity, our national unity!" Given the context, "our" can only be taken as a veiled allusion to Russia and the Russian people.

At roughly the same time that Chivilikhin gave this interview, Anatolii Cherniaev, then a worker in the Party's Central Control Commission, wrote of his wariness of those who glorify past Russian feats of arms. "All around me are myths of the irrational idea of nationality," he complained in his diary. Cherniaev was reacting to an interview he had read with the village prose writer Valentin Rasputin. Cherniaev was particularly taken aback by Rasputin's apparent belief in the immutability of ethnonational loyalties "despite all the successes of internationalism." In Rasputin's words: "in 100 years Russians will still be Russians, Tatars will still be Tatars." It was no coincidence, Cherniaev wrote, that in the same interview Rasputin described the Battle of Kulikovo Field as a "sacred" event for all Russians. After all, this battle was fought between Russians and Mongol-Tatars, who, Rasputin implied, were innately incapable of subsuming those ethnic loyalties to a larger ideal or identity. Cherniaev cited "Brezhnevism" as the main culprit behind such an ethnocentric worldview, presumably because of Brezhnev's toleration for a marginal Russocentric nationalism within the RSFSR, which mirrored the increasing ethnonational assertiveness of many non-Russian republican elites at the time.[128]

Cherniaev would soon join other critics of Brezhnevism in Gorbachev's administration, which lifted many censorship constraints in the name of "openness" and a more truthful accounting of the Soviet past. Thus, the divergent paradigms of Soviet patriotism, and the doctrine that wedded them in discursive tension, were about to become matters of public debate and scrutiny. In a limited way, of course, there had always been contests within the Party between advocates of the pan-Soviet victory myth on the one hand and of a more Russified public memory of the war on the other. Whether in discussions for early war monuments, the rhetoric of party officials, factions within planning committees for public festivals, splits within the commission to draft a new history of the war, among other forums, the establishment of a "dominant" myth was an internally contested process. However, Gorbachev's partial liberalization of Soviet life would bring these contests into the open and launch a series of renewed, Russocentric challenges to the official memory promoted by the Soviet state. These came not just from the group of pro-Soviet nationalists examined previously, but from various other proponents of

[128] Cherniaev, *Sovmestnyi iskhod*, 399–401.

a reinvented "Russia," whose views ranged from radical ethnonationalism to liberal-reformism. Such glasnost-era debates fall beyond the purview of this book – although the concluding chapter will touch on them briefly. Needless to say, there were many like Cherniaev, not to mention Gorbachev himself, who would fight to preserve the pan-Soviet victory myth as a last vestige of a shared, Soviet identity.

Conclusion

> Our Victory is not a thing of the past. It is a living Victory, facing the present as well as the future.
>
> – Mikhail Gorbachev, 1985[1]

> The chronology of this great country began primarily with 1917, giving scant attention to the thousand-year path it had traveled before. This was manifest most clearly in the postwar period: everything was, so to speak, "ancestry unknown." But the growth of national self-awareness that began in the period of perestroika gave rise very naturally to an interest in our ancestors' history and culture. This process, which I saw as beneficial, could be observed in all the republics, including the Russian Federation. But there were those who made an exception for Russia and did not approve of its thirst for rebirth.
>
> – Egor Ligachev, 1992[2]

In February 1987, members of a Russian ethnonationalist network calling itself Pamiat' (Memory), after the title of Chivilikhin's 1982 novel, rallied to the defense of a war memorial design by the sculptor Viacheslav Klykov. Klykov's design – one of nearly 400 proposals exhibited in central Moscow

[1] "Bessmertnyi podvig sovetskogo naroda," *Pravda*, May 9, 1985, 1–3. In this Victory Day address, one of his first major speeches as general secretary, Gorbachev notably reversed the trend of his predecessors and singled out the Russians, stating: "Soviet people of different nationalities fought for and defended their socialist homeland. They were inspired by the great Russian people, whose courage, endurance, and unbending character were a notable example of the unbreakable waves toward victory." This was almost certainly an attempt to win over Russocentric nationalist elements in the Party. Not only is this Russocentric emphasis absent from both his previous and subsequent public statements on the war victory, but it departed from his overwhelmingly "internationalist" agenda, signaled, for example, in the appointment of Aleksandr Yakovlev to the position of the head of the Propaganda Department. On Gorbachev's early efforts to win over Russian nationalists, see O'Connor, *Intellectuals and Apparatchiks*, 79–109. For typical examples of his previous and later public statements on the war, see Gorbachev, *Sobranie sochinenii*, 1:32, 56–66, 247–259; "Uroki voiny i Pobedy," *Pravda*, May 9, 1990, 1–2.

[2] Ligachev, *Inside Gorbachev's Kremlin*, 286.

as part of the renewed search for a "Victory" complex on Poklonnaia Hill – had incorporated a central monument that closely resembled a Russian Orthodox church. Although Klykov had conspicuously substituted a "Soviet" mother-motherland figure in place of a Christian cross, the Pamiat' activists keeping vigil around the exhibition hall saw the motif for what it was: an attempt to anchor the Soviet victory in Russian historical continuity. Klykov's church-inspired monument struck a chord with many of the other attendees as well, including some veterans and the editorial boards of sympathetic journals like *Nash sovremennik*. The nationalist fervor set off by the exhibition alarmed Soviet officials and the competition's organizers, who deemed no submission worthy of advancement. The jury remarked that Klykov's proposal lacked "the idea of the triumph of socialism over fascism, the universal meaning of this triumph and its origins in Soviet patriotism and socialist internationalism."[3] The art historian and critic Nikita Voronov echoed the jury's sentiments on the pages of *Literaturnaia Rossiia*. "Why is it," Voronov asked, "that only the Russian tradition is utilized in [Klykov's] Victory monument? After all, Victory in the Great Patriotic [War] was achieved by the whole people [*ves' narod*]."[4] *Pravda* followed suit, reminding its readers that such a monument must consist of "an artistic form that the whole people and each of us individually would perceive as our own."[5]

The history of the victory myth as it navigated the turbulent final years of the Soviet Union and its collapse, and its quasi-resurrection and reformulation in the post-Soviet space, is a matter to be considered in another time and place. But the controversy surrounding the Poklonnaia Hill memorial offers a useful encapsulation of the core themes of this book. Not only do these debates reveal the war's continued resonance amid the waning of Soviet rule, but they point to the gulf that remained between two increasingly incompatible conceptions of victory. As will be discussed briefly, the failure to locate and develop an agreed upon design for the Poklonnaia Hill memorial before the USSR's collapse stemmed in large part from these tendencies' irreconcilability outside the strictures of the Soviet people doctrine.

The criticism leveled at Klykov's church-monument prompted *Nash sovremennik* to publish an open letter signed by twenty-eight notable

[3] This account is partly based on Schleifman, "Moscow's Victory Park," qts. 14; Tumarkin, "The Story of a War Memorial," 132–133. Important to note is that Orthodox church imagery has often been associated with the projection of universal and multiethnic, and not merely Russian, themes and values. See Glebov, "The Mongol-Bolshevik Revolution," 104.
[4] Quoted in Tomilina, *Pamiatnik pobedy*, 201–203.
[5] A. Iusin, "Uroki otkrytogo konkursa," *Pravda*, Mar. 1, 1987, 3.

authors, including the village prose writers Vasilii Belov and Valentin Rasputin. Addressed to both the competition jury and the critic Voronov, the letter homed in on Voronov's plea to involve a greater number of designers from the republics in order to "give [the memorial] an international character." To this, the letter's signatories scoffed: "In that case, ... let anyone [participate], let the 'Vikings' [*variagi*], just not the Russians ... Allow no bell tower, allow no 'bell,' or any other historically significant symbols of Russian history and Russian culture." By denying Klykov's design, the authors asserted, Voronov and likeminded "internationalists" on the jury were opposing "precisely the idea of [Russian] historical continuity."[6]

The open letter drew the ire of the Central Committee's propaganda and cultural departments. A resulting CC memorandum formally reiterated the jury's assessment, noting how "the idea of the victory of socialism over fascism, of the world-historic significance of this victory, of Soviet patriotism and socialist internationalism as [the victory's] source" was entirely absent from Klykov's design. The memo then elaborated on this point, making clear that it was not simply the religious connotations that rendered the design so problematic. More troubling still was its narrow Russocentrism:

> Using the imagery of Russian church architecture, V. Klykov leaves the monument open to interpretations of an exclusively national [*natsional'nyi*] orientation ... It is no coincidence that at Manezh during the exhibition of competition entries, activists of the Pamiat' association were constantly on guard around this work and advocating on its behalf ... In an authoritarian tone, the national-Russian yet again stands in opposition to the pan-Soviet [*obshchesovetskomu*], to the international.

The CC departments were less concerned about Pamiat', which they rightly viewed as a fringe organization, than the appearance of the open letter in *Nash sovremennik*. The journal's explicit endorsement of a Russian-centered victory monument not only violated the spirit of Soviet patriotism, but it risked stoking "nationalist moods" among non-Russians, "the outbreaks of which are occurring in Ukraine, Belarus, Estonia, Kazakhstan, Kyrgyzstan, and in several other republics." The authors of the memo touted the announcement of a new design competition as a chance to launch a much broader campaign to disseminate "internationalist positions" as the basis of the war's memory.[7]

[6] "Otkrytoe pis'mo," 190–191; Tomilina, *Pamiatnik pobedy*, 201–203; Schleifman, "Moscow's Victory Park," 14–15.
[7] Tomilina, *Pamiatnik pobedy*, 201–203.

Although a new competition did take place, the Central Committee's push to cast the event as an affirmation of pan-Soviet internationalism proved a resounding failure. Not only was Klykov's design still in the running when the entries were put on public display in April 1988, but Russian national-historical motifs abounded. Several prominent submissions took as their inspiration the demolished Cathedral of Christ the Savior, which had commemorated the Patriotic War of 1812. Pamiat' agitators continued to make their presence felt as well, especially after the jury deemed only ten projects worthy of continuation to a second round. Despite the inclusion of Klykov's design among the ten, Pamiat' representatives now demanded the jury's replacement and the full-scale reconstruction of the cathedral. Nina Tumarkin, who attended the 1988 exhibition and interviewed several of the key participants, reports that although the jury had no intention of endorsing any of the church-inspired proposals, which it found "impossibly nationalistic," it advanced Klykov's design because its members were "scared of going against the tide of popular support." Quite abruptly, in late 1989, the jury determined that none of the proposals was worthy of development. The resulting decision to terminate the competition, Tumarkin correctly concluded at the time, "apparently came from higher-ups."[8]

As they had more or less since 1945, Russocentric and pan-Soviet conceptions of the nature and meaning of victory cohabitated uneasily during the twilight of the USSR. Under Stalin, these twin paradigms had been in tension with one another, enabling ideologists and Stalin himself to wield the nascent victory myth in either a Russocentric or internationalist direction as circumstances dictated. Stalin's successors retained the myth's internationalist orientation, while channeling Russocentric themes away from the war and into the narrative spheres of historical preservation and revolutionary activism. In this way, the discursive tension of Soviet patriotism persisted, but with the victory myth tied exclusively to its internationalist pole. This configuration, which we have labeled the doctrine of the Soviet people, remained the principal formula for resolving the contradictory features of Soviet patriotic identity more generally. By shining a light on the ideological tensions and inconsistencies contained within this doctrine, glasnost, like destalinization before it, opened the victory myth's competing tendencies to a degree of public debate. Of course, during the Khrushchev era, these debates took place between party-administrative factions and constituted a momentary reckoning with the personality cult before the Soviet people doctrine brought them to a decisive end. By contrast, the Gorbachev leadership in effect

8 Tumarkin, "The Story of a War Memorial," 133–143. Cf. Tomilina, 226–232.

pitted an "official" pan-Soviet myth against an increasingly "popular" Russocentric alternative, believing naïvely that the leadership's preferred version would win out. The decision to terminate the design competition followed from the late-Soviet leadership's inability to produce a suitable ideological formula that could at once harmonize the multivalent tendencies embedded in Soviet war memory while remaining faithful to the ideals of glasnost and mass public participation.

The failure of the Poklonnaia Hill competition also reflected the somewhat paradoxical disconnect between the Russian people, whom Stalin had toasted as the "decisive force" in the war, and an official myth of the war that often obscured the Russians' singular role. Certainly, as this book has demonstrated, the degree to which the myth should highlight the Russian nation's unique contribution to victory was internally contested. But in the post-Stalin era, aside from the vague nationalist parallelism tolerated under Brezhnev and a certain variability among non-Russian republics, the "dominant" victory myth maintained a consistently internationalist tenor. When Pamiat' members rallied around Klykov's church-inspired monument, disparaging the other offerings on display as "anti-Russian," they were merely articulating a Russian national resentment that had seethed below the surface of official war memory for decades. In the words of political commissar Getmanov from *Life and Fate*, which was published in the USSR amid the Poklonnaia Hill affair, "In the name of the friendship of nations we keep sacrificing the Russians ... I'm all for the friendship of nations, but not on these terms. I'm sick of it!"[9]

It would take the better part of a decade after the Soviet Union's demise for the war's memory to become a plausible symbol of Russian national unity and belonging. Following the Soviet collapse, as Poklonnaia Hill emerged as the symbolic heart of Russian war commemoration, planners established an Orthodox church at the site, in addition to a memorial mosque and synagogue, reflecting the multiconfessional, civic orientation of Russian nationhood favored by Yeltsin's administration. But the war's legacy proved an elusive basis on which to build a sense of Russian national identity in the aftermath of the USSR's dissolution.

At least in part, this was a holdover from the Soviet victory myth's consistently internationalist, postrevolutionary alignment. Indeed, a frequent refrain of post-Soviet memoirs has been the fragmentation of Russian historical memory as a distinct legacy of the Soviet culture of commemoration. For example, Vladimir Desiatnikov, an artist and war veteran of Cossack stock, blamed Communist authority for the failure of

[9] Grossman, *Life and Fate*, 221.

his long-suffering proposal for a memorial highway linking sites associated with Russia's patriotic wars. As early as the 1960s, Desiatnikov had petitioned the Party for support in developing his envisaged route of glory. Unfortunately, "as a result of protracted planning," the idea was never embraced under Brezhnev. He tried again in 1988. This time he appealed to Gorbachev directly, reminding the General Secretary that "[i]nvaders have more than once attacked our motherland along the Old Smolensk Road, and have also retreated in disgrace as many times." He received no answer. Fifteen years later, in December 2003, Desiatnikov put this issue directly before Putin during a televised question-and-answer event. Evidently, Putin was interested. The Russian Presidential Administration considered Desiatnikov's proposal, which it passed to Moscow regional authorities, where it proceeded to die a final death. But unlike perceived Communist resistance to the project, Desiatnikov credits Putin with taking his idea seriously and speculates that financial constraints ultimately prevented its implementation. Contrary to Brezhnev and Gorbachev, the new leadership at least recognized the common Russian threads connecting the country's long history of military invasion and preordained victory over enemies of all stripes.[10]

Desiatnikov's faith in Putin was not misplaced. Postmillennial commemorations have endeavored to situate achievements of the Soviet era, and especially 1941–5, within a larger Russian historical context.[11] Referring to this challenge, Putin noted in 2012 that "we need to link historical eras together and revert to understanding the simple truth that Russia did not begin in 1917, or even in 1991, but rather, that we have a single, uninterrupted history spanning over one thousand years."[12] The Putin-led resurgence of a myth of victory, one that could bridge the country's deep economic, ethnic, and political divides, has served as the cornerstone to this nation-building project.

All the while, Russian national war memory has reflected the complex and often paradoxical legacies of Soviet mythmaking, which simultaneously advocated lateral and hierarchical, postrevolutionary and transhistorical, homogenizing and variegating patriotic discourses and loyalties. Post-Soviet Russia has seen these tensions reproduced to an extent in the divide between civic-territorial (*rossiiskii*) and ethnic (*russkii*) conceptions of Russian nationhood, as well as in the more recent notion of a transnational "Russian world" (*russkii mir*). These competing official visions of Russianness have evolved from a singular

[10] Desiatnikov, *Zemnyi poklon*, 391–394.

[11] On Russia's grand myth of exceptionalism, see Carleton, *Russia: The Story of War*.

[12] Quoted in Blakkisrud, "Blurring the Boundary," 256.

focus on an inclusive, civic identity during the 1990s and early 2000s, to a brief flirtation with ethnonationalism, to the more recent approach, which involves "deliberately blurring the borders of the Russian ethnic 'self.'"[13] Notwithstanding the vastly differing political and ideological contexts, the impulse behind the Kremlin's frequent appeals to the war victory as an elastic source of patriotic identity, one capable of accommodating the fluctuations and persistent ambiguities of the "Russian idea," is a product of the Soviet era.

And yet, the dynamism that has made the war so attractive from Putin's perspective has presented its own challenges. The war's memory is contested like never before. As Roger Reese has pointed out in a provocative article, whatever the war's popularity, the official position is being challenged from across the political spectrum:

> ... on the political right in the form of: Skin-heads adopting Nazi wardrobe, symbols, and slogans, openly expressed anti-Semitism and anti-Muslim sentiments with Nazi racial undertones, and the national socialist political movement. Also on the right, the Russian Orthodox Church has its own take on the legacy that challenges the supremacy of the state in the victory. On the left the legacy is challenged by pro-democracy, anti-communist, anti-Stalinist, anti-Putin liberals. Further to the left, communists want to fully rehabilitate Stalin as a great wartime leader and savior of the nation as though that absolves him of all his misdeeds. The legacy is disputed from abroad with Europe and the Baltic States equating the Nazis and Soviets as equals in oppression. The greater part of the post-Soviet generation of Russians is simply not invested in the legacy of the war. Their parents wearied by it. In sum, Putin is failing in his efforts to use the legacy of the war as a unifying shibboleth for today's Russia.[14]

To this assessment, the author would add only that ideological multivalence has always characterized the war's remembrance. Indeed, attempts to delineate the nature and meaning of victory in Russia today are a legacy of the tensions, ambiguities, and contestations that defined the Soviet myth of the Great Patriotic War from its inception.

* * *

This book has argued that Soviet war memory encapsulated a range of contrasting patriotic ideals, centered on the Russian Question, which fostered real politics and debate throughout the postwar decades. As the preceding chapters have demonstrated, the Communist Party, bereft of

[13] See, among others, Blakkisrud, 249–274, qt. 250; Laruelle, *Russian Nationalism*; Pain, "The Imperial Syndrome," 46–74; Kolstø, "The Ethnification of Russian Nationalism," 18–45; Aktürk, *Regimes of Ethnicity*, chap. 7.

[14] Reese, "The Legacy of World War II," 209.

an evocative mobilizational repertoire, deployed highly Russocentric and national-patriotic themes and imagery in the life-or-death struggle that was the Great Patriotic War. But wartime mobilization involved a number of competing tendencies, which coalesced after 1945 around two dominant paradigms. The Russocentric paradigm advocated Russian historical exceptionalism and leadership of an ethnically diverse and hierarchically configured community of peoples. The pan-Soviet paradigm, by contrast, embodied a homogenizing tendency in that it downplayed ethnic particularities and Russian primacy in favor of an aspirational Soviet people. In order to reconcile the contradictions between these official discourses, rather than meld them into a coherent Russocentric ideology, Stalin-era authorities positioned what were two distinct ideological lines in discursive tension with one another, bestowing the Stalinist leadership with a remarkably fluid and multivalent mobilizational toolkit.

By the mid 1950s, as destalinization conflated wartime national-patriotic messaging with the excesses of the personality cult, a new doctrine of the Soviet people created distinct spheres for the articulation of the divergent patriotic discourses. The doctrine increasingly bound the Russocentric paradigm to the narratives of prerevolutionary and early Soviet social development while linking the internationalist paradigm squarely to the Soviet victory of 1945. These competing tendencies vied to define Soviet patriotic identity for decades, and sometimes overlapped, particularly as the war became the centerpiece of large-scale public commemoration in the 1960s. Although the doctrine mandated their continued compartmentalization, Russophiles, neo-Stalinists, and nationally minded republican officials perpetuated the Russocentric variant of the war's memory in a variety of ways. By the 1980s, these elements had generated a counter narrative of sorts – multiethnic and inclusive, but situated less in the revolutionary teleology than in the Russian historical longue durée.

In expounding this argument, the book has engaged one of the enduring questions of Russian history: the relationship between the Russian nation and the state to which it belonged. As the book contends, the Communist Party leadership pursued a contradictory approach to the Russian Question. It regularly subsumed Russians' unique sense of identity to the postrevolutionary "Soviet" imagined community while simultaneously celebrating Russian historical achievements and according Russians the status of first among equals. This paradoxical feature of Soviet rule became an impediment to the formation of a well-developed sense of Russian identity. Russians may have been the "*most* Soviet nation," but they were never *the* Soviet nation, a fact constantly reiterated in the war's commemoration after Stalin.[15] At the same time, this contradictory practice created the conditions for a Russian national resentment that was increasingly directed at the very state with which Russians so closely identified.

The book is indebted to the work of scholars who have long argued for the relative weakness of Russian nationalism and national expression.[16] However, in its insistence that the victory myth articulated a distinctly "Soviet" sense of imagined community, the book has departed from this body of scholarship in an important respect. Geoffrey Hosking, for example, describes the dominant ideological line from 1945 to the Soviet collapse as a merger of Marxism-Leninism and messianic Russian nationalism, suggesting that the concept of a "Soviet people" was merely a façade for what was in reality a Russian imperial project. "Soviet authorities," Hosking writes, "were never able to generate either a narrative or a commemoration of the past which would enable the Soviet peoples to feel themselves members of the same community."[17] Yet this book has shown that, despite inconsistencies and perpetual contests over its meaning, the Soviet myth of World War II offered precisely such a pan-Soviet narrative, one that was not merely an outgrowth of Russian imperial (and certainly not ethnic) aspirations, but that consistently affirmed a postrevolutionary and internationalist sense of belonging as a counterpoise to parallel, Russocentric ideological currents.

The historian Peter Blitstein once proposed that, for much of its existence, the Soviet project rested upon a contradiction, what he called an "essential tension," a notion that lies at the heart of this book. Blitstein writes:

> When we recognize that the regime was engaged in incompatible policies of *both* empire maintenance *and* nation-building, we are more likely to understand the problems the regime encountered when confronting ethnic difference. For, ultimately, the regime was pursuing fundamentally incompatible goals by means of contradictory practices. Put another way ... the basic tension inscribed in the Soviet multinational state was between the regime's need to create a culturally uniform national community and its need to maintain ethnic diversity.

[15] Stalin first used this term to describe Russians in a 1933 toast. See Plokhy, *Lost Kingdom*, 251.

[16] See, for example, Hosking, *Rulers and Victims*; Tolz, *Russia*; Szporluk, *Russia, Ukraine*; Hosking, *Russia*; Szporluk, "The Fall of the Tsarist Empire," 65–93; Rogger, "Nationalism and the State," 253–264. Important works engaging this debate that focus on the crucial years surrounding the First World War include Norris, *A War of Images*; Jahn, *Patriotic Culture*; Brooks, *When Russia Learned to Read*.

[17] Hosking, *Rulers and Victims*, 230–236, qt. 405–406.

This book has pursued Blitstein's call to "focus on the tensions inscribed in Soviet nationality policy itself," to assess "whether the incompatibility of national and imperial practices themselves created the condition for the collapse of the multinational state."[18] It was precisely the combustible tensions created by the regime's contradictory approaches to social mobilization and nation-building that animated Soviet patriotism during the forty-year period after the war. But while it was an unstable ideological formula in the longer term, the tensions of patriotism, and continual efforts to resolve their contradictions, lent a certain dynamism to the Soviet repertoire of rule, and probably did much to hold the "unbreakable union" together, even as this logic contained the seeds of its own destruction.

[18] Blitstein, "Nation and Empire," 217–218.

Bibliography

Archives (with select *fondy*)

APRK (Archive of the President of the Republic of Kazakhstan)
- f. 708 Central Committee of the Communist Party of the Kazakh SSR

ARAN (Archive of the Russian Academy of Sciences)
- f. 457 Department of History and Philosophy of the Academy of Sciences of the USSR
- f. 1577 Institute of History of the Russian Academy of Sciences
- f. 1841 Institute of History of the Academy of Sciences of the USSR

ARAN IRI (Archive of the Institute of Russian History of the Russian Academy of Sciences)
- f. 2 Commission of the History of the Great Patriotic War

GARF (State Archive of the Russian Federation)
- f. A-259 Council of Ministers of the RSFSR
- f. A-501 Ministry of Culture of the RSFSR
- f. A-639 All-Russian Society for the Protection of Historical and Cultural Monuments
- f. R-6903 State Committee of the USSR for Television and Radio Broadcasting
- f. R-7523 Supreme Soviet of the USSR
- f. R-7676 Central Committees of Trade Unions of Machine Workers
- f. R-7913 Central Committee of the Union of Marine and River Transport Workers
- f. R-8131 Prosecutor's Office of the USSR
- f. R-9548 All-Union Lecture Bureau

OKhDOPIM (Department for the Preservation of Documents of the Socio-Political History of Moscow)
- f. 3 Moscow Regional Committee of the CPSU
- f. 4 Moscow City Committee of the CPSU

RGALI (Russian State Archive of Literature and Art)
- f. 674 Union of Architects of the USSR
- f. 2466 Moscow Department of the Union of Architects
- f. 3151 Directorate of Art Funds and Monument Design

RGANI (Russian State Archive of Contemporary History)
- f. 1 Congresses of the CPSU
- f. 3 Politburo of the CC CPSU

f. 4 Secretariat of the CC CPSU
f. 5 Apparatus of the CC CPSU
f. 52 N. S. Khrushchev
f. 72 Ideological Commission of the CC CPSU
f. 89 Declassified Documents Linked to the Trial of the Communist Party
RGASPI (Russian State Archive of Social and Political History)
f. 17 Central Committee of the CPSU
f. 71 Institute of Marxism-Leninism
f. 82 V. M. Molotov
f. 88 A. S. Shcherbakov
f. 558 I. V. Stalin
f. 599 *Kommunist* Editorial Board
f. 606 Academy of Social Sciences of the CC CPSU
f. 629 P. N. Pospelov
f. M-1 Central Committee of the Komsomol
f. M-73 *Molodaia gvardiia* Editorial Board
TsGAIPD RT (Central State Archive of Historical-Political Documentation of the Republic of Tatarstan)
f. 15 Tatar Oblast Party Committee
TsGAGA (Central State Archive of the City of Almaty)
f. 116 Cultural Administration of the City of Alma-Ata
f. 174 Executive Committee of the Alma-Ata City Council of Workers' Deputies
TsGARK (Central State Archive of the Republic of Kazakhstan)
f. R-1308 Central State and Historical Museums of Kazakhstan
f. R-1660 Kazakhstan in the Great Patriotic War
f. R-1890 Ministry of Culture of the Kazakh SSR
TsMAMLS (Central Moscow Archive-Museum of Personal Collections)
f. 159 R. M. Fatuev
f. 192 V. I. Konotop
f. 236 Ia. M. Belitskii

Published Primary Sources

(newspaper citations are given in the notes)

XV s"ezd vsesoiuznogo leninskogo kommunisticheskogo soiuza molodezhi. Stenograficheskii otchet. Moscow: Molodaia gvardiia, 1966.
XX s"ezd kommunisticheskoi partii sovetskogo soiuza (14–25 fevralia 1956 goda). Stenograficheskii otchet. 2 vols. Moscow: Gospolitizdat, 1956.
XXII s"ezd kommunisticheskoi partii sovetskogo soiuza (17–31 oktiabria 1961 goda). Stenograficheskii otchet. 2 vols. Moscow: Gospolitizdat, 1962.
XXIV s"ezd kommunisticheskoi partii sovetskogo soiuza (30 marta-9 aprelia 1971 goda). Stenograficheskii otchet. 2 vols. Moscow: Politizdat, 1971.
Abdykalykov, M. A., and A. M. Pankratova, eds. *Istoriia Kazakhskoi SSR. S drevneishikh vremen do nashikh dnei.* Alma-Ata, 1943.

Abrosimov, P. "Pamiatnik slavy i pobedy russkogo naroda." *Arkhitektura i Stroitel'stvo*, no. 1 (1952): 30–32.

Adrianov, M. "Triumfal'naia Arka meniaet adres." *Stroitel'stvo i Arkhitektura Moskvy*, no. 4 (1966): 10–11.

Afanas'ev, K. N., ed. *Iz istorii sovetskoi arkhitektury 1941–1945 gg. Dokumenty i materialy*. Moscow: Nauka, 1978.

Afiani, V. Iu., et al., eds. *Ideologicheskie komissii TsK KPSS, 1958–1964: Dokumenty*. Moscow: ROSSPEN, 1998.

Aimermakher, K., V. Iu. Afiani, D. Bairau, B. Bonvech, V. P. Kozlov, and N. G. Tomilina, eds. *Doklad N. S. Khrushcheva o kul'te lichnosti Stalina na XX s"ezde KPSS. Dokumenty*. Moscow: ROSSPEN, 2002.

Anderson, M. F. "Voprosy okhrany i ispol'zovaniia voenno-istoricheskikh pamiatnikov v svete postanovleniia TsK KPSS 'O 40-letii pobedy sovetskogo naroda v Velikoi Otechestvennoi voine 1941–1945 godov'." In *Pamiatniki Velikoi Otechestvennoi voiny v patrioticheskom vospitanii trudiashchikhsia: Sbornik nauchnykh trudov*, edited by M. F. Anderson, 3–24. Moscow: Ministerstvo Kul'tury SSSR, 1985.

Anderson, R., ed. "The USSR's 1948 Instructions for the Identification, Registration, Maintenance, and Restoration of Architectural Monuments under State Protection." *Future Anterior* 5, no. 1 (2008): 64–72.

Arkin, D. E. "Monumenty geroiam Velikoi Otechestvennoi voiny. Zametki o konkurse." *Arkhitektura SSSR*, no. 5 (1944): 3–11.

Artizov, A., Iu. Sigachev, I. Shevchuk, and V. Khlopov, eds. *Reabilitatsiia: kak eto bylo. Dokumenty Prezidiuma TsK KPSS i drugie materialy*. 3 vols. Moscow: Mezhdunarodnyi fond "Demokratiia," 2000–2004.

Bagirov, M. D. "Starshii brat v sem'e sovetskikh narodov." *Kommunist*, no. 3 (1953): 64–88.

Bagramov, E. A. *The CPSU's Nationalities Policy: Truth and Lies*. Moscow: Progress Publishers, 1988.

Natsional'nyi vopros i burzhuaznaia ideologiia. Moscow, 1966.

Bekmakhanov, E. B. *Kazakhstan v 20–40-e gody XIX veka*. Alma-Ata: Kazakhskoe ob"edinennoe Gos. izd., 1947.

Belopol'skii, Ia. B. *Pamiatnik voinam Sovetskoi Armii, pavshim v boiakh s fashizmom: sooruzhen v Berline*. Moscow: Gos. izd. arkhitektury i gradostroitel'stva, 1950.

"Bol'shinstvo liudei ne znaiut slov Gimna" [Oct. 14, 1946 and Nov. 22, 1946]. *Istochnik*, no. 6 (1997): 95.

Boltin, E. "O khode raboty po sozdaniiu 'Istorii Velikoi Otechestvennoi voiny.'" *Voenno-istoricheskii zhurnal*, no. 1 (1959): 109–113.

Bondarev, I. *Goriachii sneg; Batal'ony prosiat ognia: roman, povest'*. Moscow: Sov. pisatel', 1985.

Burlatskii, F. M. *Vozhdi i sovetniki. O Khrushcheve, Andropove i ne tol'ko o nikh*. Moscow: Politizdat, 1990.

Bushin, V. *Ia posetil sei mir: Iz dnevnikov frontovika*. Moscow: Algoritm, 2012.

Bylinov, A. "Rota ukhodit s pesnei." *Novyi mir*, no. 7 (1957): 56; no. 8 (1957): 47.

Cassidy, H. C. *Moscow Dateline, 1941–1943*. Boston: Houghton Mifflin, 1943.

Chalmaev, V. "Neizbezhnost'." *Molodaia gvardiia*, no. 9 (1968): 259–289.

"Velikie iskaniia." *Molodaia gvardiia*, no. 3 (1968): 270–295.

"Chastnoe opredelenie" [28 June 1982]. *Istochnik*, no. 2 (1996): 86–87.
Cherniaev, A. S. *Moia zhizn' i moe vremia*. Moscow: Mezhdunarodnye otnosheniia, 1995.
Sovmestnyi iskhod: dnevnik dvukh epoch, 1972–1991 gody. Moscow: ROSSPEN, 2008.
Chernikhov, I. *Moi tvorcheskii put'*. Moscow: Russkii avangard, 2011.
Chivilikhin, V. *Pamiat': roman-esse*. 2 vols. Moscow: Sovremennik, 1982, 1984.
Danilevskii, V. *Dmitrii Pozharskii*. Moscow: Gospolitizdat, 1943.
Kuz'ma Minin. Moscow: Gospolitizdat, 1943.
Dement'ev, A. "O traditsiiakh i narodnosti." *Novyi mir*, no. 4 (1969): 215–235.
"Den' velikoi pobedy sovetskogo naroda." *Voenno-inzhenernyi zhurnal*, no. 5 (1947): 3–6.
Derzhavin, N. *Vekovaia bor'ba slavian s nemetskimi zakhvatchikami*. Moscow, 1943.
Desiatnikov, V. *Zemnyi poklon*. Moscow: "Sinergiia," 2008.
Dmitriev, A. I. *Dnevnik rabochego [III.1946-XII.1955]: Dokumental'naia publikatsiia*. May 9, 1948 and May 9, 1951. Permskii Gosudarstvennyi Arkhiv Noveishei Istorii. Accessed Jan. 2019. www.permgani.ru/diary/1948.html#161.
"Dogovarivaiutsia do togo, chto ne bylo zalpa 'Avrory'," *Istochnik*, no. 2 (1996): 112–21.
"Doklad I. V. Stalina o kinopovesti A. P. Dovzhenko 'Ukraina v ogne.'" In *Kino na voine: dokumenty i svidetel'stva*, edited by F. I. Fomin, 384–393. Moscow: Materik, 2005.
Dokumenty voinskoi slavy. Moscow: Tsentral'nyi muzei krasnoi armii, 1949.
Dubrovskii, S. "Pis'mo v redaktsiiu gazety 'Izvestiia.'" *Moskovskii arkhiv: istoriko-kraevedcheskii al'manakh*, no. 1 (1996): 341–42.
"Dukh ostaetsia, kak i metody polemiki." *Istochnik*, no. 1 (1997): 88–89.
Dzyuba, I. *Internationalism or Russification? A Study in the Soviet Nationalities Problem*. Edited by M. Davies. 2nd ed. London and Southampton: The Camelot Press Ltd., 1970.
Ekskursii, lektsii, konsul'tatsii, vystavki. Moscow, 1950.
Erenburg, I. *Voina: Aprel' 1942 – Mart 1943*. Moscow: Voenizdat, 2002.
Fal'sifikatory istorii (istoricheskaia spravka). Moscow: OGIZ Gospolitizdat, 1948.
"Fashizm prost, kak palka, poetomu s nim tak slozhno borotsia." *Literaturnaia gazeta*, July 9, 1997. Accessed Feb. 2018. www.alexanderyakovlev.org/fond/issues-doc/1009891.
Fursenko, A. A., et al. *Prezidium TsK KPSS, 1954–1964. Chernovye protokol'nye zapisi zasedanii, stenogrammy, postanovleniia*. 3 vols. Moscow: ROSSPEN, 2003–2008.
Ganichev, V. "'Molodaia gvardiia.' 1968–1978. Iz vospominanii." *Moskva*, no. 9 (2013): 115–146.
Gatagova, L. S., et al., eds. *TsK VKP(b) i natsional'nyi vopros, 1933–1945*. Moscow: ROSSPEN, 2009.
Golovenchenko, F. "Vysoko derzhat' znamia sovetskogo patriotizma v iskusstve i literature." *Bol'shevik*, no. 3 (1949): 39–48.
Goncharov, V., and V. Nekhotin, eds. *Prosim osvobodit' iz tiuremnogo zakliucheniia (pis'ma v zashchitu repressirovannykh)*. Moscow: Sovremennyi pisatel', 1998.

Gorbachev, M. S. *Sobranie sochinenii*. 28 vols. Moscow: Izd. "Ves' mir," 2008–2018.
Gorbatov, B. *Sobranie sochinenii v chetyrekh tomakh*. 4 vols. Moscow: Izd. "Pravda," 1988.
Gorinov, M. M., et al., eds. *Moskva poslevoennaia, 1945–1947: arkhivnye dokumenty i materialy*. Moscow: Mosgorarkhiv, 2000.
Grishin, V. V. *Ot Khrushcheva do Gorbacheva. Politicheskie portrety piati gensekov i A. N. Kosygina. Memuary*. Moscow, 1996.
Grossman, V. *Life and Fate*. Translated by Robert Chandler. New York Review of Books Classics. New York: Penguin Random House, 2006.
Gusev, N. N. *"Voina i Mir" L. N. Tolstogo – Geroicheskaia epopeia Otechestvennoi voiny 1812 goda: Bloknot lektora*. Moscow: Narkompros RSFSR, 1943.
Gusliarov, E. N. *Stalin v zhizni: sistematizirovannyi svod vospominanii sovremennikov, dokumentov epokhi, versii istorikov*. Moscow: OLMA-PRESS, 2003.
Iakovlev, A. *Omut pamiati*. Moscow: Vagrius, 2000.
"Protiv antiistorizma." *Literaturnaia gazeta*, Nov. 15, 1972, 4–5.
Sumerki. Moscow: Materik, 2003.
Tsel' zhizni. Moscow: Politizdat, 1973.
Iastrebov, A. "Pokushenie na Krasnuiu ploshchad'." *Nedelia*, Nov. 21, 1988, 12.
Ikh vospital Komsomol (O komsomol'tsakh – geroiakh otechestvennoi voiny). Saratov: Oblastnoe izd. "Kommunist," 1942.
"Istoricheskaia nauka v SSSR. Konferentsiia chitatelei zhurnala 'Voprosy istorii." *Voprosy istorii*, no. 2 (1956): 199–213.
Ivanov, V. "Natsional'nyi kharakter i literatura." *Literaturnaia gazeta*, May 7, 1969, 3–4.
Ivanov, V. "Sotsializm i kul'turnoe nasledie." *Kommunist*, no. 17 (1970): 89–100.
Kak grazhdanin Rossii. Moscow: Al'manakh "Pamiatniki Otechestva," 1997.
Kardin, V. "Legendy i fakty." *Novyi mir*, no. 2 (1966): 237–250.
Kargalov, V. "Ot nepriadvy do ugry." *Nash sovremennik*, no. 9 (1980): 160–179.
"Ratnaia slava Rossii." *Nash sovremennik*, no. 6 (1980): 172–179.
Khlevniuk, O. V., et al., eds. *Sovetskaia natsional'naia politika: ideologiia i praktiki, 1945–1953*. Moscow: ROSSPEN, 2013.
Kolesnikova, S. G. *O sovetskom patriotizme*. Moscow: OGIZ, 1947.
Kolli, N. Ia., and I. Kastel'. "Arkhitekturnye voprosy vosstanovleniia goroda Kalinina." *Arkhitektura SSSR*, no. 2 (1946): 6–16.
Konenkov, S. T., P. D. Korin, and L. M. Leonov. "Beregite sviatyniu nashu!" *Molodaia gvardiia*, no. 5 (1965): 216–219.
Korobov, V. " . . . 'Kakie byli vremena! Kakie liudi byli!'" *Nash sovremennik*, no. 5 (1975): 155–162.
Kozlov, M. M., et al., eds. *Velikaia Otechestvennaia voina 1941–1945: entsiklopediia*. Moscow: "Sovetskaia entsiklopediia," 1985.
Kratkii putevoditel' po zalam ekspozitsii. Moscow: Tsentral'nyi Muzei Krasnoi Armii, 1946.
Krivitskii, A. *28 geroev-panfilovtsev*. Moscow: OGIZ, 1942.
Kurlat, F. L., and Iu. E. Sokolovskii. *S putevoditelem po Moskve*, 3rd ed. (Moscow: Moskovskii rabochii, 1980).
Kurmacheva, M. D. "Ob otsenke deiatel'nosti Ivana Groznogo." *Voprosy istorii*, no. 9 (1956): 195–203.

Kuz'min, A. "Pisatel' i istoriia." *Nash sovremennik*, no. 4 (1982): 148–165.
Lakshin, V. *Golosa i litsa*. Moscow: Geleos, 2004.
Lashkevich, K. G. "Dnevnik: 15 iulia 1941." *Prozhito*. Accessed Jan. 10, 2019. http://prozhito.org/person/45.
"Lenin i Stalin o sovetskom patriotizme." *Agitator i propagandist Krasnoi Armii*, nos. 19–20 (1944): 15–19.
Lenin, V. I. *Polnoe sobranie sochinenii*. 5th ed. 55 vols. Moscow: Izd. politicheskoi literatury, 1967–1981.
Leonov, L. *V nashi gody. Publitsistika 1941–1948*. Moscow: "Sovetskii pisatel'," 1949.
Lert, R. *Na tom stoiu*. Moscow: Moskovskii rabochii, 1991.
Levina, S. S. *Chto chitat' o druzhbe narodov SSSR*. Moscow: Bibl. SSSR im. Lenina, 1947.
Ligachev, Y. *Inside Gorbachev's Kremlin: The Memoirs of Yegor Ligachev*. New York: Pantheon Books, 1993.
Lobanov, M. "Prosveshchennoe meshchanstvo." *Molodaia gvardiia*, no. 4 (1968): 294–306.
Luzhkov, Iu. M., et al., eds. *Moskva prifrontovaia, 1941–1942: arkhivnye dokumenty i materialy*. Moscow: Mosgorarkhiv, 2001.
Malakhieva-Mirovich, V. G. *Maiatnik zhizni moei: dnevnik russkoi zhenshchiny 1930–1954*. Moscow: Izd. AST, 2015.
Malinina, T. "Iz istorii sovetskogo monumental'nogo iskusstva. Po materialam soveshchaniia SSA SSSR i SKh SSSR, posviashchennogo voprosam memorial'noi arkhitektury. Iun' 1946 g." In *Sovetskoe izobrazitel'noe iskusstvo i arkhitektura 60–70-kh godov*, edited by M. V. Davydova et al., 249–260. Moscow: Izd. "Nauka," 1979.
Matiushkin, N. *Druzhba narodov SSSR – istochnik sily sovetskogo gosudarstva*. Moscow: OGIZ, 1947.
Mechtova, Z. A. P. "Dnevnik: 13 maia 1946." *Prozhito*. Accessed Jan. 2017. http://prozhito.org/person/160.
Meir, G. *My Life*. New York: Putnam, 1975.
Melent'ev, Iu. S. "Pole sud'by narodnoi." In *Kulikovskaia bitva v istorii i kul'ture nashei Rodiny (materialy iubileinoi nauchnoi konferentsii [8–10 sent. 1980])*, edited by B. A. Rybakov et al., 270–276. Moscow: Izd. MGU, 1983.
Metodicheskoe posobie k ekskursii k mestu podviga 28 geroev-panfilovtsev (memorial v Dubosekovo). Moscow, 1983.
Mikhaleva, A. I. *Gde vy, moi rodnye? Dnevnik ostarbaitera*. Moscow: AST, 2015.
Mints, I. *Velikaia Otechestvennaia voina sovetskogo soiuza*. Moscow: Gospolitizdat, 1947.
Mitin, M. B. *Voprosy patriotizma v svete marksistsko-leninskoi teorii*. Moscow: Moskovskii rabochii, 1946.
Modrzhinskaia, E. D. *Leninizm i sovremennaia ideologicheskaia bor'ba. "Natsional'nyi vopros" i sovremennaia ideologicheskaia bor'ba*. Moscow: Mysl', 1970.
Molotov, V. M. *O preobrazovanii Narkomata Oborony i Narkomindela iz obshchesoiuznykh v soiuznorespublikanskie narkomaty. Doklad na X sessii Verkhovnogo Soveta SSSR 1-go sozyva 1 fevralia 1944 goda*. Moscow: OGIZ, 1944.
"Monument Pobedy na meste Istoricheskogo muzeia" [20 June 1947]. *Istochnik*, no. 6 (1997): 154–156.

Nadzhafov, D. G., and Z. S. Belousova, eds. *Stalin i kosmopolitizm. Dokumenty Agitpropa TsK KPSS 1945–1953*. Moscow: MFD: Materik, 2005.
Nekrich, A. M. *1941, 22 iunia*. Moscow: Pamiatniki istoricheskoi mysli, 1995.
Nevezhin, V. A. *Stalin o voine. Zastol'nye rechi 1933–1945 gg.* Moscow: Iauza, Eksmo, 2007.
Zastol'nye rechi Stalina: Dokumenty i materialy. Moscow: AIRO-XX, 2003.
Novikov, I. "Proekty pamiatnikov geroiam i sobytiiam Velikoi Otechestvennoi voiny." *Arkhitektura SSSR*, no. 12 (1946): 22–27.
"O nekotorykh vazhneishikh zadachakh sovetskikh istorikov." *Voprosy istorii*, no. 6 (1953): 3–11.
"O podgotovke 2-go izdaniia 'Istorii Kazakhskoi SSR'." *Bol'shevik Kazakhstana*, no. 6 (1945): 49–51.
"O razrabotke istorii Velikoi Otechestvennoi voiny Sovetskogo Soiuza." *Voprosy istorii*, no. 5 (1955): 3–8.
O'Sullivan, John L. "The Great Nation of Futurity." *United States Democratic Review*, no. 6 (1839): 426–430.
"Ob ideologicheskoi rabote partorganizatsii." *Partiinoe stroitel'stvo*, nos. 15–16 (1944): 4–8.
Ortenberg, D. I. *God 1942: Rasskaz-khronika*. Moscow: Politizdat, 1988.
Osipov, V. "Bor'ba s tak nazyvaemym rusofil'stvom, ili put' gosudarstvennogo samoubiistva." *Veche*, no. 7, in *Vol'noe slovo*, nos. 17–18 (1975): 19–57.
"Otkrytoe pis'mo iskusstvovedu Nikite Voronovu i zhiuri konkursnykh proektov glavnogo monumenta pamiatnika Pobedy," *Nash sovremennik*, no. 6 (1987): 190–191.
Pankratova, A. M. *Istoriia SSSR. Chast' tret'ia. Uchebnik dlia 10 klassa srednei shkoly*. Moscow: Uchpedgiz, 1946, 1951, 1952.
Velikii russkii narod – vydaiushchaiasia natsiia i rukovodiashchaia sila sovetskogo soiuza. Stenogramma publichnoi lektsii prochitannoi 10 ianvaria 1947 goda. Moscow: Izd. "Pravda," 1947.
Velikii russkii narod. 2nd ed. Moscow: Gospolitizdat, 1952.
Parker, R. *Conspiracy against Peace: Notes of an English Journalist*. Moscow: iteraturnaya Gazeta, 1949.
Pashuto, V. T. *Aleksandr Nevskii i bor'ba russkogo naroda za nezavisimost' v XIII veke*. Moscow: Uchpedgiz, 1951.
Geroicheskaia bor'ba russkogo naroda za nezavisimost' (XIII vek). Moscow: Gospolitizdat, 1956.
Petelin, V. *Schast'e byt' samim soboi. Zhizneopisanie v vospominaniiakh, pis'makh, interv'iu, fotografiiakh*. Moscow: Golos, 1999.
Petrova, N. K., and E. M. Boltunova, eds. *Samyi pamiatnyi den' voiny. Pis'ma-ispovedi*. Moscow: Veche, 2010.
Plenum Tsentral'nogo Komiteta Kommunisticheskoi partii Sovetskogo Soiuza (18–21 iiunia 1963 goda). Stenograficheskii otchet. Moscow: Politizdat, 1964.
Pliashkevich, V. "Druzhba narodov SSSR – odin iz vazhneishikh istochnikov pobedy v Velikoi Otechestvennoi voine." *Voenno-istoricheskii zhurnal*, no. 6 (1972): 3–11.
Po sledam minuvshei voiny: pamiatnye mesta Otechestvennoi voiny v Moskve i Podmoskov'e 1941–1945 gg. Moscow: Moskovskii Rabochii, 1961.

Politicheskii dnevnik. 2 vols. Amsterdam: Fond imeni Gertsena, 1972, 1975.

Polozhenie o tsentral'nom muzee sovetskoi armii. Moscow: Voennoe izdatel'stvo voennogo ministerstva soiuza SSR, 1952.

Ponomarev, B. N. "Zadachi istoricheskoi nauki i podgotovka nauchno-pedagogicheskikh kadrov v oblasti istorii." *Vestnik Akademii Nauk SSSR*, no. 2 (1963): 3–37.

Ponomarev, B. N., et al., eds. *Istoriia Kommunisticheskoi partii Sovetskogo Soiuza*. 1st, 2nd, 3rd, and 6th eds. Moscow: Gospolitizdat, 1959, 1962, 1969, 1982.

Pospelov, P. N., et al., eds. *Istoriia Velikoi Otechestvennoi voiny Sovetskogo Soiuza 1941–1945*. 6 vols. Moscow: Voennoe izdat. Ministerstva Oborony Soiuza SSR, 1960–65.

Pospelov, P. N. *Sila sovetskogo patriotizma*. Moscow: "Pravda," 1945.

Programma Kommunisticheskoi partii Sovetskogo Soiuza. Moscow: Gospolitizdat, 1961.

"Protiv chego vystupaet 'Novyi mir'?" *Ogonek*, no. 30 (1969): 26–29.

"Radio Svoboda: materialy issledovatel'skogo otdela" [15 October 1982]. *Istochnik*, no. 2 (1996): 87–89.

Rivkina, E. M. "Dnevnik: 10 maia 1948." *Prozhito*. Accessed Jan. 2017. http://188.166.37.60/person/932.

Rodimtsev, A. I. *Gvardeitsy stoiali nasmert'*. Moscow: DOSAAF, 1969.

Rogachev, P., and M. Sverdlin. "Sovetskii narod – novaia istoricheskaia obshchnost' liudei." *Kommunist*, no. 9 (1963): 11–20.

Romanova, Iu. A. *Proshedshikh dnei ocharovanie. O tekh, kogo liubliu*. Moscow: MGO VOOPIiK, 2005.

Rybakov, A. *Deti Arbata*. Moscow: FTM, 2016.

Rybakov, B. A. "*Kulikovskaia bitva*: (rech' v Kolonnom zale Doma Soiuzov)." In *Kulikovskaia bitva v istorii i kul'ture nashei Rodiny (materialy iubileinoi nauchnoi konferentsii [8–10 sent. 1980])*, edited by B. A. Rybakov et al., 5–15. Moscow: Izd. MGU, 1983.

Rybakov, B. A., et al., eds. *Kulikovskaia bitva v istorii i kul'ture nashei Rodiny (materialy iubileinoi nauchnoi konferentsii [8–10 sent. 1980])*. Moscow: Izd. MGU, 1983.

Rykalov, V. S. "Istoricheskaia nauka za rubezhom. Obzory i retsenzii. Raboty Frantsuzskikh burzhuaznykh istorikov o Velikoi Otechestvennoi voine Sovetskogo naroda." *Voprosy istorii*, no. 11 (1963): 156–58.

Seleznev, I. "'Chtoby starye rasskazyvali, a molodye pomnili!'" *Nash sovremennik*, no. 3 (1980): 176–84.

Semanov, S. "O tsennostiakh otnositel'nykh i vechnykh." *Molodaia gvardiia*, no. 8 (1970): 308–320.

Serdtse rodiny. Moscow: Moskovskii rabochii, 1977.

Sharapov, K. "E. Bekmakhanov. Kazakhstan v 20–40-e gody XIX veka." *Voprosy istorii*, no. 4 (1949): 109–114.

Shatagin, N. I., and Z. S. Osipov. *Velikaia pobeda sovetskogo naroda: k piatoi godovshchine razgroma gitlerovskoi Germanii*. Moscow: Voennoe izd., 1950.

Shepilov, D. *Velikii sovetskii narod*. Moscow: Izd. "Pravda," 1947.

Shestakov, A. V. *Istoriia SSSR. Kratkii kurs*. Moscow: Uchpedgiz, 1937, 1945, 1951, 1955.

Shoshin, V. "Velikaia letopis' druzhby." *Nash sovremennik*, no. 12 (1972): 97–101.
Shkurko, A. I. "Voprosy muzeefikatsii pamiatnikov Kulikovskoi bitvy." In *Kulikovskaia bitva v istorii i kul'ture nashei Rodiny (materialy iubileinoi nauchnoi konferentsii [8–10 sent. 1980])*, edited by B. A. Rybakov et al., 225–233. Moscow: Izd. MGU, 1983.
Shtemenko, M. S. *General'nyi shtab v gody voiny*, 2nd ed. Moscow: Voenizdat, 1981.
Shtorm, G. *Flotovodets Ushakov*. Moscow and Leningrad: Detgiz, 1946.
Shul'gina, T. "Monumenty na istoricheskikh rubezhakh." *Stroitel'stvo i Arkhitektura Moskvy*, no. 12 (1966): 24.
Shvarts, E. L. *Zhivu bespokoino. Iz dnevnikov*. Leningrad: Sovetskii pisatel', 1990. http://royallib.com/book/shvarts_evgeniy/givu_bespokoyno_iz_dnevnikov.html.
Simonov, K. *Russkie liudi: p'esa*. Moscow: Voenizdat, 1942.
Sobranie sochinenii v desiati tomakh. 12 vols. Moscow: Khudozhestvennaia literature, 1979–87.
Stikhotvoreniia i poemy. Povesti raznykh let posledniaia rabota. Moscow: Olma-Press, 2004.
"Uroki istorii i dolg pisatelia. Zametki literatora." *Nauka i zhizn'*, no. 6 (1987): 42–48.
Skotnikov, Iu. "Pamiatniki zashchitnikam Moskvy." *Voenno-Istoricheskii Zhurnal*, no. 12 (1961): 114–118.
Slutskii, B. *Sobranie sochinenii v trekh tomakh*. 3 vols. Moscow: Khudozhestvennaia literature, 1991.
Smirnov, G. L. *Uroki minuvshego*. Moscow: ROSSPEN, 1997.
Sobolev, A. I. *O sovetskom patriotizme. Stenogramma publichnoi lektsii*. Moscow: Izd. "Pravda," 1948.
Solodovnikov, A. "Za vysokuiu ideinost' sovetskogo iskusstva." *Bol'shevik*, nos. 19–20 (1944): 52–64.
Sontag, R. J., and J. S. Beddie, eds. *Nazi-Soviet Relations: Documents from the Archives of the German Foreign Office*. Washington, DC: Government Printing Office, 1948.
Sovetskaia kul'tura v gody Velikoi Otechestvennoi voiny. Moscow: Izd. "Nauka," 1976.
Stadniuk, I. *Voina: Roman*. Moscow: Sovetskii pisatel', 1988.
Stalin, I. V. *O Velikoi Otechestvennoi voine Sovetskogo Soiuza*, 5th ed. Moscow: OGIZ, 1947.
Rech' na predvybornom sobranii izbiratelei stalinskogo izbiratel'nogo okruga g. Moskvy. Moscow: Voinizdat, 1946.
Sochineniia, vols. 1–18. Moscow: Gospolitizdat and Ogiz, 1946–2006.
Steinbeck, J. *A Russian Journal*. New York: Penguin Books, 1999.
"Stenogramma soveshchaniia po voprosam istorii SSSR v TsK VKP(b) v 1944 godu." *Voprosy istorii* 2–7, 9 (1996).
Tematika ekskursii dlia soldat i serzhantov sovetskoi armii (v pomoshch' politicheskim zaniatiiam na 1951/52 uchebnyi god). Moscow: Tsentral'nyi muzei sovetskoi armii, 1951, 1953.
"Tematiko-ekspozitsionnyi plan iubileinoi vystavki gosudarstvennogo ordena lenina istoricheskogo muzeia '600 let kulikovskoi bitvy." In *Kulikovskaia bitva v istorii*

i kul'ture nashei Rodiny (materialy iubileinoi nauchnoi konferentsii [8–10 sent. 1980]), edited by B. A. Rybakov et al., 278–280. Moscow: Izd. MGU, 1983.

Tolstoy, L. *War and Peace*. Translated by Richard Pevear and Larissa Volokhonsky. New York: Vintage Classics, 2008.

Tomilina, N. G., ed. *Pamiatnik pobedy: istoriia sooruzheniia memorial'nogo kompleksa pobedy na Poklonnoi gore v Moskve*. Moscow: Golden Bee, 2005.

Tsamerian, I. P. *Teoreticheskie problemy obrazovaniia i razvitiia sovetskogo mnogonatsional'nogo gosudarstva*. Moscow: Izd. "Nauka," 1973.

Tsentral'nyi muzei krasnoi armii. Kratkii putevoditel' po zalam ekspozitsii. Moscow, 1946, 1949.

Tvardovskii, Aleksandr. "Po sluchaiu iubileia." *Novyi mir*, no. 1 (1965): 3–19.

Vasilii Terkin (Kniga pro boitsa). Moscow: Izd. "Nauka," 1976.

Vernye podvigu ottsov. Materialy VIII plenuma TsK VLKSM. Moscow: Molodaia gvardiia, 1966.

Vozovikov, V. S. "Chto viditsia s Krasnoi ploshchadi." *Voenno-istorichiskii zhurnal*, no. 1 (1989): 3–14.

"Vsesoiuznoe soveshchanie istorikov. I. Plenarnye zasedaniia 18–19 dekabria." *Voprosy istorii*, no. 2 (1963): 3–33.

Vyshinksii, P. E. "Sovetskii patriotism – dvizhushchaia sila razvitiia sotsialisticheskogo obshchestva." In *O sovetskom sotsialisticheskom obshchestve: sbornik statei*, edited by F. Konstantinov, M. Kammari, and G. Glezerman, 422–474. Moscow: Gos. Izdat. politicheskoi literatury, 1948.

"Za leninskuiu partiinost' v istoricheskoi nauke!" *Voprosy istorii*, no. 3 (1957): 3–19.

"Zapiska KGB SSSR v TsK KPSS ob antisovetskoi deiatel'nosti S. N. Semanova" [Aug. 4, 1982]. *Istochnik*, no. 6 (1994): 110–111.

"Zapiska KGB SSSR v TsK KPSS ob antisovetskoi deiatel'nosti Ivanova A. M. i Semanova S. N." [Mar. 28, 1981]. *Istochnik*, no. 6 (1994): 108–110.

"Zapiska otdela administrativnykh organov TsK KPSS ob osvobozhdenii S. N. Semanova ot zanimaemoi dolzhnosti" [Apr. 22, 1981]. *Istochnik*, no. 6 (1994): 110.

Zhdanov, Iu. A. *Vzgliad v proshloe: vospominaniia ochevidna*. Rostov-on-Don: FENIKS, 2004.

Zhukov, G. K. *Vospominaniia i razmyshleniia*. Moscow: Izd. Agentstva pechati novosti, 1969.

Znamia Pobedy. Moscow: Voen. Izd. Voennogo Min. SSSR, 1953.

Secondary Sources

Adorno, T. W. "What Does Coming to Terms with the Past Mean?" In *Bitburg in Moral and Political Perspective*, edited by G. Hartman, translated by T. Bahti and G. Hartman, 114–129. Bloomington: Indiana University Press, 1986.

Aktürk, Şener. *Regimes of Ethnicity and Nationhood in Germany, Russia, and Turkey*. Cambridge: Cambridge University Press, 2012.

Allensworth, Wayne. *The Russian Question: Nationalism, Modernization, and Post-Communist Russia*. New York: Rowman & Littlefield, 1998.

Amar, Tarik Cyril. *The Paradox of Ukrainian Lviv: A Borderland City between Stalinists, Nazis, and Nationalists*. Ithaca and London: Cornell University Press, 2015.

Anderson, Benedict. *Imagined Communities: Reflections on the Origin and Spread of Nationalism*. London: Verso, 2006.

Anderson, Malcolm. *States and Nationalism in Europe since 1945*. London: Routledge, 2000.

Applebaum, Rachel. *Empire of Friends: Soviet Power and Socialist Internationalism in Cold War Czechoslovakia*. Ithaca: Cornell University Press, 2019.

Arad, Yitzhak (Yitshak). *In the Shadow of the Red Banner: Soviet Jews in the War Against Nazi Germany*. Jerusalem: Gefen Books, 2010.

"Stalin and the Soviet Leadership: Responses to the Holocaust." In *Remembering the Future: The Holocaust in an Age of Genocide*, edited by John K. Roth and Elisabeth Maxwell, 1: 355–370. New York: Palgrave, 2001.

Arnold, Sabine. *Stalingrad im sowjetischen Gedächtnis. Kriegserinnerung und Geschichtsbild im totalitären Staat*. Bochum: Projekt, 1998.

Ashplant, T. G., Graham Dawson, and Michael Roper. "The Politics of War Memory and Commemoration: Contexts, Structures, Dynamics." In *The Politics of War Memory and Commemoration*, edited by T. G. Ashplant, Graham Dawson, and Michael Roper, 3–85. London and New York: Routledge, 2000.

Aspaturian, Vernon. "The Non-Russian Nationalities." In *Prospects for Soviet Society*, edited by Allen Kassof, 143–198. New York: Praeger, 1968.

"The Union Republics and Soviet Diplomacy: Concepts, Institutions, and Practices." *The American Political Science Review* 53, no. 2 (1959): 383–411.

Assmann, Aleida. "Re-Framing Memory: Between Individual and Collective Forms of Constructing the Past." In *Performing the Past: Memory, History, and Identity in Modern Europe*, edited by Karin Tilmans, Frank van Vree, and Jay Winter, 35–50. Amsterdam: Amsterdam University Press, 2010.

Assmann, Jan, and John Czaplicka. "Collective Memory and Cultural Identity." *New German Critique* 65 (1995): 125–33.

Azadovskii, Konstantin, and Boris Egorov. "From Anti-Westernism to Anti-Semitism." *Journal of Cold War Studies* 4, no. 1 (2002): 66–80.

Barber, John. "The Image of Stalin in Soviet Propaganda and Public Opinion during World War 2." In *World War 2 and the Soviet People*, edited by John Garrard and Carol Garrard, 38–49. New York: St. Martin's Press, 1993.

Barber, John, and Mark Harrison, eds. *The Soviet Home Front, 1941–1945: A Social and Economic History of the USSR in World War II*. London: Longman, 1991.

Barthes, Roland. *Mythologies*. New York: The Noonday Press, 1991.

Beissinger, Mark R. "Demise of an Empire-State: Identity, Legitimacy, and the Deconstruction of Soviet Politics." In *The Rising Tide of Cultural Pluralism: The Nation-State at Bay?*, edited by Crawford Young, 93–115. Madison: University of Wisconsin Press, 1993.

Belenkaja, Marianna. "Verteidigung der Heimat ist Pflicht eines Moslems." *Russland.ru*, May 5, 2005, www.russland.news/kapitulation1/morenews.php?iditem=25.

Belenkin, B. I. "Ispravlennomu ne verit'! Destalinizatsiia na rannem etape: tret'ia redaktsiia 'Velikogo russkogo naroda' A. M. Pankratovoi." In *Posle Stalina. Reformy 1950-x godov v kontekste sovetskoi i postsovetskoi istorii*, 117–128. Moscow: ROSSPEN, 2016.

Berding, Helmut, et al., eds. *Krieg und Erinnerung: Fallstudien zum 19. und 20. Jahrhundert*. Gottingen: Vandenhoeck & Ruprecht, 2000.

Bergman, Jay. *The French Revolutionary Tradition in Russian and Soviet Politics, Political Thought, and Culture*. Oxford: Oxford University Press, 2019.

Berkhoff, Karel C. *Motherland in Danger: Soviet Propaganda during World War II*. Cambridge, MA: Harvard University Press, 2012.

"'Total Annihilation of the Jewish Population': The Holocaust in the Soviet Media, 1941–45." In *The Holocaust in the East: Local Perpetrators and Soviet Responses*, edited by Michael David-Fox, Peter Holquist, and Alexander M. Martin, 83–117. Pittsburgh: University of Pittsburgh Press, 2014.

Bernstein, Seth. *Raised under Stalin: Young Communists and the Defense of Socialism*. Ithaca: Cornell University Press, 2017.

"Remembering War, Remaining Soviet: Digital Commemoration of World War II in Putin's Russia." *Memory Studies* 9, no. 4 (2016): 422–36.

Bidlack, Richard. "Ideological or Political Origins of the Leningrad Affair? A Response to David Brandenberger." *The Russian Review* 64, no. January (2005): 90–95.

Bilinsky, Yaroslav. "The Concept of the Soviet People and Its Implications for Soviet Nationality Policy." *Annals of the Ukrainian Academy of Arts and Sciences in the United States* 14 (1981): 87–133.

Billig, Michael. *Banal Nationalism*. London: Sage, 1995.

Bittner, Stephen V. *The Many Lives of Khrushchev's Thaw: Experience and Memory in Moscow's Arbat*. Ithaca and London: Cornell University Press, 2008.

Blakkisrud, Helge. "Blurring the Boundary between Civic and Ethnic: The Kremlin's New Approach to National Identity under Putin's Third Term." In *The New Russian Nationalism: Imperialism, Ethnicity and Authoritarianism 2000–15*, edited by Pål Kolstø and Helge Blakkisrud, 249–274. Edinburgh: Edinburgh University Press, 2016.

Blight, David W. *Race and Reunion: The Civil War in American Memory*. Cambridge, MA: Belknap, 2001.

Blitstein, Peter A. "Nation and Empire in Soviet History, 1917–1953." *Ab Imperio*, no. 1 (2006): 197–219.

"Stalin's Nations: Soviet Nationality Policy between Planning and Primordialism, 1936–1953." Ph.D. diss., University of California, Berkeley, 1999.

Bodnar, John E. *Remaking America: Public Memory, Commemoration, and Patriotism in the Twentieth Century*. Princeton: Princeton University Press, 1993.

Bonwetsch, Bernd. "'Ich habe an einem vollig anderen Krieg teilgenommen': Die Erinnerung an den 'Grossen Vaterlandischen Krieg' in der Sowjetunion." In *Krieg und Erinnerung: Fallstudien zum 19. und 20. Jahrhundert*, edited by Helmut Berding, Klaus Heller, and Winfried Speitkamp, 145–167. Gottingen: Vandenhoeck & Ruprecht, 2000.

"The Purge of the Military and the Red Army's Operational Capability during the 'Great Patriotic War.'" In *From Peace to War: Germany, Soviet Russia, and the World, 1939–1941*, edited by Bernd Wegner, 395–414. Providence and Oxford: Berghahn Books, 1997.

Bouchard, Gérard. *National Myths: Constructed Pasts, Contested Presents*. New York: Routledge, 2013.

Bouvard, Josette. *Le Métro de Moscou: La Construction d'un Mythe Soviétique*. Paris: Sextant, 2005.

Brandenberger, David. "Ideologicheskie istoki sovetskogo patriotizma." Unpublished manuscript, July 2020, typescript.

National Bolshevism: Stalinist Mass Culture and the Formation of Modern Russian National Identity, 1931–1956. Cambridge, MA: Harvard University Press, 2002.

Propaganda State in Crisis: Soviet Ideology, Indoctrination, and Terror under Stalin, 1927–1941. New Haven: Yale University Press, 2012.

"Stalin, the Leningrad Affair, and the Limits of Postwar Russocentrism." *The Russian Review* 63 (April 2004): 241–255.

Stalinskii russotsentrizm. Sovetskaia massovaia kul'tura i formirovanie russkogo natsional'nogo samosoznaniia (1931–1956). Moscow: ROSSPEN, 2017.

"Stalin's Populism and the Accidental Creation of Russian National Identity." *Nationalities Papers* 38, no. 5 (2010): 723–739.

Brandenberger, David, and A. M. Dubrovskii. "Itogovyi partiinyi dokument soveshchaniia istorikov v TsK VKP(b) v 1944." *Arkheograficheskii ezhegodnik za 1998 god* (1999): 148–163.

Brandenberger, David, and Mikhail V. Zelenov. "Stalin's Answer to the National Question: A Case Study on the Editing of the 1938 *Short Course*." *Slavic Review* 73, no. 4 (2014): 859–880.

Stalin's Master Narrative: A Critical Edition of the History of the Communist Party of the Soviet Union (Bolsheviks): Short Course. New Haven: Yale University Press, 2019.

Brooks, Jeffrey. "Pravda Goes to War." In *Culture and Entertainment in Wartime Russia*, edited by Richard Stites, 9–27. Bloomington: Indiana University Press, 1995.

Thank You, Comrade Stalin!: Soviet Public Culture from Revolution to Cold War. Princeton: Princeton University Press, 2001.

When Russia Learned to Read: Literacy and Popular Literature, 1861–1917. Evanston, IL: Northwestern University Press, 2003.

Brubaker, Rogers. *Ethnicity without Groups*. Cambridge, MA: Harvard University Press, 2004.

Nationalism Reframed: Nationhood and the National Question in the New Europe. Cambridge and New York: Cambridge University Press, 1996.

Brudny, Yitzhak M. *Reinventing Russia: Russian Nationalism and the Soviet State, 1953–1991*. Cambridge, MA: Harvard University Press, 1998.

Budnitskii, Oleg. "The Great Patriotic War and Soviet Society: Defeatism, 1941–42." *Kritika* 15, no. 4 (2014): 767–98.

Burbank, Jane, and Frederick Cooper. *Empires in World History: Power and the Politics of Difference*. Princeton, NJ: Princeton University Press, 2011.

Burdei, G. D. *Istorik i voina. 1941–1945*. Saratov: Izd-vo Sarat. un-ta, 1991.

Calder, Angus. *The Myth of the Blitz*. London: Jonathan Cape, 1991.

Carleton, Gregory. *Russia: The Story of War*. Cambridge, MA: Belknap / Harvard, 2017.
Carmack, Roberto J. "History and Hero-Making: Patriotic Narratives and the Sovietization of Kazakh Front-Line Propaganda, 1941–1945." *Central Asian Survey* 33, no. 1 (2014): 95–112.
Kazakhstan in World War II: Mobilization and Ethnicity in the Soviet Empire. Lawrence: University Press of Kansas, 2019.
Caute, David. *Politics and the Novel During the Cold War*. New York: Routledge, 2010.
Chernyshova, Natalya. *Soviet Consumer Culture in the Brezhnev Era*. London: Routledge, 2013.
Chislennost' naseleniia SSSR po perepisi na 15 ianvaria 1959 goda po respublikam, kraiam, oblastiam, natsional'nym okrugam, raionam, gorodam, poselkam gorodskogo tipa, raionnym tsentram i krupnym sel'skim naselennym mestam. Moscow: TsSU pri Sovete Ministrov SSSR, 1960. Accessed Jul. 2020. www.demoscope.ru/weekly/ssp/ussr59_reg1.php.
Clark, Katerina. "Eisenstein's Two Projects for a Film about Moscow." *The Modern Language Review* 101, no. 1 (2006): 184–200.
Moscow, the Fourth Rome: Stalinism, Cosmopolitanism, and the Evolution of Soviet Culture, 1931–1941. Cambridge, MA: Harvard University Press, 2011.
The Soviet Novel: History as Ritual. 3rd ed. Bloomington: Indiana University Press, 2000.
Cohen, Aaron J. *War Monuments, Public Patriotism, and Bereavement in Russia, 1905–2015*. London: Lexington Books, 2020.
Cohen, Ariel. *Russian Imperialism: Development and Crisis*. Westport, CT: Praeger, 1996.
Cohen, Stephen F. *Rethinking the Soviet Experience: Politics and History since 1917*. Revised ed. Oxford and New York: Oxford University Press, 1986.
Colley, Linda. *Britons: Forging the Nation 1707–1837*. New Haven: Yale University Press, 2009.
Colton, Timothy J. *Moscow: Governing the Socialist Metropolis*. Cambridge, MA: Harvard University Press, 1998.
Confino, Alon. "Collective Memory and Cultural History: Problems of Method." *The American Historical Review* 102, no. 5 (1997): 1386–1403.
Conze, Susanne, and Beate Fieseler. "Soviet Women as Comrades-in-Arms: A Blind Spot in the History of the War." In *The People's War: Responses to World War II in the Soviet Union*, edited by Robert W. Thurston and Bernd Bonwetsch, 211–234. Chicago: University of Illinois Press, 2000.
Corney, Frederick C. *Telling October: Memory and the Making of the Bolshevik Revolution*. Ithaca and London: Cornell University Press, 2004.
Cosgrove, Simon. *Russian Nationalism and the Politics of Soviet Literature: The Case of Nash Sovremennik, 1981–1991*. New York: Palgrave Macmillan, 2004.
Dany, Charlotte, and Katja Freistein. "Global Governance and the Myth of Civil Society Participation." In *Myth and Narrative in International Politics: Interpretive Approaches to the Study of IR*, edited by Berit Bliesemann de Guevara, 229–248. Palgrave Macmillan, 2016.

Davies, Norman. *No Simple Victory: World War II in Europe, 1939–1945*. New York: Viking Penguin, 2007.

Davis, Vicky. *Myth Making in the Soviet Union and Modern Russia: Remembering World War Two in Brezhnev's Hero City*. New York: I. B. Tauris, 2018.

Davoliūtė, Violeta. *The Making and Breaking of Soviet Lithuania: Memory and Modernity in the Wake of War*. London and New York: Routledge, 2013.

Day, Andrew. "The Rise and Fall of Stalinist Architecture." In *Architectures of Russian Identity: 1500 to the Present*, edited by James Cracraft and Daniel Bruce Rowland, 172–192. Ithaca and London: Cornell University Press, 2003.

deGraffenried, Julie K. *Sacrificing Childhood: Children and the Soviet State in the Great Patriotic War*. Lawrence: University Press of Kansas, 2014.

Dobczansky, Markian. "Rehabilitating a Mythology: The Ukrainian SSR's Foundational Myth after Stalin." *Nationalities Papers* 47, no. 3 (2019): 366–378.

Dobrenko, Evgeny. *Late Stalinism: The Aesthetics of Politics*. Translated by Jesse M. Savage. New Haven: Yale University Press, 2020.

Stalinist Cinema and the Production of History: Museum of the Revolution: Museum of the Revolution. Edinburgh: Edinburgh University Press, 2008.

"The Disaster of Middlebrow Taste, or, Who 'Invented' Socialist Realism." In *Socialist Realism without Shores*, edited by Thomas Lahusen and Evgeny Dobrenko, 135–164. Durham: Duke University Press, 1997.

Dobson, Miriam. "Contesting the Paradigms of De-Stalinization: Readers' Responses to One Day in the Life of Ivan Denisovich." *Slavic Review* 64, no. 3 (2005): 580–600.

Khrushchev's Cold Summer: Gulag Returnees, Crime, and the Fate of Reform after Stalin. Ithaca: Cornell University Press, 2009.

Donovan, Victoria. *Chronicles in Stone: Preservation, Patriotism, and Identity in Northwest Russia*. Ithaca and London: Cornell University Press, 2019.

"'How Well Do You Know Your Krai?' The Kraevedenie Revival and Patriotic Politics in Late Khrushchev-Era Russia." *Slavic Review* 74, no. 3 (2015): 464–83.

"*Nestolichnaya kul'tura*: Regional and National Identity in Post-1961 Russian Culture." Ph.D. diss., University of Oxford, 2011.

Dreeze, Jonathon. "Stalin's Empire: Soviet Propaganda in Kazakhstan, 1929–1953." Ph.D. diss., The Ohio State University, 2019.

Druzhba, O. V. *Velikaia Otechestvennaia voina v soznanii sovetskogo i postsovetskogo obshchestva: dinamika predstavlenii ob istoricheskom proshlom*. Rostov-on-Don: Izd. DGTU, 2000.

Druzhinin, P. A. *Ideologiia i filologiia. Leningrad, 1940-e gody. Dokumental'noe issledovanie*. 2 vols. Moscow: "Novoe literaturnoe obozrenie," 2012.

Dubrovskii, A. M. "Glavnaia pesnia, ili Gosudarstvennyi gimn SSSR," *Forum noveishei vostochnoevropeiskoi istorii i kul'tury*, no. 2 (2013): 167–83.

Istorik i vlast': istoricheskaia nauka v SSSR i kontseptsiia istorii feodal'noi Rossii v kontekste politiki i ideologii (1930–1950-e gg.). Briansk: Izd. BGU, 2005.

Duncan, Peter J. S. "Ideology and the National Question: Marxism-Leninism and the National Policy of the Communist Party of the Soviet Union." In

Ideology and Soviet Politics, edited by Stephen White and Alex Pravda, 180–202. London: Macmillan Publishers, 1988.

Russian Messianism: Third Rome, Revolution, Communism and After. London and New York: Routledge, 2002.

Dunlop, John B. *The Faces of Contemporary Russian Nationalism*. Princeton: Princeton University Press, 1983.

Dunmore, Timothy. *Soviet Politics, 1945–53*. London: Macmillan, 1984.

Dzeniskevich, A. R. *Blokada i politika. Oborona Leningrada v politicheskoi kon"iunkture*. St. Petersburg: Nestor, 1998.

Edele, Mark. "Fighting Russia's History Wars: Vladimir Putin and the Codification of World War II." *History and Memory* 29, no. 2 (2017): 90–124.

"Paper Soldiers: The World of the Soldier Hero According to Soviet Wartime Posters." *Jahrbücher Für Geschichte Osteuropas* 47, no. 1 (1999): 89–108.

Soviet Veterans of the Second World War: A Popular Movement in an Authoritarian Society, 1941–1991. Oxford: Oxford University Press, 2008.

Stalin's Defectors: How Red Army Soldiers Became Hitler's Collaborators, 1941–1945. Oxford: Oxford University Press, 2017.

"The Soviet Culture of Victory." *Journal of Contemporary History* 54, no. 4 (2019): 780–98.

Edgar, Adrienne. "Bolshevism, Patriarchy, and the Nation: The Soviet 'Emancipation' of Muslim Women in Pan-Islamic Perspective." *Slavic Review* 65, no. 2 (2006): 252–72.

Tribal Nation: The Making of Soviet Turkmenistan. Princeton and Oxford: Princeton University Press, 2006.

Edmondson, Linda. "Putting Mother Russia in a European Context." In *Art, Nation and Gender: Ethnic Landscapes, Myths and Mother-Figures*, edited by Tricia Cusack and Sighle Bhreathnach-Lynch, 53–64. Burlington: Ashgate, 2003.

Ellis, Frank. *The Damned and the Dead: The Eastern Front through the Eyes of the Soviet and Russian Novelists*. Lawrence: University Press of Kansas, 2011.

Vasiliy Grossman: The Genesis and Evolution of a Russian Heretic. Oxford: Berg, 1994.

Enstad, Johannes Due. *Soviet Russians under Nazi Occupation: Fragile Loyalties in World War II*. New York: Cambridge University Press, 2018.

Epstein, Barbara. *The Minsk Ghetto, 1941–1943: Jewish Resistance and Soviet Internationalism*. Berkeley: University of California Press, 2008.

Etkind, Alexander. *Warped Mourning: Stories of the Undead in the Land of the Unburied*. Stanford, CA: Stanford University Press, 2013.

Evans, Alfred B. *Soviet Marxism-Leninism: The Decline of an Ideology*. Westport, CT: Praeger, 1993.

Fainberg, Dina, and Artemy M. Kalinovsky, eds. *Reconsidering Stagnation in the Brezhnev Era: Ideology and Exchange*. Lanham, MD: Lexington Books, 2016.

Fedenko, Panas. *Khrushchev's New History of the Soviet Communist Party*. Munich: Institute for the Study of the USSR, 1963.

Fedor, Julie. "Memory, Kinship, and the Mobilization of the Dead: The Russian State and the 'Immortal Regiment' Movement." In *War and Memory in Russia, Ukraine and Belarus*, edited by Julie Fedor, Markku Kangaspuro,

Jussi Lassila, and Tatiana Zhurzhenko, 307–344. London: Palgrave Macmillan, 2017.
Figes, Orlando. *The Whisperers: Private Life in Stalin's Russia*. London: Allen Lane, 2007.
Fieseler, Beate. *Arme Sieger: Die Invaliden des "Grossen Vaterländischen Krieges" der Sowjetunion 1941–1991*. Cologne: Böhlau-Verlag, 2019.
Finney, Patrick. "Vasily Grossman and the Myths of the Great Patriotic War – Patrick Finney, 2013." *Journal of European Studies* 43, no. 4 (2013): 312–28.
Fitzpatrick, Sheila. "Postwar Soviet Society: The 'Return to Normalcy,' 1945–1953." In *The Impact of World War II on the Soviet Union*, edited by Susan J. Linz, 129–156. Lanham, MD: Rowman & Allanheld, 1985.
Florin, Moritz. "Becoming Soviet through War: The Kyrgyz and the Great Fatherland War." *Kritika: Explorations in Russian and Eurasian History* 17, no. 3 (2016): 495–516.
Forest, Benjamin, and Juliet Johnson. "Unraveling the Threads of History: Soviet-Era Monuments and Post-Soviet National Identity in Moscow." *Annals of the Association of American Geographers* 92, no. 3 (2002): 524–547.
Fowkes, Reuben. "Soviet War Memorials in Eastern Europe, 1945–74." In *Figuration/Abstraction: Strategies for Public Sculpture in Europe, 1945–1968*, edited by Charlotte Benton, 11–32. Aldershot: Ashgate, 2004.
"The Role of Monumental Sculpture in the Construction of Socialist Space in Stalinist Hungary." In *Socialist Spaces: Sites of Everyday Life in the Eastern Bloc*, edited by David Crowley and Susan Emily Reid, 65–84. Oxford: Berg Publishers, 2002.
Fraser, Erica L. *Military Masculinity and Postwar Recovery in the Soviet Union*. Toronto: University of Toronto Press, 2019.
Froggatt, Michael. "Science in Propaganda and Popular Culture in the USSR under Khrushchev, 1953–1964." Ph.D. diss., University of Oxford, 2005.
Fürst, Juliane. *Stalin's Last Generation: Soviet Post-War Youth and the Emergence of Mature Socialism*. Oxford: Oxford University Press, 2012.
"Where Did All the Normal People Go? Another Look at the Soviet 1970s." *Kritika: Explorations in Russian and Eurasian History* 14, no. 3 (2013): 621–640.
Fürst, Juliane, and Josie McLellan, eds. *Dropping Out of Socialism: The Creation of Alternative Spheres in the Soviet Bloc*. Lanham, MD: Lexington Books, 2017.
Gabowitsch, Mischa. "Are Copycats Subversive? Strategy-31, the Russian Runs, the Immortal Regiment, and the Transformative Potential of Non-Hierarchical Movements." *Problems of Post-Communism* 65, no. 5 (2018): 297–314.
"Patron-Client Networks and the Making of Soviet War Memorials." In *Monument. Central and Eastern Europe, 1918–2018*, edited by Agnieszka Tarasiuk, 14–17. Warsaw: National Museum in Warsaw, 2019.
"Russia's Arlington? The Federal Military Memorial Cemetary near Moscow." *Journal of Soviet and Post-Soviet Politics and Society* 2, no. 2 (2016): 89–143.
"Soviet War Memorials from Berlin to Pyongyang: A Chronological and Typological Overview." In *The Palgrave Handbook on Cultural and Artistic Responses to War*, Vol. II, edited by Martin Kerby. Basingstoke: Palgrave (forthcoming).

2018. "Victory Day before Brezhnev: Soviet War Commemoration, 1945–1964." Paper presented at the 23rd Annual ASN World Convention, New York, May 2018.

Gajos, Bartłomiej. "Fading Red October: Soviet Youth and the Fiftieth Anniversary of the October Revolution." *Revolutionary Russia* 31, no. 1 (2018): 107–125.

Gallagher, Matthew P. *The Soviet History of World War II: Myths, Memories, and Realities*. Reprint ed. Westport, CT: Greenwood Press, 1976.

Garner, Ian Roland. "The Myth of Stalingrad in Soviet Literature, 1942–1963." Ph.D. diss., University of Toronto, 2018.

Garrard, John, and Carol Garrard. *The Life and Fate of Vasily Grossman*. Barnsley: Pen & Sword Military, 2012.

eds. *World War 2 and the Soviet People*. New York: St. Martin's Press, 1993.

Gati, Charles. *Failed Illusions: Moscow, Washington, Budapest, and the 1956 Hungarian Revolt*. Washington, DC: Woodrow Wilson Center Press, 2006.

Geertz, Clifford. *Local Knowledge: Further Essays In Interpretive Anthropology*. New York: Basic Books, 2008.

Geldern, James von. *Bolshevik Festivals, 1917–1920*. Berkeley and Los Angeles: University of California Press, 1993.

Gellner, Ernest. *Nations and Nationalism*. 2nd ed. Ithaca and New York: Cornell University Press, 2008.

Gilburd, Eleonory. *To See Paris and Die: The Soviet Lives of Western Culture*. Cambridge, MA: Harvard University Press, 2018.

Gill, Graeme. *Symbols and Legitimacy in Soviet Politics*. Cambridge and New York: Cambridge University Press, 2011.

Gillis, John R. "Introduction: Memory and Identity." In *Commemorations: The Politics of National Identity*, edited by John R. Gillis, 3–26. Princeton: Princeton University Press, 1994.

Glantz, David M. *Colossus Reborn: The Red Army at War, 1941–1943*. Lawrence: University Press of Kansas, 2005.

Goff, Krista A., and Lewis H. Siegelbaum. "Introduction: Belonging in the Eurasian Borderlands: Interrogating Empire and Nation." In *Empire and Belonging in the Eurasian Borderlands*, edited by Krista A. Goff and Lewis H. Siegelbaum, 1–16. Ithaca and London: Cornell University Press, 2019.

Golsan, Richard J. "The Legacy of World War II in France: Mapping the Discourses of Memory." In *The Politics of Memory in Postwar Europe*, edited by Richard Ned Lebow, Wulf Kansteiner, and Claudio Fogu, 73–101. Durham: Duke University Press, 2006.

Gorlizki, Yoram, and Oleg Khlevniuk. *Cold Peace: Stalin and the Soviet Ruling Circle, 1945–1953*. Oxford and New York: Oxford University Press, 2004.

Gorsuch, Anne E., and Diane P. Koenker, eds. *The Socialist Sixties: Crossing Borders in the Second World*. Bloomington: Indiana University Press, 2013.

Gruner, Frank. "'Russia's Battle against the Foreign': The Anti-Cosmopolitanism Paradigm in Russian and Soviet Ideology." In *Cosmopolitanism, Nationalism and the Jews of East Central Europe*, edited by Michael L. Miller and Scott Ury, 109–136. London and New York: Routledge, 2015.

Hahn, Werner. *Postwar Soviet Politics: The Fall of Zhdanov and the Defeat of Moderation, 1946–53*. Ithaca: Cornell University Press, 1982.

Halbwachs, Maurice. *On Collective Memory*. Translated by Lewis A. Coser. Chicago: University of Chicago Press, 1992.

Halfin, Igal. *From Darkness to Light: Class, Consciousness, and Salvation in Revolutionary Russia*. Pittsburgh: University of Pittsburgh Press, 2000.

Terror in My Soul: Communist Autobiographies on Trial. Cambridge, MA: Harvard University Press, 2003.

Harris, Adrienne M. "Memorializations of a Martyr and Her Mutilated Bodies: Public Monuments to Soviet War Hero Zoya Kosmodemyanskaya (1942-the Present)." *The Journal of War and Culture Studies* 5, no. 1 (2012): 73–90.

"No Nastas'ias on the Volga: Soviet Women Veterans and Folkloric Self-Representations." *Folklorica* 17–18 (2013): 99–130.

Hasanli, Jamil. *Khrushchev's Thaw and National Identity in Soviet Azerbaijan, 1954–1959*. Boulder and New York: Lexington Books, 2015.

Hellbeck, Jochen. *Revolution on My Mind: Writing a Diary Under Stalin*. Cambridge, MA: Harvard University Press, 2006.

Stalingrad: The City That Defeated the Third Reich. Translated by Christopher Tauchen. New York: PublicAffairs, 2015.

Hellberg-Hirn, Elena. *Soil and Soul: The Symbolic World of Russianness*. Aldershot: Ashgate, 1998.

Herf, Jeffrey. *Divided Memory: The Nazi Past in the Two Germanys*. Cambridge, MA: Harvard University Press, 1997.

Herzog, Philipp. "'National in Form and Socialist in Content' or Rather 'Socialist in Form and National in Content"? The 'Amateur Art System' and the Cultivation of 'Folk Art' in Soviet Estonia." *Nar. Umjet.* 47, no. 1 (2010): 115–140.

Hill, Ronald J. "The 'All-People's State' and 'Developed Socialism.'" In *The State in Socialist Society*, edited by Neil Harding, 104–128. London: Macmillan Publishers, 1984.

Hirsch, Francine. *Empire of Nations: Ethnographic Knowledge and the Making of the Soviet Union*. Ithaca: Cornell University Press, 2005.

Hnatiuk, Ola. "How the Soviet Union Suppressed the Holocaust to Fight 'Nationalism.'" *The Odessa Review*, November 16, 2017. http://odessareview.com/soviet-union-suppressed-holocaust-fight-nationalism/.

Hobsbawm, Eric. *Nations and Nationalism since 1780: Programme, Myth, Reality*. 2nd ed. Cambridge: Cambridge University Press, 2012.

"Introduction: Inventing Traditions." In *The Invention of Tradition*, edited by Eric Hobsbawm and Terence Ranger, 1–14. Cambridge: Cambridge University Press, 1992.

Hoffmann, David L. *Stalinist Values: The Cultural Norms of Soviet Modernity, 1917–1941*. Ithaca: Cornell University Press, 2003.

"Was There a 'Great Retreat' from Soviet Socialism? Stalinist Culture Reconsidered." *Kritika* 5, no. 4 (2004): 651–674.

Hoisington, Sona Stephan. "'Ever Higher': The Evolution of the Project for the Palace of Soviets." *Slavic Review* 62, no. 1 (2003): 41–68.

Hopkins, A. G. *American Empire: A Global History*. Princeton and Oxford: Princeton University Press, 2019.

Hornsby, Robert. *Protest, Reform and Repression in Khrushchev's Soviet Union.* Cambridge and New York: Cambridge University Press, 2013.

"Soviet Youth on the March: The All-Union Tours of Military Glory, 1965–87." *Journal of Contemporary History* 52, no. 2 (2017): 418–445.

Hosking, Geoffrey. *Rulers and Victims: The Russians in the Soviet Union.* Cambridge, MA: Belknap Press, 2009.

"The Second World War and Russian National Consciousness." *Past and Present* 175, no. 1 (2002): 162–187.

Hosking, Geoffrey A. *Russia: People and Empire, 1552–1917.* Cambridge, MA: Harvard University Press, 1997.

Hroch, Miroslav. "From National Movement to the Fully-Formed Nation: The Nation-Building Process in Europe." In *Mapping the Nation*, edited by Gopal Balakrishnan, 78–97. Verso Books, 2012.

Hunt, Lynn. *Politics, Culture, and Class in the French Revolution: Twentieth Anniversary Edition, With a New Preface.* Berkeley: University of California Press, 2004.

Huyssen, Andreas. *Twilight Memories: Marking Time in a Culture of Amnesia.* New York: Routledge, 1994.

Jahn, Hubertus. *Patriotic Culture in Russia during World War I.* Ithaca: Cornell University Press, 1998.

Jenks, Andrew L. *The Cosmonaut Who Couldn't Stop Smiling: The Life and Legend of Yuri Gagarin.* DeKalb: Northern Illinois University Press, 2013.

Johnson, Emily D. "Jubilation Deferred: The Belated Commemoration of the 250th Anniversary of St. Pestersburg/Leningrad." In *Rites of Place: Public Commemoration in Russia and Eastern Europe*, edited by Julie Buckler and Emily D. Johnson, 81–102. Evanston, IL: Northwestern University Press, 2013.

Johnson, Jeremy. "Speaking Soviet with an Armenian Accent: Literacy, Language Ideology, and Belonging in Early Soviet Armenia." In *Empire and Belonging in the Eurasian Borderlands*, edited by Krista A. Goff and Lewis H. Siegelbaum, 129–144. Ithaca and London: Cornell University Press, 2019.

Jones, Polly. *Myth, Memory, Trauma: Rethinking the Stalinist Past in the Soviet Union, 1953–70.* New Haven: Yale University Press, 2013.

Revolution Rekindled: The Writers and Readers of Late Soviet Biography. Oxford: Oxford University Press, 2019.

Judson, Pieter M. *The Habsburg Empire: A New History.* Cambridge, MA: Harvard University Press, 2016.

Kaiser, Robert J. *The Geography of Nationalism in Russia and the USSR.* Princeton, NJ: Princeton University Press, 1994.

Kalashnikov, Antony. 2018. "Stalinist War Monuments and the 'Immortalization of Memory': Actors and Motives." Paper presented at the annual ASEEES convention, Boston, 2018.

Kammen, Michael G. *In the Past Lane: Historical Perspectives on American Culture.* Oxford: Oxford University Press, 1999.

Kan, A. S. "Anna Pankratova i 'Voprosy istorii'. Novatorskii i kriticheskii istoricheskii zhurnal v Sovetskom Soiuza v 1950-e gody." In *Istorik i vremia. 20–50-e gody XX veka. A.M. Pankratova: (Sbornik)*, edited by Iu. S. Kukushkin, 85–100. Moscow: Izd. RUDN, 2000.

Kauffman, Jesse. *Elusive Alliance: The German Occupation of Poland in World War I*. Cambridge, MA: Harvard University Press, 2015.
Kazarkin, A. "Pamiat' – Ekologiia kul'tury: (k 60-letiiu V. Chivilikhina)." *Sibirskie ogni*, no. 3 (1988): 156–62.
Kaziev, S. Sh. "Natsional'naia politika v Kazakhstane (1941–1953 gg.)." *Uchenye zapiski Orlovskogo gos. univ.* 1, no. 64 (2015): 29–34.
Kelly, Catriona. "The Motherland and the Fight with Fascism: War Cult and War Film under Brezhnev (1965–1982)." Unpublished Manuscript, 2019.
"The Shock of the Old: Architectural Preservation in Soviet Russia." *Nations and Nationalism* 24, no. 1 (2018): 88–109.
Kenez, Peter. *A History of the Soviet Union from the Beginning to the End*. 2nd ed. Cambridge and New York: Cambridge University Press, 2006.
Khalid, Adeeb. "Backwardness and the Quest for Civilization: Early Soviet Central Asia in Comparative Perspective." *Slavic Review* 65, no. 2 (2006): 231–51.
Khaniutin, Iurii. *Preduprezhdenie proshlogo*. Moscow: Iskusstvo, 1968.
Khrushchev, Sergei, ed. *Memoirs of Nikita Khrushchev. Vol. 1*. 3 vols. University Park: The Pennsylvania State University Press, 2005.
Kikeshev, Nikolai Ivanovich. "Slavianskoe dvizhenie v SSSR: 1941–1948 gody." Candidate diss., Institute of Russian History of the Russian Academy of Sciences, 2008.
Kirschenbaum, Lisa A. "'Our City, Our Hearths, Our Families': Local Loyalties and Private Life in Soviet World War II Propaganda." *Slavic Review* 59, no. 4 (2000): 825–47.
The Legacy of the Siege of Leningrad, 1941–1995: Myth, Memories, and Monuments. Cambridge: Cambridge University Press, 2006.
Kivelson, Valerie A., and Ronald Grigor Suny. *Russia's Empires*. Oxford: Oxford University Press, 2017.
Klein, L. S. *Voskreshenie Peruna: k rekonstruktsii vostochnoslavianskogo iazychestva*. Saint Petersburg: Evraziia, 2004.
Klumbytė, Neringa, and Gulnaz Sharafutdinova. "Introduction: What Was Late Socialism?" In *Soviet Society in the Era of Late Socialism, 1964–1985*, edited by Neringa Klumbytė and Gulnaz Sharafutdinova, 1–14. Lanham, MD: Lexington Books, 2013.
Knischewski, Gerd, and Ulla Spittler. "Memories of the Second World War and National Identity in Germany." In *War and Memory in the Twentieth Century*, edited by Martin Evans and Kenneth Lunn, 239–254. Oxford: Berg, 1997.
Kolstø, Pål. "The Ethnification of Russian Nationalism." In *The New Russian Nationalism: Imperialism, Ethnicity and Authoritarianism 2000–2015*, edited by Pål Kolstø and Helge Blakkisrud, 18–45. Edinburgh: Edinburgh University Press, 2016.
Konradova, Natal'ia and Anna Ryleva. "Geroi i Zhertvy: Memorialy Velikoi Otechestvennoi." In *Pamiat' o voine 60 let spustia: Rossiia, Germaniia, Evropa*, edited by M. Gabovich, 241–261. Moscow: Novoe Literaturnoe Obozrenie, 2005.
Koonz, Claudia. "Between Memory and Oblivion: Concentration Camps in German Memory." In *Commemorations: The Politics of National Identity*, edited by John R. Gillis, 258–280. Princeton: Princeton University Press, 1994.

Köpstein, Helga. *Die sowjetischen Ehrenmale in Berlin*. Berlin: ROSSI, 2006.
Koshar, Rudy. *From Monuments to Traces: Artifacts of German Memory, 1870–1990*. Berkeley: University of California Press, 1994.
Kostyrchenko, G. V. *Tainaia politika Stalina: vlast' i antisemitizm*. Moscow: Mezhdunarodnye otnosheniia, 2001.
V plenu krasnogo faraona: politicheskie presledovaniia evreev v SSSR v poslednee stalinskoe desiatiletie. Moscow: Mezhdunarodnye otnosheniia, 1994.
Kotkin, Stephen. *Armageddon Averted: The Soviet Collapse, 1970–2000*. 2nd ed. Oxford and New York: Oxford University Press, 2008.
Magnetic Mountain: Stalinism as a Civilization. Berkeley: University of California Press, 1997.
Kozhevnikov, A. Iu. *Russkii patriotizm i sovetskii sotsializm*. Moscow: Prometei, 2017.
Kozlov, Denis. "Naming the Social Evil: The Readers of Novyi Mir and Vladimir Dudintsev's Not by Bread Alone, 1956–59 and Beyond." In *The Dilemmas of De-Stalinization: Negotiating Cultural and Social Change in the Khrushchev Era*, edited by Polly Jones, 80–98. London and New York: Routledge, 2006.
"The Historical Turn in Late Soviet Culture: Retrospectivism, Factography, Doubt, 1953–91." *Kritika: Explorations in Russian and Eurasian History*, 2001, 577–600.
The Readers of Novyi Mir: Coming to Terms with the Stalinist Past. Cambridge, MA: Harvard University Press, 2013.
Kozlov, N. D. *Obshchestvennoe soznanie v gody Velikoi Otechestvennoi voiny (1941–1945)*. Saint Petersburg: LOIUU, 1995.
Kozlov, Vladimir A. *Mass Uprisings in the USSR: Protest and Rebellion in the Post-Stalin Years*. Translated by Elaine McClarnand MacKinnon. London and New York: Routledge, 2015.
Kreindler, Isabelle T. "Soviet Language Planning since 1953." In *Language Planning in the Soviet Union*, edited by Michael Kirkwood, 46–63. London: Macmillan-SSEES, 1989.
Krivosheev, G. F. *Rossiia i SSSR v voinakh XX veka: poteri vooruzhennykh sil: statisticheskoe issledovanie*. Moscow: OLMA-Press, 2001.
Krylova, Anna. "Dancing on the Graves of the Dead." In *Memory and the Impact of Political Transformation in Public Space*, edited by Daniel Walkowitz and Lisa Maya Knauer, 83–102. Durham: Duke University Press, 2004.
Soviet Women in Combat: A History of Violence on the Eastern Front. Cambridge and New York: Cambridge University Press, 2010.
Kumar, Krishan. *Visions of Empire: How Five Imperial Regimes Shaped the World*. Princeton: Princeton University Press, 2017.
Lagrou, Pieter. *The Legacy of Nazi Occupation: Patriotic Memory and National Recovery in Western Europe, 1945–1965*. Cambridge: Cambridge University Press, 1999.
Lane, Christel. "Legitimacy and Power in the Soviet Union through Socialist Ritual." *British Journal of Political Science* 14, no. 2 (1984): 207–17.
The Rites of Rulers: Ritual in Industrial Society – The Soviet Case. Cambridge: Cambridge University Press, 1981.

LaPierre, Brian. *Hooligans in Khrushchev's Russia: Defining, Policing, and Producing Deviance during the Thaw*. Madison: University of Wisconsin Press, 2012.

Laruelle, Marlene. *Russian Nationalism: Imaginaries, Doctrines, and Political Battlefields*. New York: Routledge, 2019.

Lehmann, Maike. "Apricot Socialism: The National Past, the Soviet Project, and the Imagining of Community in Late Soviet Armenia." *Slavic Review* 74, no. 1 (2015): 9–31.

Lenoe, Matthew E. *Closer to the Masses: Stalinist Culture, Social Revolution, and Soviet Newspapers*. Cambridge: Harvard University Press, 2004.

Leong, Albert. *Centaur: The Life and Art of Ernst Neizvestny*. Oxford: Rowman & Littlefield, 2002.

Lewin, Moshe. *The Soviet Century*. London: Verso, 2005.

Liber, George O. *Alexander Dovzhenko: A Life in Soviet Film*. London: British Film Institute, 2002.

Lieven, Anatol. "The Weakness of Russian Nationalism." *Survival* 41, no. 2 (1999): 53–70.

Linz, Susan J., ed. *The Impact of World War II on the Soviet Union*. Lanham, MD: Rowman & Allanheld, 1985.

Liuks, L. "Evreiskii vopros v politike Stalina." *Voprosy istorii*, no. 7 (1999): 41–59.

Livshin, A. Ia., and I. B. Orlov. "Propaganda i politicheskaia sotsializatsiia." *Otechestvennaia istoriia*, no. 1 (2008): 99–105.

Lovell, Stephen. *The Shadow of War: Russia and the USSR, 1941 to the Present*. Oxford: Wiley-Blackwell, 2010.

The Soviet Union: A Very Short Introduction. Oxford: Oxford University Press, 2009.

Maddox, Steven. *Saving Stalin's Imperial City: Historic Preservation in Leningrad, 1930–1950*. Bloomington: Indiana University Press, 2015.

"These Monuments Must Be Protected! The Stalinist Turn to the Past and Historic Preservation during the Blockade of Leningrad." *The Russian Review* 70 (2011): 608–626.

Makhnyrev, A. L. "Izmenenie roli mesta istoricheskikh iubileev v obshchestvenno-politicheskoi zhizni SSSR: ot poslevoennogo stalinizma k khrushchevskoi 'ottepeli.'" *Vestnik MGOU*, no. 3 (2014): 133–153.

"Rol' i mesto istoricheskikh iubileev v obshchestvenno-politicheskoi zhizni SSSR (1945–1964 gg.)." Candidate diss., Moscow City Pedagogical University, 2015.

Malia, Martin. *The Soviet Tragedy: A History of Socialism in Russia*. New York: Simon and Schuster, 1996.

Malinina, Tat'iana Glebovna. "Khudozhestvennyi obraz pamiatnika Velikoi Otechestvennoi voiny (po materialam konkursov i vystavok 1942–1945 godov)." Candidate diss., Scientific Research Institute of the Theory and History of Fine Arts of the Academy of Arts of the USSR, 1984.

Manley, Rebecca. *To the Tashkent Station: Evacuation and Survival in the Soviet Union at War*. Ithaca: Cornell University Press, 2012.

Mann, Yan. "Contested Memory: Writing the Great Patriotic War's Official History during Khrushchev's Thaw." Ph.D. diss., Arizona State University, 2016.

Markwick, Roger D. *Rewriting History in Soviet Russia: The Politics of Revisionist Historiography, 1956–1974*. London: Palgrave Macmillan, 2001.

"Thaws and Freezes in Soviet Historiography, 1953–64." In *The Dilemmas of De-Stalinization: Negotiating Cultural and Social Change in the Khrushchev Era*, edited by Polly Jones, 173–192. London and New York: Routledge, 2006.

Markwick, Roger D., and Charon Cardona, eds. *Soviet Women on the Frontline in the Second World War*. Basingstoke: Palgrave Macmillan, 2012.

Martin, Barbara. *Dissident Histories in the Soviet Union: From De-Stalinization to Perestroika*. New York: Bloomsbury Publishing, 2019.

Martin, Terry. "Modernization or Neo-Traditionalism? Ascribed Nationality and Soviet Primordialism." In *Stalinism: New Directions*, edited by Sheila Fitzpatrick, 348–367. London and New York: Routledge, 2000.

The Affirmative Action Empire: Nations and Nationalism in the Soviet Union, 1923–1939. Ithaca: Cornell University Press, 2001.

McGlynn, Jade. "Historical Framing of the Ukraine Crisis through the Great Patriotic War: Performativity, Cultural Consciousness and Shared Remembering." *Memory Studies* 13, no. 6 (2018): 1058–1080.

Medvedev, Roy A. *On Stalin and Stalinism*. Oxford: Oxford University Press, 1979.

Merlin, Aude. "Remembering and Forgetting in Chechnya Today: Using the Great Patriotic War to Create a New Historical Narrative." In *Chechnya at War and Beyond*, edited by Anne Le Huérou, Aude Merlin, Amandine Regamey, and Elisabeth Sieca-Kozlowski, 37–57. London and New York: Routledge, 2014.

Merridale, Catherine. *Ivan's War: Life and Death in the Red Army, 1939–45*. New York: Metropolitan Books, 2006.

Red Fortress: History and Illusion in the Kremlin. New York: Metropolitan Books, 2013.

Mijnssen, Ivo. *Russia's Hero Cities: From Postwar Ruins to the Soviet Heroarchy*. Bloomington: Indiana University Press, 2021.

Mikhalev, S. N. *Liudskie poteri v Velikoi Otechestvennoi voine 1941–1945 gg.: Stat. issled.* Krasnoyarsk: Krasnoyarsk Pedagogical University, 2000.

Mitrokhin, Nikolai. *Russkaia partiia: dvizhenie russkikh natsionalistov v SSSR, 1953–1985 gody*. Moscow: Novoe literaturnoe obozrenie, 2003.

Monger, David. *Patriotism and Propaganda in First World War Britain: The National War Aims Committee and Civilian Morale*. Liverpool: Liverpool University Press, 2012.

Mosse, George L. *Fallen Soldiers: Reshaping the Memory of the World Wars*. Oxford: Oxford University Press, 1991.

Musil, Robert. "Monuments." In *Posthumous Papers of a Living Author*, translated by Peter Wortsman, 64–68. Brooklyn: Archipelago, 2006.

Nahaylo, Bohdan, and Victor Swoboda. *Soviet Disunion: A History of the Nationalities Problem in the USSR*. New York: The Free Press, 1990.

Naimark, Norman M. "Ethnic Cleansing Between War and Peace." In *Landscaping the Human Garden: Twentieth-Century Population Management in a Comparative Framework*, edited by Amir Weiner, 218–235. Stanford: Stanford University Press, 2003.

Nekrich, Aleksandr M. *The Punished Peoples: The Deportation and Fate of Soviet Minorities at the End of the Second World War*. New York: WW Norton, 1978.

Nora, Pierre. "General Introduction: Between Memory and History." In *Realms of Memory: Rethinking the French Past*, edited by Pierre Nora, 1–20. New York: Columbia University Press, 1996.

Norris, Stephen M. *A War of Images: Russian Popular Prints, Wartime Culture, and National Identity, 1812–1945*. DeKalb: Northern Illinois University Press, 2006.

"Memory for Sale: Victory Day 2010 and Russian Remembrance." *The Soviet and Post-Soviet Review* 38, no. 2 (2011): 201–29.

O'Connor, Kevin. *Intellectuals and Apparatchiks: Russian Nationalism and the Gorbachev Revolution*. Lanham, MD: Lexington Books, 2008.

Orlov, I. B. "Natsional'nyi i internatsional'nyi komponenty sovetskoi voennoi propagandy." In *Sovetskie natsii i natsional'naia politika v 1920–1950-e gody: Materialy VI mezhdunarodnoi konferentsii, Kiev, 10–12 oktiabria 2013*. Moscow: Fond "Prezidentskii tsentr B. N. El'tsina," 2014: 406–415.

Oushakine, Serguei Alex. *The Patriotism of Despair: Nation, War, and Loss in Russia*. Ithaca: Cornell University Press, 2009.

Pain, Emil. "The Imperial Syndrome and Its Influence on Russian Nationalism." In *The New Russian Nationalism: Imperialism, Ethnicity and Authoritarianism 2000–2015*, edited by Pål Kolstø and Helge Blakkisrud, 46–74. Edinburgh: Edinburgh University Press, 2016.

Palmer, Scott W. "How Memory Was Made: The Construction of the Memorial to the Heroes of the Battle of Stalingrad." *The Russian Review* 68, no. 3 (2009): 373–407.

Parthé, Kathleen F. *Russian Village Prose: The Radiant Past*. Princeton, NJ: Princeton University Press, 1992.

Passerini, Luisa. *Fascism in Popular Memory: The Cultural Experience of the Turin Working Class*. Cambridge: Cambridge University Press, 1987.

Peri, Alexis. *The War Within: Diaries from the Siege of Leningrad*. Cambridge, MA: Harvard University Press, 2017.

Perrie, Maureen. *The Cult of Ivan the Terrible in Stalin's Russia*. New York: Palgrave Macmillan, 2001.

"The Tsar, the Emperor, the Leader: Ivan the Terrible, Peter the Great and Anatolii Rybakov's Stalin." In *Stalinism: Its Nature and Aftermath. Essays in Honour of Moshe Lewin*, edited by Nick Lampert and Gabor T. Rittersporn, 77–100. London: Macmillan, 1992.

Persak, Krzysztof. "The Polish-Soviet Confrontation in 1956 and the Attempted Soviet Military Intervention in Poland." *Europe-Asia Studies* 58, no. 8 (2006): 1285–1310.

Petrone, Karen. *Life Has Become More Joyous, Comrades: Celebrations in the Time of Stalin*. Bloomington: Indiana University Press, 2000.

The Great War in Russian Memory. Bloomington: Indiana University Press, 2011.

Petrov, N., and O. Edel'man. "Novoe o sovetskikh geroiakh." *Novyi mir*, no. 6 (1997): 140–51.

Pinsky, Anatoly. "The Individual after Stalin: Fedor Abramov, Russian Intellectuals, and the Revitalization of Soviet Socialism, 1953–1962." Ph.D. diss., Columbia University, 2011.

Plamper, Jan. *The Stalin Cult: A Study in the Alchemy of Power*. New Haven: Yale University Press, 2012.

Platt, Kevin M. F., and David Brandenberger, eds. *Epic Revisionism: Russian History and Literature as Stalinist Propaganda*. Madison: University of Wisconsin Press, 2006.

Plokhy, Serhii. *Lost Kingdom: The Quest for Empire and the Making of the Russian Nation*. New York: Basic Books, 2017.

Popoff, Alexandra. *Vasily Grossman and the Soviet Century*. New Haven: Yale University Press, 2019.

Popov, V. P. *Bol'shaia nich'ia: SSSR ot Pobedy do raspada*. Moscow: ENAS, 2005.

Qualls, Karl D. *From Ruins to Reconstruction: Urban Identity in Soviet Sevastopol After World War II*. Ithaca: Cornell University Press, 2009.

Rakowska-Harmstone, Teresa. "Chickens Coming Home to Roost: A Perspective on Soviet Ethnic Relations." *Journal of International Affairs* 45, no. 2 (1992): 519–48.

Raleigh, Donald J. *Soviet Baby Boomers: An Oral History of Russia's Cold War Generation*. New York: Oxford University Press, 2012.

Ree, Erik van. "Stalin as Marxist: The Western Roots of Stalin's Russification of Marxism." In *Stalin: A New History*, edited by Sarah Davies and James Harris, 159–80. Cambridge: Cambridge University Press, 2005.

The Political Thought of Joseph Stalin: A Study in Twentieth Century Revolutionary Patriotism. London and New York: Routledge, 2002.

Reese, Roger R. "The Legacy of World War II for Putin's Russia." *South Central Review* 35, no. 1 (2018): 196–212.

Why Stalin's Soldiers Fought: The Red Army's Military Effectiveness in World War II. Lawrence: University Press of Kansas, 2011.

Remnick, David. *Lenin's Tomb: The Last Days of the Soviet Empire*. New York: Vintage Books, 1994.

Risch, William Jay. *The Ukrainian West: Culture and the Fate of Empire in Soviet Lviv*. Cambridge, MA: Harvard University Press, 2011.

Roberts, Geoffrey. *Stalin's General: The Life of Georgy Zhukov*. New York: Random House, 2012.

Rogger, Hans. "Nationalism and the State: A Russian Dilemma." *Comparative Studies in Society and History* 4, no. 3 (1962): 253–64.

Rolf, Malte. *Soviet Mass Festivals, 1917–1991*. Translated by Cynthia Klohr. University of Pittsburgh Press, 2013.

Roth-Ey, Kristin. *Moscow Prime Time: How the Soviet Union Built the Media Empire That Lost the Cultural Cold War*. Ithaca: Cornell University Press, 2011.

Rousso, Henry. *The Vichy Syndrome: History and Memory in France since 1944*. Translated by Arthur Goldhammer. Cambridge, MA: Harvard University Press, 1994.

Rubenstein, Joshua. *The Last Days of Stalin*. New Haven: Yale University Press, 2016.

Rudling, Per Anders. "'For a Heroic Belarus!': The Great Patriotic War as Identity Marker in Lukashenka and Soviet Belarusian Discourses." *Sprawy Narodowościowe/Nationalities Affairs* 32 (2008): 43–62.

Sadomskaya, Natalia. "New Soviet Rituals and National Integration in the USSR." In *Soviet Nationality Policies: Ruling Ethnic Groups in the USSR*, edited by Henry R. Huttenbach, 94–120. London: Mansell Publishing Limited, 1990.

Sanborn, Joshua A. *Drafting the Russian Nation: Military Conscription, Total War, and Mass Politics, 1905–1925*. DeKalb: Northern Illinois University Press, 2003.

Schechter, Brandon M. "'The Language of the Sword': Aleksandr Bek, the Writers Union and Baurdzhan Momysh-Uly in Battle for the Memory of Volokolamskoe Shosse." Berkeley Working Papers. Berkeley, 2009. https://iseees.berkeley.edu/sites/default/files/u4/2009%2008-Shechter.pdf.

"'The People's Instructions': Indigenizing The Great Patriotic War Among 'Non-Russians.'" *Ab Imperio* 2012, no. 3 (2012): 109–33.

The Stuff of Soldiers: A History of the Red Army in World War II through Objects. Ithaca and London: Cornell University Press, 2019.

Schleifman, Nurit. "Moscow's Victory Park: A Monumental Change." *History and Memory* 13, no. 2 (2001): 5–34.

Scott, R. Erik. *Familiar Strangers: The Georgian Diaspora and the Evolution of Soviet Empire*. Oxford and New York: Oxford University Press, 2016.

Service, Robert. *Stalin: A Biography*. Cambridge, MA: Belknap, 2005.

Shaw, Charles David. "Soldiers' Letters to Inobatxon and O'g'ulxon: Gender and Nationality in the Birth of a Soviet Romantic Culture." *Kritika: Explorations in Russian and Eurasian History* 17, no. 3 (2016): 517–52.

"Making Ivan-Uzbek: War, Friendship of the Peoples, and the Creation of Soviet Uzbekistan, 1941–1945." Ph.D. diss., University of California, Berkeley, 2015.

Sherman, Daniel J. *The Construction of Memory in Interwar France*. Chicago: University of Chicago Press, 1999.

Shin, Boram. "Red Army Propaganda for Uzbek Soldiers and Localised Soviet Internationalism during World War II." *The Soviet and Post-Soviet Review* 42, no. 1 (2015): 39–63.

Semanov, Sergei. *Andropov. 7 tain genseka s Lubianki*. Moscow: Veche, 2001.

Shein, I. A. *Voina 1812 goda v otechestvennoi istoriografii*. Moscow: Nauchno-politicheskaia kniga, 2013.

Sidorova, L. A. *Ottepel' v istoricheskoi nauke. Sovetskaia istoriografiia pervogo poslestalinskogo desiatiletiia*. Moscow: Pamiatniki istoricheskoi mysli, 1997.

Siegelbaum, Lewis H. *Stakhanovism and the Politics of Productivity in the USSR, 1935–1941*. Cambridge: Cambridge University Press, 1990.

Siegelbaum, Lewis H., and Leslie Page Moch. "Transnationalism in One Country? Seeing and Not Seeing Cross-Border Migration within the Soviet Union." *Slavic Review* 75, no. 4 (2016): 970–86.

Simon, Gerhard. *Nationalism and Policy Toward the Nationalities in the Soviet Union*. Boulder: Westview Press, 1991.

Slepyan, Kenneth. *Stalin's Guerrillas: Soviet Partisans in World War II*. Lawrence: University Press of Kansas, 2006.

Slezkine, Yuri. *Arctic Mirrors: Russia and the Small Peoples of the North*. Ithaca and London: Cornell University Press, 1994.

The Jewish Century. Princeton: Princeton University Press, 2004.

"The USSR as a Communal Apartment, or How a Socialist State Promoted Ethnic Particularism." *Slavic Review* 53, no. 2 (1994): 414–52.

Smelser, Ronald, and Edward J. Davies II. *The Myth of the Eastern Front: The Nazi-Soviet War in American Popular Culture*. Cambridge and New York: Cambridge University Press, 2008.

Smith, Anthony D. "The 'Golden Age' and National Renewal." In *Myths and Nationhood*, edited by George Schopflin and Geoffrey Hosking, 36–59. London: Routledge, 1997.

Smith, Jeremy. *Red Nations: The Nationalities Experience in and after the USSR*. Cambridge and New York: Cambridge University Press, 2013.

"The Battle for Language: Opposition to Khrushchev's Education Reform in the Soviet Republics, 1958–59." *Slavic Review* 76, no. 4 (2017): 983–1002.

The Bolsheviks and the National Question, 1917–23. New York: St. Martin's Press, 1999.

Smith, Kathleen E. *Mythmaking in the New Russia: Politics and Memory in the Yeltsin Era*. Ithaca and London: Cornell University Press, 2002.

Smolkin, Victoria. *A Sacred Space Is Never Empty: A History of Soviet Atheism*. Princeton and Oxford: Princeton University Press, 2018.

Stangl, Paul. "The Soviet War Memorial in Treptow, Berlin." *Geographical Review* 93, no. 2 (2003): 213–236.

Statiev, Alexander. "'La Garde meurt mais ne se rend pas!' Once Again on the 28 Panfilov Heroes." *Kritika: Explorations in Russian and Eurasian History* 13, no. 4 (2012): 769–798.

Stites, Richard, ed. *Culture and Entertainment in Wartime Russia*. Bloomington: Indiana University Press, 1995.

Stronski, Paul. *Tashkent: Forging a Soviet City, 1930–1966*. Pittsburgh: University of Pittsburgh Press, 2010.

Suny, Ronald Grigor. "Stalin and His Stalinism: Power and Authority in the Soviet Union, 1930–53." In *Stalinism and Nazism: Dictatorships in Comparison*, edited by Ian Kershaw and Moshe Lewin, 26–52. Cambridge: Cambridge University Press, 1997.

"The Contradictions of Identity: Being Soviet and National in the USSR and After." In *Soviet and Post-Soviet Identities*, edited by Mark Bassin and Catriona Kelly, 17–36. Cambridge and New York: Cambridge University Press, 2012.

The Making of the Georgian Nation. 2nd ed. Bloomington: Indiana University Press, 1994.

The Revenge of the Past: Nationalism, Revolution, and the Collapse of the Soviet Union. Stanford, CA: Stanford University Press, 1993.

Szporluk, Roman. *Russia, Ukraine, and the Breakup of the Soviet Union*. Stanford, CA: Hoover Institution Press, 2000.

"The Fall of the Tsarist Empire and the USSR: The Russian Question and Imperial Overextension." In *The End of Empire? The Transformation of the USSR in Comparative Perspective*, edited by Karen Dawisha and Bruce Parrott, 65–93. London: M.E. Sharpe, 1997.

Taubman, William. *Khrushchev: The Man and His Era*. New York and London: W. W. Norton & Company, 2004.

Thomson, Alistair. *Anzac Memories: Living With the Legend*. Oxford: Oxford University Press, 1994.
Tikhonov, Vitalii Vital'evich. "'Koleso istorii rabotaet v nashu pol'zu': istorik kak propagandist v gody Velikoi Otechestvennoi voiny." *Bylye gody* 3, no. 25 (2012): 58–67.
"Stalinskaia premiia kak instrument konstruirovaniia obshchei istorii narodov SSSR." *Istoricheskii zhurnal: nauchnye issledovaniia*, no. 2 (2016): 177–185.
Tillett, Lowell. *The Great Friendship: Soviet Historians on the Non-Russian Nationalities*. Chapel Hill: University of North Carolina Press, 1969.
Timasheff, Nicholas S. *The Great Retreat: The Growth and Decline of Communism in Russia*. New York: E. P. Dutton & Co., 1946.
Tishkov, Valery. *Chechnya: Life in a War-Torn Society*. Berkeley and Los Angeles: University of California Press, 2004.
Titov, Alexander. "The 1961 Party Programme and the Fate of Khrushchev's Reforms." In *Soviet State and Society Under Nikita Khrushchev*, edited by Melanie Ilic and Jeremy Smith, 8–26. London: Routledge, 2009.
Tolz, Vera. *Russia: Inventing the Nation*. London: Arnold, 2001.
Tsipursky, Gleb. *Socialist Fun: Youth, Consumption, and State-Sponsored Popular Culture in the Soviet Union, 1945–1970*. Pittsburgh: University of Pittsburgh Press, 2016.
Tucker, Robert C. *Stalin in Power: The Revolution from Above, 1928–1941*. New York: Norton, 1992.
Tumarkin, Nina. *The Living & the Dead: The Rise And Fall of the Cult of World War II In Russia*. New York: Basic Books, 1995.
"The Story of a War Memorial." In *World War 2 and the Soviet People*, edited by Carol Garrard and John Garrard, 125–46. Basingstoke: Macmillan, 1993.
Ulam, Adam Bruno. *Stalin: The Man and His Era*. Beacon Press, 1989.
Unowsky, Daniel L. *The Pomp and Politics of Patriotism: Imperial Celebrations in Habsburg Austria, 1848–1916*. West Lafayette, IN: Purdue University Press, 2006.
Vail', Petr, and Aleksandr Genis. *60-e mir sovetskogo cheloveka*. Moscow: Novoe literaturnoe obozrenie, 1996.
Vdovin, A. I. *Russkie v XX veke*. Moscow: OLMA, 2004.
Vihavainen, Timo. "Nationalism and Internationalism: How Did the Bolsheviks Cope with National Sentiments." In *The Fall of an Empire, the Birth of a Nation: National Identities in Russia: National Identities in Russia*, edited by Chris J. Chulos and Timo Piirainen, 75–97. Aldershot: Ashgate, 2000.
Vujačić, Veljko. *Nationalism, Myth, and the State in Russia and Serbia: Antecedents of the Dissolution of the Soviet Union and Yugoslavia*. Cambridge: Cambridge University Press, 2015.
"Stalinism and Russian Nationalism: A Reconceptualization." *Post-Soviet Affairs* 23, no. 2 (2007): 156–183.
Walicki, Andrzej. *Marxism and the Leap to the Kingdom of Freedom: The Rise and Fall of the Communist Utopia*. Palo Alto, CA: Stanford University Press, 1995.
Walker, Shaun. *The Long Hangover: Putin's New Russia and the Ghosts of the Past*. Oxford: Oxford University Press, 2018.

Weiner, Amir. "In the Long Shadow of War: The Second World War and the Soviet and Post-Soviet World." *Diplomatic History* 25, no. 3 (2001): 443–456.

Making Sense of War: The Second World War and the Fate of the Bolshevik Revolution. Princeton: Princeton University Press, 2002.

"Nature, Nurture, and Memory in a Socialist Utopia: Delineating the Soviet Socio-Ethnic Body in the Age of Socialism." *The American Historical Review* 104, no. 4 (1999): 1114–1155.

"The Making of a Dominant Myth: The Second World War and the Construction of Political Identities within the Soviet Polity." *The Russian Review* 55, no. 4 (1996): 638–660.

"When Memory Counts: War, Genocide, and Postwar Soviet Jewry." In *Landscaping the Human Garden: Twentieth-Century Population Management in a Comparative Framework*, edited by Amir Weiner, 167–188. Stanford: Stanford University Press, 2003.

Weiner, Douglas R. *A Little Corner of Freedom: Russian Nature Protection from Stalin to Gorbachev*. Berkeley: University of California Press, 2002.

Werfel, Franz. *Twilight of a World*. Translated by H. T. Lowe-Porter. New York: The Viking Press, 1937.

Werth, Alexander. *Russia at War, 1941–1945*. New York: Dutton, 1964.

Westwood, J. N. *Russia, 1917–1964*. New York: Harper & Row, 1966.

Whittington, Anna. "'For the Soviet Person, New Rituals': Religion, Civic Rites, and Soviet Identity." In *Konstruiruia "Sovetskoe"? Politicheskoe Soznanie, Povsednevnye Praktiki, Novye Identichnosti. Materialy Desiatoi Mezhdunarodnoi Konferentsii Studentov i Aspirantov 22–23 Aprelia 2016 Goda, Sankt-Peterburg*, 167–74. Saint Petersburg: EUSP, 2016.

"Making a Home for the Soviet People: World War II and the Origins of the Sovetskii Narod." In *Empire and Belonging in the Eurasian Borderlands*, edited by Krista A. Goff and Lewis H. Siegelbaum, 147–161. Ithaca: Cornell University Press, 2019.

Winter, Jay. *Remembering War: The Great War Between Memory and History in the Twentieth Century*. New Haven: Yale University Press, 2006.

Sites of Memory, Sites of Mourning: The Great War in European Cultural History. Cambridge: Cambridge University Press, 1998.

"The Performance of the Past: Memory, History, Identity." In *Performing the Past: Memory, History, and Identity in Modern Europe*, edited by Karin Tilmans, Frank van Vree, and Jay Winter, 11–34. Amsterdam: Amsterdam University Press, 2010.

Winter, Jay, and Emmanuel Sivan. "Setting the Framework." In *War and Remembrance in the Twentieth Century*, edited by Jay Winter and Emmanuel Sivan, 6–39. Cambridge: Cambridge University Press, 2000.

Wojnowski, Zbigniew. "De-Stalinization and the Failure of Soviet Identity Building in Kazakhstan." *Journal of Contemporary History, De-Stalinization and the Failure of Soviet Identity*, 52, no. 4 (2016): 999–1021.

The Near Abroad: Socialist Eastern Europe and Soviet Patriotism in Ukraine, 1956–1985. Toronto: University of Toronto Press, 2017.

Wolfe, Thomas C. "Past as Present, Myth, or History? Discourses of Time and the Great Fatherland War." In *The Politics of Memory in Postwar Europe*, edited by Richard Ned Lebow, Wulf Kansteiner, and Claudio Fogu, 249–283. Durham: Duke University Press, 2006.

Woll, Josephine. *Real Images: Soviet Cinemas and the Thaw*. London: I. B. Tauris, 2000.

Wortman, Richard S. *Scenarios of Power: From Peter the Great to the Abdication of Nicholas II*. Princeton: Princeton University Press, 2006.

Yanov, Alexander. *The Russian Challenge and the Year 2000*. New York: Basil Blackwell, 1987.

The Russian New Right: Right-Wing Ideologies in the Contemporary USSR. Berkeley: Institute of International Studies, University of California, 1978.

Yekelchyk, Serhy. "Celebrating the Soviet Present: The Zhdanovshchina Campaign in Ukrainian Literature and the Arts." In *Provincial Landscapes: Local Dimensions of Soviet Power, 1917–1953*, edited by Donald J. Raleigh, 255–275. University of Pittsburgh Press, 2001.

"Stalinist Patriotism as Imperial Discourse: Reconciling the Ukrainian and Russian 'Heroic Pasts,' 1939–1945." *Kritika: Explorations in Russian and Eurasian History* 3, no. 1 (2002): 51–80.

Stalin's Empire of Memory: Russian-Ukrainian Relations in the Soviet Historical Imagination. Toronto: University of Toronto Press, 2014.

Yilmaz, H. "History Writing as Agitation and Propaganda: The Kazakh History Book of 1943." *Central Asian Survey* 31, no. 4 (2012): 409–423.

Young, James E. *The Texture of Memory: Holocaust Memorials and Meaning*. New Haven: Yale University Press, 1994.

Youngblood, Denise J. *Russian War Films: On the Cinema Front, 1914–2005*. Lawrence: University Press of Kansas, 2006.

Yurchak, Alexei. *Everything Was Forever, Until It Was No More: The Last Soviet Generation*. Princeton: Princeton University Press, 2013.

Zaslavsky, Victor. *The Neo-Stalinist State: Class Ethnicity & Consensus in Soviet Society*. Armonk, NY: M.E. Sharpe, 1982.

Zelnik, Reginald E. *Perils of Pankratova: Some Stories from the Annals of Soviet Historiography*. Seattle: University of Washington Press, 2005.

Zhuk, Sergei I. *Rock and Roll in the Rocket City: The West, Identity, and Ideology in Soviet Dniepropetrovsk, 1960–1985*. Baltimore: Johns Hopkins University Press, 2010.

Zubkova, Elena. *Russia after the War: Hopes, Illusions, and Disappointments, 1945–1957*. Armonk, NY: M.E. Sharpe, 1998.

Zubok, Vladislav M. *A Failed Empire: The Soviet Union in the Cold War from Stalin to Gorbachev*. Chapel Hill: University of North Carolina Press, 2007.

Zhivago's Children: The Last Russian Intelligentsia. Cambridge, MA: Harvard University Press, 2009.

Index